Power and Interdepen

in

ONE WEEK LOAN

2 8 0r~ ...

Power is an inescapable feature of human existence. It plays a role in all social contexts and is particularly important in the functioning of organizations and work groups. Organizational researchers have certainly recognized the importance of power but have traditionally focused on its negative aspects. Yet power can also have very positive effects. *Power and Interdependence in Organizations* capitalizes on significant developments in social science over the past twenty years to show how managers and employees can manage power in order to make it a constructive force in organizations. Written by a team of international academics, the book explores both the positive and negative aspects of power, identifying opportunities and threats. It shows that harnessing the positive aspects of power, as well as controlling its more destructive effects, has the potential to revolutionize the way that organizations function, making them both more humane and productive.

DEAN TJOSVOLD is the Henry Y. W. Fong Chair Professor of Management at Lingnan University, Hong Kong.

BARBARA WISSE is Associate Professor of Organizational Psychology at VU University Amsterdam.

Power and Interdependence in Organizations

Edited by

DEAN TJOSVOLD

AND

BARBARA WISSE

CAMBRIDGE
UNIVERSITY PRESS

CAMBRIDGE UNIVERSITY PRESS
Cambridge, New York, Melbourne, Madrid, Cape Town, Singapore, São Paulo, Delhi

Cambridge University Press
The Edinburgh Building, Cambridge CB2 8RU, UK

Published in the United States of America by Cambridge University Press, New York

www.cambridge.org
Information on this title: www.cambridge.org/9780521703284

First published 2009

Printed in the United Kingdom at the University Press, Cambridge

A catalogue record for this publication is available from the British Library

ISBN 978-0-521-87859-3 hardback
ISBN 978-0-521-70328-4 paperback

To my lovely son, Alexander, who empowers me.

BW

To my wonderful sons and daughters, Jason, Wesley, Lena and Colleen: They grow and stay united.

DT

Contents

Figures

Tables

Foreword

Mark Twain made a very simple observation to do with leaders and power in life generally, "keep away from people who try to belittle your ambitions. Small people always do that, but the really great make you feel that you, too, can somehow become great." As the Editors of this outstanding and timely volume indicate, leadership and power permeate all aspects of our life, both inside and outside of organizations. From an organizational behavior and behavioral science point of view, we need to better understand the nature of this power and its interdependence with other aspects of organizational life. In terms of the latter, James MacGregor Burns (2003: 240) suggested in his book *Transforming Leadership*, for example, that "transforming change flows not from the work of the great man who single-handedly makes history but from the collective achievement of a great people."

Whereas in the 1960s and 1970s the literature was replete with leadership studies, the 1980s and 1990s saw a slight decline in popularity in this subject, as other related subjects took hold (i.e. TQM [total quality management]). But with a different global business scene today involving the emergence of India, China, Russia, and other formerly underdeveloped countries, with differing political traditions and systems in a multimedia age, the issues of leadership, power and "leading with others" has come to "front of stage" once again. And although we have an academic tradition of understanding leadership in the context of the last half of the twentieth century, we have never fully understood the concept of power in the context of the twenty-first century and beyond (Burke and Cooper 2006). This volume brings together some of the world's leading thinkers to explore various aspects of power, participative leadership, exchange dynamics, influence models, and the concept of "leading with values," in a way that highlights not only the current literature and reflections of the thought leaders in the field but also the implications for the future of organizational development.

We feel that this book makes an enormous contribution to the literature in the field, to help us understand where we are, where we are likely to go and the implications of these reflections on how we should get to where we might want to go to achieve organizational and individual objectives. The Editors ought to be congratulated on putting together a coherent, innovative, and scholarly volume of distinguished international scholars. We hope that this book will stimulate debate on issues of grave significance to all of us working in and with organizations over the next decades. Without the uninhibited reflections on these issues prevalent in this book, the old adage would apply "if you always do what you always did – you'll always get what you always got!"

Series Editors

Cary L. Cooper,
CBE, Lancaster University Management School, England
Jone Pearce,
University of California, Irvine, USA

References

Burke, R. and Cooper, C. L. (2006) *Inspiring leaders*, London and New York, N.Y. Routledge.

Burns, J. M. (2003) *Transforming leadership: A new pursuit of happiness*, New York, N.Y.: Atlantic Monthly.

Introduction

The sole advantage of power is that you can do more good.
                            Baltasar Gracian, *The Art of Worldly Wisdom*, 1647

Nearly all men can stand adversity, but if you want to test a man's character, give him power.
                            Abraham Lincoln (1809–1865)

Power tends to corrupt, and absolute power corrupts absolutely.
                            Lord Acton, Letter to Bishop Mandell Creighton, 1898

Power pervades everyday life in organizations and society and can be highly constructive but also very destructive. The powerful overcome adversities to unite and liberate countries; the powerful also suppress and demoralize. Power can mobilize us to rescue people from tragedies but also to bring havoc. Power helps us get things done that we cannot do alone, for good and for evil. It affects our dealing with crises but also our everyday activities. Power is inevitable in our organizations: the issue we confront is to understand when it is constructive and when it is destructive.

Power plays a key role in organizations and groups, indeed in all social contexts. Organizations – with their hierarchical structure, inter-dependent relationships, and the potential goal incompatibilities of the parties – are major arenas where power processes occur. Chapters in this book explore the positive and negative faces of power and inter-dependence in organizations; they identify opportunities and threats. Together the chapters advocate the need to manage power in order to take advantage of it and guard against its destructiveness.

The need to manage power crosses all boundaries; we need knowledge developed worldwide to help us manage power constructively. This book advances our understanding of power by providing a forum for research-ers from many countries to review their findings and develop their perspectives. Understanding power provides us with directions for how we can make power work for ourselves and our organizations and world.

Defining power

A critical first step to understand and manage power is to have a useful definition. Ideally, this definition is agreed upon so that we communicate accurately in our discussions and in our research. Using one term to mean many things breeds confusion. Knowledge should be cumulative in that researchers are all documenting the dynamics of the "same" thing.

Unfortunately, power is such a pervasive phenomenon and involves many important issues, including moral ones, that agreeing on a definition of power has proved difficult; imposing a definition is impossible. Indeed, even holding a discussion about it is a challenge. Some researchers seem to assume that defining power is too obvious even to specify; others just give up. This section briefly reviews major alternatives. Chapter authors generally use one of these definitions though they may emphasize different aspects.

Before zooming in on the different alternatives, let us try to capture those issues on which there appears to be consensus. First, researchers recognize that power involves perceptions and meaning rather than the objective state of affairs. People's beliefs and perceptions directly influence actions in social situations. Of course, the objective situation has an impact on these understandings and thereby on people's actions. Second, it is generally acknowledged that power is social in that it occurs and is exercised in interdependent settings. People have power within and as part of a social situation. Even power considered as an individual difference involves other people. Individual power needs are typically defined in terms of wanting to have an impact on other people and are exercised in social situations (McClelland 1970). Power is a subjectively experienced phenomenon that occurs in social, interdependent situations.

Alternative views of power are based on two major disagreements. The first is that some researchers consider power as a capacity (also called potential and ability), whereas others consider power as actual or realized influence. Another major difference is whether power is considered to affect outcomes (costs and benefits) or to involve influence where the target actually complies with action. The term "action" is a broad one and includes "thought" actions (such as attitudes and beliefs), affective states (such as sentiments, moods and emotions), and overt behaviors.

These different assumptions result in several definitions of power. In our explanation of the definitions we focus on dyadic situations. Of course, power processes take place in and between groups as well.

1. Power as the potential to influence another's actions. This definition implies that a high-power person could influence a low-power person to perform a behavior if the high-power person wants to.
2. Power as the potential to overcome resistance. This implies that a high-power person could influence another person even though this person does not want to perform the targeted action. This is a more restrictive definition than potential to influence another's actions.
3. Power as the potential to affect outcomes. According to this definition, high-power persons have resources that can affect the benefits and costs (the goal movement in field theory terms, success or failure in popular terms) of others. This definition implies that the high-power person has power bases, that is, resources valued by the low-power person; the low-power person values these resources because they can affect his or her outcomes.
4. Power as the potential to bring about desired change. Here the high-power individual has the ability to make things happen in a social setting, that is, to implement the change that the person in power desires. The power-holder may work with or against others to accomplish desired ends.
5. Power as actual influence: The person in power has successfully influenced another person. This definition involves actual influence. It requires that the power is exercised, that it be done.
6. Power as actually overcoming resistance. The power-holder has successfully influenced another person to do as the power-holder wants even though this person prefers not to do the targeted action. Note that this is a more restrictive definition of the previous definition.

The Editors prefer Definition 3: Power is the potential to affect outcomes. Powerful persons have resources that are valued because they can affect the extent to which the ones subject to power can achieve their goals. Powerful people can make the life of those subject to power better or worse, though they may not be able to get them to do their bidding. The capacity to affect outcomes is a basis for influence, for affecting the other's actions, but having the capacity does not insure that it is skillfully and successfully implemented to influence others. However, this definition preference is just that of the editors! Chapter authors have chosen their own definitions that often lead directly to the aspect of power they explore.

Power and interdependence in organizations

Managers, employees, and colleagues are interdependent in that they have power over and with each other. That we depend upon each other is perhaps the most basic reality of organizations and our social lives. We each have ideas, knowledge, effort, money, and opinions that others value, and others have abilities that we value. We have resources that can help and frustrate others' goals and aspirations but they have resources that affect our goals too. To be successful, people in organizations must coordinate and make use of each other's abilities and recourses.

Individual workers, including entry-level ones, are clearly dependent on others for job opportunities and rewards, but, you might ask, are they also powerful? They are hired because they are thought to have valued resources that can be applied to get things done. Why hire them if they are not able to assist? Some people are even hired because of who they know; they have the ability to find other people who have knowledge and authority that can help get things done.

Chief executive officers (CEOs) surely have resources that others value, but are CEOs also dependent? One might argue that CEOs are in a way the most dependent of all in an organization. They need everyone to do their job and to coordinate with each other if they are going to fulfill their goal of having a prosperous organization. Employees who do not contribute frustrate the CEO's objectives. Those who behave unethically can tarnish the CEO's reputation.

Power is part of how an economy and society as a whole work. Organizations have power over each other as they depend upon each other. Manufacturers rely upon suppliers for quality, cost-efficient parts delivered in a timely manner; suppliers need manufacturers as their customers. In the global marketplace, the lines of interdependence have expanded. Korean manufacturers rely on Indian suppliers as well as marketing organizations in North America. Financial and trade markets in one country also depend on those in another. Some Hong Kong brokers must be at work at dawn to discuss with their New York colleagues; others have to stay late into the night to coordinate with Europe. Increasingly, what happens "over there" also affects what happens "here."

Power is very much a part of relationships where people affect each other and depend upon each other, including the relationships between boss and employee, among team members, and between departments, organizations, and countries. As our chapters document, the quality of the relationships greatly affects how power is managed and its impact.

The need to manage power

Power and interdependence are major themes for organizations of the twenty-first century, critical both for developing our theoretical understanding and promoting organizational effectiveness. We must manage power as it has both a constructive and destructive face. How can we develop the positive aspects of power and control its destructiveness? So far managers and employees have been given little help to manage power.

Commentators, researchers, and managers both in the USA and elsewhere have traditionally elaborated on the negative view of power (Tjosvold 1967). Professional and academic discussions tend to rephrase the negative dynamics of power with some references to positive forms of power and empowerment. Power differences are often thought to frustrate direct, honest discussion and mutual relationships. Managers may feel obligated to protect their superior position and to assert their superior competence by trying to dominate employees (Argyris and Schon 1978; Kipnis 1976; McClelland 1970, 1975). Employees, feeling intimidated and vulnerable because they feel they have little recourse to their bosses' arbitrary decisions, restrict themselves to that which supports the boss, leaving them unable to discuss their conflicts openly and constructively (Hurwitz et al. 1968; Solomon 1960).

Wouldn't life be better without power or with everyone having equal power so that its effects can be neutralized? But power cannot be wished away or neutralized. Although seldom is power one-way (i.e. employees have resources valued by even dictatorial bosses), it is unrealistic that organizational members have the same power over each other. Even within a cohesive small group, members will have diverse resources that become valued at different times. Equal power in the sense of mutual power is not only possible but also common. But equal in the sense of identical or the same amount is unrealistic and in many cases undesirable. There is no reasonable alternative to managing our power.

Chapters in this book develop theorizing guided by empirical research to document the value of power and to identify the organizational and individual conditions under which power promotes individuals and organizations. As you will discover reading the chapters, developing the positive face of power as well as controlling its negative face has great potential for making our organizations more humane and more productive. However, learning to make power in our organizations a constructive force will be a challenge for many years to come.

The book

I have no patience with scientists who take a board of wood, look for its thinnest part, and drill a great number of holes where drilling is easy.

Albert Einstein

The fact that a problem will certainly take a long time to solve, and that it will demand the attention of many minds for several generations, is no justification for postponing the study. And, in times of emergency, it may prove in the long run that the problems we have postponed or ignored, rather than those we have failed to attack successfully, will return to plague us. Our difficulties of the moment must always be dealt with somehow; but our permanent difficulties are difficulties of every moment.

T. S. Eliot

Recent years have witnessed a reemerging interest in the origins and consequences of power and interdependence. However, the literature is fragmented, and our research progress is halting; interesting studies appear but few perspectives are empirically and theoretically systematically developed.

The book provides a forum for active researchers to develop their approaches to understanding power and interdependence in organizations, to summarize what is known, to identify obstacles to our efforts, and to point to how we might proceed. It revisits the enduring issue of power in a fresh way. Chapter authors capitalize on the developments over the past twenty years and point to innovative and inspiring ideas very much needed as organizations cope with the demands of our global, interconnected marketplace and world. The book brings together researchers from Europe, North America, and Asia with academic backgrounds in psychology, business, and sociology. As a consequence, the book offers many different perspectives on power and interdependence.

The chapters are the core of the book and its rationale. They are organized into five sections:

1. Relationships to manage the faces of power.
2. Participative leadership: leading with others.
3. Exchange dynamics and outcomes.
4. Power to influence.
5. Leading with values.

You can compare and contrast how authors have approached major issues of power. You will see the diversity and controversies within this research.

These sections are not, by the way, the ones originally proposed and distributed to the authors. Chapter authors, like everyone else but even more so, make up their own minds. And well they should, for these chapters are opportunities for them to develop their emerging research perspective, not to "cover" a particular issue deemed relevant by the editors.

Relationships to manage the faces of power

Chapters in this section outline approaches to developing relationships within and between organizations for constructive power. Based on his long-term commitment to the study and teaching of power, Jeffrey Pfeffer argues that we have made progress but our attitudes toward power are still highly ambivalent. Researchers should identify both the structural, socio-logical drivers of power dynamics and the psychological, individual aspects. An in-depth understanding of power will be invaluable for organizations and highly useful for our students as they manage their careers.

David Winter also brings considerable experience to bear on the positive and negative faces of power, in particular the taming of its destructive face. He shows that religion, love, and responsibility can tame power but they can also feed its havoc. He proposes that "historical generative consciousness" convinces the powerful to use their potential constructively. In addition to their immediate group, these leaders include diverse out-groups as part of their community, recognizing that the welfare of their own group cannot be long sustained without the support of other groups. He also shows that social scientists can write beautifully crafted chapters!

Barbara Wisse and Daan van Knippenberg describe how individuals see themselves very much affects their relationships with others and in particular how they approach power. People can develop a personal self-construal when they emphasize that they have a unique identity; they can also emphasize their collective, interdependent self where they see themselves as part of a group. Personal self-concepts may lead to an emphasis that interests are distinct and incompatible and thereby to using power to promote oneself at the expense of others. In contrast, assuming that their interests match, people with an inter-dependent self use their power to help each other be productive and to support each other. Selecting and orienting people to construe their own identity in terms of being an organization member should then very much contribute to the positive face of power.

Joris Lammers and Adam D. Galinski similarly emphasize that whether people consider themselves as collectivistic or individualistic very much affects the dynamics and outcomes of power. Their findings also identify legitimacy as another major condition that affects the extent that power can be constructive. When people believe power is reasonable and potentially useful for helping others accomplish valu-able goals, power helps the powerful feel secure and free to act. Believing that power is for mutual purposes rather than to promote self-interest also contributes to making power constructive; collectivist values reinforce the positive effects of power.

Dean Tjosvold and Peiguan Wu argue that the kind of interdepend-ence very much affects the dynamics and outcomes of power and use theory and research on cooperation and competition to examine these effects. Experimental and field studies show that organizational mem-bers, both when they have similar or unequal status, apply their power resources for mutual benefit, strengthen their relationships, and recog-nize and appreciate each other's power when they believe their goals are positively related but not when they believe they have competitive, incompatible goals. Studies specifically document that collectivist values have their constructive impact on power dynamics by strength-ening cooperative goals. Developing cooperative relationships, by such methods as assigning common tasks and training in the skills of open-minded discussion, is a practical way to make power constructive.

Participative leadership: leading with others

Chapters in this section focus on the power relationship between man-agers and employees and, more specifically, on how they can work together to make decisions and manage. George Graen integrates leader-member exchange research showing the value of high-quality relationships for effective leadership with a network perspective. He proposes that leaders and employees focus on "relationship sharing" where they develop mutually respectful and powerful relationships within their teams. Ideally, they develop competent networks that can not only accomplish challenging projects but also strengthen individuals and promote their careers.

David De Cremer and Marius van Dijke relate important implications of procedural justice research for understanding power. Integrating research from power and justice, they argue that subordinates are typically highly concerned about the potential abuse of power. Managers can allay these concerns and consequently secure their power and control by involving employees in decision-making and giving them voice. Studies also indicate that leaders who confront instability are concerned about how others view them and have a high sense of power and are especially motivated to reaffirm their power through procedural justice.

Also, arguing that giving employees voice contributes to organizational decision-making and indeed may solidify managers' positions, Peter T. Coleman wonders why so few managers involve employees. Coleman found that their implicit theories make leaders reluctant to use participation despite research and professional practice indicating its value. Managers tend to assume that power is limited; if employees are powerful, then they must be less powerful. Key then to leaders being more open and participative is for them to understand that power is expandable, that when employees become more powerful, they can be more effective and more appreciated.

Exchange dynamics and outcomes

Exchange theorists directly examine how the powerful and those subject to power treat each other in terms of how they use their power to reward and punish. Following the sociologists Peter Blau and Richard Emerson, they use the basic idea of exchange to understand the complex ways that the powerful and less powerful interact.

Linda Molm summarizes that reciprocal exchanges result in trust, positive evaluations, feelings of solidarity and fairness. Noting that exchange theorists have traditionally examined the exchange of benefits, she suspected that exchanging punishments would not simply yield mirror-image effects. Although the power to reward leads to its use, the power to punish does not. Her research also underlines that while the powerful may resist change, the disadvantaged typically work to alter the power imbalance. They use networks to form alliances to increase their power and form coalitions to reduce the powerful's alternatives.

Edward J. Lawler and Chad A. Proell have elaborated on the exchange perspective by highlighting that it can be both non-zero-sum and cooperative, or zero-sum and competitive. They have begun the difficult but potentially highly useful integration of exchange theory perspective on power with emotions. Exchanges are between people who react, not just with calculations of exchanging benefits and punishments but with strong feelings when they have and use power to solve problems. Indeed, expressing emotions can increase power. They propose a broad model of power that includes how power affects the powerful's freedom and motivation to act and strategies to use power.

Alice H. Eagly and Agneta Fischer are not exchange theorists but they have organized and documented pervasive unequal exchange dynamics and relationships, specifically, the exchange between women and men in organizations worldwide. Their evidence is more than a basis for recognizing an injustice: It is a stinging indictment and call for action. They and their evidence do not suggest that change is easy or will come quickly. But there is hope. Indeed, as exchange theorists have argued, the disadvantaged are working to alter the inequality and are making progress.

Power to influence

Previous chapters have reviewed research indicating that power can affect relationships, motivation, and emotions even without influence attempts. Authors in this section have studied how power affects the choice of influence tactics and their success. They have drawn upon considerable research to offer several frameworks for understanding power's role in influencing others.

Gary Yukl has developed his framework over decades of focused research for understanding power as the capacity to influence attitudes and actions in desired ways. His chapter reviews the different types of influence tactics that have been identified. His research points toward core effective influence tactics, namely rational persuasion, consultation, collaboration, and inspirational appeals that result not just in compliance but also in internal commitment.

French and Raven's work (1959) on the power bases of reference, expertise, legitimate, reward, and coercion is arguably the most influential study of power in organizations. M. Afzalur Rahim has integrated this work with recent advances in influence. His research suggests an elegant model: Expert and reference power influence have direct constructive effects both on employee performance and satisfaction. Coercive, reward, and legitimate power can have their constructive impact to the extent that they lead to expert and reference power influence attempts.

Also building on French and Raven's work on power bases (1959), Meni Koslowsky and Joseph Schwarzwald propose a framework to identify key influence tactics. Their instrument was found to measure these tactics reliably. Research is testing and developing the usefulness of this framework.

John E. Barbuto Jr. and Gregory T. Gifford identify influence attempts from the perspective of the person being influenced rather than the powerful and the kind of power base employed. Targets of influence are not passive receivers but are partners in the influence processes. They classify these influence triggers into those derived from power, relationships, and values. Surely influence attempts come in many forms; identifying and classifying them are complex projects.

Randall S. Peterson and Sarah Harvey identify critical influence strategies whereby leaders can use their power to help teams manage conflict constructively and take advantage of the potential benefits of conflict. They summarize research indicating that leaders should use indirect expressions of power: Specifically, they should manage group process rather than outcomes, develop the right structure, and manage how the group interacts with its external environment. Direct expressions of power elicit reactance from team members and foster relationship risks whereas indirect influence promotes psychological safety.

Lourdes Munduate and Francisco J. Medina describe how to use power to influence organizational change processes. They examine how the use of power by the agents directly involved in change processes may induce a proactive attitude toward change. Specifically, they argue that the use of personal power, a power base that is highly dependent on the quality of the relationship between power-holder and those subjected to power, facilitates a positive disposition toward change.

Leading with values

Power involves how people should relate to each other and have an impact on each other, both to support and to harm. Power then has a moral dimension: How should leaders use their power and to what effect? Authors in this section outline moral prescriptions justifying and detailing how managers should lead.

Dirk van Dierendonck, Inge Nuijten, and Imke Heeren argue that leaders should strive to serve. As servants, they are motivated to promote the capabilities of each employee. They persuade and empower their employees, but they do not aim to manipulate for compliance or even commitment. Servant-leaders satisfy their own needs for competence and relationships through promoting their employees.

Noting scandals involving top management greed and misconduct, Annebel H. B. De Hoogh and Deanne N. Den Hartog urge leaders to use their power responsibly and ethically. Leaders should seek to further the welfare of their employees, not their own. They may develop pro-social goals, indeed not just for their employees but also for other organizational stakeholders. The authors identify a number of issues in clarifying the nature of ethical leadership and call for more research on its effects.

Ping Ping Fu and Caroline Fu discuss how the Eastern philosophical perspective of Taoism has universal implications for leaders; indeed, their arguments reinforce those outlined by other chapters in this section. Deeply concerned about their followers, Taoist leaders work to develop them. But Taoism holds that leaders need not choose the welfare of their employees over their own; rather, they work to integrate these interests. Realizing that they become truly powerful when employees internalize leader values, leaders should begin with themselves by refining their virtues and formulating their own values to inspire followers.

The book's chapters attest to our progress in understanding power and integrating power research with other management theories. Our knowledge base though is insufficient; the challenges to managing power and the consequent need for power knowledge appear to intensify much faster than power research progresses. Authors offer ideas and possibilities that should be explored more. This book will succeed to the extent that it stimulates you and other readers to take power seriously and to join the effort to enhance the likelihood that power aids in making our teams and organizations more alive and potent. Positive power offers the potential of making our organizations more able to solve our pressing, global problems and, simultaneously, to help our leaders and followers become more fulfilled and confident.

References

Argyris, C. and Schon, D. A. (1978) *Organizational learning: A theory of action perspective*, Reading, Mass.: Addison-Wesley.

French, J. R. P. Jr. and Raven, B. H. (1959) The bases of social power. In D. Cartwright and A. F. Zander (Eds.), *Studies in social power* (pp. 150–167), Ann Arbor, Mich.: Institute for Social Research.

Hurwitz, J. I., Zander, A. F., and Hymovitch, B. (1968) Some effects of power on the relations among group members. In D. Cartwright and A. Zander (Eds.), *Group dynamics* (pp. 291–297), New York, N.Y. Harper & Row.

Kipnis, D. (1976) *The power-holders*, Chicago, Ill.: University of Chicago Press.

McClelland, D. C. (1970) The two faces of power. *Journal of Affairs*, **24**, 29–47.

(1975) *Power: The inner experience*, New York, N.Y.: Irvington Publishers, Inc.

Solomon, L. (1960) The influence of some types of power and game strategies upon the development of interpersonal trust. *Journal of Abnormal and Social Psychology*, **61**, 223–230.

Tjosvold, D. (1967) The American Revolution pamphleteers: Conservators of seventeenth century English radicalism. Senior thesis, Princeton University, Princeton, N. J.

PART I

Relationships to manage the faces of power

1 | *Understanding power in organizations*

JEFFREY PFEFFER

Almost thirty years ago, Rosabeth Kanter (1979) wrote that power was the organization's last dirty secret. She argued that discussions of power and influence were circumscribed both in the workplace and even in the research literature. Asking workplace colleagues or interview respondents questions such as "who (or what department) has the most power" would earn opprobrium rather than praise, something that Salancik and I experienced personally when we began our research on the effects of departmental power on resource allocations in universities (Pfeffer and Salancik 1974). Power, except for occasional discussion of the bases of power (French and Raven 1968), was largely missing from management textbooks and also from the research literature on organizations and management.

Research on power has recently enjoyed some resurgence, particularly in social psychology, as I will discuss below. And although there are now a number of schools that offer elective courses on understanding power and political dynamics inside companies, nonprofits, and government agencies, such electives are seemingly less common than courses on negotiation, for instance. That is the case even though the two topics are highly complementary. Negotiations classes for the most part focus on how to obtain an agreement when interests conflict, how to claim value, and integrative and distributive bargaining over outcomes in circumstances where the parties already have established strengths and weaknesses and interests. Meanwhile, the study of power and influence, focusing on both structural sources of power and interpersonal tactics such as communications strategies and influence skills, can help people develop stronger positions and more allies and resources in advance of entering into negotiations.

In this chapter I discuss some possible reasons for the ambivalence about power. I argue that because power affects so many aspects of social and organizational life, we need to overcome that ambivalence in both our teaching and our research. I conclude by describing some ways

of both understanding power and influence and surmounting our mixed
emotions about the topic.

Why "power" makes people uncomfortable

We are clearly ambivalent about power. As Gandz and Murray (1980:
244) noted, most people agree with the statements "successful executives must be good politicians" and "the existence of workplace politics
is common in most organizations," and few believe that "powerful
executives don't act politically." But at the same time, their sample of
managers held the views that "organizations free of politics are happier
than those where there are a lot of politics" and "politics in organizations are detrimental to efficiency." Similar sentiments come from
students – even MBA students who voluntarily elect to enroll in a course
that has been variously titled "power and politics in organizations" or
"paths to power". Many may, in fact, enroll as a reflection of their own
ambivalence about power. As a colleague, Deborah Gruenfeld,
remarked to me, it was her observation that, even though most people
spend most of their working lives in hierarchical organizations, a large
fraction have trouble with hierarchical relationships. Some individuals
are counterdependent, rebelling against the efforts of those senior in the
hierarchy to direct or manage them and resisting the influence and
direction of others. Some individuals are reluctant to use their own
formal authority or, for that matter, to develop informal influence to
get others to comply with their requests, believing that they don't have
the "right" to tell others what to do or direct their behavior. Both
counterdependence and a reluctance to use power creates difficulties
for people in their careers, precisely because hierarchy is a fact of social
life and people spend a lot of time in hierarchical structures, so being
effective in hierarchical relationships is important. Moreover, individuals' conflicted feelings about power and its use can affect behavior at
work and possibly the stress that many people experience working in
political environments.

   There are a number of possible reasons for this ambivalence and the
conflicted feelings people have about power and politics in organizations, although few of these explanations have been empirically
explored. Understanding the causes and sources of people's discomfort
with power and its effects remains an important research task. Ferris
et al. (1996) suggested that workplace politics is a source of stress.

Politics may be important for organizational success, but because people are often unskilled and unschooled in building and exercising influence, this discrepancy between their need to do something and their perceived ability to navigate organizational politics effectively could be a source of discomfort.

Another possibility may result from the cultural context and its implications for how people see their social roles. The respondents to Gandz and Murray's survey and the students Gruenfeld and I encounter are largely Western, many from the USA, others from Western Europe. Even those who have very different cultural backgrounds may be somewhat "Westernized" by the time they reach North American companies or business schools. One of the most prominent differences across cultures is individualism. As noted by Markus and Kitayama (1991), Asian cultures emphasize the relatedness of individuals to each other, while, in American culture, individuals seek to maintain their independence from others. The individual ethos of Western culture, combined with the emphasis on individual achievement in school where grading on the curve is common, can suggest to people that they should succeed on the basis of what they do as individuals. This cultural understanding can create the idea that independence and self-sufficiency are both descriptive of others and normatively desirable – ideas that contrast with interdependence and being in relationship with others and getting things done by influencing those others. This line of argument suggests that ambivalence about and reactions to power and interdependence are in part determined by culture and cultural teachings and values.

The idea that power is a basis for success violates some other important social psychological principles as well. As Lerner (e.g., Lerner 1980; Lerner and Simmons 1966) described long ago, people have a need to believe that the world is just. Such a belief provides a feeling of more control over events and comports with social values of fairness and justice. Because of the belief in a just world, people will re-evaluate the characteristics of individuals depending on what happens to them, derogating victims and elevating the skills and worth of people who may enjoy accidental good fortune (Lerner and Simmons 1966; Hafer 2000). There is evidence that unjust situations create discomfort for people (Hafer 2000) and affect their political judgments, for instance, about income redistribution (e.g., Benabou and Tirole 2006).

For many people, success that is based on political skill or power violates the sense of a just world, since few people seem to believe that possession of political skills and the acquisition of power ought to be sufficient to entitle people to good outcomes. The sense of injustice and unfairness from people succeeding on the basis of networking skills, the ability to strategically influence relationships, and similar political tactics is evident in the reactions of students to both readings and cases that illustrate advancement and success on the basis of political skill and is completely consistent with the just-world effect. This reasoning suggests that just-world beliefs should mediate the relationship between success or failure based on political or networking skills or their absence and people's psychological reactions to those situations.

Another observation that may explain the ambivalence and discomfort associated with observing political behavior in organizations is that people, including business people and students, seem to make distinctions between what might be seen as acceptable and even normatively prescribed behavior at the level of organizations or organizational units and the same behavior if exhibited by individuals in the context of interpersonal relationships. So, for instance, the idea of engaging in industrial espionage, such as the reports of employees of Oracle going through competitors' trash to see if they could glean useful information, is viewed less negatively than the same behavior if undertaken by an individual to obtain some advantage over a competitor for a promotion. Similarly, we teach courses in business schools on strategy and strategic moves – including entering the markets of others to encourage mutual forbearance and other elements of game theory, which has now become part and parcel of many strategy courses. But strategic behavior undertaken at an individual level and focused on people who are competitors seems to elicit greater feelings of inappropriateness. Companies, for instance, engage in advertising campaigns in which they attack the relative merits of competitors' products and engage in other forms of public-relations activities. Except possibly in the domain of political life and elections, such behavior is much less socially acceptable when undertaken by individuals against organizational competitors.

It seems as if personal relations are viewed as being more natural and less "strategic," or at least many people appear to view interpersonal relationships as if they *should* be more honest and authentic than relations among organizational actors. In part this may be because viewing interpersonal relationships from a strategic frame requires more vigilance, calculation, and effort than most people are willing to expend. In part, however, it is also because there is something somehow unseemly about using tactics that would be perfectly acceptable at a more "macro" level against others in interpersonal competition. Why, and the extent to which this is true, remain topics that deserve additional study.

And yet another social psychological process, self-enhancement, may be implicated in the observed ambivalence and discomfort with power and politics in organizations. There is evidence that, in most circumstances, people tend to see themselves as possessing more of good qualities and attributes and fewer negative traits (Krueger 1998). To the extent that being successful on the basis of merit and ability is a normatively valued and socially desirable outcome, believing that one has succeeded because of political skills rather than "merit" is a threat to people's positive self-perceptions.

Finally, when confronted with difficult trade-offs, people are understandably ambivalent. Power and influence ideas can cause people to think about the trade-off, for instance, between being popular and well liked versus being powerful and effective and getting things done. One way to avoid confronting such difficult choices is to pretend that they do not exist – that success does not require such decisions – or avoiding thinking about topics, such as organizational politics, that make such trade-offs salient.

Why understanding power and influence is important – for individuals and organizations

Although people may be ambivalent about power, understanding power and influence is important because power and knowledge about power help account for many outcomes of theoretical and substantive interest. Krackhardt (1990) showed that knowing about distributions of influence can be helpful for one's career and is useful if not essential for targeting sales efforts focused on companies.[1] Power as a

---

[1] Alston Gardner, co-founder and former CEO of an industrial sales-training company, was one of the largest purchasers of *Managing with Power* (Pfeffer 2002). As part of a three-day sales-training program, most of one day was spent helping sales people diagnose organizational power distributions so they could focus their influence efforts on those most crucial for affecting the final purchase decision.

concept is useful for understanding resource allocations in organizations (e.g., Pfeffer and Moore 1980; Pfeffer and Salancik 1974), career advancement (Moore and Pfeffer 1980; Standing and Standing 1999), people's wages (Pfeffer and Konrad 1991), and decisions ranging from organizational computer purchases (Pettigrew 1973) to CEO succession (Fligstein 1987; Ocasio 1994; Ocasio and Kim 1999).

Power also has profound effects on those with power and on their relationships with others (e.g., Galinsky et al. 2003; Keltner et al. 2003; Kipnis, 1972). Research shows that when people feel they are more powerful their action orientation increases, they tend to focus more on their own needs, they display anger more readily (Tiedens 2000), they increase their social distance from others, and they are less constrained by social mores and conventions – they are more disinhibited in their behavior.

Power and influence are also important topics for understanding some aspects of organizational performance. One of the biggest problems managers confront is the ability to actually get things done. The recent spate of books on execution (e.g., Bossidy et al. 2002; Hartman 2003) is evidence that people recognize that planning and strategic brilliance are, by themselves, insufficient to achieve organizational success. Political leaders such as Richard Nixon have lamented their seeming inability to get government bureaucracy to bend to their will and carry out policies and dictates. Senior corporate leaders, particularly in large organizations, also bemoan how difficult it apparently is to change organizational cultures and to get the myriad people throughout a company on the same page.

Clearly, the ability to get things done requires skill at influencing others. Although measures and incentives are one approach to this influence task, particularly for those with the hierarchical authority to impose such interventions, other interpersonal influence techniques (e.g., Cialdini 1988) are also crucial for inducing people to do what needs to get done to ensure high levels of performance. The importance of influence skills for making things happen, and the importance of execution to business success, is one reason that Kanter (1979) argued that power skills were essential to making companies successful.

Power and influence skills are crucial for individuals. As Keith Ferrazzi (Ferrazzi and Raz 2005) has commented, contrary to what people may have been told or to some conventional wisdom, individuals are not responsible for their own careers. Their own hard work and drive will not, in and of itself, make them successful. In order to be successful, particularly in larger organizations where climbing a hierarchy is the path to career advancement, other people, such as bosses, determine someone's success. Therefore, for individuals to be successful in promotion tournaments, it is important that they be able to get others in their organization interested in their success and willing to spend effort advocating on their behalf. Anyone who has witnessed promotion discussions in law firms, management consulting organizations, investment banks, or, for that matter, academic departments will immediately recognize the truth of this statement.

Lyndon Johnson's enormous political success, first in the US House of Representatives and then in the Senate, depended in no small measure on his ability to first locate where the power was and who held it and then build relationships with these older men – sometimes referred to as Johnson being a "professional son" – that would cause them to want to help Johnson be successful in his endeavors (e.g., Caro 1982). This advocacy by others for someone's success requires, obviously, skill at playing organizational politics and influencing those others to be supporters.

Individuals also need political skills and understanding of power because their success depends on getting things done, too. It is not just at a more macro level of analysis where the ability to solve problems and make things happen is a source of success – this is also true at the level of the individual and his or her career. Frank Stanton (Smith 1990) rose rapidly through the ranks at CBS because he could provide answers – even if those answers just came from *The World Almanac*, about economic and demographic factors that could help CBS make better programming decisions and sell advertising more effectively. Robert Moses, the New York City Parks Commissioner (Caro 1974) got along with his many powerful bosses, including New York Governor Al Smith and New York City Mayor LaGuardia, because he was willing and able to accomplish things, even those things that raised a ruckus. As Al Smith's son said in a television interview, politicians were quite willing to take credit for the public works such as parks, playgrounds, and swimming pools that Moses built even if they clucked in public about his tough methods. As one observer of the New York political scene commented:

Every morning when a mayor comes to work, there are a hundred problems that must be solved. And a lot of them are so big and complex that they just don't seem susceptible to solution. And when he asks guys for solutions, what happens? Most of them can't give him any ... But you give a problem to Moses and overnight he's back in front of you – with a solution, all worked out down to the last detail ... He had solutions when no else had solutions. (Caro 1974: 463)

Some people erroneously believe that the more collegial, team-oriented settings so prevalent today in high technology and other knowledge work environments have reduced the need for individuals to possess political skills. But quite the contrary. In organizations where hierarchy matters a lot, one can get things done through recourse to formal authority and the rules and processes that constitute the organization's ways of doing things. In less formalized systems, where collaboration and teamwork are the norm, disagreements about what to do and how to do it can, and often do, still occur. These disagreements about the appropriate course of action must still be resolved in order for decisions to get made and things to get accomplished. But now, instead of dictating decisions through fiat, issues will need to be negotiated and influence used to resolve disagreements and move things along. Ironically, then, the more team-based and flatter hierarchies that are so much in the news and the diminished reliance on formal controls and rewards and punishments require more influence skills on the part of organizational members, not less. In more lateral structures and in roles such as project management, getting things done requires being able to influence others without having formal authority over them.

Some ways of overcoming ambivalence and understanding power and influence

Because power is at once important but provokes ambivalence, it is important to find ways to overcome the reluctance of both scholars and students to take power seriously. With respect to research orientations, power represents a theoretical orientation that speaks to the potency of interests, both individual and group, and strategic, intentional actions. Power is notably absent from many theoretical literatures, including population ecology (Hannan and Freeman 1989), many strands of institutional theory (cf. DiMaggio 1988), and transactions cost economics (Williamson and Ouchi 1981) that see environments and their rules and constraints as givens and view human agency and intentional, adaptive action as limited in their explanatory power.

In the fifteen years since writing *Managing with Power* (Pfeffer 1992), colleagues and I have taught numerous sections of material on power and influence, both at Stanford and at other universities, not just in the USA. but also around the world. That experience, as well as the additional research that has appeared over the years, leads to some interrelated conclusions about how to understand power and influence in organizations and how to help others be comfortable with that task.

The most fundamental idea is that hierarchies are ubiquitous in social relationships including in both informal groups and formal organizations (Tiedens and Fragale 2003). Hierarchies among humans facilitate cooperation and coordination. And in order to determine hierarchical relationships, behaviors that create dominance help in making decisions, distributing power, and claiming resources. Therefore, understanding power relations is essential in understanding omnipresent hierarchies, and diagnosing how dominance and influence get both acquired and used is a fundamental task for analysts of social systems and social relations.

At a theoretical level, there are two complementary approaches to understanding the sources of power, each of which is important and necessary. One approach for understanding the sources of power and influence, and for that matter, their use, focuses on structure, including network structure and the structure of situations. Burt's (1992) work on structural holes represents one research stream in this tradition. Burt found that people who occupy bridging positions between two otherwise unconnected or at best very weakly connected networks – people who, in other words, occupy a structural hole between more densely connected networks of others – can reap the benefits of brokerage by bringing together resources and mediating the interests and objectives of the two separate networks. The idea of brokerage or standing between built on earlier and less sophisticated ideas about the importance of being central in networks. The insight was that centrality, per se, might be less important depending on how connected the other people were to each other, and that what mattered for acquiring power and influence was being able to provide value or benefits to people by accessing information or social ties that they could not.

Other research emphasizing the importance of structural position includes the body of work that argues that one important source of power comes from the control over resources. Such resources include obviously money and budgets – one source of Robert Moses' power was that in his position as Parks (and later Bridge) Commissioner, he hired lawyers, floated bonds with their underwriting fees, and built public works, thereby providing money to both contractors and the workers and their unions who worked on the projects (Caro 1974). In fact, during the Great Depression, his access to engineering talent that could build public works permitted him to wind up spending a disproportionate amount of WPA (Works Progress Administration) money in New York. But other important resources include information, access to people and their calendars, often controlled by assistants, and physical equipment and physical space and offices. Certainly, in many universities, laboratory space is at a premium, and those with space have power as a consequence of this fact.

Yet another structural source of power is the influence that comes from occupying a formal position. Positions in organizations, particularly in hierarchical organizations, come with authority rights – the right to make decisions and to allocate tasks and resources. Those positions and their associated influence rights come to be institutionalized (Scott 1995), in the sense of being taken for granted and seldom questioned or challenged. Thus, CEOs have power simply because of their title, as, to a lesser degree, do academic administrators such as deans. Cialdini (1988) has noted how we are conditioned to obey authority, which is why uniforms – sometimes a signal of authority – can be so important. Such deference is often almost automatic and mindless. Thus, titles and positions matter and convey power regardless of the particular qualities of the individual occupying a particular position.

The second source of power derives from individual actions and behaviors, taken, obviously, within structural contexts but not completely constrained by or subject to those contexts. People can gain influence above and beyond what they might be expected to have on the basis of their structural position by what they do, how they act, and how they communicate to others.

As one example, people can, through their effort and insight, find or create resources that become important out of almost nothing. Caro (1982) described how, as a young Congressional aide, Lyndon Johnson took control of a virtually moribund organization of Congressional secretaries, the Little Congress. Having gotten control of the organization, he then made it an important place by inviting prominent politicians to speak, by having debates that attracted media attention because reporters figured out this was a good setting to preview the arguments that would be made about pending legislation, by leveraging the press coverage to get even more prominent people to speak, and, by so doing, elevating his visibility as the organization's leader. Or, to take another example, Klaus Schwab was a not very successful academic until he created a forum in Europe for business leaders to get together and discuss important political and economic issues. That organization evolved into the World Economic Forum, and Schwab's institutional entrepreneurship has provided him with a position of enormous visibility and access as well as one that has permitted him to become reasonably wealthy. On a less grand but still important scale, a junior McKinsey consultant told me how he obtained visibility and access, important sources of power, by taking on the task of organizing seminars for the office, something that others did not want to do.

As a second example, people can enhance their influence through how they behave. Behavior that expresses strong emotion, such as anger, or that otherwise conveys power can produce attributions of power to the individual on the part of others. For instance, recent research shows how the expression of emotions can affect the conferral of status. Tiedens (2001) found that people who expressed anger were more likely to be seen as high status than those who expressed sadness. The basic theoretical argument is straightforward and is based on ideas from attribution theory. In order to express strong emotions, and particularly negative emotions such as anger, it is presumed that people must have the power that provides them the freedom to express those strong, negative emotions. Consequently, when people do display anger, for instance, as contrasted with sadness, others perceive them to have more power and confer more status and power on them. In another study, Tiedens and Fragale (2003) reported that when exposed to a dominant confederate, subjects tended to exhibit a diminished postural stance, again demonstrating how acting as though one had power can actually provide some advantages in acquiring power.

Finally, effective communication can also enhance an individual's power and influence above and beyond what structural conditions might dictate. There is almost certainly no more vivid example of this than Oliver North's testimony in front of a joint Congressional investigating committee looking into the Iran–Contra scandal during the presidency of Ronald Reagan. Accused of violating federal law in providing aid to the Nicaraguan resistance (the Contras) and also of running a covert foreign policy out of the White House that entailed supplying arms to the Iranians in exchange for the promise to release hostages, and observed by justice department attorneys to be shredding documents (destroying evidence), North was able to win over the American people through a masterful use of language. He framed his actions in terms of achieving higher aims such as saving lives or protecting the interests of the USA. He never appeared defensive or embarrassed about what he did. And he stressed that he always told his superiors what he was doing, and why.

As the literature on conversation analysis and political discourse demonstrates, there are "rules" for giving speeches and for how to frame talk that are more likely to elicit applause and agreement, and conversational gambits that produce power. For instance, interruption, when successful, both creates power and is more likely to be done by those with more power. Studies of cross-gender conversations, for instance, have traditionally found that men are more likely to interrupt women than vice versa. And studies of physicians' interaction with patients found that after about forty-five seconds, doctors tended to interrupt what their patients were saying.

In addressing an audience, be it one person or many, the influence technique of flattery (Cialdini 1988) can be embedded in discourse, praising the audience and telling them how intelligent and perceptive they are. This will generate liking and leave the audience more susceptible to influence. Murray Edelman's perceptive analysis (1964: 123) of political language noted that "political argument, when it is effective, calls the attention of a group with shared interests to those aspects of their situation which make an argued for line of action *seem* consistent with the furthering of their interests."

Atkinson's (1984) analysis of political speeches and what makes them effective found that political language produces emotion rather than thoughtful analysis and, in fact, often precludes rational analysis. Effective political language promotes identification and affiliation with the speaker and his or her ideas. This can be accomplished, for instance, by using "us" versus "them" references as a way of building shared social identity. Atkinson also found that using lists of at least three items was effective in persuasion because it provided the aura of comprehensiveness, and that the use of contrasts, inviting explicit comparisons, was also effective in persuading others.

Much of the research on power and influence adopts either the structural or human-action perspective. Few studies have explored the extent to which structures themselves can be changed by what people do – although Burt's research speaks to this possibility – and few studies of interpersonal influence techniques have placed those techniques in structural context to, for instance, explore the conditions under which they will be more or less effective, or for that matter, the conditions under which they are more or less likely to be used. In both research and teaching, it would seem to be important to incorporate a more comprehensive view of power and political action in organizational contexts.

The idea that power depends on both structure and action also has implications for how we teach these ideas to students. Structure can be analytically understood. So, too, can the various strategies and techniques of interpersonal influence. However, as pointed out elsewhere (Pfeffer and Sutton 2000), there is a tendency to separate knowing and doing, and nowhere is this more problematic than in professional schools where competence in professional practice virtually demands that people have not only the knowledge of relevant ideas and theories but also the practice of using those ideas. This line of argument suggests that having people practice "doing power" – for instance, by using various influence techniques in organizations such as student clubs or part-time employers – while they are learning the concepts will lead to more engagement with the material and more learning and retention of the ideas.

Conclusion

Thirty years ago there was little discussion of power in management textbooks or courses or, for that matter, in the management literature. What discussion there was tended to proceed from French and Raven's (1968) typology of the bases of power. Although over the ensuing years our understanding of social-influence processes has increased dramatically through more research and teaching activity, power and politics in organizations retains a somewhat problematic position in our courses and our scholarly activities. The ambivalence about power that affects our students also affects the scholarly community as its members decide what theoretical ideas and empirical research to advocate and pursue.

Because of this fact, I have argued here that we ought to directly study and understand the sources of the ambivalence about power and politics.

That study and the insight it can produce may have some benefit in helping us, and our students, surmount the reluctance to directly engage with the important topics of organizational power and politics.

I have also argued for a more multidimensional approach to both our scholarship and our teaching, recognizing both structural and behavioral sources of power and power strategies and advocating the need for more studies that incorporate both aspects. People act in context, and their structural positions affect their opportunities for leverage. But that context is created by what people do, and even with given constraints, there is wide variation in individual effectiveness in negotiating those constraints. The dichotomy between action and structure pervades much of sociology, and its resolution has been an important theoretical and empirical topic. Such should also be the case in studies of power and politics in organizational settings.

Finally, I have maintained that the literature suggests that power and political skill have important effects on organizational decisions and individual outcomes, including career outcomes. Because of the importance of these effects, it behooves us to understand power in organizations and to develop even more effective ways of helping our students to understand it, also.

References

Atkinson, M. (1984) *Our master's voices: The language and body language of politics*, London: Methuen.

Benabou, R. and J. Tirole (2006) Belief in a just world and redistributive politics. *Quarterly Journal of Economics*, **121**, 699–746.

Bossidy, R., R. Charan, and C. Burk (2002) *Execution: The discipline of getting things done*, New York, N.Y.: Crown Business.

Burt, R. S. (1992) *Structural holes: The social structure of competition*, Cambridge, Mass.: Harvard University Press.

Caro, R. (1974) *The power broker: Robert Moses and the fall of New York*, New York, N.Y.: Random House.

   (1982) *The path to power: The years of Lyndon Johnson*, New York, N.Y.: Knopf.

Cialdini, R. B. (1988) *Influence: Science and practice*, 2nd edn, Glenview, Ill.: Scott Foresman.

DiMaggio, P. J. (1988) Interest and agency in institutional theory. In L. G. Zucker (Ed.), *Institutional patterns and organizations* (pp. 3–21), Beverly Hills, Calif.: Sage.

Edelman, M. (1964) *The symbolic uses of politics*, Urbana, Ill.: University of Illinois Press.

Ferrazzi, K. and T. Raz (2005) *Never eat alone*, New York, N.Y.: Doubleday Currency.

Ferris, G. F., D. W. Frink, M. C. Galang, J. Zhou, K. M. Kacmar, and J. L. Howard (1996) Perceptions of organizational politics: Prediction, stress-related implications, and outcomes. *Human Relations*, 49, 233–266.

Fligstein, N. (1987) The interorganizational power struggle: Rise of finance personnel to top leadership in large corporations 1919–1979. *American Sociological Review*, 52, 44–58.

French, J. R. P. Jr. and B. Raven (1968) The bases of social power. In D. Cartwright and A. Zander (Eds.), *Group Dynamics*, 3rd edn (pp. 259–269), New York, N.Y.: Harper & Row.

Galinksy, A., D. H. Gruenfeld, and J. C. Magee (2003) From power to action. *Journal of Personality and Social Psychology*, 85, 453–466.

Gandz, J. and V. V. Murray (1980) The experience of workplace politics. *Academy of Management Journal*, 23, 237–251.

Hafer, C. L. (2000) Do innocent victims threaten the belief in a just world? Evidence from a modified Stroop task. *Journal of Personality and Social Psychology*, 79, 165–173.

Hannan, M. and Freeman, J. (1989) *Organizational ecology*, Cambridge, Mass.: Harvard University Press.

Hartman, A. (2003) *Ruthless execution: What business leaders do when their companies hit the wall*, London: FT Press.

Kanter, R. (1979) Power failure in management circuits. *Harvard Business Review*, 57 (4), 65–75.

Keltner, D., D. H. Gruenfeld, and C. Anderson (2003) Power, approach, and inhibition. *Psychological Review*, 110, 265–284.

Kipnis, D. (1972) Does power corrupt? *Journal of Personality and Social Psychology*, 24, 33–41.

Krackhardt, D. (1990) Assessing the political landscape: Structure, cognition and power in organizations. *Administrative Science Quarterly*, 35, 342–369.

Krueger, J. (1998) Enhancement bias in descriptions of self and others. *Personality and Social Psychology Bulletin*, 24, 505–516.

Lerner, M. J. (1980) *The belief in a just world: A fundamental delusion*, New York, N.Y.: Plenum.

Lerner, M. J. and C. H. Simmons (1966) Observer's reactions to the "innocent victim": Compassion or rejection? *Journal of Personality and Social Psychology*, 4, 203–210.

Markus, H. R. and S. Kitayama (1991) Culture and the self: Implications for cognition, emotion, and motivation. *Psychological Review*, 98, 224–253.

Moore, W. L. and J. Pfeffer (1980) The relationship between departmental power and faculty careers on two campuses: The case for structural effects on faculty salaries. *Research in Higher Education*, **13**, 291–306.

Ocasio, W. (1994) Political dynamics and the circulation of power: CEO succession in US industrial corporations 1960–1990. *Administrative Science Quarterly*, **39**, 586–611.

Ocasio, W. and H. Kim (1999) The circulation of corporate control: Selection of functional backgrounds of new CEOs in large US manufacturing firms 1981–1992. *Administrative Science Quarterly*, **44** (3), 532–562.

Pettigrew, A. M. (1973) *Politics of organizational decision-making*, London: Tavistock.

Pfeffer, J. (1992) *Managing with power*, Boston, Mass.: Harvard Business School Press.

Pfeffer, J. and A. M. Konrad (1991) The effects of individual power on earnings. *Work and Occupations*, **18**, 385–414.

Pfeffer, J. and W. L. Moore (1980) Power in university budgeting: A replication and extension. *Administrative Science Quarterly*, **25**, 637–653.

Pfeffer, J. and G. R. Salancik (1974) Organizational decision making as a political process: The case of a university budget. *Administrative Science Quarterly*, **19**, 135–151.

Pfeffer, J. and R. I. Sutton (2000) *The knowing-doing gap: How smart companies turn knowledge into action*, Boston, Mass.: Harvard Business School Press.

Scott, W. R. (1995) *Institutions and organizations*, Thousand Oaks, Calif.: Sage.

Smith, S. B. (1990) *In all his glory: The life of William S. Paley*, New York, N. Y.: Simon & Schuster.

Standing, C. and S. Standing (1999) The role of politics in IS career progression. *Systems Research and Behavioral Science*, **16**, 519–531.

Tiedens, L. Z. (2000) Powerful emotions: The vicious cycle of social status positions and emotions. In N. Ashkanasy, W. Zerbe, and C. Hartel (Eds.), *Emotions in the workplace: Research, theory, and practice* (pp. 71–81), Westport, Conn.: Quorum Books.

(2001) Anger and advancement versus sadness and subjugation: The effect of negative emotion expressions on social status conferral. *Journal of Personality and Social Psychology*, **80**, 86–94.

Tiedens, L. Z. and A. R. Fragale (2003) Power moves: Complementarity in dominant and submissive nonverbal behavior. *Journal of Personality and Social Psychology*, **84**, 558–568.

Williamson, O. E. and W. G. Ouchi (1981) The markets and hierarchies program of research: Origins, implications, prospects. In A. H. Van de Ven and W. F. Joyce (Eds.), *Perspectives on Organizational Design and Behavior* (pp. 347–370), New York, N. Y.: Wiley.

2 | *How can power be tamed?*

DAVID G. WINTER

Power is essential for any successful human organization, whether a family organized for mutual material and emotional support, an economic enterprise organized for the production and distribution of goods and services, or a political structure organized to keep the peace and create cooperation among diverse groups. Yet any serious analysis of power immediately confronts its dual nature: On the one hand, power makes it possible to coordinate human activity so that organizations can accomplish what individuals cannot. That coordination requires people who have the desire and skill to seek power. As Russell (1995: 190–191) argued, "democracy, if it is to exist psychologically as well as politically, demands organization of the various interests [...] by men who enjoy whatever influence is justified [...]." Moreover, the power of charismatic leaders can make us feel that "our hearts burn within us, while he talked with us by the way" (Luke 24:32; see also House et al. 1991; McClelland and Burnham 1976).

On the other hand, power can destroy: turning persons into dehumanized objects (Kipnis 1976), leaders into demagogues, and organized society into a totalitarian prison. Hitler was only the most memorable of the many charismatic leaders who led their people to aggressive war. As Bertrand Russell (1995: Chapter 18) argued, taming power is the central moral and ethical problem of human social existence – a concern to the ancient Confucians and Greeks and a leitmotif of Western social science, from organizational theory and normative political science to laboratory experimentation in psychology (Lee-Chai and Bargh 2001).

How do we claim the "good" of power while protecting ourselves from the "bad"? One obvious way is to separate good and bad, then set good power free to destroy the bad. Americans may be particularly prone to this kind of moral dualism; for example, in 1917, Woodrow Wilson called for a declaration of war on Germany because "the world must be made safe for democracy." Such a Manichaean approach is not without risk, for it may become one of the subtle corruptions of power,

leading to places like Dresden, Hiroshima, My Lai, and Abu Ghraib –
or, for that matter, to the Twin Towers of the World Trade Center.
What starts out as good power turns, often beneath our notice, to bad.
As Lord Acton (1948: 364) observed in his letter to Bishop Creighton,
"power tends to corrupt, and absolute power corrupts absolutely. Great
men are almost always bad men."

Psychologists have proposed a wide variety of ways in which power
might be tamed. A recent catalogue (Lee-Chai and Bargh 2001) suggests
various mechanisms: prosocial goals, a communal (versus exchange)
orientation, interdependent self-construal, high self-esteem, "soft" (versus "hard") power tactics, effortful (versus effortless) information processing, low power distance, and institutional transparency. Yet even
these laboratory mechanisms are not without ambiguity. For example,
does a "communal orientation" simply promote *communal* wars, as in
the former Yugoslavia, Rwanda, and Iraq? And at the end of the day,
how applicable are such laboratory manipulations to real-life power
dilemmas: diplomats trying to decide whether to defuse a nuclear crisis
by deterrence or appeasement, teachers balancing punishment and
diversion in dealing with a schoolyard bully, or harassed parents trying
to cope with the conflicting demands of job, family, and children. In this
chapter, I draw on politics, history, and literature in addition to psychological research to sketch the topic of taming power in broad
outline.

How might power be tamed?

First let us review four ways in which power might be tamed: by love,
reason, religion, and responsibility. Drawing on psychological research,
politics, and history, I argue that each has a mixed record: Each is often
successful, *but* each is also vulnerable to being "hijacked" by power
itself. Then I introduce the concept of *generative historical consciousness* as yet another way in which power might be tamed. Because there
are no magical solutions, we need to explore every possible concept.

Power tamed by love and affiliation?

Freud believed that power (i.e. the destructive instincts) could be tempered by Eros, or love. In an exchange with Einstein (Freud 1964: 212),
he wrote that "If willingness to engage in war is an effect of the

destructive instinct, the most obvious plan will be to bring Eros, its antagonist, into play against it." Some modern research confirms the role of love or affiliation in taming power drives. Among individuals, the aggressive manifestations of the power motive[1] are reduced or eliminated by the affiliation motive, which promotes health (McClelland 1989) and long-term adjustment (McAdams and Valliant 1982). At the societal level, high levels of affiliation motivation predict concessions and compromise (Langner and Winter 2001), thus deflecting power motivation away from war and toward peace (McClelland 1975: Chapter 9; Winter, 2007).

Yet, under some circumstances, affiliation and love actually intensify the bad effects of power. Thus, most soldiers fight because of affiliative bonds with fellow soldiers, rather than for power or ideology (Williams 1989). Scorned love, or an unfaithful lover, can ignite murderous rage, as in Shakespeare's *Othello*. At the conclusion of the epic "Ring" cycle of operas, Wagner's Brünnhilde believed that her lover Siegfried had betrayed her and so asked the gods to "teach me revenge as has never been tamed" (*Götterdämmerung*, Act III). She then arranged for Siegfried to be murdered, seized a firebrand from his funeral pyre and flung it toward Valhalla, thus setting the whole world on fire. If, in the words of political theorist Morgenthau (1962: 248), "power is redeemed by an irreducible residue of love," so also "love is corrupted by an irreducible residue of power."

Power tamed by reason and intellect?

Believing that power can be tamed by reason and intellect, Plato proposed that his ideal *Republic* should be ruled by specially trained intelligent and rational Guardians.[2] Similarly, Russell believed that the scientific temper ("a half-way house between skepticism and dogmatism") could combat autocratic power (1995: 203). Psychologists have attempted to translate these broad concepts into specific variables such as self-regulation (Kuhl 2000), self-control (Baumeister et al.

---

[1] As used in this chapter, "motive" and "motivation" are conceptualized and measured in the tradition of David McClelland and colleagues (Winter 1998; see also Smith 1992).

[2] *The Republic*, Section 473 c–d.

1994), or self-regulation and attentional control competencies (Mischel and Ayduk 2002: 115ff).

Yet it is well to remember that reason and the intellect have also been seduced into the service of power. At the beginning of World War I, intellectuals and scientists of both sides exchanged manifestos ("Britain's destiny and duty," 1914; "To the civilized world," 1914/1915). And scientific reason gave the world nuclear weapons. On the day that the U.S.A. destroyed Hiroshima by the first military use of an atomic bomb, President Harry Truman enthusiastically remarked that "this is the greatest thing in history!" (Walker 2004: 78). Over sixty years later, however, nuclear weapons are not an unambiguous case of scientific restraint on power. As Baumann and Kuhl (2005: 467) noted, intellect, self-control, and self-regulation facilitate people's "behavior according to their emotional preferences," meaning that these qualities are no better or worse than the preferences they serve. To the ancient Greeks, Athena was the goddess of wisdom and reason, but she was also the goddess of war.

Power tamed by religion?

With its focus on ultimate concerns and submission of human will to divine forces, religion can give people the will and strength to tame their power drives. In the Christian tradition, Jesus resisted the temptations of power before beginning his public ministry, as the Gospel of Luke records: "And the devil said unto him, All this power will I give thee [...] if thou therefore wilt worship me, all shall be thine. And Jesus answered and said unto him, 'Get thee behind me, Satan'" (Luke 4:5–8). Many religious groups are indeed pacifistic, emphasizing the "soft power" of persuasion rather than the "hard power" of force.

Yet religion has also been hijacked by power – especially during wartime, as in the Crusades or the religious wars of the sixteenth and seventeenth centuries. Speaking after four years of bloody civil war, Abraham Lincoln (1865) began his second inaugural address with the ironic observation that "both [sides] read the same Bible, and pray to the same God; and each invokes His aid against the other."

Responsibility

Responsibility is an important concept in diverse domains of thought. In psychology, the concept of responsibility involves variables such as impulse control and altruism. Drawing on these perspectives, Winter and Barenbaum (1985) empirically developed an implicit measure of responsibility, based on content analysis of Thematic Apperception Test (TAT) stories. The measure includes five categories:

1. moral or legal standards;
2. obligation;
3. concern for others;
4. concern about consequences of actions;
5. self-judgment.

This measure has shown some promise in taming power drives and so will be discussed at length here. Each of the five categories would appear to exert a restraining influence on power. Moral and legal standards define the appropriate abstract ends for which power might be used, obligations and concern for others suggest duty and altruism as restraints, and concern about consequences engages prudence and foresight. Finally, self-judgment involves monitoring, evaluation, and feedback.

Construct validity of the responsibility measure

Secondary analyses of data from two longitudinal studies provide construct validation for the responsibility measure. Table 2.1 presents results from a 1977 follow-up by McClelland et al. (1982) of adults who were in first grade when their mothers were interviewed in the Sears et al. (1957) *Patterns of Childrearing* study. For these grown-up children, responsibility was measured by a TAT given in the follow-up. The correlates of adult responsibility are somewhat different for women and men. High-scoring women scored high on two *cognitive* measures that suggest responsibility and self-control: the "principled thinking" scale (Stages 5A, 5B, and 6) of Rest's Defining Issues Test (1976), constructed to measure Kohlberg's stages of moral development (1963); and the self-control scale of the Adjective Check List, which identifies "serious, sober individuals, interested in and responsive to their obligations" (Gough and Heilbrun 1965: 6). In contrast, high-scoring men report greater inhibition of impulsive and irresponsible *actions*. That is, they respond more often with "haven't done but would like to" (that is, they inhibit) to a list of impulsive, aggressive actions such as "threw things around the room," "stayed up all night

Table 2.1 Adult correlates of responsibility measure.

	Correlation with responsibility TAT scores		
Variable	Total	Men	Women
From adult follow-up of Sears et al. (1957) *study*[a]	(*n* = 78)	(*n* = 38)	(*n* = 40)
Principled thinking[b]	.18	.04	.35*
Self-control scale of adjective checklist	.15	−.01	.35*
Inhibition of aggressive actions	.38***	.62***	−.03
From the Grant Study of Adult Development[c]		(*n* = 60)	
Career success cluster		.30*	
Personal well-being cluster		.05	

+ *p* < .10
* *p* < .05
** *p* < .01
*** *p* < .001
[a] McClelland et al. (1982).
[b] Stages 5A, 5B, and 6 of Defining Issues Test (Rest, 1976).
[c] Vaillant (1977).

for no reason," and "didn't show up for a day's work because you just didn't feel like it" (see Winter 1973: 135).

Table 2.1 also presents results from a secondary analysis of data from sixty male Harvard graduates of the Grant Study of Adult Development (Vaillant 1977). Responsibility scores from TATs written at around age thirty significantly predicted a clinician's ratings fifteen to eighteen years later on a cluster of variables suggesting career success (e.g., income, advancement, enjoying job) but were unrelated to another rating cluster involving personal well-being (e.g., recreation, low substance use, few psychiatric visits).

Responsibility tames power motivation

Table 2.2 shows that from an early age responsibility moderates or channels power motivation. Among adults scoring high in responsibility, adult power motivation scores were significantly correlated with variables reflecting "prosocial aggression" measured when they were twelve years old. Sears (1961: 471) describes these variables as

Table 2.2 How responsibility moderates the expression of power motivation.

Variable	Correlation with power motivation if responsibility is:	
	High	Low
Pre-adolescents[a]		
Prosocial aggression	.41+	−.38
Antisocial aggression	−.18	.34
Self-aggression	−.51*	.13
College students[b]		
Conscientious student cluster:		
women	.27	−.44**
Profligacy cluster:		
Men	−.71***	.40
Women	.03	.41*
Adults[b]		
Responsible versus profligate style:		
Men	.64*	−.49*
Women	.49*	−.46*

+ $p < .10$
* $p < .05$
** $p < .01$
*** $p < .001$
[a] Data from Sears (1961) follow-up of Sears et al. (1957) sample.
[b] Adapted from Winter and Barenbaum (1985).

"aggression used in a socially approved way for purposes that are acceptable to the moral standards of the group" (e.g., "When a person has broken an important rule, he should definitely be punished for it"). Their negative correlation with self-aggression (impulses toward suicide, self-punishment from sources outside the self, and accidents) suggests that high-scorers sublimate aggressive power concerns rather than internalizing them. In contrast, among adults scoring low in responsibility, adult power motivation was correlated with twelve-year-old "antisocial aggression" variables – acts or sentiments "that are normally unacceptable socially in the formal pattern of our culture" (e.g., "Sometimes an actual fight is the only way to settle an argument").

Among college students and adults, as shown in the lower parts of Table 2.2, responsibility channels power motivation into responsible behaviors such as conscientious academic work or being a leader, whereas low responsibility channels the same motive into "profligate impulsive" behaviors such as drinking, verbal and physical aggression, and sexual exploitation.

Other studies suggest that responsibility plays a similar moderating role in two major domains of adult life: family and work. In a study of 100 custodial mothers of divorcing families, Stewart et al. (1997) found that among women *low* in responsibility, power motivation predicted blaming the former spouse and not one's self for the divorce, using conflict tactics that involved verbal aggression and violence, filing more legal motions, and drawing their children into "loyalty strains". For women high in responsibility, power motivation was not related to any of these variables.

Winter (1991) carried out a secondary analysis of data from a longitudinal study (by Howard and Bray, 1988) of 142 AT&T managers in nontechnical administration or sales positions, finding that men who showed a combination of high power motivation and high responsibility had advanced to higher management levels sixteen years later ($\chi^2 = 5.42$, $p < .02$).

Origins of responsibility

Secondary analyses also suggest some antecedents of responsibility. Once again the results are different for women and men, as shown in Table 2.3. Women's responsibility appears to be socialized by *cognitive verbal means*. When they were children, their mothers reported using verbal discipline involving evaluation of the child's action or mention of negative consequences and contingencies rather than appealing to higher authorities such as father, police, or the bogeyman. In contrast, men's responsibility socialization appears to involve *behaviors* – assigning chores such as making one's bed, taking care of clothes, or caring for younger siblings. These childhood antecedents of responsibility appear to be quite narrow and specific, whereas two of the major clusters of maternal treatment variables in the *Patterns of Childrearing* study show only nonsignificant trend relationships – maternal warmth (positive) and restrictiveness (negative) – to adult responsibility.

Table 2.3 Childrearing antecedents of responsibility.

| Variable | Correlation with responsibility scores: | | |
	Total $(n = 78)$	Men $(n = 38)$	Women $(n = 40)$
Childhood antecedents[a]			
Explanatory verbal discipline	.23*	.09	.36*
Responsibility tasks	.37***	.69***	.16
	Correlation with gain in responsibility score during college		
College antecedents[b]			
Rated contributions to learning from:			
Formal academic demands	.18	.11	.24+
Informal social life	.19+	−.34*	.09

+ $p < .10$
* $p < .05$
** $p < .01$
*** $p < .001$
[a] Data from Sears et al. (1957) study.
[b] Data from Winter et al. (1981) study of "Ivy College".

A similar pattern of gender difference appears to continue in college. Among the women and men of the "Ivy" College class of 1978 studied by Winter et al. (1981), those women who reported great contributions to learning from formal academic work (e.g., classes, assigned reading, labs, thesis) showed a near-significant trend toward higher gains in responsibility scores from first to senior year. For men, involvement in informal social life (dorm life, bull sessions) predicted significantly lower gains (or actual declines) in responsibility scores over the course of college. In college as in childhood, then, women's responsibility appears to be socialized through cognitive mechanisms, whereas for men behavior training (or inhibition) tends to be more important.

The paradoxical role of responsibility in international crises

Although responsibility clearly tames power at the individual level, its effect is quite different at the international level. Winter (2007) scored

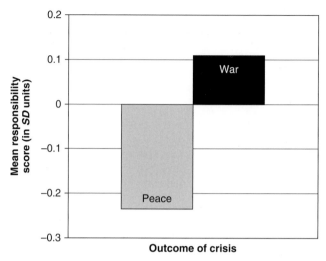

Figure 2.1 Means of averaged responsibility scores (standardized within pairs) for eight matched pairs of war and peace crises.

documents such as government-to-government communications, speeches, and media commentary from international crises that escalated to war and matched crises that were peacefully resolved. As shown in Figure 2.1, responsibility scores were significantly higher in the war crises, especially those involving one or more major powers. (The overall mean d across the eight pairs of studies was .401, which is a moderate effect size, $p = .038$.)

Thus in the fog of crisis and war, with emotions unleashed and the stakes running high, the same variable that restrains individual power can easily be enlisted to justify violent collective power. This surprising result can be understood by examining the responsibility scoring categories. For example, *moral and legal standards* ("good/bad," "right/ wrong") are applied to the other side rather than the self, so that they rationalize aggressive power: *They* become an "axis of evil". The sense of *impersonal obligation* becomes a fatalistic "we have no choice," as Holsti (1972) found in his study of communications during the July 1914 crisis. *Concern for other people* is narrowed to a focus on protecting one's own people, and *concern for consequences* arouses visions of worst-case scenarios. Thus US National Security Adviser Condoleezza Rice (2003) said in a television interview six months before the 2003 US invasion of Iraq that "we don't want the smoking gun to be a mushroom cloud."[3] Finally, *self-judgment* evolves into a sense that "history will judge us" if we shrink from aggression. Speaking for British intervention at the beginning of World War I, Foreign Secretary Sir Edward Grey (1914/1916, p. 95) argued that

If, in a crisis like this, we run away from those obligations of honour and interest as regards the Belgian treaty, I doubt whether, whatever material force we might have at the end, it would be of very much value in face of the respect that we should have lost.[4]

During some international crises, then, going to war may appear the "responsible" choice: to deter an aggressor, protect one's citizens, and secure the survival of one's core values. Most people would accept that after Hitler violated the Munich Agreement by occupying Prague in March 1939, Neville Chamberlain did the "responsible" thing by resisting further German conquests and declaring war after Germany invaded Poland. On the other hand, aggression is sometimes rationalized – perhaps privately as well as publicly – with the language of responsibility. Thus, on the day of that invasion, Hitler spoke of his "duty [...] that our people shall live, that Germany shall live" (Domarus 1990: III, 1755). Thus even responsibility is subject to hijacking by power itself.

Return of the repressed

What is the mechanism by which responsibility, religion, reason, and love – mechanisms and processes that ordinarily tame power – are subverted into the service of untamed power? Freud (1959: 35) described this process as a particular form of the "return of the repressed": "[by] a piece of malicious treachery. It is precisely what was chosen as the instrument of repression [...] that becomes the vehicle for the return [...]. When what has been repressed returns, it emerges from the repressing force itself." Perhaps such a return is aided by the lowering of inhibition that often accompanies the possession and expression of power (see Keltner, Gruenfeld, and Anderson, 2003).

The taming mechanisms of love, science and wisdom, religion, and responsibility can become the very means by which power defeats

---

[3] See http://transcripts.cnn.com/TRANSCRIPTS/0209/08/le.00.html.
[4] See http://net.lib.byu.edu/~rdh7/wwi/1914/greytalk.html.

taming. In the name of love, we seek vengeance; in the name of rationality, we unleash chaos; in the name of the creator, we kill other creatures. Finally, in the name of responsibility, we join with Caesar's spirit and "cry 'havoc!' and let slip the dogs of war" (Mark Antony, in Shakespeare's *Julius Caesar*, Act III, Scene 1, line 276).

A new approach: "generative historical consciousness"[5]

Since no mechanism is foolproof, it is important to identify other concepts that can be brought to bear in taming power. In the last part of this chapter, I therefore introduce a new concept of *generative historical consciousness* for that purpose. Here I only sketch a broad outline; if the concept has merit, precise definitions and measures will eventually follow.

Historical consciousness

How was World War III avoided in 1962? The concept of generative historical consciousness begins with a reflection on the Cuban Missile Crisis of October 1962. In the judgment of historians Fursenko and Naftali (1997: ix), it was the only moment in the second half of the twentieth century "when a third world war seemed possible." At the time, President Kennedy estimated the chances of a thermonuclear war as "somewhere between one out of three and even" (Sorensen 1965: 705).

One reason such a calamity did not happen is reflected in a theme running through the words and deeds of leaders on both sides: a sense of how their actions would look in historical perspective, or *historical consciousness*.[6] For example, shortly before the crisis, Kennedy had read *The Guns of August*, Barbara Tuchman's (1962) account of the outbreak of World War I, and so he was determined to avoid a 1914-style rush to disaster (Blight 1990: 99). And, as Kennedy's advisers debated an air strike, they were haunted by the realization that they would be repeating the Japanese surprise attack on Pearl Harbor. ("Pearl Harbor" was mentioned at least ten times during the

---

[5] I am indebted to Joshua Berman for discussions in developing this concept.
[6] This is *not* the same thing as the "lessons of history," which often turn out to be wrong.

deliberations of the Executive Committee of the National Security Council during the crisis; see May and Zelikow 1997.)

On the Soviet side, Chairman Khrushchev recalled his own experience of war in his letter to Kennedy at the height of the crisis: "I have participated in two world wars and know that war ends when it has rolled through cities and villages, everywhere sowing death and destruction" (US Department of State 1996: 236). Years after the crisis, he recalled his thinking to an American editor: "What good would it have done me in the last hour of my life to know that though our great nation and the United States were in complete ruins, the national honor of the Soviet Union was intact?" (Cousins 1977: 22).

In his autobiography, Bill Clinton (2004: 952) recounted that contemplating a rock brought back from the moon gave him a sense of historical consciousness that he would use to smooth over more everyday power conflicts: "Whenever arguments in the Oval Office heated up beyond reason, I would interrupt and say, 'You see that rock? It's 3.6 billion years old. We're all just passing through. Let's calm down and go back to work.'"

Intimations of mortality

In the long run of history, of course, we will be dead. People deal with the undoubted fact of their personal mortality in different ways, and the way we view the prospect of our own death affects whether and how we can tame our power drives. Some people experience the prospect of their own death as diminishing and threatening, creating a desperate determination to force a final "victory" of their power before their time runs out. For example, as Adolf Hitler's health concerns increased, his foreign policy became increasingly reckless (Kershaw 2000: 36–37). An observer recorded Hitler's words at a 1937 secret military conference (Domarus 1990: 959):

He, Hitler, would not live much longer [...]. In his family, men did not grow old. Also both his parents had died young. It was hence necessary to face the problems which absolutely had to be resolved (*Lebensraum*) as quickly as possible – so that this would occur while he was still alive.

Just three days before the German invasion of Poland in September 1939, Hitler spoke to his entourage (Kershaw 2000: 228, 907, n. 324): "I'm now 50 years old, still in full possession of my strength. The problems must be solved by me, and I can wait no longer. In a few years I will be physically and perhaps mentally, too, no longer up to it."

According to former US Secretary of State Henry Kissinger (2005), China's Chairman Mao Zedong suffered similar anxieties, as reflected in a 1972 conversation with US President Richard Nixon:

> Mao answered: "All I have changed is Beijing and a few suburbs." It was a nightmare for him that after 20 years of fighting and all those efforts to found a communist society, he had achieved so little of lasting value. That is what led him to sacrifice more and more lives to achieve his work within his lifetime. He believed that otherwise his legacy would be destroyed.[7]

However, not every political leader responds to intimations of personal mortality in this way (see Florian and Mikulincer 1998; Routledge and Arndt 2005). For example, it was only *after* they each suffered heart attacks that Egyptian President Anwar Sadat and Israeli Prime Minister Menahem Begin reversed previous policies, achieving a measure of reconciliation between Egypt and Israel that culminated in the 1978 Camp David agreement. And in South Africa, an aging Nelson Mandela opted for reconciliation rather than revenge when he assumed the Presidency in 1994.

Generativity

Shakespeare's character of Prospero in *The Tempest* is a striking literary example of how acceptance of personal mortality leads to taming power drives. Having been unjustly deposed and exiled, Prospero employed magical powers to get revenge, exulting that "At this hour lies at my mercy all mine enemies" (Act IV, Scene 1, Lines 262–263). Yet, suddenly he renounced his powers and spoke his famous soliloquy about mortality:

> Yea, all which it inherit, shall dissolve;
> And, like this insubstantial pageant faded,
> Leave not a rack behind. We are such stuff
> As dreams are made on, and our little life
> Is rounded with a sleep.
>
> (Act IV, Scene 1, Lines 154–158)

Why the change? Shortly before, he arranged for the marriage of Prospero's daughter Miranda to Ferdinand, son of the King of Naples

---

[7] Interview with *Der Spiegel*: see www.spiegel.de/international/spiegel/ 0,1518,379165,00.html (accessed February 3, 2007).

(one of the conspirators who exiles him). After successfully rearing and launching his daughter, Prospero is able to accept his mortality, give up his power, and get off the stage.

Prospero's loving care of Miranda is an example of *generativity*. Erikson (1950: Chapter 7; 1982) introduced this concept to describe the midlife developmental stage when people rear the next generation and enhance cultural institutions, and in recent years psychologists have elaborated and refined it (see de St. Aubin et al. 2004; Hofer et al. 2008; McAdams and de St. Aubin 1998; Stewart and Vandewater, 1998). Generative actions take many forms: parenting, mentoring, leadership, creating new products or ways of understanding. In each case, the generative person *surrenders control* of that legacy, thereby creating a legacy or symbolic immortality. I suggest that generativity is the third component of generative historical consciousness.

Generative historical consciousness is currently a conceptual framework for future research, though measures exist of some components such as implicit time-span (Lasane and O'Donnell 2005) and implicit generativity (Peterson and Stewart 1990).

Summary characterization

One of the most eloquent statements ever made by a US president embodies all three elements of generative historical consciousness in four brief sentences. Speaking at American University, John F. Kennedy (1964: 462) called on Americans to "re-examine our own attitude" – toward peace, the Soviet Union, and the Cold War:

So, let us not be blind to our differences – but let us also direct attention to our common interests and to the means by which those differences can be resolved. And if we cannot end now our differences, at least we can help make the world safe for diversity. For, in the final analysis, our most basic common link is that we all inhabit this small planet. We all breathe the same air. We all cherish our children's future. And we are all mortal.

References

Acton, Lord (J. E. E. Dalberg Acton) (1948) Letter to Mandell Creighton, April 5, 1887. Reprinted in G. Himmelfarb (Ed.), *Essays on freedom and power* (pp. 358–367), Glencoe, Ill.: Free Press.

Baumann, N. and Kuhl, J. (2005) How to resist temptation: The effects of external control versus autonomy support on self-regulatory dynamics. *Journal of Personality*, **73**, 443–470.

Baumeister, R. F., Heatherton, T. F., and Tice, D. M. (1994) *Losing control: How and why people fail at self-regulation*, Orlando, Fla.: Academic Press.

Blight, J. G. (1990) *The shattered crystal ball: Fear and learning in the Cuban Missile Crisis*, Savage, Md.: Rowman & Littlefield.

"Britain's destiny and duty" (1914, September 18) *The Times*, p. 3.

Clinton, B. (2004) *My life*, New York, N.Y.: Knopf.

Cousins, N. (1977) The Cuban Missile Crisis: An anniversary. *Saturday Review*, October 15, pp. 4, **22**.

de St. Aubin, E., McAdams, D. P., and Kim, T.-C. (Eds.) (2004) *The generative society: Caring for future generations*, Washington, D.C.: American Psychological Association.

Domarus, M. (1990) *Hitler: Speeches and proclamations 1932–1945*, 3 vols., Wauconda, Ill.: Bolchazy-Carducci Publishers.

Erikson, E. H. (1950) *Childhood and society*, New York, N.Y.: Norton.

(1982) *The life-cycle completed*, New York, N.Y.: Norton.

Florian, V. and Mikulincer, M. (1998) Symbolic immortality and the management of the terror of death. *Journal of Personality and Social Psychology*, **74**, 725–734.

Freud, S. (1959) Delusion and dream in Jensen's *Gradiva*. In J. Strachey (Ed.), *The standard edition of the complete psychological works of Sigmund Freud* (Vol. IX, pp. 1–95), London: Hogarth. (Original work published 1907.)

(1964) Why war? The correspondence with Einstein. In J. Strachey (Ed.), *The standard edition of the complete psychological works of Sigmund Freud* (Vol. XXII, pp. 199–215), London: Hogarth. (Original work published 1933.)

Fursenko, A. and Naftali, T. (1997) *"One hell of a gamble": Khrushchev, Kennedy, and Castro 1958–1964*, New York, N.Y.: Norton.

Gough, H. G. and Heilbrun, A. B. Jr. (1965) *The adjective check list manual*, Palo Alto, Calif.: Consulting Psychologists Press.

Grey, E. (1916) Speech to the House of Commons, August 3, 1914. In E. von Mach (Ed.), *Official documents relating to the outbreak of the European war* (pp. 89–96), New York, N.Y.: Macmillan. (Original work published 1914.)

Hofer, J., Busch, H., Chasiotis, J., Kärtner, J., and Campos, D. (2008) Concern for generativity and its relation to implicit pro-social power motivation, generative goals, and satisfaction with life: A cross-cultural investigation. *Journal of Personality*, **76**, 1–30.

Holsti, O. (1972) *Crisis, escalation, war*, Montreal: McGill-Queen's University Press.

House, R. J., Spangler, W. D., and Woycke, J. (1991) Personality and charisma in the US presidency: A psychological theory of leader effectiveness. *Administrative Science Quarterly*, **36**, 364–396.

Howard, A. and Bray, D. (1988) *Managerial lives in transition: Advancing age and changing times*, New York, N.Y.: Guilford.

Keltner, D., Gruenfeld, D. H., and Anderson, C. (2003) Power, approach, and inhibition. *Psychological Review*, **110**, 265–284.

Kennedy, John F. (1964) *Public papers of the Presidents: John F. Kennedy 1963*, Washington, D.C.: Government Printing Office.

Kershaw, I. (2000) *Hitler 1937–1945: Nemesis*, New York, N.Y.: Norton.

Kipnis, D. (1976) *The power-holders*, Chicago, Ill.: University of Chicago Press.

Kissinger, H. A. (2005) Henry Kissinger on Europe's falling out with Washington (Interview with *Der Spiegel*), October 10. Retrieved September 7, 2008, from: www.spiegel.de/international/spiegel/ 0,1518,379165,00.html.

Kohlberg, L. (1963) The development of children's orientations toward a moral order. I. Sequence in the development of moral thought. *Vita Humana*, **6**, 11–33.

Kuhl, J. (2000) A functional-design approach to motivation and self-regulation: The dynamics of personality systems and interactions. In M. Boekaerts, P. R. Pintrich, and M. Zeidner (Eds.), *Handbook of self-regulation* (pp. 111–169), Orlando, Fla.: Academic Press.

Langner, C. and Winter, D. G. (2001) The motivational basis of compromise and concessions: Archival and experimental studies. *Journal of Personality and Social Psychology*, **81**, 711–727.

Lasane, T. P. and O'Donnell, D. A. (2005) Time orientation measurement: A conceptual approach. In A. Strathman and J. Joireman (Eds.), *Understanding behavior in the context of time: Theory, research, and application* (pp. 11–30), Mahwah, N. J.: Erlbaum.

Lee-Chai, A. Y. and Bargh, J. A. (Eds.) (2001) *The use and abuse of power: Multiple perspectives on the causes of corruption*, Philadelphia, Pa.: Psychology Press.

Lincoln, A. (1865) Second inaugural address. Retrieved September 6, 2008, from: www.bartleby.com/124/pres32.html.

May, E. R. and Zelikow, P. D. (1997) *The Kennedy tapes: Inside the White House during the Cuban Missile Crisis*, New York, N.Y.: Norton.

McAdams, D. P. and de St. Aubin, E. (Eds.) (1998) *Generativity and adult development: How and why we care for the next generation*, Washington, D.C.: American Psychological Association.

McAdams, D. P. and Vaillant, G. E. (1982) Intimacy motivation and psychosocial adjustment: A longitudinal study. *Journal of Personality Assessment*, **46**, 586–593.

McClelland, D. C. (1975) *Power: The inner experience*, New York, N.Y.: Irvington.

(1989) Motivational factors in health and disease. *American Psychologist*, **44**, 675–683.

McClelland, D. C. and Burnham, D. H. (1976) Power is the great motivator. *Harvard Business Review*, March–April, 100–110, 159–166.

McClelland, D. C., Constantian, C. A., Pilon, D. A., and Stone, C. (1982) Effects of child-rearing practices on adult maturity. In D. C. McClelland (Ed.), *The development of social maturity* (pp. 209–248), New York, N.Y.: Irvington.

Mischel, W. and Ayduk, O. (2002) Self-regulation in a cognitive-affective personality system: Attentional control in the service of the self. *Self and Identity*, **1**, 113–120.

Morgenthau, H. J. (1962) Love and power. *Commentary*, **33**(3), 247–251.

Peterson, B. E. and Stewart, A. J. (1990) Using personal and fictional documents to assess psychosocial development: A case study of Vera Brittain's generativity. *Psychology and Aging*, **5**, 400–411.

Rest, J. R. (1976) New approaches in the assessment of moral judgment. In T. Lickona (Ed.), *Moral development and behavior: Theory, research, and social issues* (pp. 198–218), New York, N.Y.: Holt, Rinehart, & Winston.

Rice, C. (2002) Interview on CNN with Wolf Blitzer, September 7. Retrieved September 6, 2008, from: http://transcripts.cnn.com/TRANSCRIPTS/0309/07/le.00.html.

Routledge, C. and Arndt, J. (2005) Time and terror: Managing temporal consciousness and the awareness of mortality. In A. Strathman and J. Joireman (Eds.), *Understanding behavior in the context of time: Theory, research, and application* (pp. 59–84), Mahwah, N.J.: Erlbaum.

Russell, B. (1995) *Power: A new social analysis*, New York, N.Y.: Norton. (Original work published 1938.)

Sears, R. R. (1961) Relation of early socialization experiences to aggression in middle childhood. *Journal of Abnormal and Social Psychology*, **63**, 466–492.

Sears, R. R., Maccoby, E. E., and Levin, H. (1957) *Patterns of childrearing*, Evanston, Ill.: Row Peterson.

Smith, C. P. (Ed.) (1992) *Motivation and personality: Handbook of thematic content analysis*, New York, N.Y.: Cambridge University Press.

Sorensen, T. C. (1965) *Kennedy*, New York, N.Y.: Harper & Row.

Stewart, A. J. and Vandewater, E. (1998) The course of generativity. In D. P. McAdams and E. de St. Aubin (Eds.), *Generativity and adult development* (pp. 75–100), Washington, D.C.: American Psychological Association.

Stewart, A. J., Copeland, A. P., Chester, N. L., Malley, J. E., and Barenbaum, N. B. (1997) *Separating together: How divorce transforms families*, New York, N.Y.: Guilford.

"To the civilized world." (1915) *Current history: A monthly magazine: The European war*. Vol. I: From the Beginning to March 1915 (pp. 185–187), New York, N.Y.: The New York Times Company. (Original work published 1914.)

Tuchman, B. W. (1962) *The guns of August*, New York, N.Y.: Macmillan.

US Department of State (1996) *Foreign relations of the United States 1961–1963, Vol. XI: Cuban Missile Crisis and aftermath*, Washington, D.C.: Government Printing Office.

Vaillant, G. E. (1977) *Adaptation to life*, Boston, Mass.: Little, Brown.

Walker, J. S. (2004) *Prompt and utter destruction: President Truman and the use of atomic bombs against Japan* (rev. edn), Chapel Hill, N.C.: University of North Carolina Press.

Williams, R. M. (1989) *The American soldier*: An assessment, several wars later. *Public Opinion Quarterly*, 53, 160–166.

Winter, D. G. (1973) *The power motive*, New York, N.Y.: Free Press.

(1991) A motivational model of leadership: Predicting long-term management success from TAT measures of power motivation and responsibility. *Leadership Quarterly*, 2 (2), 67–80.

(1998) "Toward a science of personality psychology": David McClelland's development of empirically derived TAT measures. *History of Psychology*, 1, 130–153.

(2007) The role of motivation, responsibility, and integrative complexity in crisis escalation: Comparative studies of war and peace crises. *Journal of Personality and Social Psychology*, 92, 920–937.

Winter, D. G. and Barenbaum, N. B. (1985) Responsibility and the power motive in women and men. *Journal of Personality*, 53, 335–355.

Winter, D. G., McClelland, D. C., and Stewart, A. J. (1981) *A new case for the liberal arts: Assessing institutional goals and student development*, San Francisco, Calif.: Jossey-Bass.

3 Power and self-construal
How the self affects power processes

BARBARA WISSE AND
DAAN VAN KNIPPENBERG

Power plays a role in all social contexts, and it plays a key role in organizations and work groups. More specifically, one might argue that the particulars of the social context largely determine the way that (lack of) power is experienced, the way that people think or feel about power (e.g., the positive or negative connotations of power), and the way in which power differentials manifest themselves (e.g., Tjosvold 1984, 1985; van Knippenberg et al. 2001). Because power derives its meaning from the social context in which it exists, we expect that factors that affect a person's relational or social orientation may greatly influence power processes. One of the central aspects of an individual's relationship with others is the individual's self-definition in the relationship. Therefore, this chapter focuses on the question if the extent to which a person sees himself or herself as a distinctive individual (i.e. differentiated from the other party) or more as psychologically connected to the other party (i.e. incorporating the other[s] into perceptions of the self) may affect power processes. We will use theoretical insights from the field of self and identity to present a framework to understand power processes in organizations. Building on prior research concerning the development of levels at which the self may be construed, and on the existing empirical work on the influence of (proxies and correlates of) self-conception on power and influence processes, we outline how theory development and research endeavors may benefit from employing a self-construal perspective to power. First, however, we briefly overview theory on the self that is relevant to the present chapter.

The self-concept

The self-concept can be seen as the way that we perceive ourselves or as the knowledge we have about ourselves. This knowledge greatly influences the way we feel, what we think, how we behave and memorize, and the things we aim to achieve (for an overview, see Leary and Tangney 2003), and is therefore also highly relevant to organizational behavior (Lord et al. 1999; van Knippenberg et al. 2004). Importantly, as we will elaborate on later, we assert that it may also help to explain power processes.

A major point in relation to a self-concept analysis of power processes is that self-conception may differ in the *level of inclusiveness* at which the self is construed (Aron et al. 1991). People may perceive themselves or think about themselves in more personal terms or in more social terms. The personal form of self-construal is activated when an individual's sense of unique identity, differentiated from others, is the basis of self-definition (the *personal self*). At this level of inclusiveness, people's motivations have a primarily egocentric character which may make them focus more on self-benefit. The self may also be expanded, incorporating others into it (Aron et al. 1991; Aron and Fraley 1999; Brewer and Gardner 1996; Sedikides and Brewer 2001). The *interdependent self*, or the *social self*, focuses on the individual in the context of relationships and group memberships, thus embedding the individual in a larger social whole (Lee et al. 2000; Markus and Kitayama 1991). Interdependent self-construal may imply a psychological merging of self and group that leads individuals to see the self as similar to other members of the collective, to ascribe group-defining characteristics to the self, and to take the collective's interest to heart (Sedikides and Brewer 2001; Turner et al. 1987; van Knippenberg and Hogg 2003). This form of interdependent self-construal is sometimes referred to as the *collective self* (Brewer and Gardner 1996; Sedikides and Brewer 2001), or as *social identity* (Hogg and Abrams 1988; Tajfel and Turner 1986). Interdependent self-construal may also imply a psychological merging of self and other (sometimes referred to as the *relational self*; Brewer and Gardner 1996; Markus and Kitayama 1991; Sedikides and Brewer 2001) and is then based more on the individual's roles in relationships with significant others, such as one's family or close friends. For the interdependent self, the basic social motivation is to strive for collective or mutual welfare and enhancement and to maintain a respectful and agreeable relationship with others (Brewer and Gardner 1996; Lee et al. 2000; Turner et al. 1987). Important to our discussion of the relationship between power and self-construal is the notion that the more inclusive the self is, the more that the included person's resources and perspectives are viewed as belonging to the self (Aron et al. 2004).

Note that the self is not an unidimensional construct: People generally have multiple selves (Leary and Tangney 2003; Markus and Wurf 1987). A person can have an identity for each of the different personal and social positions or role relationships that this person may hold. Thus, self as manager is an identity, self as employee of organization X is an identity, and self as a spouse is an identity. Even though people may have many distinct selves, and even though different levels of self-representation coexist within the same individual, only one self tends to be salient or activated. This activated portion of the self-concept may be referred to as the working self-concept (Lord and Brown 2004; Markus and Wurf 1987), or salient identity (Turner et al. 1987). Which part or level of the self-concept will be activated is dependent on point in time, and situational, individual or cultural differences (Leary and Tangney 2003; Sedikides and Brewer 2001; Turner et al. 1987). For instance, a person's identity as a supervisor of some team may be salient when working in the office, while a person's identity as a student may be salient when attending classes on an art course.

In view of the evidence that self-construal is a core aspect of inter-personal and individual–group relationships, affecting both attitudes and behavior, and the fact that power is a key feature of social relation-ships, an obvious question is how theory on self-construal may explain power processes. The remainder of this chapter explores this question. Below, we will first provide a theoretical reflection on how self-construal may inform motivations, goals, and perspectives related to power. Thereafter we will discuss the scarce empirical evidence that may sub-stantiate our reasoning. However, we hope that our discussion of the empirical evidence may demonstrate the importance of including the self-concept in theories and studies of power by highlighting some (probable) prominent effects.

Theoretical outlook on power processes and the self

For all practical purposes we will conceptualize power in the present chapter as a social phenomenon that takes place between interdepend-ent people. Clearly thus, one might argue that organizations – with their common hierarchical structure of departments and persons, the interdependent relationships between people and groups, and the potential goal incongruencies of the multiple parties – are one of the more likely arenas for power processes to take place. Although the revitalization of the power concept has not yet yielded consensus on the nature and the definition of power, we speak of power when a person (i.e. the power-holder) is capable of affecting the outcomes or behavior of (an) other person(s) (Fiske et al. 1996; Goodwin et al. 1998; Pruitt and Carnevale 1993; Tjosvold et al. 2003). Thus, power is seen as a potential; a resource that may or may not be used. Our conceptualization of power entails that power is a feature of social interactions. Because power derives its meaning from the social context in which it exists, we expect that the level of inclusiveness at which the self is construed may greatly influence power processes. After all, as we have seen, self-construal greatly affects one's social orientation, motivation, behavior and outlook on relationships.

Power and the personal self

Power has had a bad reputation. For centuries, power has been viewed as something that corrupts, that is inherently a bad thing, or that is only deemed of importance to Machiavellians with questionable motives. Of course, this perspective on power is rather one-sided, and power may just as well be used by moral people who intend to do good. Yet, this negative outlook on power does have its origins somewhere. Sometimes people do use power only for their own good, paying little attention to others. As we will explain, it may be the power processes that take place at the personal level of self-construal that have added to power's bad reputation. When the personal form of self-construal is activated, an individual's sense of unique identity, differentiated from others, is the basis of self-definition. At this level of inclusiveness, people's motivations have a primarily egocentric character (Brewer and Gardner 1996). Power processes at the personal level of self-construal may thus be characterized by an eye on the differences between self and other and on a strong focus on own outcomes. Depending on perceived interdependence, power processes may be characterized by relative indifference toward the other party, by a competitive orientation toward the other party or by a cooperative orientation toward the other party. As we will explain, two out of these three orientations may lead to destructive power processes. Unfortunately, as the personal self may be characterized by ample attention to the differences between self and other, these two orientations may be the most likely to be developed.

When parties perceive little interdependence, power may be infrequently used. However, if power is employed, it will be governed by
self-interest motives. When parties with a salient personal self perceive
themselves to be interdependent, they may be conscious of the fact that
own goals may be incompatible with the other parties' goals.

When own and others' goals are perceived to be negatively related to
one another, power may be wielded as a means to ensure benefits for
oneself, at the expense of the outcomes of the other party. Power
processes at the individual level of self-construal may then best be
described as a tough, competitive process, in which little attention is
reserved for the other party's interests. As Tjosvold and Wu (see
Chapter 5 of this book) explain, a competitive orientation may lead to
mutual hostility, restricted communication, closed-mindedness, resistance to being influenced, and goal frustration.

However, when own and others' goals are perceived to be positively
related to one another, power may also be wielded as a means to ensure
benefits for oneself, but this time aiding the other is in the best interest of
the self. This in turn, may lead to a more cooperative orientation which
may be characterized by positive regard, openness, mutual trust, and
mutual goal productivity (see Chapter 5 by Tjosvold and Wu).

Power and the social self

When the self is more extended, including others, the basic social
motivation is to strive for collective or mutual welfare and enhancement
and to maintain harmony with others (Brewer and Gardner 1996; Lee
et al. 2000; Turner et al. 1987). Aron, McLauglin-Volpe, et al. (2004),
focusing more on the relational self, argue that people may be motivated
to include others in the self, because it may give them the opportunity
for self-expansion (cf. Aron, Aron, et al. 2004). That is, it may help them
to acquire goals, perspectives, and identities that enhance their ability to
accomplish goals. When the other is included in the self, the other's
resources, perspectives, and identities are also included in the self. This
means that the other's resources (e.g., possessions, competencies, information, social assets) are perceived as one's own. Aron, McLauglin-
Volpe, et al. (2004: 105) state that "helping other is helping self:
Interfering with other is interfering with self. This analysis also implies
that the other's acquisition and loss of resources is experienced to some
extent as if the acquisition or loss was with regard to one's own

resources." Power use within close relationships is thus governed by the power-holder's belief that promoting the other party's interest is in fact promoting own self-interest. Moreover, power may be wielded more as a means to ensure joint benefits: The outcomes of the other party are taken into account because the other party's outcomes are perceived as own outcomes. Power processes at the relational level of self-construal may thus best be described as cooperative. Note that it is important to distinguish the relational self from concepts such as positive goal inter-dependence or goal alignment. These latter concepts lack the self-defining component, and they could refer to any situation in which a person happens to have goal congruency with the power-holder.

Just like self-construal at the relational level blunts the distinction between self and other, because self and other become a more integrated whole, self-construal at the collective level reduces the distinction between self and group and turns the group into part of the self (Smith and Henry 1996; Tropp and Wright 2001; van Knippenberg and Hogg 2003). Theories such as social identity theory and self-categorization theory explain how an individual's conception of the self is affected by his or her membership of social groups, such as organizations (Hogg 2003; Hogg and Abrams 1988; Tajfel and Turner 1986; Turner et al. 1987). It is argued that the conception of the self as a group member provides the basis for the perceptual, attitudinal, and behavioral effects of group membership. The more one conceives of oneself in terms of the membership of a group, that is, the more one identifies with a group, the more one's attitudes and behavior are directed by this group membership. We propose that if the level of self-representation shifts toward the collective level, the use of power reflects the transformation of the group into part of the self, just as a shift to relational self-construal is reflected in the use of power. Like the relational self that is motivated to foster relationships with signifi-cant others, the collective self is motivated to foster harmonious rela-tionships with the group and its members. Moreover, when the group is included in the self, the group's resources, perspectives, and identity are also included in the self (cf. Aron, McLaughlin-Volpe, et al. 2004). Thus, employing power in a way that might endanger the relationship between self and group is less attractive (cf. van Knippenberg and van Knippenberg 2003). Moreover, for people with a salient collective self, power use is governed to a large extent by the power-holder's belief that promoting the group's interests is in fact promoting own self-interest.

Power may be wielded more as a means to ensure collective benefits: The outcomes of the group are a focal point because the group's outcomes are perceived as own outcomes.

Power processes at the social level of self-construal may thus be more cooperative than power processes at the personal level of self-construal. At the personal level of self-construal, people are focused on self-benefit and will only be inclined toward cooperation when they believe that own goals and other's goals are positively related.

Empirical findings concerning the role of the self in power processes

Unfortunately, only a limited number of studies focus on the relationship between power and self-construal. Empirical studies on power hardly ever focus explicitly on the influence of the extent to which the power-holders have a salient personal self. They sporadically focus on the relational self, and they sometimes focus on the collective self. To assess the potential value of a focus on self-construal for our understanding of power process, we will therefore also discuss studies that investigated proxies and (probable) correlates of self-construal. However, we acknowledge the fact that it would be preferable to discuss empirical evidence that directly concerns the link between self-construal and power processes.

The self, cooperation, and competition

Although the personal self is hardly ever the explicit focus in power studies, probably the majority of them are situated in a context in which the personal level of self-construal is likely to be salient. Power dynamics in, for instance, competitive task settings, conflict, or negotiation (Kim et al. 2005; Pruitt and Kim 2004; see also Tjosvold and Wu, Chapter 5) have in common that differences in goal orientation between the self and the other may be highlighted (Deutsch 1973), which may enhance the likelihood that the personal self is activated (cf. Brewer and Gardner 1996; Turner et al. 1987). So, although negative interdependence and the salience of the personal self do not necessarily go hand in hand (i.e. the personal self may also be salient when parties perceive themselves to be independent or cooperatively interdependent), competition is likely to trigger personal self-construal. Several studies show that power dynamics in competitive task settings, conflict or negotiation contexts are often characterized by parties' relatively strong focus on self-enhancement, the development of negative attitudes toward one another, less helping behavior, and less trust (Olekalns et al. 2005; Tjosvold 1981, 1984, 1995; Tjosvold et al. 2005; van Knippenberg et al. 2001). Steinel and de Dreu (2004) also showed that provision of accurate and inaccurate information may be used as a power tool in cooperation and competition. Less accurate and more inaccurate information were given when the other decision-maker was competitive rather than cooperative (especially when participants had a prosocial rather than selfish value orientation). Participants thus engaged in strategic misrepresentation to trick competitive others into damaging their own outcomes and increasing the participant's outcomes.

Interestingly, there is also some evidence for the idea that the salience of the personal self is more likely to instigate a competitive power orientation than a cooperative one. Tarr et al. (2005) predicted that personal self-construal would lead to a higher likelihood of using more assertive predicament responses such as justifications or denials. They also proposed that social self-construal would lead to the higher likelihood of using more mitigating predicament responses such as apologies and excuses. Clearly, responses such as apologies and excuses are more focused on establishing a cooperative relationship with the other party than responses such as denials and justifications. They found partial support for their line of reasoning. Tjosvold et al. (2003) focused on the relation between collectivistic and individualistic values and cooperation and competition. Although collectivism and individualism are not equal to the social self and the personal self, it has been argued that the situations that an individualistic culture affords should over time lead to stronger representation of the personal (vs. collective) self, whereas situations that a collectivistic culture affords should over time lead to a stronger representation of the collective (vs. personal) self (Markus and Kitayama 1991; Wagar and Cohen 2003). Tjosvold et al. (2003) found that collectivistic and individualistic values predicted cooperative and competitive goal interdependence, which, in turn, affected group interaction and outcomes. Collectivistic values reinforced cooperative goals and an open-minded discussion of views leading to strong relationships and team productivity. Individualistic values had contrasting effects through the fostering of competitive goals and closed-minded discussion (for similar results also compare Cai et al. 2000; Ohbuchi et al. 1999).

In a similar vein, Chen et al. (2001) examined the hypothesis that power is mentally associated with different goals for individuals with a communal versus an exchange relationship orientation (Clark and Mills 1979). As communals are more relationship-oriented and more likely to pay attention to the others' needs, high communals may be more likely to have a salient social self, whereas individuals with a high exchange orientation, having a strong focus on self-interest, may be more likely to have a salient personal self. Chen et al. predicted that communals associate power with social-responsibility goals, whereas exchangers link power with self-interest goals. Thus, when power is activated, distinct goals should be activated for communals and exchangers. Indeed, they found that power-primed communals responded in socially responsible ways, whereas power-primed exchangers acted more in line with their self-interests. For more definite conclusions regarding the role of self-construal in this respect, however, we would need a comparable line of research focusing on self-construal rather than relationship orientation (i.e. the latter we should only with some caution assume to reflect differences in self-construal).

Aron et al. (1991) conducted several experiments in which they showed that a close other's resources may indeed be included in the self. In their studies they gave participants the power to allocate resources to others. Results showed that others were given an equal or even larger amount of resources than the self when this other was a close friend, but not when the other had a more distal relationship with the participant. A salient relational self thus seems to promote a focus on others' well-being and on a cooperative use of power resources.

The self and the use of openness to influence tactics

Van Knippenberg and van Knippenberg (2003) discuss several studies on influence tactics (see Yukl, Chapter 12, on power and interpersonal influence in organizations for a thorough discussion on influence tactics) and social influence that also suggest that a cooperative power orientation is more likely when the relational self is salient than when the personal self is salient. For instance, several studies show that relational strength predicts the number of hard-influence tactics as compared to the number of soft-influence tactics that are used

(Farmer et al. 1997; van Knippenberg and Steensma 2003; van Knippenberg et al. 1999). Because the use of hard-influence tactics allows the target of influence little leeway in accepting or resisting the influence attempt, hard tactics communicate less respect and usually place more strain on the relationship between power-holder and target than do soft tactics (Tjosvold and Sun 2001; van Knippenberg and Steensma 2003). The lessened use of hard tactics thus points to power-holders' motivation to uphold agreeable relationships and to take the other party's perspective into account.

Studies in social influence furthermore suggest that relational as opposed to personal self-construal renders individuals more open to the other's influence attempts. The influence process Kelman (1958) labeled "identification," and the power base that French and Raven (1959) labeled "reference" (i.e. influence based on a sense of oneness with the influencing agent) seem to reflect influence grounded in relational self-construal. Studies of group-based influence suggest that targets of influence attempts are more open to the agent's influence when agent and target have a shared social identity (for reviews, see Turner 2005; van Knippenberg 1999).

We also would expect that as the collective self becomes salient, a power-holder will be more willing to be cooperative vis-à-vis the target, and thus also use fewer hard- as compared to soft-influence tactics. Two studies addressed this issue. Bruins (1997) and Schwarzwald et al. (2005) focused on the extent to which the sharing of a social identity affected tactic use. Both studies seem to corroborate our line of reasoning. Fu et al. (2004) focus on the relationship between collectivism-individualism and tactic use and find similar results.

To conclude

In this chapter, we used theoretical insights into self and identity to present a framework that helps understand power processes in social contexts. Because power is something that derives its meaning from the social context in which it exists, factors that affect a person's relational or social orientation are prone to be important determinants of power processes. Because one of the central aspects of an individual's relationship with others is the individual's self-definition in the relationship, we proposed that the extent to which a person sees himself or herself as a distinctive individual (i.e. the personal self) or more as psychologically connected to the other party (i.e. the relational or collective self) may affect power processes. We argued that because both the relational self and the collective self are motivated to maintain harmonious bonds with the target of influence (which may be an individual or a group), and are likely to regard others' resources, perspectives, and identity as their own, they are expected to develop a cooperative power orientation. The personal self, in contrast, is motivated by self-interest and less likely to regard others' resources, perspectives and identity as belonging to self. As a consequence, a competitive power orientation is more likely to evolve for people with a salient personal self.

The abuse of power by people in leadership positions is a concern to many organizations as well as to society at large. In this respect, the current analysis suggests that the obvious implication for practice is that organizations that seek to foster the use of power for ends that benefit the organization and society rather than the power-holders should seek to engender power-holder self-construal that incorporates the organization and its external environment. This may for instance be achieved by selecting individuals to positions of power who have well-established ties with the organization and are well embedded in the organization's environment, and who have a sense of common history and common future with the organization and the communities within which it is embedded. While this may be easier said than done, it does not seem to be something that is high on the agenda of the selection and development for powerful leadership positions. More emphasis on these aspects in the selection and development of individuals for leadership positions may make a contribution to the more constructive use of power in organizations.

However, as already noted in the introduction to our theoretical analysis, the amount of empirical evidence for the relationship between self-construal and influence tactics is still small and indirect. Much is left to be discovered. What we seem to need especially is research that employs solid measures or manipulations of self-construal. Most of the studies we discussed in the above focused on proxies or probable correlates of self-construal. To assess the potential promise of our theoretical perspective, however, we need more direct evidence. Research in power has a long history but seems to miss focus and direction. Perhaps the inclusion of the self-concept in theory and research may provide a welcome integrative framework for the study of power.

References

Aron, A., Aron, E. N., Tudor, N., and Nelson, G. (1991) Close relationships as including other in the self. *Journal of Personality and Social Psychology*, **60**, 241–253.

Aron, A., Aron, E. N., and Norman, C. (2004) Self expansion model of motivation and cognition in close relationships and beyond. In M. B. Brewer and M. Hewstone (Eds.), *Self and social identity* (pp. 99–123), Oxford: Blackwell.

Aron, A. and Fraley, B. (1999) Relationship closeness as including other in the self: Cognitive underpinnings and measures. *Social Cognition*, **17**, 140–160.

Aron, A., McLaughlin-Volpe, T., Mashek, D., Lewandowski, G., Wright, S. C., and Aron, E. N. (2004) Including others in the self. *European Review of Social Psychology*, **15**, 101–132.

Brewer, M. B. and Gardner, W. (1996) Who is this "we"? Levels of collective identity and self representations. *Journal of Personality and Social Psychology*, **71**, 83–93.

Bruins, J. (1997) *Predicting the use of influence tactics: A classification and the role of group membership*. Paper presented at the European Congress on Work and Organizational Psychology, Verona, Italy.

Cai, D. A., Wilson, S. R., and Drake, L. E. (2000) Culture in the context of intercultural negotiation: Individualism-collectivism and paths to integrative agreements. *Human Communication Research*, **26**, 591–617.

Chen, S., Lee-Chai, A. Y., and Bargh, J. A. (2001) Relationship orientation as a moderator of the effects of social power. *Journal of Personality and Social Psychology*, **80**, 173–187.

Clark, M. S. and Mills, J. (1979) Interpersonal attraction in exchange and communal relationships. *Journal of Personality and Social Psychology*, **37**, 12–24.

Deutsch, M. (1973) *The resolution of conflict*, New Haven, Conn.: Yale University Press.

Farmer, S. M., Maslyn, J. M., Fedor, D. B., and Goodman, J. S. (1997) Putting upward influence strategies in context. *Journal of Organizational Behavior*, **18**, 12–42.

Fiske, S. T., Morling, B., and Stevens, L. E. (1996) Controlling self and others: A theory of anxiety, mental control, and social control. *Personality and Social Psychology Bulletin*, **22**, 115–123.

French, J. R. P. and Raven B. H. (1959) The bases of social power. In D. Cartwright (Ed.), *Studies in social power* (pp. 150–167), Ann Arbor, Mich.: Institute for Social Research.

Fu, P. P., Kennedy, J., Tata, J., Yukl, G., Bond, M. H., Peng, T. K., et al. (2004) The impact of societal cultural values and individual social beliefs on the perceived effectiveness of managerial influence strategies: A meso approach. *Journal of International Business Studies*, 35, 284–305.

Goodwin, S. A., Operario, D., and Fiske, S. T. (1998) Situational power and interpersonal dominance facilitate bias and inequality. *Journal of Social Issues*, 54, 677–698.

Hogg, M. A. and Abrams, D. (Eds.) (1988) *Social identifications: A social psychology of intergroup relations and group processes*, London: Routledge.

Hogg, M. A. (2003) Social identity. In M. R. Leary and J. P. Tangney (Eds.), *Handbook of self and identity* (pp. 462–479), New York, N.Y.: The Guilford Press.

Kelman, H. C. (1958) Compliance, identification, and internalization: Three processes of attitude change. *Journal of Conflict Resolution*, 2, 51–60.

Kim, P. H., Pinkley, R. L., and Fragale, A. R. (2005) Power dynamics in negotiation. *Academy of Management Review*, 30, 799–822.

Leary, M. R. and Tangney, J. P. (2003) *Handbook of self and identity*, New York, N.Y.: The Guilford Press.

Lee, A. Y., Aaker, J. L., and Gardner, W. L. (2000) The pleasures and pains of distinct self-construals: The role of interdependence in regulatory focus. *Journal of Personality and Social Psychology*, 78, 1122–1134.

Lord, R. G. and Brown, D. J. (2004) *Leadership processes and follower identity*, Mahwah, N. J.: Erlbaum.

Lord, R. G., Brown, D. J., and Freiberg, S. J. (1999) Understanding the dynamics of leadership: The role of follower self-concept in the leader/follower relationship. *Organizational Behavior and Human Decision Processes*, 78, 167–203.

Markus, H. and Kitayama, S. (1991) Culture and the self: Implications for cognition, emotion and motivation. *Psychological Review*, 98, 224–253.

Markus, H. and Wurf, E. (1987) The dynamic self-concept: A social psychological perspective. *Annual Review of Psychology*, 38, 299–337.

Ohbuchi, K., Fukushima, O., and Tedeschi, J. T. (1999) Cultural values in conflict management: Goal orientation, goal attainment, and tactical decision. *Journal of Cross-Cultural Psychology*, 30, 51–71.

Olekalns, M., Robert, C., Probst, T., Smith, P. L., and Carnevale, P. (2005) The impact of message frame on negotiators' impressions, emotions, and behaviors. *International Journal of Conflict Management*, 16, 379–402.

Pruitt, D. G. and Carnevale, P. J. (1993) *Negotiation in social conflict*, Buckingham: Open University Press.

Pruitt, D. G. and Kim, S. H. (2004) *Social conflict: Escalation, stalemate, and settlement*, 3rd edn, New York, N.Y.: McGraw-Hill.

Schwarzwald, J., Koslowsky, M., and Allouf, M. (2005) Group membership, status, and social power preference. *Journal of Applied Social Psychology*, 35, 644–665.

Sedikides, C. and Brewer, M. B. (2001) *Individual self, relational self, collective self*, Philadelphia, Pa.: Psychology Press.

Smith, E. R. and Henry, S. (1996) An in-group becomes part of the self: Response time evidence. *Personality and Social Psychology Bulletin*, **22**, 635–642.

Steinel, W. and De Dreu, C. K. W. (2004) Social motives and strategic misrepresentation in social decision making. *Journal of Personality and Social Psychology*, **86**, 419–434.

Tajfel, H. and Turner, J. C. (1986) The social identity theory of intergroup behavior. In S. Worchel and W. G. Austin (Eds.), *Psychology of intergroup relations* (pp. 7–24), Chicago, Ill.: Nelson Hall.

Tarr, N. D., Kim, M. S., and Sharkey, W. F. (2005) The effects of self-construals and embarrassability on predicament response strategies. *International Journal of Intercultural Relations*, **29**, 497–520.

Tjosvold, D. (1981) Unequal power relationships within a cooperative or competitive context. *Journal of Applied Social Psychology*, **11**, 137–150.

  (1984) Influence strategy, perspective taking, and relationships between high- and low-power individuals in cooperative and competitive contexts. *The Journal of Psychology*, **116**, 187–202.

  (1985) Power and social context in superior-subordinate interaction. *Organizational Behavior and Human Decision Processes*, **35**, 281–293.

  (1995) Effects of power to reward and punish in cooperative and competitive contexts. *The Journal of Social Psychology*, **135**, 733–736.

Tjosvold, D., Coleman, P. T., and Sun, H. F. (2003) Effects of organizational values on leaders' use of informational power to affect performance in China. *Group Dynamics: Theory, Research, and Practice*, **7**, 152–167.

Tjosvold, D., Law, K. S., and Sun, H. F. (2003) Collectivistic and individualistic values: Their effects on group dynamics and productivity in China. *Group Decision and Negotiation*, **12**, 243–263.

Tjosvold, D. and Sun, H. F. (2001) Effects of influence tactics and social contexts in conflict: An experiment on relationships in China. *International Journal of Conflict Management*, **12**, 239–258.

Tjosvold, D., Sun, H. F. F., and Wan, P. (2005) An experimental examination of social contexts and the use of power in a Chinese sample. *Journal of Social Psychology*, **145**, 645–661.

Tropp, L. R. and Wright, S. C. (2001) Ingroup identification as inclusion of ingroup in the self. *Personality and Social Psychology Bulletin*, **27**, 585–600.

Turner, J. C. (2005) Explaining the nature of power: A three-process theory. *European Journal of Social Psychology*, **35**, 1–22.

Turner, J. C., Hogg, M., Oakes, P. J., Reicher, S., and Wetherell, M. (1987) *Rediscovering the social group: A self-categorization theory*. Oxford: Blackwell.

Van Knippenberg, B. and Steensma, H. (2003) Future interaction expectation and the use of soft and hard influence tactics. *Applied Psychology: An International Review*, 52, 55–67.

Van Knippenberg, B. and van Knippenberg, D. (2003) Leadership, identity, and influence: Relational concerns in the use of influence tactics. In D. van Knippenberg and M. A. Hogg (Eds.), *Leadership and power: Identity processes in groups and organizations* (pp. 123–137), London: Sage.

Van Knippenberg, B., van Knippenberg, D., Blaauw, E., and Vermunt, R. (1999) Relational considerations in the use of influence tactics. *Journal of Applied Social Psychology*, 29, 806–819.

Van Knippenberg, B., van Knippenberg, D., and Wilke, H. A. (2001) Power use in cooperative and competitive settings. *Basic and Applied Social Psychology*, 23, 293–302.

Van Knippenberg, D. (1999) Social identity and persuasion: Reconsidering the role of group membership. In D. Abrams and M. A. Hogg (Eds.), *Social identity and social cognition* (pp. 315–331), Oxford: Blackwell.

Van Knippenberg, D. and Hogg, M. A. (2003) A social identity model of leadership effectiveness in organizations. *Research in Organizational Behavior*, 25, 245–297.

Van Knippenberg, D., van Knippenberg, B., de Cremer, D., and Hogg, M. A. (2004) Leadership, self, and identity: A review and research agenda. *The Leadership Quarterly*, 15, 825–856.

Wagar, B. M. and Cohen, D. (2003) Culture, memory, and the self: An analysis of the personal and collective self in long-term memory. *Journal of Experimental Social Psychology*, 39, 468–475.

4 The conceptualization of power and the nature of interdependency

The role of legitimacy and culture

JORIS LAMMERS AND ADAM D. GALINSKY

Power is often considered the central animating force of human interaction. Who has power, who is affected by power, and how that power is exercised provide the foundation for understanding human relations (Russell 1960). Although it is difficult to give both a parsimonious and a complete definition of power (Fiske and Berdahl 2007; Lukes 1974), power is often defined as the ability to control resources, own and others, a definition rooted in theories of dependency and interdependency (Thibaut and Kelly 1959). Because those who possess power depend less on the resources of others than vice versa, the powerful are more easily able to satisfy their own needs and desires. Given this asymmetric interdependence, many models of power typically describe it as an inherently social variable.

Although power emerges from a specific set of social relations, the possession of power has a transformative impact on an individual's psychological state, leading the powerful to roam in a very different psychological space than the powerless (Keltner et al. 2003; Kipnis 1972). An explosion of research has demonstrated that the possession of power has metamorphic effects on the mental states of individuals and can lead to both positive and negative consequences. Fueling the positive perspective on power are findings that the powerful, compared to the powerless, are more likely to help others (Chen et al. 2001), less likely to fall prey to conformity pressures (Anderson et al. 2000; Cast 2003, Galinsky et al. 2007), are more creative in their thinking (Galinsky et al. 2007), see the big picture (Smith and Trope 2006), are more agentic (Galinsky et al. 2003; Magee et al. 2007), behave more like their personalities and consistent with their attitudes (Anderson et al. 2001; Bargh et al. 1995; Chen et al. 2001; Galinsky et al. 2007), think more abstractly while being more flexible in their attention (Guinote 2007; Smith and Trope 2006), are overall more goal-focused (Galinsky et al. 2003; Smith and Bargh 2008) and are more likely to take action to make the world a better place (Galinsky et al. 2003).

In contrast, other research has demonstrated a host of power's negative side effects. Power has been related to selfish, corrupt, and risky behavior (Anderson and Galinsky 2006; Chen et al. 2001; Galinsky et al. 2003; Kipnis, 1972; Maner et al. 2007), reduced empathy and less openness to the perspectives, emotions, and attitudes of others (Anderson et al. 2000; Galinsky et al. 2006; Snodgrass 1992; Van Kleef et al. 2006), and a tendency to objectify and stereotype others (Goodwin et al. 2000; Gruenfeld et al. 2008). Power has even been identified as a springboard to sexual harassment (Bargh et al. 1995).

Why would the experience of power have such seemingly contradictory effects? When does power inspire malevolence versus beneficence? We argue that prior models have failed to provide a parsimonious framework to explain the full range of the effects of power because they have largely ignored the fact that power is not a unitary construct. We contend that power is rooted in the very nature of dependency and interdependency and as a result its effects on cognition and behavior emerge from the meaning given to the power relationship, which is partly determined by how power is acquired and exercised. In this chapter we argue that the psychological consequences of power depend on how it is conceptualized, on the evaluative connotations attached to it, on the very nature of the interdependence between the powerful and the powerless. We point to two separate conceptual dichotomies of power and how each of these distinctions alters the psychological consequences of power and powerlessness.

The first dichotomy contrasts a functional view from a conflict view of power, and we claim that these two conceptualizations differ in the degree to which power differences are viewed as legitimate. We describe two sets of studies documenting that the psychological effects of power and powerlessness reverse when the hierarchy is tinged with illegitimacy. The second dichotomy contrasts an entitlement and capacity to influence view of power with one anchored in a sense of responsibility and of interdependency. These two conceptualizations also relate to the two primary ways in which different cultures mentally represent and conceptualize the self. We review work demonstrating that the cultural context moderates the typical effects of power. In independent cultures, power is associated with entitlement and competition but in interdependent cultures, power is linked to responsibility and within group cooperation.

In our conclusion, we explore how these conceptualizations of power not only help to determine when power has its effects, but also *why* power has the effects it does. We claim that the psychological consequences of power emerge not just from the amount of resources one possesses but on how power is conceptualized, acquired, and wielded.

Two conceptualizations of power: functionalist vs. conflict

A duality inherent in views of power is whether power is conceived as a positive or negative social force. In Western philosophy there are two philosophical traditions that have opposing views on power. One tradition, with roots that date back to Aristotle (1996), argues that power differences are something positive and legitimate because they allow order and stability. Hobbes for example (1998) believed that people should combine their individual strengths into a powerful monarch, because this is the only way to prevent endless civil war. In modern sociology, this view on power is coined the *functionalist view*, because hierarchy generates legitimate order and allows society to function in an organized and effective manner (Parsons 1967; Arendt 1969).

A second philosophical tradition, however, builds on the writings of Plato (1998) to argue that power differences are something negative and inherently illegitimate. Rousseau (1997) for example argued that because all men are created equal, power differences necessarily lead to social inequality; in essence, hierarchy corrupts human nature. More recently, Mills (1956) pointed to the adverse effects of power by arguing that America after World War II is ruled by a "power elite," a clique of political, military, and economic leaders who secretly decide on the course of the country and severely undermine democracy. From this view, power leads to domination, suppression and violations of the interests of the powerless. For this reason, this view is often termed the *conflict theory* of power (Lenski 1966).

These contrasting conceptualizations of power are also mirrored in the distinct views that religious traditions have held on the nature and role of power (Lenski 1966). For example, the Hebrew Bible and Old Testament have a divergent view of power from that of Hindus. Reflecting the conflict theory of power, in the Old Testament, Micah describes the powerful rulers of Israel as those who "pervert equity," "covet fields" and "oppress a man." "Therefore thus saith the Lord: Behold, against this family do I devise an evil" (Micah 2:2–3). Here, wielding power goes against the will of God. Hindus, on the other hand, worship Manu, the Great Lawgiver, who separated the people into more and less powerful castes, each with different roles and social positions. Social inequality and power differences do not go against the will of the gods but are in fact part of a divine plan, suggesting an inherently more functionalist view of power.

Legitimacy moderates the effects of power

We believe that rather than one view on power being correct and the other false, both point to equally important ways to conceptualize power (Hindess 1996; Lenski 1966). As a consequence, how power is conceptualized by the powerful and by the powerless will have differential downstream effects on behavior and cognition. At their core, the functionalist and the conflict conceptualizations of power differ in the degree to which power differences are thought to be inherently legitimate. In the functionalist view, power is generally seen as legitimate, as a positive force that helps people to cooperate in a coordinated fashion and do things they would be unable to do alone. In the conflict view, power is disliked because power leads to abuse and corruption. Therefore, the legitimacy of power should determine how the powerful and the powerless think, feel, and behave.

Lammers et al. (2008) conducted a series of studies to explore how power and legitimacy affect the basic tendencies associated with power. According to the approach/inhibition theory of power (Keltner et al. 2003) the possession of power triggers the relative activation of the behavioral approach (Carver and White 1994), which is posited to regulate behavior associated with rewards. In contrast, powerlessness is said to activate the behavioral inhibition system, which has been equated to an alarm system that triggers avoidance and response inhibition. Lammers et al. reasoned that the power–approach link would be tempered by the perceived legitimacy of power. Although legitimate power puts a focus on gains (approach) and legitimate powerlessness on preventing losses (inhibition), under conditions of illegitimacy this effect of power could be diminished. Because illegitimacy signals the possibility of change, the powerless may focus on potential gains (approach), whereas the powerful may focus on avoiding losses (inhibition). Thus, they predicted that power would lead to more approach than powerlessness but only when the power-relationship was considered to be legitimate.

Lammers et al. (2008) manipulated power and legitimacy in three different ways to establish that the power–approach link is not invariant: recalling an experience with power, activating concepts associated with power and legitimacy, and assigning participants to legitimate or illegitimate high or low power roles. In their first study, participants recalled a time in which they had power or were in a state of low power and that power was either legitimate or illegitimate. Although legitimate power led to more approach tendencies, as measured by the BAS/BIS scale (Carver and White 1994), than legitimate powerlessness, the opposite effect occurred under conditions of illegitimacy: Illegitimate powerlessness led to more behavioral approach than illegitimate power. A second study using the same manipulations found that legitimate power led to a greater propensity to negotiate than legitimate powerlessness, replicating the results of Magee et al. (2007). Illegitimate powerlessness, however, led to more desire to negotiate than illegitimate power. In their final two studies, they explored how legitimacy and power interacted to affect preferences for risk. In one study, power and legitimacy were primed by unobtrusively exposing participants to power(lessness) and (il)legitimacy related words (Chen et al. 2001), and, in the other, power was manipulated by either granting participants power over someone else or by having someone else have power over them, and legitimacy was manipulated by either basing these assignments on merit or by explicitly violating merit. In both studies, they found exactly the same pattern: Legitimate power led participants to choose a risky plan more often than legitimate powerlessness (which replicated the results of Anderson and Galinsky [2006]), but this difference disappeared under illegitimacy. Across these studies, legitimate power consistently led to more approach but when power was conceived or expressed under the shadow of illegitimacy, the powerful no longer showed more approach than the powerless.

Lammers et al. (2007) followed up this investigation by exploring the role of power and legitimacy on the tendency to cooperate. They noticed that the literature was littered with opposing findings, with some studies finding that the powerless are more inclined to cooperate than the powerful (Tjosvold and Okun 1979) and other studies demonstrating the opposite pattern of the powerful being more inclined to cooperate (Camerer and Thaler 1995; Van Dijk and Vermunt 2000; Van Knippenberg et al. 2001). A closer look at the various findings suggests that these effects may depend on the degree to which the various power manipulations were seen as legitimate. Lammers et al. (2007) therefore tested whether legitimacy also moderates the effect of power on cooperative intentions and behavior.

In their first experiment, they orthogonally manipulated power and legitimacy with a role manipulation and subsequently measured preference for cooperation by asking participants to rate the desirability of cooperative and non-cooperative games. In their next two experiments, they manipulated power and legitimacy with a recall task and subsequently measured the degree to which participants wanted to cooperate with a fellow participant. A fourth experiment replicated these findings with a semantic priming task. All four studies showed the exact same pattern of results: When power was seen as legitimate, the powerful cooperated less than the powerless but when power was seen as illegitimate the powerful cooperated more than the powerless. The effect of power on cooperation was fully moderated by legitimacy, regardless of whether power was manipulated through power-related roles, memories or semantic primes. Importantly, across both projects by Lammers and colleagues, the effect of legitimacy had equal and opposite effects on approach, risk, and cooperation for the powerful and for the powerless.

These studies have important implications not only for when power leads to approach and cooperation but also for why power produces its effects. Before we turn to the question of why, we will first review another line of research demonstrating the important role of how power is conceptualized. In these studies, power is conceived not in terms of its legitimacy but in terms of the cultural differences attached to the meaning of power.

Two conceptualizations of power: influence vs. responsibility

Central to power are the concepts of influence and interdependency. On the one hand, power often involves putting pressure on others to engage in behaviors that will help the powerful accomplish their own objectives, with a sense of entitlement being part and parcel of having power. Thus, many people have defined power as the capacity to influence others (French and Raven 1959; Weber 1947). In fact, some have even defined power as actual influence, such that power occurs only when one person directly causes or alters the behavior of another person (Simon 1957) In these formulations, power is linked to energy, both metaphorically (Russell 1960) and literally (Galinsky et al. 2003), and one can think of control over resources as a potential source of influence in the same way energy can be stored and later released. Power, it could also be said, is the ability to be uninfluenced by others (Galinsky et al. 2007). Without power – when one's behavior is influenced and one's outcomes are determined by others – one is constrained. With power, one is relatively free of such constraint, at least within the context of the specific power relationship.

On the other hand, power is also rooted in interdependency and responsibility. From this perspective, the powerful should not just influence others but attend and care to their needs, a view summarized eloquently in the infamous Spiderman quote, "With great power comes great responsibility." For example, parents have enormous, almost dictatorial, control over their children but typically demonstrate great sacrifice and generosity toward their children's best interests.

Culture moderates the effects of power

These twin aspects – influence and interdependency – form two seemingly opposite aspects of the same concept (Giddens 1968; Parsons 1967). We suggest that these two very different views of power are captured in cultural differences. Although, in every culture, power is an important determinant of thought and behavior, cultures differ in their conceptualizations of power. As Zhong et al. (2006) recently speculated, different, centuries-old philosophical ideas have created very different conceptualizations of power and speculated that previously demonstrated associations between power and attention to rewards and assertive action are actually culturally circumscribed. The Western philosophical tradition of Nietzsche (1966, 1968) suggests that to have power is to have freedom and the enviable ability to satisfy one's own desires. In contrast, Eastern philosophy has talked about the importance of inhibition for the powerful. In the phrase "conquer with inaction," Lao Tsu proposed that the supreme exercise of will is restraint and power should increase people's responsibility for and obligations to those who submit to their power.

We have argued above that the very nature of interdependency moderates the effects of power. In fact, cultures differ widely on how interdependent the self is with others and in their construals of the self. Self-construals refer to the way in which people mentally represent the self and research has identified two primary modes of self-representation: independence and interdependence (e.g., Markus and Kitayama 1991; Brewer and Gardner 1996). Those individuals who have independent self-construals tend to think of themselves as autonomous individuals and define themselves in terms of their unique personal traits (e.g., Cousins 1989). In contrast, individuals with interdependent self-construals are more likely to think of themselves in the context of the larger social world, tending to define themselves in terms of their group memberships and relationships with others. On average, Westerners tend to construe themselves as relatively more independent, whereas East Asians tend to construe themselves relatively interdependently.

Based on these different self-construals, Zhong et al. (2006) suggested that (a) power is conceptually and experientially connected to the dominant values of one's culture and (b) culture therefore produces different cognitive and behavioral outcomes of power. Essentially, they argued that the experience of power accentuates cross-cultural differences: It increases Westerners' focus on the self and on action, whereas it broadens East Asians' consideration of interpersonal constraints and highlights how their behavior might negatively impact others. Power not only makes people think and act more in line with their personalities (Anderson et al. 2001) but it also makes them more consistent with their cultural background, leading them to become truer representations of their cultures' underlying values.

Zhong et al. (2006) first set out to demonstrate that individuals from different cultural backgrounds have different associations between the concepts of power on the one hand and reward, responsibility, and restraint on the other. In two studies, they subliminally primed the concept of power (vs. paper) in a lexical decision task to determine individuals' subsequent associations with words related to rewards and responsibility. They found that the basic associations with power differed by cultural background. Westerners who were primed with power (vs. paper) responded more quickly to reward-related words but more slowly to responsibility-related words. East Asians showed the exact opposite strength of association with power: greater accessibility of responsibility-related words and weaker accessibility to reward-related words following a subliminal power prime.

In follow-up behavioral studies, Zhong et al. (2006) explored whether East Asians would show restraint in a common dilemma, a situation in which self-interested claiming often leads to rapid depletion of common resources. Galinsky et al. (2003) had shown that among Westerners power increases self-interested claiming. In contrast, Zhong et al. found that the experience of power by East Asians reduced claiming and hence increased the potential preservation of a commonly shared resource. In another study they investigated whether an individual difference measure of power would differentially predict cooperation among East Asians and Westerners. They measured power using the generalized version of the Sense of Power scale (Anderson and Berdahl 2002; Anderson and Galinsky 2006), which asks participants to report their generalized beliefs about the power they have in their relationships with others. For Westerners, power was negatively correlated with cooperation, but for East Asians a sense of power was positively related to cooperation. These results suggest that the distinct associations with power that Westerners and East Asians have produce different behavioral consequences.

These results further support our overall contention that the effects of power depend on how it is conceived and understood. Culture moderates the psychological effects of power because its members, based in different levels of chronic interdependency and self-construals, define the very nature of power in fundamentally different ways.

Conclusion

By showing that legitimacy and culture moderate the effects of power on cognition and behavior, these studies have important implications for our understanding of power. First, they provide insight into *what* effects a power difference has, and *when* it has a specific effect. Second, these studies have more theoretical implications for *why* power produces its effects.

When does power have what effects?

In social psychology, the idea that the effects of power are dependent on how the power-holder conceptualizes his or her power is not entirely new. A number of researchers have found that individual approaches or contextual variations alter the effects of power. For example, Chen et al. (2001) demonstrated that power leads to selfish behavior only for people with an exchange-relationship orientation; for those with a communal-relationship orientation, power leads to action that promotes the interests of others. Overbeck and Park (2001, 2006) show that if a powerful position requires one to obtain an accurate image of one's subordinates, then the powerful will invest more, rather than less, effort in understanding their subordinates.

These various findings suggest that the effects of power should not be seen as fixed and rigid but depend on how people perceive and conceptualize their power position. Nonetheless, until recently the exact effects of such conceptualizations remained unexamined. We have argued that the effects of power depend not only on how it is conceptualized but also on the meaning and connotations attached to it, and ultimately on the very nature of the interdependence between the powerful and the powerless. This more fine-grained view of power can help illuminate past findings on when the effects of power are expected to lead to positive consequences and when they should be expected to lead to negative results.

Indeed, the findings presented in this chapter clearly demonstrate that both positive and negative effects of power can be elicited depending on how that power is conceptualized, either because of legitimacy (Lammers et al. 2007, 2008) or because of cultural differences (Zhong et al. 2006). For example, we reported evidence showing that whereas legitimate power leads to more behavioral approach and greater propensity to negotiate, it also leads to less cooperation on the part of the powerful. And yet, when power is tinged with illegitimacy, the exact opposite pattern is found. Similarly, when power is embedded in an interdependent self-construal, the powerful lean toward responsibility, cooperation, and less self-interested claiming compared to when power is entrenched in an independent self-construal. Thus, the effects of power on approach and cooperation are not invariant but context dependent, determined by how power is conceived, acquired, and exercised.

The opposing positive and negative effects of power raise an interesting question: Is it possible to harness the good functional view of power without dragging along the less savory aspects, to make the powerful simultaneously assertive and cooperative? The research described in this chapter suggests that the positive effects of power can emerge depending on how power is conceptualized. When the powerful view the hierarchical relationships through a lens of interdependence and responsibility, the powerful cooperate, assist, and act for the benefit of others. Similarly, when managers are less overconfident about the legitimacy of their power position, they are more likely to cooperate for the organizational good and less likely to act only in terms of competition and self-interest. On the other hand, if those in power are too unsure of the legitimacy of their position, this can make them inhibited and overly cautious. Thus, here it seems that perceptions of legitimacy by the powerful need to achieve a Goldilocks balance: not too much insecurity and not too much confidence.

It is not only important to harness the good in power, but researchers need also to discover how to inspire the powerless. One means of motivating contribution and commitment is to conceive and exercise the power relationship legitimately. For example, we have shown that one way in which legitimacy produces positive organizational outcomes by the powerless is through increased cooperation. When an organizational hierarchy is perceived to be legitimate, the lower strata of an organization will display more cooperative intentions and behaviors (cf. McAllister 1995). This can be of critical importance as cooperation among employees is essential to the performance of almost any organization (Smith et al. 1995).

Why does power have such effects?

The studies presented in this chapter have important implications for *why* power has its effects on cognition and behavior. We noted at the beginning of this chapter that the dominant models of power talk about control over resources. For example, Keltner et al. (2003) argued that power drives psychological approach because the powerful have access to rewards and are less dependent on others, whereas the powerless lack resources and are more subject to social threats. The various lines of research reviewed in this chapter qualify their reasoning.

The results of Chen et al. (2001) and Overbeck and Park (2001, 2006) provided the first evidence that the effects of power change if that position of power is conceptualized differently, either because of personality differences, or because of different expectations for the position of power. The results obtained by Lammers et al. (2007, 2008), that the effect of power is blocked or even reversed if power is viewed as illegitimate, and the results of Zhong et al. (2006), that cultural conceptualizations of power lead to opposite patterns, further weaken the idea that the effects of power are caused by materialistic differences. Indeed, these studies manipulated legitimacy or measured culture without referring to differences in resource control.

Importantly, illegitimate power does not lead to fewer resources: people who illegitimately obtain or use power are typically not poorer than those with legitimate power. In fact, they may acquire equal or even more resources (e.g., the mafia boss versus the head of an equally large corporation). In addition, illegitimate powerlessness is likely associated with even more social threats than legitimate powerlessness. Nonetheless, illegitimate power leads to less approach than legitimate power. Similarly, in East Asian cultures, power hierarchies are typically more pronounced, characterized by greater power distance (Hofstede 1979) than in Western cultures, resulting in the powerful having control over a larger and more enduring share of resources. Yet, East Asians show an automatic association between power on the one hand and restraint, responsibility, and cooperation on the other.

The collection of findings suggests that the effects of power depend on what being powerless or powerful means in a given relationship. Being the powerless party in a legitimate power relationship means something different to lacking power under the shadow of illegitimacy. In a situation of legitimate powerlessness one should follow the leader (i.e. cooperate) and delay gratifying one's own desires (i.e. inhibition). In a situation of illegitimate powerlessness, however, people are inclined to revolt against the status quo (act and compete). Similarly, having legitimate power means something quite different compared to when power is acquired or exercised illegitimately. Under conditions of legitimacy, the powerful will approach and lead the way, whereas lacking legitimacy drives the powerful to be more concerned about protecting one's power position and can even lead to a focus on reconciliation (e.g., through cooperation). Thus, the effect of power can better be explained by taking into account the symbolic value and meaning attached to positions of power or powerlessness.

The moderation of the associations with and the effects of power by culture further strengthen the important role of the meaning and conceptualization attached to power. Whereas the West conceptualizes power as being associated with assertive and individual action, power is associated with responsibility and personal restraint in the Far East (Zhong et al. 2006). As a result, power makes participants more likely to focus on their own interests in the West (Galinsky et al. 2003), but leads East Asians toward cooperation and generosity.

We have tried in these pages to reassert the social aspect of power. Ultimately, the effects of power are not just about the amount of resources possessed. Rather, the psychological consequences of power depend on its meaning, on the nature of interdependency, on how power is conceived and conceptualized, on how it is acquired and wielded. The effects of power cannot be reduced to quantitative calculations of relative resources but require a qualitative appreciation for how power emerged, for what purpose, and to what end.

References

Anderson, C. and Berdahl, J. L. (2002) The experience of power: Examining the effects of power on approach and inhibition tendencies. *Journal of Personality and Social Psychology*, 83, 1362–1377.

Anderson, C. and Galinsky, A. D. (2006) Power, optimism, and risk-taking. *European Journal of Social Psychology*, 36, 511–536.

Anderson, C., John, O. P., Keltner, D., and Kring, A. M. (2001) Who attains social status? Effects of personality and physical attractiveness in social groups. *Journal of Personality and Social Psychology*, 81, 116–132.

Anderson, C., Keltner, D., and John, O. P. (2000) Emotional convergence between people over time. *Journal of Personality and Social Psychology*, 84, 1054–1068.

Arendt, H. (1969) *On violence*, New York, N.Y.: Harcourt, Brace & World.

Aristotle (1996) *The politics and the constitution of Athens*, trans. S. Everson, Cambridge: Cambridge University Press.

Bargh, J. A., Raymond, P., Pryor, J. B., and Strack, F. (1995) Attractiveness of the underling: An automatic power → sex association and its consequences for sexual harassment and aggression. *Journal of Personality and Social Psychology*, 68, 768–781.

Brewer, M. B., and Gardner, W. (1996) Who is this we? Levels of collective identity and self representations. *Journal of Personality and Social Psychology*, 71, 83–93.

Camerer, C. and Thaler, R. H. (1995) Anomalies: Ultimatums, dictators and manners. *The Journal of Economic Perspectives*, 9, 209–219.

Carver, C. S. and White, T. L. (1994) Behavioral inhibition, behavioral activation, and affective responses to impending reward and punishment: The BIS/BAS scales. *Journal of Personality and Social Psychology*, 67 (2), 319–333.

Cast, A. D. (2003) Power and the ability to define the situation. *Social Psychology Quarterly*, 66, 185–201.

Chen, S., Lee-Chai, A. Y., and Bargh, J. A. (2001) Relationship orientation as moderator of the effects of social power. *Journal of Personality and Social Psychology*, 80, 183–187.

Cousins, S. D. (1989) Culture and self-perception in Japan and the United States. *Journal of Personality and Social Psychology*, 56, 124–131.

Fiske, S. T. and Berdahl, J. L. (2007) Social power. In A. Kruglanski and E. T. Higgins (Eds.), *Social psychology: A handbook of basic principles* (pp. 678–692), New York, N.Y.: Guilford Press.

French, J. R. P. Jr. and Raven, B. H. (1959) The bases of social power. In D. Cartwright (Ed.), *Studies in social power* (pp. 118–149), Ann Arbor, Mich.: Institute of Social Research.

Galinsky, A. D., Gruenfeld, D. H., and Magee, J. C. (2003) From power to action. *Journal of Personality and Social Psychology*, 85, 453–466.

Galinsky, A. D., Magee, J. C., Gruenfeld, D. H, Whitson, J., and Liljenquist, K. A. (2007) Power and immunity to constraint on cognition: Implications for creativity, conformity, and dissonance. Manuscript submitted for publication.

Galinsky, A. D., Magee, J. C., Inesi, M. E., and Gruenfeld, D. H. (2006) Power and perspectives not taken. *Psychological Science*, 17, 1068–1074.

Giddens, A. (1968) Power in the recent writing of Talcott Parsons. *Sociology*, 2, 257–272.

Goodwin, S. A., Gubin, A., Fiske, S. T., and Yzerbyt, V. Y. (2000) Power can bias impression processes: Stereotyping subordinates by default and by design. *Group Processes and Intergroup Relations*, 3, 227–256.

Gruenfeld, D. H, Inesi, M. E., Magee, J. C., and Galinsky, A. D. (2008) Power and the objectification of social targets. *Journal of Personality and Social Psychology*, 95, 111–27.

Guinote, A. (2007) Power and goal pursuit. *Personality and Social Psychology Bulletin*, 33, 1076–1087.

Hindess, B. (1996) *Discourses of power, From Hobbes to Foucault*, New York, N.Y.: Blackwell.

Hobbes, T. (1998) *Leviathan*, Oxford: Oxford University Press. (Original work published 1651.)

Hofstede, G. (1979) Hierarchical power distance in forty countries. In C. J. Lammers and D. J. Hickson (Eds.), *Organizations alike and unlike: Towards a comparative sociology of organizations* (pp. 97–119), London, Routledge & Kegan Paul.

Keltner, D., Gruenfeld, D. H., and Anderson, C. (2003) Power, approach and inhibition. *Psychological Review*, 110 (2), 265–284.

Kipnis, D. (1972) Does power corrupt? *Journal of Personality and Social Psychology*, 24, 33–41.

Lammers, J., Galinsky, A. D., Gordijn, E. H., and Otten, S. (2007) Power and cooperation: The moderating effect of legitimacy. Manuscript submitted for publication.

(2008) Legitimacy moderates the effects of power on approach. *Psychological Science*, **19**, 558–564.

Lenski, G. E. (1966) *Power and privilege: A theory of social stratification*, New York, N.Y.: McGraw-Hill.

Lukes, S. (1974) *Power, A radical view*, London: Macmillan.

Magee, J. C., Galinsky, A. D., and Gruenfeld, D. H. (2007) Power, propensity to negotiate, and moving first in competitive interactions. *Personality and Social Psychology Bulletin*, **33**, 200–212.

Maner, J. K., Gailliot, M. T., Butz, D., and Peruche, B. M. (2007) Power, risk, and the status quo: Does power promote riskier or more conservative decision-making? *Personality and Social Psychology Bulletin*, **33**, 451–462.

Markus, H. R. and Kitayama, S. (1991) Culture and the self: Implications for cognition, emotion, and motivation. *Psychological Review*, **98**, 224–253.

McAllister, D. J. (1995) Affect- and cognition-based trust as foundations for interpersonal cooperation in organizations. *Academy of Management Journal*, **38**, 24–59.

Mills, C. W. (1956) *The power elite*, Oxford: Oxford University Press.

Nietzsche, F. (1966) *Beyond good and evil*, trans. W. Kaufmann, New York, N.Y.: Vintage Books. (Original work published 1886.)

(1968) *The will to power*, trans. W. Kaufmann, New York, N.Y.: Vintage Books. (Original work published 1901.)

Overbeck, J. R. and Park, B. (2001) When power does not corrupt: Superior individuation processes among powerful perceivers. *Journal of Personality and Social Psychology*, **81**, 549–565.

(2006) Powerful perceivers, powerless objects: Flexibility of power-holders' social attention. *Journal of Personality and Social Psychology*, **99**, 227–243.

Parsons, T. (1967) *Sociological theory and modern society*, New York, N.Y.: Free Press.

Plato (1998) *The Republic*, trans. R. Waterfield, Oxford: Oxford University Press.

Rousseau, J. J. (1997) *The social contract, and the first and second discourses*, trans. V. Gourevitch, Cambridge: Cambridge University Press. (Original work published 1762.)

Russell, B. (1960) *Power, a new social analysis*, London: Allen & Unwin. (Original work published 1938.)

Simon, H. A. (1957) *Models of man*, New York, N.Y.: Wiley.

Smith, K. G., Carroll, S. J., and Ashford, S. J. (1995) Intra- and interorganizational cooperation: Toward a research agenda. *Academy of Management Journal*, **38**, 7–23.

Smith, P. K. and Bargh, J. A. (2008) Nonconscious effects of power on basic approach and avoidance tendencies. *Social Cognition*, **26**, 1–24.

Smith, P. K. and Trope, Y. (2006) You focus on the forest when you're in charge of the trees: Power priming and abstract information processing. *Journal of Personality and Social Psychology*, **90** (4), 578–96.

Snodgrass, S. E. (1992) Further effects of role versus gender on interpersonal sensitivity. *Journal of Personality and Social Psychology*, **62** (1), 154–158.

Thibaut, J. W. and Kelley, H. H. (1959) *The social psychology of groups*, New York, N.Y.: Wiley.

Tjosvold, D. and Okun, M. (1979) Effects of unequal power on cooperation in conflict. *Psychological Reports*, **44**, 239–242.

Van Dijk, E. and Vermunt, R. (2000) Strategy and fairness in social decision making: Sometimes it pays to be powerless. *Journal of Experimental Social Psychology*, **36**, 1–25.

Van Kleef, G. A., De Dreu, C. K. W., Pietroni, D., and Manstead, A. S. R. (2006) Power and emotion in negotiation: Power moderates the interpersonal effects of anger and happiness on concession making. *European Journal of Social Psychology*, **36**, 557–581.

Van Knippenberg, B., Van Knippenberg, D., and Wilke, H. A. (2001) Power use in cooperative and competitive settings. *Basic and Applied Social Psychology*, **23**, 291–300.

Weber, M. (1947) *The theory of social and economic organization*, trans. A. M. Henderson and T. Parsons, New York, N.Y.: Oxford University Press.

Zhong, C., Magee, J. C., Maddux, W. W., and Galinsky, A. D. (2006) Power, culture, and (in)action: Considerations in the expression and enactment of power in East Asian and Western society. In Y. Chen (Ed.), *Research on managing groups and teams: National culture and groups* (pp. 53–73), Greenwich, Conn.: Elsevier Science Press.

5 | Power in cooperation and competition

Understanding the positive and negative faces of power

DEAN TJOSVOLD AND PEIGUAN WU

In the office in which I work there are five people of whom I am afraid. Each of these five people is afraid of four people (excluding overlaps), for a total of twenty and each of these twenty people is afraid of six people, making a total of one hundred and twenty people who are feared by at least one person. Each of these one hundred and twenty people is afraid of the other one hundred and nineteen, and all of these one hundred and forty-five people are afraid of the twelve men at the top who helped found and build the company and now own and direct it.

Joseph Heller, *Something Happened.*

The men who make power make an indispensable contribution to the Nation's greatness, but the men who question power make a contribution just as indispensable, especially when questioning is disinterested, for they determine whether we use power or power uses us.

John F. Kennedy, October 26, 1963

Our task is not to learn where to place power; it is how to develop power [...] Genuine power can only be grown, it will slip from every arbitrary hand that grasps it; for genuine power is not coercive control, but co-active control. Coercive power is the curse of the universe; co-active power, the enrichment and advancement of every human soul.

Mary Parker-Follett (1924)

Power has traditionally been considered a destructive force in organizations, corrupting those with power and demoralizing those without it (Ashforth 1997; Kipnis 1976; Rudolph and Peluchette 1993). Power oppresses individuals and makes being organized and being human incompatible (Argyris and Schon 1978; Hogan et al. 1994). Suspicion of power is not restricted to the West. Theorizing about leadership in such societies as China has emphasized the distance between those with power and those subject to power (Hofstede 1993: 80; Leung 1997). Yet power has a positive as well as a negative face (Daily and Johnson 1997; Follett 1924; Kanter 1979, 1977; McClelland 1975; Pfeffer 1994). Power struggles may help critical people and groups obtain the additional resources needed to be productive (Pfeffer and Moore 1980; Welbourne and Trevor 2000). Leaders want to empower their employees so that they feel valued and contribute (Burke 1986; Conger and Kanungo 1988). However, power itself is neither destructive nor constructive; how it is managed determines its outcomes.

Power is central to understanding interdependence between persons and groups as it involves the extent to which people are dependent upon each other. Team members may believe that they very much need each other's ideas, information, and other resources to reach their goals or that they can rely on themselves. Researchers have tended to focus on the effects of the amount of power that one person has over another (Kanter 1979, 1977; Pfeffer 1994). Less appreciated is that the kind of dependence can very much differ; the powerful and those subject to power can reach much different conclusions about the nature of their dependence, and these conclusions have dramatic effects on the use and outcomes of power; dependence differs in kind as well as in degree.

Considering the amount and kind of dependence together is critical for understanding how persons with power over each other interact and the effects of this interaction. This chapter proposes that the theory of cooperation and competition can identify major kinds of dependence that the powerful and those subject to power can experience; whether they conclude that their dependence is cooperative or competitive very much affects the dynamics and outcomes of power.

The chapter first reviews the research on the effects of cooperative and competitive goal interdependence on the expectations and use of power. It identifies the value of cooperative power relationships for organizations and individuals, but studies also document that managers confront difficulties in developing these relationships. The chapter then reviews research on the conditions that promote cooperative, constructive power relationships. The final section summarizes major practical implications for how managers can make power constructive in their organizations. Although power equalization has often been proposed as the best way to manage power (Walton 1987), this chapter argues that developing cooperative, mutual power relationships provides an effective, practical approach to managing power in organizations.

Power is defined as the control over resources that can affect the other's goals (French and Raven 1959; Raven 1993; Thibaut and Kelley 1959); the person subject to power values the knowledge, abilities, and other resources of the powerful person because these resources can affect the extent of reaching his or her goals. Power then implies dependence: The greater the power, the greater the dependence of those subject to power. Typically, power involves interdependence in that people can affect each other's goals as each has resources that the other values. Power has most often been investigated when dependence is unequal; the high-power person can affect the other's goals more than the low-power person can affect the high-power person's goals.

Power in cooperative and competitive contexts

Managing power effectively requires research that identifies the conditions under which power develops its constructive and destructive dynamics. This section discusses how beliefs concerning how their goals are related dramatically affect the interaction and relationship of the powerful and those subject to power.

Dependent persons not only value the abilities and resources of the powerful person but can make quite different conclusions about the nature of their dependence. The theory of cooperation and competition identifies alternative ways in which people conclude they depend upon others. Assuming that dependence is typically mutual, though often unequal, Deutsch (1973) theorized that how people consider their goals are related to each other affects their expectations and thereby how they interact and the outcomes of their interaction. This theory and its considerable research can help identify the conditions and dynamics for constructive and destructive power.

Alternative goal interdependencies

In cooperation, people perceive their goals are positively related so that as one person moves toward goal attainment, others move toward reaching their goals as well (Deutsch 1973; Johnson and Johnson 2005). They understand one's goal attainment helps others reach their goals; as one succeeds, others succeed. People in cooperation appreciate that they want each other to pursue their goals effectively, for the other's effectiveness helps all of them reach their goals.

In contrast, people may believe that their goals are competitive, that is, one's goal attainment precludes, or at least makes less likely, the goal attainment of others. If one succeeds, others must fail. If one "wins," others "lose." People with competitive goals conclude that they are better off when others act ineffectively. When others are productive, they are less likely to be successful themselves. Competitive teammates want to prove they are the most capable and their ideas superior; they are frustrated when others develop useful ideas and work hard. Competitive work pits self-interests against each other in a fight to win.

Goal independence occurs when people believe their goals are unrelated. The goal attainment of one neither helps nor hinders the goal attainment of others. Success by one means neither failure nor success for others. People in perceived goal independence conclude that it means little to them if others act effectively or ineffectively. Independent work creates disinterest and indifference.

Expectations of power use

Whether people conclude their goals are primarily cooperative or competitive, Deutsch (1973) theorized, profoundly affects their orientation and intentions toward each other. Specifically, goal interdependence affects their expectations about how others will use their power.

When powerful Person B believes her goals are cooperatively related to Person A, dependent Person A can realistically expect that B wants A to succeed. Person A concludes that Person B will provide her resources so that A can act effectively in pursuit of his goals because, as he succeeds, then B also moves toward her goals. It is to B's self-interest to promote A's goal attainment; consequently, B then shares information, gives advice, rewards and in other ways applies her abilities to make Person A more effective.

Person A can therefore trust that Person B will use her abilities supportively, and, in turn, Person A is likely to reciprocate and use his abilities to enhance B (Lewicki et al. 1998). They believe they can rely upon each other.

These mutual expectations of reliance promote ongoing efforts to support and assist each other (Deutsch 1973; Johnson and Johnson 1989, 2005; Johnson et al. 1981; Stanne et al. 1999). This kind of promotive interaction results in relationships characterized by positive regard, openness, and productivity. Specifically, Deutsch theorized that cooperation leads to "inducibility" where people are willing to be influenced and to comply with requests.

When powerful Person B believes her goals are competitively aligned with dependent Person A's goals, Person A concludes that B will work toward her own goals at the expense of his. It is to B's own self-interest that A fails to reach his goals because that makes it more likely that B will succeed. Person A cannot realistically expect B to provide information, ideas, and rewards to help A act effectively for that would frustrate her own goal attainment. Person A has grounds to be suspicious of B and be reluctant to apply his abilities to assist B's goal attainment; indeed, A may be tempted to use them to obstruct B's success.

Expectations of goal obstruction restrict information and resource exchange. People withhold information and ideas in the expectation that they can win the competition and outdo each other (Deutsch 1973; Johnson and Johnson 1989; Johnson et al. 1981; Stanne et al. 1999). These interaction patterns result in mutual hostility, restricted communication, and goal frustration. Specifically, competition results in closed-mindedness and resistance to being influenced.

Dependent persons who believe that B considers her goals as independent are likely to conclude that B has little interest in using her abilities and resources either to promote or frustrate A's goal-directed efforts. Goal independence leads people to have few incentives to communicate and exchange resources. Generally, independence has been found to have similar though not as strong effects on interaction and productivity as competition (Deutsch 1973; Johnson and Johnson 1989, 2005; Johnson et al. 1981).

Empirical studies on social context and power

Experiments in North America and in mainland China have tested the idea that goal interdependence affects the dynamics and outcomes of power. They randomly assigned participants to four conditions: cooperative or competitive goals with high or low power (Tjosvold 1981; Tjosvold and Sun 2001). Participants taking the role of managers and assigned to the cooperative condition understood that, consistent with their company's history of managers and employees working together, they would earn more chances in a lottery depending on how well both they and the employees performed their tasks. Managers in the competitive condition believed that their company had a history in which managers and employees try to outdo each other, and they would receive more chances in the lottery to the extent that they did their own task more successfully than the employee. Participants indicated that these inductions did affect their conclusions about the kind of dependence they had.

High-power managers were given the employee problem, three hints that would help the employee solve the problem, and its answer. Managers in the low-power condition were given the problem without the hints or answer. Participants in the high-power condition indicated that they could affect the other's goals more than those in the low-power condition.

Results support the reasoning that power provides the capacity to assist employees but that cooperative, not competitive, goals facilitate the motivation of managers to use their power to support employees and managerial conclusions that employees are capable and appreciative. These and related experiments indicate that a cooperative compared to a competitive context induces actual assistance and supportive comments from the power-holders to those subject to power (Lawler and Yoon 1993, 1995; Tjosvold 1985a, 1985b; Tjosvold et al. 2003). Studies have demonstrated that cooperative compared to competitive goals induce greater support, more persuasion, and more trusting and friendly attitudes between high- and low-power persons. Power leads to the capacity to affect another; power by itself does not much induce using resources to support or obstruct the efforts of dependent persons.

Consistent with this experimental research, field studies indicate that with cooperative goals leaders use their power to assist and promote employees (Tjosvold 1989; Tjosvold et al. 1991). Hong Kong leaders and employees with cooperative goals discussed their opposing views directly, resulting in productive work, experiencing the leader as democratic, and believing that both the leader and employee were powerful (Tjosvold et al. 1998).

Powerful units are expected to use their leverage to obtain needed organizational resources (Pfeffer 1981). Budget teams in Hong Kong fought in tough, closed-minded ways to decide how to distribute scarce resources when they had competitive goals (Poon et al. 2001). However, managers and employees with cooperative goals integrated their ideas and perspectives, which resulted in high-quality budgets. A cooperative context promotes an effective distribution of scarce resources.

Power bases and social context

Social-context research can supplement the power bases approach to power that proposes that the kind of resource – reward, coercive, legitimacy, referent, and expertise – determines power effects (French and Raven 1959). Social context research suggests that, in addition to any effects because of the nature of the power base, the impact of a power base depends upon whether it is used cooperatively or competitively (Tjosvold 1995). A manager's ability to give a bonus – a reward power base in the French and Raven conceptualization – is not inevitably used cooperatively. Reward power can be experienced as competitive when the employees believe their manager is giving them a bonus to perform duties good for the manager but against their own long-term interests. Employees then react negatively to the reward power (Tjosvold 1995).

The value of cooperative power relationships

Interdependence is a basic characteristic of organizations where people value and depend upon each other's resources, although often not equally. A manager has knowledge and rewards that can help employees work effectively to accomplish their goals but employees typically have information that can help managers make effective decisions. Indeed, mistakes by front-line employees, such as pilots whose ship spills tons of oil in the sea, can very much affect the lives and reputations of CEOs.

Organizations have complex layers of interdependence, that is, mutual power. Within departments and teams, employees have specialized effort and expertise that, when integrated, help them reach their goals. Departments have different expertise that must be coordinated for effective organizational performance. The hierarchy distributes unequal power throughout the organization. Hierarchy poses a particularly challenging issue for managing power. Managers are tempted to assume that only they have significant power; employees, to fear that.

Equalizing power has been the traditional approach to managing power in organizations (Walton 1987). Organizational members should have, if not equal, at least not widely disparate amounts of power to avoid the temptations to use power exploitatively; everyone should have power to check and counter each other.

Social-context research, however, provides a realistic, constructive alternative to power equalization. It suggests that power should be constructively employed and that this can be accomplished when organizational members enhance their power and use each other's power for mutual benefit. They see each other as resourceful and are prepared to employ their resources so that they all succeed. This section reviews research on the value of cooperative power relationships for organizations and for people.

Utility for organizations

Organizations are turning to new product and other types of groups to accomplish important tasks (Deming 1993; Kanter 1983; Kouzes and Posner 1987; Pfeffer 1994; West 2002). In new product teams, specialists from research and development, production, engineering, and marketing are expected to combine their ideas into developing a new product that can be manufactured and sold profitably. Managers are expected to assist and in other ways empower these teams so that employees believe they are competent and efficacious and have the autonomy and responsibility to complete their own course of action (Kirkman and Rosen 1999; Spreitzer et al. 1997). Then these teams can solve organizational problems.

Utility for individuals

Mutual power can be constructive for individuals as well as for organizations. Knowing that they have abilities that others value develops social acceptance. Dependence may also be useful: Feeling dependent upon the abilities of others can strengthen feelings of social support and reduce stress when these abilities are expected to promote mutual benefit (Johnson and Johnson 1989, 2005).

Psychologists have argued that interdependence is a foundation for psychological maturity and competence (Breger 1974). As they develop, people shift between the extremes of independence and dependence; immature people unrealistically demand independence but later feel highly dependent. Successful psychological development depends on integrating these opposing tendencies. Competent adults recognize and manage their interdependence. They see themselves as both powerful and dependent; they are ready to use their power as they seek the power of others. More research is needed to investigate directly the effects of cooperative power on individual development as well as organizational performance.

Obstacles to developing cooperative power relationships

Although managers and employees usually are mutually dependent, the temptation is to focus on who has power and who does not, who are the winners and who are the losers. The inability to develop mutual power may be an important reason that organizations often find implementing effective teamwork difficult. Research has identified obstacles to using power for mutual benefit.

Elaborating upon the idea that power corrupts managers, Kipnis (1976) argued that superior power tempts managers to exert unilateral control over employees. To support this coercion, the powerful come to see employees as people who can be controlled and, because of cultural values on the importance of self-control, they devalue employees (Fiske 1993; Kipnis 1976; Kipnis et al. 1980; Rind and Kipnis 1999; Scholl 1999). The powerful view employees as pawns and thereby unworthy of respect. These negative attitudes in turn reinforce the powerful to use their power to control and to dismiss the abilities of those subject to power.

McClelland (1970, 1975) found that managers with high personal power needs try to dominate subordinates; they use their position to meet their needs to assert themselves and to feel in charge. Argyris and Schon (1996, 1978) argued that managers typically adopt Model I values of being in control, suppressing emotions, and trying to win interpersonally (Argyris and Schon 1996, 1978). These values disrupt effective work relationships and, in particular, the feedback that could direct and motivate managers to develop mutually enhancing relationships.

How managers conceptualize power may also induce their coercion and undermine effective mutual power. Building upon the work of Follett (1924), Coleman (2006) argued that viewing power as limited makes it unlikely that managers will employ participation despite its advantages. Those managers who emphasized that power is scarce and that the more power employees had the less they had were found to avoid involving employees in decision-making.

Enhancing power relationships

Rejecting the notion that power itself corrupts, Rosabeth Kanter (1977, 1979) argued that power is often a highly productive force in organizational life. Power does not frustrate employee involvement but promotes participation. It is the more powerful managers who assist and support their subordinates, the less powerful who resist employee influence. Powerful managers have the confidence as well as ability to aid their subordinates and to influence them collaboratively. Even in high-power distance cultures such as China, superiors have been found to use their power to assist, support, and empower (Pye 1985; Spencer-Oatey 1997). This section reviews research on the conditions that facilitate cooperative power relationships.

Collaborative influence

Managerial needs and values do not necessarily result in coercion and disrupted relationships. McClelland (1975, 1970) found that managers can have high social-power needs, not just personal needs to dominate. These needs involve wanting to have a positive impact on others by being noticed, recognized, and remembered. When combined with self-control, managers with high social-power needs encourage and promote employees. Powerful, successful managers do not take power from employees but energize them with power (McClelland 1975).

Managers can eschew Model I values of being in control and embrace Model II values of mutual influence, open management of feelings, and joint determination. Argyris demonstrated that managers with these Model II values develop open, productive relationships with employees (Argyris and Schon 1996, 1978).

Research using a variety of methods supports the theorizing that collaborative influence can be effective and mutually enhancing. In an experiment, collaborative influence communicated respect and encouraged openness both to the influencer as a person and to his or her position (Tjosvold and Sun 2001). Controlling influence was experienced as disrespectful and fostered closed-mindedness and rejection of the other. Managers who relied on controlling-influence methods did not have much impact on their employees and disrupted their relationships with them (Yukl et al. 1999; Yukl and Tracey 1992).

Social context can be useful for understanding coercive and collaborative influence. Superiors were found to rely on collaborative methods to influence when they had cooperative goals with employees but to use coercive methods when they had competitive goals (Tjosvold et al. 1981). Leaders with cooperative goals conclude that, as their employees are open to influence, collaborative influence is appropriate and effective and they need not coerce; collaborative influence reinforces cooperative goals and mutual benefit.

Expandable power

Mary Parker Follett (1924) wanted organizations and society to expand power and use it for promoting the common good. Coleman (2006) found that managers who viewed power as expandable so that both the leader and the follower can enhance their power involved employees in decision-making and developed constructive relationships. In an experiment, power-holders who believed that power is expandable compared to limited provided support and resources, especially when employees lacked the ability to perform well (Tjosvold et al. 2003).

Evidence indicates that social context can shed light on how viewing power as expandable has its effects (Tjosvold et al. 2003). Viewing power as limited, managers are apt to see their relationship with employees as competitive; whatever employees gain comes at their manager's expense. Understanding power as expandable encourages the development of cooperative links between managers and employees. Managers believe by helping employees be more able and successful, they can also be more powerful and successful.

Orientation and methods of influence and views of power can very much affect power management. Collaborative influence and conceptualizing power as expandable appear to reinforce cooperative goal interdependence as major conditions that promote the positive face of power. In contrast, the temptation to control unilaterally and viewing power as limited can promote competitive goals and the negative face of power.

Leading with power

Leadership has been considered part of the positive side of organization and power part of the dark side. Contemporary leaders are trying to empower their employees to solve problems and get things done through redesigning organizations, restructuring governance, and changing their style. Rather than command and control, they are helping employees develop the abilities and confidence to exercise their judgment and make decisions (Christopher et al. 2000).

Research reviewed and other studies suggest how leaders can develop cooperative power relationships, where employees search out each other's abilities and appreciate their contributions, negotiate and collaboratively influence each other to exchange resources that will help them both be more productive, and encourage each other to develop and enhance their strengths (Tjosvold et al. 2006). These positive power patterns occur as employees work on common tasks with cooperative goals.

Cooperative interdependence

Strengthening cooperative goals lays the foundation for constructive power relationships. Managers and employees have common tasks such as to develop a new product and solve a customer problem. The manager wants employees to integrate their ideas and develop one solution. Each person signs off on the final product indicating that he or she has contributed and supports it.

Managers and employees can strengthen cooperative goals by recognizing they have complementary responsibilities and roles, all of which are needed to succeed. Tangible rewards as well as praise are given to all those who contribute. Individuals receive a bonus based on the performance of the department and the profitability of the company. Managers recognize all members of a cross-functional team, and their accomplishments are written up in the company newsletter. Similarly, everyone is held accountable for unproductive performance. Common tasks, joint effort, and shared rewards can convince people their important goals are positively related.

Recognition and appreciation

With cooperative goals, managers and employees are prepared to identify and value each other's power because they expect that abilities will be used for mutual benefit. They help each other be aware of their ideas, information, skills, and other abilities so that they are in a better position to do their jobs and reach goals.

Collaborative influence

Avoiding coercion, managers and employees indicate that they are open to being influenced as they try to influence each other. Secure in their expectations of each other, they agree to exchange their resources and strengthen their work relationships. They encourage, guide, and give tangible assistance that aid productivity.

Development and learning

Understanding that power is expandable, managers and employees indicate that they want to help each other develop valued abilities. Explaining and teaching help them cognitively process and organize information, engage in higher-level reasoning, attain insights, and become personally committed to achieving. They challenge each other's reasoning that promotes curiosity, motivation to learn, reconceptualization of what one knows, and higher quality decision-making (Johnson and Johnson 1989, 2005).

Concluding comments

Understanding the opposing faces of power is both intellectually challenging and practically significant. Research has begun to answer fundamental questions: What drives power to be used in ways that wreck havoc on people and their relationships? What are the conditions where power builds mutual confidence and facilitates common effort?

Power research has emphasized the degree of power and power differences. Little integrated into the power research is that dependent persons can reach very different conclusions about the nature of their dependence on the powerful. Studies in the West and in China have documented that how they conclude that their goals are related very much affects their expectations for how they will use their power and thereby their interaction and outcomes. When people with power over each other, even if unequal, believe that their goals are cooperatively rather than competitively related, they have been found to expect and to use their resources for mutual benefit and thereby strengthen their relationship and performance.

Organizations and groups are often blamed for using power to suppress individuals. Americans have long celebrated individual struggle against collective tyranny. But power and organizations are not going away; there is no realistic alternative to constructive power management. Leaders and employees need validated ideas to understand power and how they can make power facilitate their common efforts. This chapter has demonstrated the utility of the theory of cooperation and competition to understand the diverse dynamics and outcomes of power and shown how strengthening cooperative goals, recognizing resources, influencing collaboratively, and developing abilities contribute significantly to the positive face of power.

References

Argyris, C. and Schon, D. A. (1978) *Organizational learning: A theory of action perspective*, Reading, Mass.: Addison-Wesley.
   (1996) *Organizational learning II: Theory, method, and practice*, Reading, Mass.: Addison-Wesley.
Ashforth, B. E. (1997) Petty tyranny in organizations: A preliminary examination of antecedents and consequences. *Canadian Journal of Administrative Sciences*, **14**, 126–140.
Breger, L. (1974) *From instinct to identity: The development of personality*, Englewood Cliffs, N. J.: Prentice-Hall.
Burke, W. (1986) Leadership as empowering others. In S. Srivastva (Ed.), *Executive power* (pp. 51–77), San Francisco, Calif.: Jossey-Bass.
Christopher, R., Probst, T. M., Martocchio, J. J., Drasgow, F., and Lawler, J. J. (2000) Empowerment and continuous improvement in the United States, Mexico, Poland, and India: Predicting fit on the basis of the dimensions of power distance and individualism. *Journal of Applied Psychology*, **85**, 643–658.
Coleman, P. (2006) Power and conflict. In M. Deutsch, P. T. Coleman, and E. C. Marcus (Eds.),*The handbook of conflict resolution: Theory and practice*, 2nd edn (pp. 120–143), San Francisco, Calif.: Jossey-Bass.
Conger, J. A. and Kanungo, R. N. (1988) The empowerment process: Integrating theory and practice. *Academy of Management Review*, **13**, 471–482.
Daily, C. M. and Johnson, J. L. (1997) Sources of CEO power and firm financial performance: A longitudinal assessment. *Journal of Management*, **23**, 97–117.
Deming, W. E. (1993) *The new economics for industry, government, education*, Cambridge, Mass.: Massachusetts Institute of Technology, Center for Advanced Engineering Study.
Deutsch, M. (1973) *The resolution of conflict*, New Haven, Conn.: Yale University Press.
Fiske, S. T. (1993) Controlling other people: The impact of power on stereotyping. *American Psychologist*, **48**, 709–726.
Follett, M. P. (1924) *Creative experience*, New York, N.Y.: Longmans Green.

French, J. R. P. Jr. and Raven, B. H. (1959) The bases of social power. In D. Cartwright and A. F. Zander (Eds.), *Studies in social power* (pp. 150–167), Ann Arbor, Mich.: Institute for Social Research.

Hofstede, G. (1993) Cultural constraints in management theories. *The Academy of Management Executive*, 7, 81–94.

Hogan, R., Curphy, G. J., and Hogan, J. (1994) What we know about leadership: Effectiveness and personality. *American Psychologist*, 49, 493–504.

Johnson, D. W. and Johnson, R. T. (2005) New developments in social interdependence theory. *Psychological Monographs*, 131, 285–358.

   (1989) *Cooperation and competition: Theory and research*, Edina, Minn.: Interaction Books.

Johnson, D. W., Maruyama, G., Johnson, R. T., Nelson, D., and Skon, L. (1981) Effects of cooperative, competitive and individualistic goal structures on achievement: A meta-analysis. *Psychological Bulletin*, 89, 47–62.

Kanter, R. M. (1983) *The change masters*, New York, N.Y.: Simon & Schuster.

   (1979) Power failure in management circuits. *Harvard Business Review*, July–August, 65–75.

   (1977) *Men and women of the corporation*, New York, N.Y.: Basic Books.

Kipnis, D. (1976) *The power-holders*, Chicago, Ill.: University of Chicago Press.

Kipnis, D., Schmidt, S. M., and Wilkinson, I. (1980) Intraorganizational influence tactics: Explorations in getting one's way. *Journal of Applied Psychology*, 65, 440–452.

Kirkman, B. L. and Rosen, B. (1999) Beyond self-management: Antecedents and consequences of team empowerment. *Academy of Management Journal*, 42, 58–74.

Kouzes, J. M. and Posner, B. Z. (1987) *The leadership challenge*, San Francisco, Calif.: Jossey-Bass.

Lawler, E. J. and Yoon, J. (1993) Power and the emergence of commitment behavior in negotiated exchange. *American Sociological Review*, 58, 465–481.

   (1995) Structural power and emotional processes in negotiation: A social exchange approach. In R. M. Kramer and D. M. Messick (Eds.), *Negotiation as a social process* (pp. 143–165), Thousand Oaks, Calif.: Sage Publications.

Lewicki, R. J., McAllister, D. J., and Bies, R. J. (1998) Trust and distrust: New relationships and realities. *Academy of Management Review*, 23, 438–458.

Leung, K. (1997) Negotiation and reward allocations across cultures. In P. C. Earley and M. Erez (Eds.), *New perspectives on international industrial/organizational psychology* (pp. 640–675), San Francisco, Calif.: Jossey-Bass.

McClelland, D. C. (1970) The two faces of power. *Journal of Affairs*, 24, 29–47.

(1975) *Power: The inner experience*, New York, N.Y.: Irvington.

Pfeffer, J. (1981) *Power in organizations*, Boston, Mass.: Pittman.

(1994) *Competitive advantage through people: Unleashing the power of the work force*, Boston, Mass.: Harvard Business School Press.

Pfeffer, J. and Moore, W. L. (1980) Power in university budgeting: A replication and extension. *Administrative Science Quarterly*, **24**, 637–653.

Poon, M., Pike, R., and Tjosvold, D. (2001) Budget participation, goal interdependence and controversy: A study of a Chinese public utility. *Management Accounting Research*, **12**, 101–118.

Pye, L. W. (1985) *Asian power and politics: The cultural dimensions of authority*, Cambridge, Mass.: Harvard University Press.

Raven, B. H. (1993) The bases of power: Origins and recent developments. *Journal of Social Issues*, **49**, 227–252.

Rind, B and Kipnis, D. (1999) Changes in self-perceptions as a result of successfully persuading others. *Journal of Social Issues*, **55**, 141–156.

Rudolph, H. R. and Peluchette, J. V. (1993) The power gap: Is sharing or accumulating power the answer? *Journal of Applied Business Research*, **9**, 12–20.

Scholl, W. (1999) Restrictive control and information pathologies in organizations. *Journal of Social Issues*, **55**, 101–118.

Spencer-Oatey, H. (1997) Unequal relationships in high and low power distance societies: A comparative study of tutor-student role relations in Britain and China. *Journal of Cross-Cultural Psychology*, **28**, 284–302.

Spreitzer, G. M., Kizilos, M. A., and Nason, S. W. (1997) A dimensional analysis of the relationship between psychological empowerment and effectiveness, satisfaction, and strain. *Journal of Management*, **23**, 679–704.

Stanne, M. B., Johnson, D. W., and Johnson, R. T. (1999) Does competition enhance or inhibit motor performance: A meta-analysis. *Psychological Bulletin*, **125**, 133–154.

Thibaut, J. W. and Kelley, H. H. (1959) *The social psychology of groups*, New York, N.Y.: Wiley.

Tjosvold, D. (1981) Unequal power relationships within a cooperative or competitive context. *Journal of Applied Social Psychology*, **11**, 137–150.

(1985a) Effects of attribution and social context on superiors' influence and interaction with low performing subordinates. *Personnel Psychology*, **38**, 361–376.

(1985b) Power and social context in superior–subordinate interaction. *Organizational Behavior and Human Decision Processes*, **35**, 281–293.

(1989) Interdependence and power between managers and employees: A study of the leader relationship. *Journal of Management*, **15**, 49–64.

(1995) Effects of power to reward and punish in cooperative and competitive contexts. *Journal of Social Psychology*, **135**, 723–736.

Tjosvold, D., Andrews, I. R., and Struthers, J. (1991) Power and interdependence in work groups: Views of managers and employees. *Group and Organization Studies*, **16**, 285–299.

Tjosvold, D., Leung, K., and Johnson, D. W. (2006) Cooperative and competitive conflict in China. In M. Deutsch, P. T. Coleman, and E. Marcus (Eds.), *The Handbook of Conflict Resolution: Theory and Practice* (pp. 671–692), San Francisco, Calif.: Jossey-Bass.

Tjosvold, D., Coleman, P. T., and Sun, H. (2003) Effects of organizational values on leaders' use of information power to affect performance in China. *Group Dynamics: Theory, Research, and Practice*, **7**, 152–167.

Tjosvold, D., Hui, C., and Law, K. S. (1998) Empowerment in the leader relationship in Hong Kong: Interdependence and controversy. *Journal of Social Psychology*, **138**, 624–637.

Tjosvold, D., Johnson, D. W., and Johnson, R. T. (1981) Effect of partner's effort and ability on liking for partner after failure on a cooperative task. *The Journal of Psychology*, **109**, 147–152.

Tjosvold, D. and Sun, H. (2001) Effects of influence tactics and social contexts: An experiment on relationships in China. *International Journal of Conflict Management*, **12**, 239–258.

Walton, R. (1987) *Managing conflict: Interpersonal dialogue and third-party roles*, 2nd edn, Reading, Mass.: Addison-Wesley.

Welbourne, T. M. and Trevor, C. O. (2000) The role of departmental and position power in job evaluation. *Academy of Management Journal*, **43**, 761–771.

West, M. A. (2002) Sparkling fountains or stagnant ponds: An integrative model of creativity and innovation implementation in work groups. *Applied Psychology: An International Journal*, **51**, 355–424.

Yukl, G., Kim, H., and Chavez, C. (1999) Task importance, feasibility, and agent influence behavior as determinants of target commitment. *Journal of Applied Psychology*, **84**, 137–143.

Yukl, G. and Tracey, J. B. (1992) Consequences of influence attempts used with subordinates, peers, and the boss. *Journal of Applied Psychology*, **77**, 525–535.

PART II

Participative leadership
Leading with others

6 | Growing powerful using cherry-picking strategies
Coworker networks as cherry trees

GEORGE B. GRAEN

Introduction

"Boys, we may have a problem with the New York family. How much juice can we beg, borrow, or steal to placate their Don and avoid a war?"

Tony Soprano

The answers to this question require Tony's captains to search their social networks for "juice" to satisfy the offended Don. What is this thing they call "juice"? Where do they look for it? How is it grown and stored? Can you identify "juice" by its smell, sight, sound, taste, or touch? When and how can it be used effectively? This chapter is about these questions that can be stated easily but must be answered carefully in terms that make clear what we understand and what needs more research. The approach taken in this chapter is to explore people networks that cannot be commanded or controlled yet supply the life-saving flows of influence. Clearly, sometimes it is not what you know, but who you know that saves the day and keeps your hopes alive.

Although scholars and researchers use the concept of power in many different ways, Tony Soprano's captains know what he means by the term "juice". They know that juice may include material objects, such as money and property, and human services of many kinds, both positive and negative. Juice may be receiving something attractive or avoiding or stopping something aversive. Tony's captains also know where to look for "juice" in their social networks. Every person, in his or her respective social network, is a potential supplier of some useful "juice". All of the captains' business associates are grist for the juice mill, but only a few can render useful "juice". After the captains return to Tony with their potential juice for the New York Don, Tony has a meeting with the Don or his representative(s) and negotiates the shape of the "juice package". In the negotiation, it becomes crystal clear that the New York Don has much greater "juice" than Tony. Tony must swallow his pride and apologize to the Don and humbly render the negotiated "juice" package. Tony's business network failed this test and needs to be strengthened. But how should he proceed?

Some scholars would define power as perceived potential to influence the Don as seen by Tony and his captains. Other scholars would require more and define power as the outcome of the Don forcing Tony to apologize and render the juice package. We prefer to use perceived potential to influence another's actions, as *potential*, and the demonstration of such as *actual* power. Perceived potential can be self-perception and others' perception. This leads to the question of disagreement between the two perceptions that will become apparent during negotiations. Actual power can be analyzed in terms of the costs and benefits for each party as a consequence of the actual deal. Miscalculations in the use of "juice" can lead to disastrous results. Clearly, "juice" has a "nitro" danger and must be handled with knowledge and care. This probably is part of the reason for the attraction of *The Sopranos* TV show and the aversion of scholars to the area of power in organizations. Many people are interested in the dark side of power, but the subject of naked power tends to be only slightly more researched than torture.

This chapter is about the nature of informal power in organizations and how an employee attains it and uses it to make a difference. As the knowledge era's sun rises in the East, the traditional twentieth-century engineering process organizations are becoming progressively less competitive relative to the new knowledge-driven corporations. Knowledge power is the new driver of organizations. Those who can exercise knowledge will be the new fast-track stars of the era. Be prepared for the changes, because they will shake our world.

Formal and informal power

Formal power is based on some legally enforceable standard in a court of law, and informal power is based on some perceived social consequences (See Table 6.1). For example, owners have a legal bases in property rights under the law to demand due diligence from their agents managing their property. This legitimate authority is delegated from owners to those managing their property. Managers sign contracts (up) with owners (down) with employees (employment contracts) and (horizontal) with other organizations. Ultimately, this process of delegation of authority relies on enforcement in the courts.

Table 6.1 Formal and informal bases of power (juice).

Formal	Informal
Ownership rights	Societal norms and roles
Managership rights	Psychological employment contract
Employment contracts	Social and work networks
Standard operating procedures	Educational and training
Special operating procedures	Personal charisma
Court systems	Family connections
	Religious connections

Informal power (Barnard 1938) typically cannot be enforced in the courts, but it can influence behavior nonetheless by having social consequences. Social norms and roles are rules of social conduct that may have severe repercussions for offenders in a social group. Psychological employment contracts (Rousseau 1995) are based on the individual's expectations for fair and reasonable treatment on the job over and above the clauses in an employment contract. Social and work networks offer social capital beyond those of a single person. Social networks tend to comprise strictly friendship relations, but work networks tend to involve greater influence-growing opportunities at work. Education and training may convince others to attribute additional influence based on know-how. Charisma or "force of personality" may also serve the influence attribution function as may family and church connections. These are not exhaustive lists of either formal or informal bases of power. Several others could be mentioned and many more specific bases could be listed.

Considering behavior in organization, formal bases of power account for perhaps 80–90 percent of observed behavior (Mintzberg 1983). Most people in organizations do their job as prescribed most of the time. This is functional for the welfare of the organization. But, we should not forget the remaining 10–20 percent that is not prescribed. These actions are necessary for the organization to survive and prosper, but they are under-determined, unpredictable, and not understood by formal organizational theory. These actions require the use of the informal bases of power to begin to understand and predict these systems for innovation and change. For many of these systems we find that the most useful guide to the informal bases of power is the network-process approach. Employees who use this approach survey the organization for the most influential network, called the "competence network," and seek methods to join it and make a difference (Graen 1989).

Power networks

Just as Tony's captains searched their social networks for greater "juice", people in work organizations search their social networks for enhanced potential influence in the face of power struggles, because the team with the more powerful networks has an advantage in these negotiations. These power struggles go on in most organizations periodically, and the preparation for them is critical to, if not determining of, success. Quite often network power trumps formal influence sources for good or ill. Let us review the nature of networks in organizations.

Networks

Recent research shows that, about 85 percent of the time, people prefer to get advice from other people rather than from relevant databases (Doz et al. 2001). As people are such an important source of information, networks – involving a sender, a link, and a receiver – need to be constructed carefully one link at a time. Beginning with the first day on the job, network opportunities emerge. Although needing a help network is clear, only the foolish new employees would commit to any network until they understand the reputation of the various networks. Membership in some networks may be detrimental to one's career by aligning one with a discredited network. Before any link is forged with a colleague, the wise new employee assesses the attached network for hidden costs. If an error is made after careful investigation, it should be severed quickly and called an error.

As shown in Figure 6.1, an ego network represents the focal person, and those people who are directly connected in the network of communications. An extended ego network includes all those people who are connected to the ego by at least two lengths. In the example, Mike is linked to the leader via the link with Marcus (two links) and the leader, Marty and Marcus represent a tirade (three-way link). Note that no links directly connect Mike with Marty or the two with Jessie or connects Jessie, Marty, Mike or Marcus. These missing links are called network holes. The leader and Marcus are most central with the most links and Jessie and Mike are isolates with only one link to the core. These networks can be analyzed easily by available computer programs

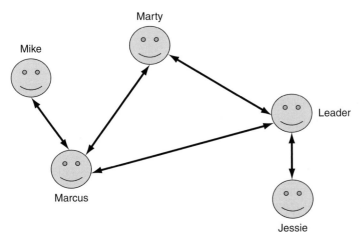

Figure 6.1 Dyads, triads, indirect relationships.

(Krackhardt and Hanson 1993). We argue that employees' managers and executives must learn to think in terms of networks of different kinds and the overlap between and among them (Gibbons and Grover 2006).

Leadership-sharing networks

Now that we understand how networks are described in terms of links or relationships, we shall focus on the critical informal instrumental influence links. These links may become the web that leads into competence networks. A competence network is an informal network of people who get the impossible done and keeps the organization functioning. It is comprised of real doers who know how to successfully bypass formal dead ends and accomplish things in extra-organizational manners. If you wish to make a difference in your career, you need to get accepted by joining successive competence networks. These networks are difficult to join because new candidates must prove themselves worthy under fire (Graen 1989). The tests for membership in competence networks are unannounced and often unfair, but you need to pass them or at least make a sincere effort to pass them.

Competence networks are constructed from informal, instrumental links by sharing leadership on a project or a job problem. The development of such an informal link often originates in offering to or requesting of work assistance or work advice of a colleague and his or her acceptance. Such offers or requests may grow into a shared leadership relationship over repeated exchanges through offering work assistance or advice on a job problem to a colleague and having it accepted and their reciprocating your kindness. This informally accepted interdependence usually starts with specific small problems and can successively grow to include much larger missions. As the exchanges become increasingly more complex, mutual respect and trust expands until the metamorphoses of the exchanges from mutually instrumental to mutually fulfilling. At this point, the leadership-sharing (LS) is between close friends. Such relationships once established may last over the entire lives of the two people (Graen, Dharwadkhar, et al. 2006).

At the center of this process are networks of dyads (two-person links). These include those that depend on each other to solve their very lives, such as surgical teams, soldiers, fire-rescue workers, and police. Such missions put people in harm's way, and LS at the highest level is demanded. Less extreme are organizations in crisis. Below this are highly competitive units of organizations in turbulent environments. Lower still are the situations of career cooperation and competition in our life. Below this are professional sports teams. We understand that our careers are a series of progressively more difficult competitions with our peers and yet we must cooperate with them. The answer to this conundrum is that we cooperate within our LS networks and compete with our peers outside of them. Our studies of entire careers of college graduates who joined the same large, multinational corporation in 1972 and retired in 2002 showed that those who most effectively practiced LS networking were most successful throughout their careers in terms of speed of promotion and compensation (Graen et al. 2006).

A person's LS should begin with the most significant people, and this usually begins with the direct report (supervisor). It proceeds to the next most significant person and then the next and so on. Periodically new relationships will be added as needed until one's LS network covers all ego-relevant functions inside and outside the employing organization. One way to look at your LS networks is that these are the people who will help you when you need them the most. Those outside of your networks likely will turn you and your problems away with "sorry that's not my job," but those inside will assure you that "your problem is my problem and we'll get it solved somehow."

The main difference between an informal network of high-efficacy people that can make the bureaucracy work despite its self-defeating rules (competence network) and a LS network that may help or hinder an organization's attempts to adapt to its change context is that competence network spreads through an organization and may not get involved in local-area issues, whereas a LS network is more concentrated and based on local-area issues.

Leadership-sharing relationships in which the parties agree to share roles about who leads and who follows on various parts of projects augment the power of the formal organization to get things done. In these LS exchanges, who leads and who follows frequently is based on who has the needed appropriate skills, information, and influence resources. In these networks, all get to lead some of the time. A network of these is called a *leadership-sharing (LS) network*. These networks are the keys to understanding emergent events, because when organizations are faced with new opportunities, whether positive or negative, the relevant LS networks are activated to cope. These networks, once activated, can be monitored to identify and map the organization's reaction. The wise employee can enhance his or her career progress by identifying, monitoring, and joining local networks (Nebus 2006).

The beginning links will be with a new employee's direct supervisor, unit peers, and those whose work is interdependent. Choices of links must be made quickly, but the offers should be carefully assessed for the long term. How can a new employee make such career relevant decisions quickly? Below are some things that may help.

Supervisor strategies

Supervisors have three strategies for relationship development, and employees reporting to supervisors also have three categories according to Graen (2006) as shown in Figure 6.2. Supervisors may be categorized based on their strategies for LS communications with their team. The *team maker* (a) makes initial offers to all team members; the *cherry picker* (b) makes offers only to the chosen few; and the *isolate* (c) makes no offer to any team member. The first strategy is the most work for both the supervisor and the team members who accept. The second strategy is less work but returns less benefit. Finally, the no-offer strategy is no work and has no benefits. In contrast, when the supervisor focuses on his or her nonteam members in the organization, the strategy of choice may be different. For many situations the supervisor should use strategy *a* for the team and strategy *b* for outside the team, because

Leader LS strategy

Follower LS strategy	Team Maker	Cherry Picker	Isolate	For person
Team Maker	• Best for leader • Caveat for follower	• Okay for leader • Okay for follower	• Poor for leader and follower	More risk & mixed rewards
Cherry Picker	• Okay for leader • Okay for follower	• Okay for leader • Best for follower	• Poor for leader and follower	Less risk & more rewards
Non-accept-ER	• Okay for leader • Poor for follower	• Okay for leader • Poor for follower	• Poor for leader and follower	No risk & no reward
For team	More work and more benefit	Less work and less benefit	No work and no benefit	

Figure 6.2 Leadership-sharing strategies of leader and follower.

we find a supervisor should be seen as fair beyond a doubt with his or her team but selective outside the team (Graen et al. 2006).

Follower's strategies

Followers have three strategies: team maker, cherry picker and nonacceptor. Employees who report directly to a supervisor should make offers to selective people including the supervisor and use the *cherry picker* strategy. The shotgun strategy of offering to all is too risky, because some choices have negative consequences regarding future opportunities. Therefore, the cherry-picker strategy implies that one picks carefully based on respect of capabilities and trust in dependability. Those colleagues who do not pass the tests at any point are dropped from one's network. Next we turn to some dos and don'ts.

Dos and don'ts

Some dos and don'ts for the newcomers are as follows.

1. Do join the correct LS networks as soon as feasible but choose wisely.
2. Don't join the wrong LS networks, because some links can be poison to your future opportunities.

3. Do commit to chosen LS network links until proven faulty and then cut ties quickly and publicly.
4. Do nurture valuable LS network links to grow them to maturity.
5. Do maintain mature links by visiting regularly.
6. Don't forget to forge triads and teams within your networks.
7. Do grow ever larger and more diverse LS networks inside and outside of your organization.
8. Do understand that LS networks keep the entire organization functioning and that they change over time.
9. Don't forget that this is a well-researched theory but it must be applied carefully and that everyone makes mistakes.

Graen and his associates (2006) have developed a measure that taps into the magnitude of sharing leadership expectation (SLX) with six sensitive statements you ask yourself about each and every member of your personal network at work. The higher your score when you are brutally honest the greater your chance of developing a shared-leadership relation. Start with your immediate supervisor; next do each of those who report to you; and continue with all those people who depend on you or who you depend on at work. For each of the six statements, the responses are

Strongly disagree = 1
Disagree = 2
Don't know = 3
Agree = 4
Strongly agree = 5.

The six statements are as follows.

1. My (colleague, supervisor, or subordinate) is satisfied with my work.
2. My (colleague, supervisor, or subordinate) would help me with my job problem.
3. My (colleague, supervisor, or subordinate) has confidence in my ideas.
4. My (colleague, supervisor, or subordinate) has trust that I would carry my workload.
5. My (colleague, supervisor, or subordinate) has respect for my capabilities.
6. I have an excellent working relationship with my (colleague, supervisor, or subordinate).

When you add your six scores, the range of scores is 6 to 36, and the higher your score, the greater your chance of developing a LS link. If your score with, say, your supervisor, is low (24 or below), you should act quickly to correct this unfavorable situation. Clearly, the six questions should help you identify the areas that need your immediate attention. When you first start your job, your score should be about 24, because you don't know. Test yourself at appropriate intervals and act to improve the problem areas. As you successively test your ties, you can more validly answer the above questions, and these tools should help you in your quest to become a high-power person in your organization and make a difference.

Research findings

New approaches for cultivating and nourishing power have produced a number of generalizations about organizational behavior.

1. Most behavior of humans in organizations is overdetermined by the rules and procedures of the formal organization enforced by legal contracts and agreements. That being stated, the most interesting and beneficial behavior is underdetermined and is called "informal". Both are necessary for an organization's survival. Informal organization is governed by the nature of humans as self-aware, need-satisfying, social creatures with limited rationality, imperfect information, creative imaginations, and deep-seated hopes and fears (Graen 1989; Weick 1995).
2. Informal influence can be mapped in terms of networks of expertise, information, influence, and social capital at any point in time and over time in terms of flows sensing relevant events, sense making, and implementation throughout the organization and its environments. As Orton and Dhillon (2006) described the flows of strategy, formulation goes from micro-actions (low levels) to meso-options (middle levels) to macro-strategy (top levels of organization) for the purpose of continuously improving the organization's future. One key to this mapping process is the rigorous measurement of relationships between formal and informal influences on individual, team and network flows of behavior.
3. Informal influence relationships are granted between employees in exchange and in proportion for shared leadership (Sparrowe and

Liden 2005). Thus, for a person to grow his or her leadership influence to get the right things done the right way with others, he or she must find a way to share leadership with those ready and willing to invest it properly. People who understand this multiplier effect we find are those who are most successful over their entire careers (Graen et al. 2006).

4. Those who understand that LS among members creates social capital throughout networks should encourage their associates and followers to do so for the good of their organization and their careers (Uhl-Bien et al. 2000).

5. Missteps can destroy social capital. Those who understand this and respect it will benefit from social capital (Krackhardt and Hanson 1993).

6. Those who successfully grow influence in their networks also agree that those in their networks can in turn influence them. It is reciprocal (Krackhardt and Hanson 1993).

7. Certain people in organizations can form a competence network for a focal person. This is an influence network made up of people with abundant social capital that get "impossible" things done in bureaucracies (Graen 1989).

8. We support the marriage of power theory and network analysis theory and hope that the new theory of LS in teams and networks is a step in that direction. Our early research showed that one's leader's relationship with his or her boss can limit the influence and social capital of a focal person (Graen et al. 1977). LS up the chain of command made a difference for lower participants in that resources flowed better when the network was strong between all three links in the chain of responsibility.

9. The impact of what a leader says to his or her follower depends on the particular LS link between the two (Wang et al. 2004). A leader may use any of a number of transformation leadership styles, but the proof of the pudding is in the critical sharing of leadership. We shouldn't be fooled by the ease of training leaders to talk the transformation talk to followers and forget about the critical process of using authentic LS to grow leadership and other social capital (Bass and Avolio 1997). Clearly, it doesn't matter what the leader says about say vision, if followers do not really listen and buy in. Also, this would apply to making offers up or horizontal. We need more research before we can understand how to develop authentic leadership (Hackman 1990; Hansen et al. 1999).

Clearly, a primary source of power in organizations is generated through relationships of the kind described above. Any person seeking to make a difference in an organization should understand that the more LS relationship with people who have large LS networks the better. In the literature, these LS relationships are called "strong ties" and the ordinary nonsharing relationships are called "weak ties," because the former are sources of power and the latter are not (Gibbons and Grover 2006).

In addition, the colleagues at work can see who are the more influential in their organization as shown by the research of Sparrowe and Liden (2005). In one study, those judged more powerful in the organization relative to their level in the organization had leadership-exchange relationships with their respective supervisor and belonged to the same competence network as their supervisor. As mentioned above, competence networks are those composed of people who get things done effectively and are networked to others who do the same. Acceptance into such a network multiplies one's informal power in an organization (Salancik and Pfeffer 1978).

Attributions are keys

It may not come as a surprise, but developing these informal power-generating relationships may not be straightforward at times (Seers 2004). People in competence networks hate to be fooled by people who ingratiate for selfish career purposes and hence attempt to sort out these phonies. A study by Lam et al. (2006) showed that supervisors were less inclined to allow LS relationships with those who they judged to be self-serving. In fact, the harder these people tried, the greater the rejection. In contrast, those judged team players were allowed LS relations, and the harder they tried the more successful they were. Clearly, supervisors do not want to be fooled by drama kings and queens.

In addition, those who achieved LS relations with their supervisor were the higher performers. Lam and his associates speculate that performance feedback seeking may be self-ingratiation or self-improvement oriented, and supervisors' judgment of which of these two is operating makes a difference in who gets to develop a LS relationship and who does not. Those who achieve the latter perform at a higher level than those who do not.

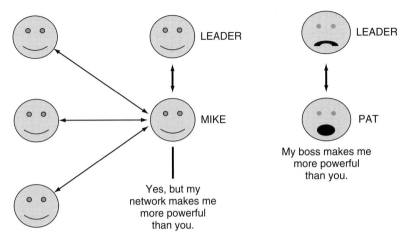

Figure 6.3 It takes a network.

Finally, as depicted in Figure 6.3, even the strongest tie with one's leader (Pat) can be trumped by the sum of another's extended network ties (Mike). Thus, it is folly to coast and not bother to develop strong ties with competence network members that you must depend upon to successfully complete your mission. Wise leaders understand that the network influence garnered by their team members are net human resources for their teams. A team with strong ties to its networks has greater potential for success than a team with weak ties. Which kind of team would you choose for yourself as leader or member?

Conclusion

Let's return to Tony Soprano's power struggle with the head of the New York family. Tony's captains bring in numerous suggestions for relevant power mechanisms, but their total falls short of that possessed by the Don. Clearly, Tony must bow to the superior power, but he now knows that his family must enhance its network influence or be taken over by the more powerful. Tony will beg, borrow, and steal to overcome his helpless condition.

In more lawful potential power struggles, the parties generally seek accommodations so that all parties compromise. In legitimate organizations, people acquire potential power by developing relationships of a particular kind. This kind we call LS relationships because the adhesion that holds the relationship together is the act of mutually sharing leadership with the other person. This act is not done easily in that it requires that a good deal of trust and respect has been developed between the parties and this trust and respect cannot be bought or sold. Trust and respect must be earned and freely granted. As a famous organizational consultant stated:

> In business and innovation, communications have one primary, overriding purpose – to build relationships. Not to inform or persuade, not to plan or contract, not to document or account, not to direct or report, not to buy or sell, but to build lasting relationships. Hard to accept, isn't it? That means that product brochures are not really about products. Business plans not about businesses. Project reviews not about projects. Sales calls not about sales. (Gary Lindquist [2006])

References

Barnard, C. (1938) *The functions of the executive*, Cambridge, Mass.: Harvard University Press.

Bass, B. M. and Avolio, B. J. (1997) *Full range leadership development: Manual for the multifactor leadership questionnaire*, Palo Alto, Calif.: Mind Garden.

Doz, Y., Santos, J., and Williamson, P. (2001) *From global to metanational*, Boston, Mass.: Harvard Business School Press.

Gibbons, D. E. and Grover, S. L. (2006) Network factors in leader–member relationships. In G. B. Graen and J. A. Graen (Eds.), *Sharing network leadership, LMX leadership: The series* (Vol. IV, pp. 63–93), Greenwich, Conn.: Information Age.

Graen, G. B. (1989) *Unwritten rules for your career: 15 secrets for fast-track success*, New York, N.Y.: John Wiley & Sons.

(2006) Post Simon, March, Weick, and Graen. In G. B. Graen and J. A. Graen (Eds.), *Sharing network leadership, LMX leadership: The series* (Vol. IV, pp. 269–278), Greenwich, Conn.: Information Age.

Graen, G. B., Dharwadkar, R., Grewal, R., and Wakabayashi, M. (2006) Japanese career progress over the long haul: An empirical examination. *Journal of International Business Studies*, 37, 148–161.

Graen, G. B., Cashman, J., Ginsburg, S., and Schiemann, W. (1977) Effects of linking-pin quality on the quality of working life of lower participants. *Administrative Science Quarterly*, 22, 491–504.

Graen, G. B., Hui, C., and Taylor, E. (2006) Experience-based learning about LMX leadership and fairness in project teams: A dyadic directional approach. *Academy of Management Learning and Education*, 5(4), 448–460.

Hackman, J.R. (1990) *Leading groups in organizations*, San Francisco, Calif.: Jossey-Bass.

Hansen, M., Nohria, N., and Tierney, T. (1999) What's your strategy for managing knowledge? *Harvard Business Review*, **77** (2), 106–116.

Krackhardt, D. and Hanson, J. (1993) Informal networks: The company behind the chart. *Harvard Business Review*, July–August, 104–111.

Lam, W., Huang, X., and Snape, E. (2006) Why doesn't my feedback seeking improve my relationship with my boss? Academy of Management Meeting, Atlanta, Ga., August.

Lindquist, G. (2006) Personal communications, August 7.

Mintzberg, H. (1983) *Power in and around organizations*, Englewood Cliffs, N.J.: Prentice-Hall.

Nebus, J. (2006) Building collegial information networks: A theory of advice network generation. *Academy of Management Review*, **31** (3), 615–637.

Orton, J.D. and Dhillon, G. (2006) Macrostrategic, mesostrategic, and microstrategic leadership processes in loosely coupled networks. In G.B. Graen and J.A. Graen (Eds.), *Sharing network leadership, LMX leadership: The series* (Vol. IV, pp. 137–167), Greenwich, Conn.: Information Age Publishing.

Rousseau, D. (1995) *Psychological contracts in organizations: Understanding written and unwritten agreements*, Thousand Oaks, Calif.: Sage Publications.

Salancik, G. and Pfeffer, J. (1978) A social information processing approach to job attitudes and task design. *Administrative Science Quarterly*, **23**, 224–253.

Seers, A. (2004) Interpersonal workplace theory at a crossroads. In G.B. Graen (Ed.), *New frontiers of leadership, LMX leadership: The series* (Vol. II, pp. 1–31), Greenwich, Conn.: Information Age.

Sparrowe, R.T. and Liden, R.C. (2005) Two routes to influence: Integrating leader–member exchange and network perspectives. *Administrative Science Quarterly*, **50** (4), 505–535.

Uhl-Bien, M., Graen, G.B., and Scandura, T.A. (2000) Leader–member exchange (LMX) for strategic human resource management systems: Relationships as social capital for competitive advantage. *Research in Personnel and Human Resources Management*, **18**, 137–185.

Wang, H., Law, K.S., Hackett, R.D., Wang, D., and Chen, Z.X. (2004) Leader–member exchange as a mediator of the relationship between transformational leadership and followers' performance and organizational citizenship behavior. *Academy of Management Journal*, **48** (3), 420–432.

Weick, K.E. (1995) *Sensemaking in organizations*, Newbury Park, Calif.: Sage Publications.

7 Acting fairly to be the boss

Procedural justice as a tool to affirm power relationships with subordinates

DAVID DE CREMER AND MARIUS VAN DIJKE

The issue of social justice is a dominating theme in our daily lives. In fact, concerns about the value of justice in our social lives go back to ancient moral philosophers such as Plato and Socrates (Rawls 1971). Indeed, the concept of social justice is related to humanitarian and ethical standards that describe how we should act and treat others (e.g., Miller 2001). Social justice can take many forms (e.g., fair distributions of outcomes, respectful treatment, fair communication of decisions and so forth), but in the past two decades considerable attention has been devoted to the issue of *procedural justice*. This focus in attention was primarily motivated by Lind and Tyler's (1988: 1) influential book in which they argued that fairness judgments (and related responses) are influenced more strongly by procedures than by outcomes, as such emphasizing the importance of procedures as a core element of social justice. Procedural justice can be defined as the fairness of procedures enacted by an authority when making allocation decisions (i.e. granting voice or not, being accurate and consistent in evaluations and so forth; see Leventhal 1980 for an overview of different procedural rules) and the respectful treatment associated with it (De Cremer et al. 2004).

To date, an impressive amount of literature exists pointing out the importance of procedural justice in promoting a wide variety of psychological outcomes relevant to the functioning of our social lives (see De Cremer and Tyler 2005; Greenberg and Colquitt 2005; Van den Bos and Lind 2002, for overviews). For instance, when people believe they are being fairly treated by authorities such as organizational managers or judges, they are more willing to accept decisions, obey laws, and exert extra effort to achieve organization goals (i.e. organization citizenship behavior; Moorman 1991). The belief that one has been treated unfairly prompts negative effect, antisocial behaviors such as revenge and theft (for recent meta-analyses, see Cohen-Charash and Spector

2001; Colquit et al. 2001), and it even negatively affects physical health (e.g., it increases chances of cardiovascular diseases; Elovainio et al. 2006).

The type of procedure that to date has received the greatest attention in the procedural justice literature is referred to as voice (Folger 1977). Voice includes the opportunity that people have to express their opinion during a decision-making process. Overall, studies show that people react more positively (e.g., positive emotions, cooperation, high fairness judgments) when they receive voice compared to when they are denied voice (Van den Bos 1999). Other types of procedural justice that recent empirical studies have started to focus on are the procedure of accuracy (i.e. evaluating every piece of information available), bias suppression, and acting consistently across time and people (De Cremer 2003a, 2004).

In the present chapter, we propose that social justice and procedural justice in particular has strong innate connections with the concept of power. As we will show, subordinates often view procedures as protection tools against abuse by power-holders. However, the main argument that we develop in this chapter aims to show that power and procedural fairness are connected not only from the perspective of subordinates, but also from the perspective of power-holders (an approach that has been neglected in the literature). More precisely, we take the perspective of the power-holder and develop a framework showing that those in power may wish to enact fair procedures to affirm their power position toward subordinates. In addition, we will elaborate on the conditions that facilitate the use of such impression-management strategies by power-holders, and which type of individuals in power are most successful in this practice.

Power and procedural justice

In the present chapter, we consider power as *social power*, which is a possibility or capacity to affect others, even if these others would resist such influence attempts. This perspective is in line with views on power suggesting that targets comply because they are dependent on the power-holder for outcomes, such as money, avoidance of punishment, information, or task support (e.g., Anderson and Berdahl 2002; Emerson 1962; Fiske 2001; French and Raven 1959; Galinsky et al. 2003; Keltner et al. 2003). As such, an actor has a power advantage, relative to a target, when this actor is less dependent on the target than the target is on the actor on a variety of dimensions (Emerson 1962; Van Dijke and Poppe 2004, 2006).

The conception of social power as being grounded in dependence, thus stressing that power-holders can abuse their power has led to the belief that power may corrupt. This is nicely illustrated by Kipnis' seminal study (1972) on the corrupting nature of power: Having power made superiors devalue the performance of their subordinates; instead, they attributed positive subordinate performance to themselves. Ever since that study, social psychologists have concerned themselves with the corrupting influence of having power (see, for instance, Georgesen and Harris 1998, for a meta-analysis of the effects of power on derogative subordinate evaluation). Noteworthy, this line of thinking is still vibrant in two theoretical traditions that have recently inspired much power research: The first is Fiske's (2001) "power as control model," which stresses that power leads to stereotyping of subordinates (among other reasons, to legitimize the power difference). The second is Keltner et al.'s model (2003) that views power as increasing action orientation (see Anderson and Berdahl 2002; Galinsky et al. 2003; see Overbeck and Park 2001, 2006 for different views). This model stresses that the increased action orientation increases the likelihood of socially inappropriate behavior.[1]

Acknowledging that social power installs the possibility of abuse and thus can corrupt power-holders makes the relationship with procedural justice very apparent. Indeed, the enactment of the formal and informal organizational procedures can make power-holders accountable. Such procedures are therefore an important protection tool against abuse by power-holders (Aquino et al. 2006; Thibaut and Walker 1975). In fact, the formal and informal procedural fairness rules in organizations have been argued to define what constitutes power abuse because they form a standard against which the actions of power-holders can be evaluated (Bies and Tripp 1995).

A first illustration of how procedural fairness connects with power abuse is found in empirical evidence showing that people indeed consider procedural fairness rules as protection from power abuse: Aquino

---

[1] It should however be noted that these authors recognize that whether having power results in abuse depends, among other things, on dispositional factors (cf., Chen et al. 2001; Guinote et al. 2002; Van Dijk and De Cremer 2006).

et al. (2006, see also Aquino et al. 2001) found that victims of offence by high-status offenders were less likely to engage in revenge when the procedural justice climate in the organization was perceived as favorable (i.e. clear norms about what constitutes fair decision-making and fair treatment), presumably because they trusted the organization to punish the offender. When the organizational justice climate was viewed as less favorable, victims were much more willing to repay an offence with revenge, presumably because they did not feel protected and thus believed that they themselves had to respond.

A second illustration of how procedural justice and protection against power abuse are interrelated can be found in the extensively studied procedural fairness rule of receiving voice in the decisions of authorities. If organizational rules demand that subordinates are given voice in the decisions of their supervisors, such rules actually demand that supervisors share their power with their subordinates to a certain extent. This act of power-sharing should therefore decrease the likelihood of power abuse. Research shows that subordinates want to share power with superiors in power (by increasing their power over their superior) in order to decrease dependence on the power-holder (Van Dijke and Poppe 2006).

Viewing voice in the decisions of authorities as an instance of power-sharing between authorities and subordinates also gives an opportunity to illustrate how procedural fairness norms can vary, resulting in varying definitions of what constitutes power abuse: Brockner et al. (2001) showed that people's reactions to the voice in decisions they receive depend on a cultural norm about how power should be distributed. Specifically, a series of studies showed that people were more likely to react negatively to low levels of voice in cultures in which no voice is considered to be a violation of social norms (i.e. low-power distance cultures). In cultures in which it is accepted and normative for people in positions of power to take decisions without much regard for input from low-power people, the negative effects of no voice were clearly less pronounced.

The above examples suggest that subordinates consider fair procedures as important because they provide them with a sense of control that may help them protect against power abuse. An issue that is at least as important is whether power-holders will indeed use fair procedures and, by that, allow their subordinates some control. Surprisingly, to date, the psychology literature has hardly devoted any attention to this question. In this chapter, we develop the argument that power-holders' decision to enact fair procedures or not is also related to control concerns. More precisely, we argue that the use of fair procedures may help power-holders to gain or sustain control in their relationship with subordinates. From this perspective, procedures can thus be seen by power-holders as valuable resources that can be used to affirm their power position.

In fact, several theories have focused on the tendency of those high in hierarchy to monitor power relationships and, if necessary, to undertake actions to preserve them. For example, social dominance orientation (SDO) theory points out that people differ in their general attitude toward favoring social inequality (Pratto et al. 1994). Those who favor social inequalities are considered to be high in SDO, and these individuals have been shown to be highly motivated to maintain or sustain their privileged status. The primary mechanism by which this is achieved is the adoption of hierarchy legitimizing myths that are remarkably easily accepted by those in lower hierarchical positions (Pratto et al. 1994). Interestingly, those high in SDO have also been shown to value the use of fair procedures (De Cremer et al., in press).

All in all, these studies suggest that those in power have a strong desire to maintain or sustain the status quo because they believe that hierarchical differences are justified and need to be maintained. This idea is nicely reflected in system justification theory (SJT; Jost and Banaji 1994; Jost et al. 2004). SJT argues that there is a strong motive "to defend and justify the status quo and to bolster the legitimacy of the existing social order" (Jost et al. 2004: 887). Thus, following the above, we suggest that those in power may be motivated to enact fair procedures to affirm their power and appearing fair may help in reaching this goal (e.g., to enhance compliance with the hierarchical status; Falbe and Yukl 1992; Greenberg et al. 1991). Why may the use of fair procedures be a useful tool to affirm one's power position?

Benefits of using fair procedures: the case of legitimacy and competence

We argue that enacting fair procedures may help power-holders to maintain or affirm their power because beliefs of *legitimacy* and *competence* are created (cf. Van Knippenberg et al. 2007). Below, we will briefly elaborate on how this may be the case.

As we noted earlier, power over others often derives from *dependence* of these others on what power-holders control, such as money, social support, or information (e.g., Emerson 1962; Ng 1980). However, the role division in power-holders and subordinates can also be accepted by both parties, which implies that subordinates comply with power-holders out of a sense of obligation. Such perceptions of legitimacy thus refer to people's belief that the person (e.g., authority, leader or interaction partner) is the appropriate and just decision-maker. Being viewed as legitimate is of high importance for power-holders. The reason for this is that influencing others through "raw" dependency-based power is very ineffective: It stirs up resistance and it requires constant observation of subordinates (Willer et al. 1997). Legitimacy has been shown to invite compliance with authorities' thoughts, feelings, and actions (Tyler 2006). Indeed, if authorities or leaders are perceived as legitimate (as compared to using "raw power") then people will more easily go along with the wishes and desires of this person and experience less doubt in the intentions of this other person (Kelman 1974, 2001).[2] This is where the concepts of power and fairness are most obviously connected, because an impressive range of studies, in a diversity of domains, such as work organizations and law courts, has shown that leaders' legitimacy is particularly enhanced by their procedural justice (see Tyler 2006, for an overview).

In addition to legitimacy, the perception of competence will also be important. Indeed, appearing fair secures the power-holder's position because being fair is often viewed as a desirable behavior (Bies and Tripp 1995). As a matter of fact, the perceived competence of those higher in the hierarchy in directing the group or organization toward its goals may, at least partly, be attributable to perceptions of such leaders as being procedurally fair (Calder 1977; Hinkin and Schriesheim 1990). This connection between procedural justice and competence becomes clearer when taking Leventhal's procedural fairness rules into account: People find it hard to believe that the group progresses toward its goals when leaders are unable to suppress personal biases or when they

---

[2] When leaders attempt to influence subordinates by means of an explicit appeal to the legitimacy of their request (i.e. "I am entitled to ask you this, and you are expected to comply"), resistance may also result (as for instance compared to rational appeals; see Ambrose and Harland 1995 for an overview). Falbe and Yukl (1992) proposed that resistance can result when legitimizing tactics are used in an arrogant manner.

violate the rule of accuracy (when leaders are incapable of basing decisions on as much available information as possible). Interesting in this respect is that Bruins et al. (1999) showed that competent leaders are allowed to strongly exercise their power: Whether they frequently or infrequently overruled their subordinate's decisions, they were considered equally legitimate. Moreover, participants were more inclined to engage in power-seeking (by taking over the leader position) when competent leaders infrequently exercised their power than when they frequently exercised their power.

Taken together, using fair procedures and thus installing an impression of fair management may help power-holders to affirm their power position because it makes them more legitimate and competent in the eyes of others. Subsequently, subordinates may then be more accepting of the power-holder and comply and cooperate with the directives and decisions of the power-holder. Of course, the strategy to use fair procedures to affirm one's power position will only be effective if the subordinates view the enactment of fair procedures as sincere.

For example, fairly enacted procedures such as voice are more likely to be seen as sincere when the decision to grant voice to subordinates stems from an authority that can be trusted to decide and act in ways that benefit those with whom they are dealing (Tyler and Huo 2002). This perception of a trustworthy authority in terms of being benevolent and willing to protect the interests of others, resulting in the use of the procedural rule of voice being viewed as sincere consequently promotes cooperation with the power-holder (De Cremer and Tyler 2007).

If, on the other hand, subordinates recognize that the use of fair procedures is a mere impression-management strategy that lacks sincerity, then one runs the risk that one's power position becomes threatened. Indeed, unsuccessful attempts of appearing fair may lead to a negative reputation of not being trustworthy (De Cremer et al. 2001) and, in turn, may motivate subordinates to display negative behavior toward the power-holder. For example, under circumstances of unfair procedures, subordinates may have a strong psychological need to defend themselves aggressively against personal insults (e.g., Aquino et al. 2001, 2006). Also, they can, for instance, attempt to leave the situation or attempt to increase their power by forming coalitions in order to contain the power-holder (see Emerson 1962).

Power promoting procedural justice: the case of unstable relationships, identifiability and sense of power

When will the need for enacting fair procedures to affirm power relations in unstable relationships be most strong? Here, we will present three variables that may influence this process: two situational (i.e. stability of the relationship and identifiability) and one individual difference (i.e. sense of power) variable.

First of all, the need to affirm one's power position is most likely to be promoted when subordinates represent a threat to the position of the power-holder. Indeed, unstable relationships with subordinates represent an aversive situation because it threatens the power-holder's position in the hierarchy. In such situations, high-power individuals are frequently engaged in monitoring their position, while low-power individuals attempt to improve their power positions (Georgesen and Harris 2006). In fact, most status hierarchies are considered dynamic rather than stable, and, therefore, it follows that power positions are often unstable, motivating those in power to monitor their positions closely. For example, recent research by Georgesen and Harris (2006) showed that threatened superiors were more likely to believe that they deserved to be the boss and, consequently, were more inclined to control the interaction. In other words, these superiors legitimized their power themselves and acted upon it. In terms of enacting fair procedures, it thus follows that those in power will be more likely to use fair procedures when their power relationship with subordinates is unstable relative to stable.

Second, in the present chapter, we advocate that the power-affirming strategy as discussed above is used to establish positive and fair perceptions among the subordinates and the social environment at large. Consequently, this perspective implies that procedural justice is a tool that affects social evaluation of others. Therefore, we predict that power-holders will be motivated most to use procedural justice as a power-affirming tool when they are under social scrutiny (i.e. when the public image of the power-holder is evaluated). The literature on accountability is very relevant to the present research, because it specifically addresses how social situations or interactions can influence how individuals feel and behave (Lerner and Tetlock 1999; Sedikides et al. 2002). This literature specifically shows that when individuals feel accountable (i.e. actions are identifiable and others know about one's own actions and decisions), they are concerned about how others view their actions and decisions. That is, accountability is assumed to activate concerns about one's public self-image or social reputation (Lerner and Tetlock 1999).

Accountability is assumed to be a multi-component construct (Lerner and Tetlock 1999: 255). Recent research has revealed that one specific component that is most responsible for the effects accountability reveals is identifiability (see Sedikides et al. 2002). If actions are identifiable to others, people become concerned about conforming to normative social influences, and, as a consequence, are concerned about their social reputation. Under such circumstances, we expect that the use of fair procedures will be serving the power-holder's position because perceptions of legitimacy and competence will contribute positively to the social reputation of the power-holder. In turn, such positive social reputation may then increase leeway for the power-holder in his or her decisions and actions.

Of course, those in power do not all possess the same psychological properties. That is, objective indicators exist to indicate who has more versus less power (e.g., a formal appointment as CEO or department head), but, at the same time, power-holders may also differ in the extent to which they experience a subjective sense of power in their relationships with others (Anderson and Berdahl 2002). It may exactly be this subjective sense of power that makes people display actions and attitudes that are representative of power motives. Recent research by Anderson and colleagues (Anderson and Galinsky 2006) has shown that this subjective sense of power relative to others may generalize across situations and relationhips, or, in other words, power-holders may individually differ in the extent to which they experience this sense of power. Here, we argue that if power-holders have a high sense of power they will strongly believe that they are able to influence others and thus wish to maintain their power position. For this reason, these individuals will particularly be motivated to use fair procedures as an important impression-management strategy.

Which power-holders will be most effective in this management strategy?

As we argued earlier, this strategy to use procedural justice as a power-affirming tool needs to be managed effectively, because subordinates may otherwise display very negative reactions toward the power-holder thereby promoting further threat to the power position. Which individuals are more skilled in managing power dynamics and perceptions in social settings?

One type of individual trait that may affect how skillful power-holders will be in this process is self-monitoring (Snyder 1987). According to the theory of self-monitoring, people differ in the extent to which they can and do regulate their behavior according to situational circumstances; that is, some people are more motivated than others to obtain, and are more skilled than others in obtaining, public appearances by regulating their expressive behavior and self-presentation. Indeed, when classified by their responses to the self-monitoring scale (SMS; Snyder and Gangestad 1986), high self-monitors appear to be very much aware of their own behavior and its social consequences. These individuals tend to look outside themselves for cues about how to respond to different situations and, thus, are more situationally oriented. In contrast, low self-monitors tend to be more committed to their internal values and, as such, openly display their traits and attitudes.

Recent research by Flynn et al. (2006) may be informative with respect to this issue. These authors tested the assumption that self-monitoring influences the extent to which individuals are (a) sensitive to how one's social actions and decisions have status implications in the eyes of others; and (b) effective in managing their relationships with others to be regarded as high in status. More precisely, their studies showed that high self-monitors were more accurate than low self-monitors in recognizing power and status dynamics in social-exchange relationships. This ability to make accurate evaluations with respect to status dynamics is a skill that generally leads to power and a positive reputation (Kilduff and Krackhardt 1994; Krackhardt and Kilduff 1999). Moreover, high self-monitors were also found to be more social pragmatists than low self-monitors in a way that they were more effective in establishing a positive and generous image of themselves in social exchanges, which, in turn enhanced their own social status. Thus, building on the findings of Flynn et al. (2006), we suggest that power-holders high in self-monitoring will be especially effective in creating a sincere procedural justice climate, which will grant them with legitimacy and thus affirm their existing power base.

Conclusion

The aim of the present chapter was to make clear that the power literature to date primarily has adopted a "subordinates' perspective" in which procedures are evaluated in terms of their potential to protect subordinates against power abuse (i.e. to gain control over their interaction with the power-holder). We argue that power-holders may also have a strong need to acquire control. Under these circumstances, those in power may use fair procedures to affirm their power position. Indeed, using fair procedures makes power-holders appear legitimate and competent decision-makers, consequently revealing positive influence among others. This strategy to use fair procedures to affirm one's power position is most likely to emerge under conditions when relationships with subordinates are unstable, when one's actions are identifiable and when one has a high sense of power. Importantly, we suggest that high self-monitors may be most successful and effective in using this power-affirming strategy.

References

Ambrose, M. L. and Harland, L. K. (1995) Procedural justice and influence tactics: Fairness, frequency, and effectiveness. In R. Cropanzano and M. Kacmar (Eds.), *Organizational Politics, justice, and support: Managing social climate at work* (pp. 97–130), Westport, Conn.: Quorum Press.

Anderson, C. P. and Berdahl, J. L. (2002) The experience of power: Examining the effects of power on approach and inhibition tendencies. *Journal of Personality and Social Psychology*, **83**, 1362–1377.

Anderson, C. P. and Galinsky, A. D. (2006) Power, optimism, and risk-taking. *European Journal of Social Psychology*, **36**, 511–536.

Aquino, K., Tripp, T. M., and Bies, R. J. (2001) How employees respond to personal offence: The effects of blame attribution, victim status, and offender status on revenge and reconciliation in the workplace. *Journal of Applied Psychology*, **86**, 52–59.

(2006) Getting even or moving on? Power, procedural justice, and types of offence as predictors of revenge, forgiveness, reconciliation, and avoidance in organizations. *Journal of Applied Psychology*, **91**, 653–668.

Bies, R. J. and Tripp, T. M. (1995) The use and abuse of power: Justice as social control. In R. Cropanzano and M. Kacmar (Eds.), *Organizational Politics, justice, and support: Managing social climate at work* (pp. 131–146), Westport, Conn.: Quorum Press.

Brockner, J., Ackerman, G., Greenberg, J., Gelfand, M. J., Fancesco, A. M., Xiong Chen, Z., Leung, K., Bierbrauer, G., Gomez, C., Kirkman, B. L., and Shapiro, D. (2001) Culture and procedural justice: The influence of power distance on reactions to voice. *Journal of Experimental Social Psychology*, **37**, 300–315.

Bruins, J. J., Ellemers, N., and De Gilder, D. (1999) Power use and differential competence as determinants of subordinates' evaluative and behavioural responses in simulated organizations. *European Journal of Social Psychology*, **29**, 843–870.

Calder, B. J. (1977) An attribution theory of leadership. In B. M. Shaw and G. R. Salanic (Eds.), *New directions in organizational behavior* (pp. 179–204), Chicago, Ill.: St. Clair Press.

Chen, S., Lee-Chai, A. Y., and Bargh, J. A. (2001) Relationship orientation as a moderator of the effects of social power. *Journal of Personality and Social Psychology*, **80**, 173–187.

Cohen-Charash, Y. and Spector, P. E. (2001) The role of justice in organizations: A meta-analysis. *Organizational Behavior and Human Decision Processes*, **86**, 278–321.

Colquitt, J. A., Conlon, D. E., Wesson, M. J., Porter, COLH, and Yee, K. (2001) Justice at the millennium. A meta-analytic review of 25 years of organizational justice research. *Journal of Applied Psychology*, **86**, 425–445.

De Cremer, D. (2003a) Why inconsistent leadership is regarded as procedurally unfair: The importance of social self-esteem concerns. *European Journal of Social Psychology*, **33**, 535–550.

    (2004) The influence of accuracy as a function of leader's bias: The role of trustworthiness in the psychology of procedural justice. *Personality and Social Psychology Bulletin*, **30**, 293–304.

De Cremer, D., Cornelis, I., and Van Hiel, A. (2008) To whom does voice matter in groups? Effects of voice on affect and judgments as a function of social dominance orientation. *Journal of Social Psychology*, **148**, 61–76.

De Cremer, D., Snyder, M., and Dewitte, S. (2001) The less I trust, the less I contribute (or not?): Effects of trust, accountability and self-monitoring in social dilemmas. *European Journal of Social Psychology*, **31**, 91–107.

De Cremer, D. and Tyler, T. R. (2005) Managing group behavior: The interplay between procedural justice, sense of self, and cooperation. In M. P. Zanna (Ed.), *Advances in experimental social psychology*, (Vol. 37, pp. 151–218), San Diego, Calif.: Elsevier Academic Press.

    (2007) The effects of trust in authority and procedural fairness on cooperation. *Journal of Applied Psychology*, **92**, 639–649.

De Cremer, D., van Knippenberg, D., van Dijke, M., and Bos, A. E. R. (2004) How self-relevant is fair treatment? Social self-esteem moderates interactional justice effects. *Social Justice Research*, **17**, 407–419.

Elovainio, M., Leino-Arjas, P., Vahtera, J., and Kivimäki, M. (2006) Justice at work and cardiovascular mortality: A prospective cohort study. *Journal of Psychosomatic Research*, **61**, 271–274.

Emerson, R. M. (1962) Power dependence relations. *American Sociological Review*, 27, 31–41.

Falbe, C. and Yukl, G. (1992) Consequences for managers of using single influence tactics and combinations of tactics. *Academy of Management Journal*, 35, 638–652.

Fiske, S. T. (2001) Effects of power on bias: Power explains and maintains individual, group and societal disparities. In A. Y. Lee-Chai and J. A. Bargh (Eds.), *The use and abuse of power: Multiple perspectives on the causes of corruption* (pp. 181–193), Philadelphia, Pa.: Psychology Press.

Flynn, F. J., Reagans, R. E., Amanatullah, E. T., and Ames, D. R. (2006) Helping one's way to the top: Self-monitors achieve status by helping others and knowing who helps whom. *Journal of Personality and Social Psychology*, 91, 1123–1137.

Folger, R. (1977) Distributive and procedural justice: Combined impact of "voice" and improvement of experienced inequity. *Journal of Personality and Social Psychology*, 35, 108–119.

French, J. R. P. and Raven, B. (1959) The bases of social power. In D. Cartwright (Ed.), *Studies in social power* (pp. 259–269), Ann Arbor, Mich.: Institute for Social Research.

Galinsky, A. D., Gruenfeld, D. H., and Magee, J. C. (2003) From power to action. *Journal of Personality and Social Psychology*, 85, 453–466.

Georgesen, J. and Harris, M. J. (1998) Why's my boss always holding me down? A meta-analysis of power effects on performance evaluations. *Personality and Social Psychology Review*, 2, 184–195.

(2006) Holding onto power: Effects of power-holders' positional instability and expectancies on interactions with subordinates. *European Journal of Social Psychology*, 36, 451–468.

Greenberg, J., Bies, R. J., and Eskew, D. E. (1991) Establishing fairness in the eye of the beholder. Managing impressions of social justice. In R. A. Giacalone and P. Rosenfeld (Eds.), *Applied impression management: How image-making affects managerial decisions* (pp. 111–132), Thousand Oaks, Calif.: Sage Publications.

Greenberg, J. and Colquitt, J. A. (2005) *Handbook of organizational justice*, Mahwah, N. J.: Lawrence Erlbaum Associates Publishers.

Guinote, A., Judd, C. M., and Brauer, M. (2002) Effects of power on perceived and objective group variability: Evidence that more powerful groups are more variable. *Journal of Personality and Social Psychology*, 82, 708–721.

Hinkin, T. R. and Schriesheim, C. A. (1990) Relationships between subordinate perceptions of supervisor influence tactics and attributed bases of supervisor power. *Human Relations*, 43, 221–237.

Jost, J. T. and Banaji, M. R. (1994) The role of stereotyping in system-justification and the production of false consciousness. *British Journal of Social Psychology*, 33, 1–27.

Jost, J. T., Banaji, M. R., and Nosek, B. A. (2004) A decade of system justification theory: Accumulated evidence of conscious and unconscious bolstering of the status quo. *Political Psychology*, 25, 881–920.

Kelman, H. C. (1974) Further thoughts on the processes of compliance, identification and internalization. In J. T. Tedeschi (Ed.), *Perspectives on social power* (pp. 125–177), Chicago, Ill.: Aldine.

(2001) Reflections on social and psychological processes of legitimization and delegitimization. In J. T. Jost and B. Major (Eds.), *The psychology of legitimacy: Emerging perspectives on ideology, justice, and intergroup relations* (pp. 54–73), New York, N.Y.: Cambridge University Press.

Keltner, D., Gruenfeld, D. H., and Anderson, C. (2003) Power, approach, and inhibition. *Psychological Review*, 110, 265–284.

Kilduff, M. and Krackhardt, D. (1994) Bringing the individual back in: A structural analysis of the internal market for reputation in organizations. *Academy of Management Journal*, 37, 87–108.

Kipnis, D. (1972) Does power corrupt? *Journal of Personality and Social Psychology*, 24, 33–41.

Krackhardt, D. and Kilduff, M. (1999) Whether close or far: Social distance effects on perceived balance in friendship networks. *Journal of Personality and Social Psychology*, 76, 770–782.

Lerner, J. S. and Tetlock, P. E. (1999) Accounting for the effects of accountability. *Psychological Bulletin*, 125, 255–275.

Leventhal, G. S. (1980) What should be done with equity theory? New approaches to the study of fairness in social relationships. In K. Gergen, M. Greenberg, and R. Willis (Eds.), *Social exchange: Advances in theory and research* (pp. 27–55), New York, N.Y.: Plenum.

Lind, E. A. and Tyler, T. R. (1988) *The social psychology of procedural justice*, New York, N.Y.: Plenum Press.

Miller, D. T. (2001) Disrespect and the experience of injustice. *Annual Review of Psychology*, 52, 527–553.

Moorman, R. H. (1991) Relationship between organizational justice and organizational citizenship behaviors: Do fairness perceptions influence employee citizenship? *Journal of Applied Psychology*, 76, 845–855.

Ng, S. H. (1980) *The social psychology of power*, London and New York, N. Y.: Academic Press.

Overbeck, J. R. and Park, B. (2001) When power does not corrupt: Superior individuation processes among powerful perceivers. *Journal of Personality and Social Psychology*, 81, 549–565.

(2006) Powerful perceivers, powerless objects: Flexibility of power-holders' social attention. *Organizational Behavior and Human Decision Processes*, **99**, 227–243.

Pratto, F., Sidanius, J., Stallworth, L. M., and Malle, B. F. (1994) Social dominance orientation: A personality variable predicting social and political attitudes. *Journal of Personality and Social Psychology*, **67**, 741–763.

Rawls, J. (1971) *A theory of justice*, Cambridge, Mass.: Belknap Press of the Harvard University Press.

Sedikides, C., Herbst, K. C., Hardin, D. P., and Dardis, G. J. (2002) Accountability as a deterrent to self-enhancement: The search for mechanisms. *Journal of Personality and Social Psychology*, **83**, 592–605.

Snyder, M. (1987) *Public appearances, private realities: The psychology of self-monitoring*, New York, N.Y.: Freeman and Company.

Snyder, M. and Gangestad, S. (1986) On the nature of self-monitoring: Matters of assessment, matters of validity. *Journal of Personality and Social Psychology*, **51**, 125–139.

Thibaut, J. and Walker, L. (1975) *Procedural justice: A psychological analysis*, Hillsdale, N. J.: Lawrence Erlbaum Associates.

Tyler, T. R. (2006) Psychological perspectives on legitimacy and legitimation. *Annual Review of Psychology*, **57**, 375–400.

Tyler, T. R. and Huo, Y. J. (2002) *Trust in the law*, New York, N.Y.: Russell-Sage.

Van den Bos, K. (1999) What are we talking about when we talk about no-voice procedures? On the psychology of the fair outcome effect. *Journal of Experimental Social Psychology*, **35**, 560–577.

Van den Bos, K. and Lind, E. A. (2002) Uncertainty management by means of fairness judgments. In M. P. Zanna (Ed.), *Advances in experimental social psychology* (Vol. 34, pp. 1–60), San Diego, Calif.: Academic Press.

Van Dijk, E. and De Cremer, D. (2006) Putting one's own interest first or not: Leader-follower effects and social value orientations. *Personality and Social Psychology Bulletin*, **32**, 1352–1361.

Van Dijke, M. H. and Poppe, M. (2004) Social comparison of power: Interpersonal versus intergroup effects. *Group Dynamics*, **8**, 13–26.

(2006) Personal power motives as a basis for social power dynamics. *European Journal of Social Psychology*, **36**, 537–556.

Van Knippenberg, B., Van Knippenberg, D., and De Cremer, D. (2007) Why people resort to coercion: The role of utility and legitimacy. *European Journal of Social Psychology*, **37**, 276–287.

Willer, D., Lovaglia, M. J., and Markovsky, B. (1997) Power and influence: A theoretical bridge. *Social Forces*, **76**, 571–603.

8 | A tale of two theories
Implicit theories of power and power-sharing in organizations

PETER T. COLEMAN

In an attempt to avoid layoffs at a company in the United States, a large majority of the employees agreed to cut their own salaries by 20 percent. The offer was rejected by the CEO, who chose instead to fire 20 percent of the workforce. He said "it was very important that management's prerogative to manage as it saw fit not be compromised by sentimental human considerations"

(Harvey 1989: 275)

Why would any CEO ever choose to share his or her power? Why would he or she withhold it? Do the ways managers think about power, how they conceive of its nature and the assumptions they make about how it operates in organizations affect their willingness to empower others? And what are the conditions that make it more or less likely that people will share power? These are the central questions addressed in this chapter.

Starting with the early studies of participative leadership by Lewin et al. (1939) and Coch and French (1948), scholars have been investigating the organizational consequences of power-sharing. Since that time, the benefits of power-sharing in organizations and the conditions under which it tends to be most effective, have been well documented (Likert 1967; Vroom and Jago 1988, 2007; Walls 1990; Argyris 1964; McGregor 1960; Bradford and Cohen 1984; Kanter 1983; Peters and Austin 1985; Peters and Waterman 1982; Hollander and Offermann 1990; Yukl 1994; Tjosvold 1981, 1985a, 1985b; Stewart and Barrick 2000). Today, organizations around the globe are seeking to empower their employees in order to increase job satisfaction and commitment, to improve the pace and efficiency of problem-solving, and to compete better in a demanding global marketplace (Deming 1993; Kirkman and Rosen 1999).

However, a fundamental problem facing workforce empowerment initiatives is the tendency of those in positions of authority in organizations to remain unwilling to share power (decision-making authority, information, resources, etc.; Argyris and Schon 1996, 1978; Jesaitis and Day 1992; O'Toole 1995; Stewart and Manz 1997). Resistance to empowerment from managers or supervisors may be due, to some degree, to the beliefs about power and authority that they bring with them to their work or that are unwittingly fostered in many organizations (Argyris and Schon 1996; Burke 1986; Coleman 2004; Conger and Kanungo 1988; Tjosvold et al. 2003).

This chapter presents a tale of two implicit theories of organizational power: competitive power and cooperative power. It suggests that basic differences in our assumptions about power can be significant determinants of our behavior as supervisors, managers and leaders. This is particularly so when such assumptions operate automatically, out of our conscious awareness. Information at this level of cognitive processing is often taken as fact, as a given, and therefore can go a long way in shaping our perceptions of and preferences for a host of organizational functions – including how we take up roles of authority. This chapter provides an overview of two contrasting implicit theories of power and summarizes the research and practical implications of these differences for organizational life.

The problem of power

Power is as essential to our understanding of organizational dynamics as it is confusing. As a construct it is abstract, ambiguous, and pervasive – affecting and being affected by virtually everything else in organizational life. Consequently, there are about as many conceptualizations of power as there are authors who have written on the subject. This is largely due to the fact that our understanding of power is filtered through our personal experiences (such as the relative level of power that we enjoy in our lives) and our basic assumptions about human nature and the nature of relations between people. This diversity of meaning also stems from differences in our training (in psychology, management, international affairs, community activism, etc.) as they shape our thinking through their associated paradigms, theories, and models, which tend to orient us to specific aspects and levels of power.

Working effectively with the construct of power requires that we hone our sense of the problem of interest (in this chapter, power-sharing and empowerment) and then specify the aspects of power that seem most relevant to our understanding of the problem. Power can be defined generally as *a capacity to produce effects* (Follet 1924).

However, such effects can be intended or unintended, and such capacities can be employed effectively or ineffectively in achieving one's goals. Thus, we will work with a slightly more specific definition of *power* proposed by Salancik and Pfeffer (1977: 3) as "the ability to bring about desired outcomes."

While employee empowerment is a complex phenomenon consisting of various sub-dimensions (see Spreitzer and Mishra 2002), which are determined by a variety of organizational and psychological factors (see Appelbaum et al. 1999; Yukl 1994), in essence it involves the redistribution and sharing of power (Leana 1987). Here, I define *power-sharing* as *activities that enhance, support, or facilitate another's ability to bring about outcomes he or she desires* (Coleman 2004: 299).

Power-sharing in organizations

The concept of power-sharing is closely associated with the acts of collective decision-making and shared leadership (Home 1991), yet its theoretical roots are unclear (Leana 1987). The most abundant literature in this area is the research on subordinate participation in decision-making, which traces its theoretical roots to the human-relations approach to management and to the values of democracy, power equality and social interaction (Likert 1967). Other forms of organizational power-sharing include participation in goal-setting, policy-making, problem-solving and change; delegation of authority; worker autonomy; structural decentralization; information-sharing; and sharing rewards, profits, and other valued outcomes (Burke 1986; Yukl 1994; Leana 1987).

Miles (1965) articulated two basic arguments in support of such initiatives. One, the human-relations argument, claims that if subordinates can contribute to group goals and strategies, they satisfy their own needs for self-esteem and achievement, leading to higher levels of job satisfaction and organizational commitment. The second rationale, the human-resources argument, holds that because knowledge and expertize are widely distributed throughout work groups and organizations, increased worker participation leads to higher quality decisions and better group performance resulting in greater employee satisfaction. Following this logic, many companies have invested in empowerment initiatives such as structural decentralization and self-managing teams (Cohen and Ledford 1994).

Research on organizational empowerment points to a variety of positive outcomes. Higher levels of empowerment have been found to motivate employees to display more customer-oriented behavior (Peccei and Rosenthal 2001), to engage in more innovative work behavior (Janssen et al. 1997), and to boost productivity and corporate competitiveness (Weiss 2002). Empowerment has also been found to increase organizational attachment, leading to less voluntary turnover (Spreitzer and Mishra 2002; Kim 2002). In addition, researchers in both public and private sectors agree that participative management practices improve employee job satisfaction (Kim 2002) and can be beneficial to worker's mental health (Spector 1986; Miller and Monge 1986; Fisher 1989). The willingness to share power with others is also a common theme in the profile of successful managers and organizations studied by Waterman (see Bogner 2002) and O'Toole (1995).

Nevertheless, research has not consistently supported the value of empowerment initiatives (see Latham et al. 1994; Leana et al. 1992; Leana et al. 1990; Locke and Schweiger 1979). Contradictory findings seem based in part upon the lack of clarity regarding the conditions necessary for employees to have the ability and motivation to participate in solving organizational problems (Glew et al. 1995; Tjosvold 1987), and in part to the tensions which can arise in organizations between needs for efficiency (typically achieved through hierarchical control) and the values of employee participation (Coleman and Voronov 2003).

Despite the many positive outcomes associated with empowerment initiatives, supervisors frequently resist sharing power with subordinates, thereby hindering the successful implementation of such programs (Argyris and Schon 1996, 1978; Jesaitis and Day 1992; O'Toole 1995, Stewart and Manz 1997). Resistance to all types of organizational change initiatives has been found to be partially accounted for by the constraints posed by well-established, ingrained schema (Labianca et al. 2000). Thus, one key to addressing managerial resistance to power-sharing may lie in understanding the cognitive structures of supervisors and managers (Stewart and Manz 1997).

Implicit theories

Social psychologists have long suggested that a major determinant of personality and interpersonal relations are the naive models or assumptions that individual's hold about the self and their social reality (Kelly

1955; Heider 1958). These *implicit theories* function much like scientific models in that they focus attention and guide the way people process and comprehend information about the self and other people. They are derived from people's own personal history of social interaction and experiences with certain types of social behavior. For example, if a child attends a school that stresses competition in most areas – for grades, for positions of leadership in the school, and for excellence in sports – you would expect that over time he or she would develop an understanding of school life as inherently win-lose. This understanding would considerably influence many of the child's decisions and choices in school and subsequent peer relations. In this way, the formation of strong implicit theories contributes to the development of a meaning system with regard to specific phenomenon (such as organizational power), which creates a motivational framework – orienting people toward particular goals, strategies, reactions, and interpretations of events (Dweck 1996).

Implicit theories differ from other individual difference variables (e.g. authoritarianism, need for power) in that they tend to be domain-specific conceptual frameworks. In other words, people can hold different theories about the various aspects of their self and their social reality. For example, a person may conceive of power relations in organizations as highly competitive and destructive but believe them to be of a very benign nature in his or her personal relations. In recent years, there has been a strong interest in how such theories can play a key role in the understanding of an array of work-related processes including leadership (Offerman et al. 1994; Dastmalchian et al. 2001), organizational performance (Schleicher and Day 1998), ability (Levy et al. 1999; Gervey et al. 1999), creativity and wisdom (Sternberg 1985), and affirmative action (Nacoste 1996).

The exact composition of these theories can differ. On the one hand, there is research on differences that individuals hold in their implicit *beliefs* of certain phenomenon that have been shown to affect people's goals, judgments and reactions to others. For example, research on differences in implicit beliefs of intelligence (incremental theories vs. entity theories) has accounted for differences in goal-orientations and major patterns of adaptive (mastery-oriented) and maladaptive (helpless) behavior (Dweck and Leggett 1988; Dweck et al. 1995; Henderson and Dweck 1990). Other research on implicit beliefs includes people's conceptions of personality and moral character (Dweck et al. 1993; Dweck 1996), and of creativity and wisdom (Sternberg 1985).

In contrast to this, research in organizations has focused on the implicit *ideals* or standards that individuals hold in their implicit theories of superior and subordinate performance. Research on *implicit leadership theories* has demonstrated that followers' unarticulated standards for ideal leadership traits and behaviors (e.g. competence and consideration) can influence the perceptions they have and the attributions they make concerning the behavior of their leaders. These theories can also bias followers' evaluations of leader behavior (Calder 1977; Eden and Leviathan 1975; Lord et al. 1984; Rush et al. 1977; Offerman et al. 1994). Similar claims have been made about implicit theories of subordinate performance held by superiors (Borman 1987).

A substantial body of research by Carol Dweck and her associates (see Dweck 1996, 2006; Dweck et al. 1995; Dweck and Leggett 1988; Hong et al. 1999) has identified a fundamental dimension of many implicit theories which appears to distinguish people in terms of their basic view of the nature of people and of social reality. In essence, it differentiates those individuals who see a more static social reality (entity theorists) from those who believe in a more dynamic one (incremental theorists). In other words, people can believe that the world and people in general have fixed natures, that we live in a static world, or, alternatively, they can view the world, its institutions, and its people as being dynamic and able to change and develop (Chiu et al. 1997). This research has shown that people can have chronic differences along this entity-incremental dimension in a particular domain (such as human nature) or hold a combination of both theories but are also influenced by the salience and relevance of different theories which are determined by aspects of the context (see Levy et al. 1998; Coleman 2004).

The entity-incremental distinction has been shown to be far-reaching (see Dweck 2006). Entity theorists and entity-orientations (compared to incremental theorists) have been shown to evidence more maladaptive (helpless) behavior (Dweck and Leggett 1988; Dweck et al. 1995; Henderson and Dweck 1990), make more ability vs. effort attributions which can negatively affect coping strategies (Hong et al. 1999), draw stronger inferences from behavior (Chiu et al. 1997), blame themselves more following failure (Erdley et al. 1997), and form and endorse more extreme group stereotypes (Levy et al. 1998). So, what might be the implications of the entity-incremental distinction for understanding organizational power?

Two theories of power in organizations

Although managers' core assumptions about organizational power remain mostly unstated and untested (Hollander and Offermann 1990), scholars contend that most managers hold traditional, win-lose views of power (Argyris and Schon 1996, 1978; Bennis and Nanus 1985; Burke 1986; Follett 1973; Kanter 1979; Tjosvold 1981). In fact, many organizational theorists derive their thinking on power relations from the definition of power offered by Robert Dahl (1957: 158), who proposed that power involves "an ability to get another person to do something that he or she would not otherwise have done." This ability is often linked with the capacity to overcome the resistance of the other and has been influential with many eminent social theorists, past (Weber 1947; Lasswell and Kaplan 1950; Cartwright 1959; French and Raven 1959) and present (see Kipnis 1976; Pfeffer 1981; Raven et al. 1998; Rahim 1989). In essence, this view holds that power and authority relations between people in organizations are intrinsically competitive: the more power A has, the less power available for B.

A basic assumption underlying the competitive view of organizational power is that power is a fixed-pie or entity (Deutsch 1973; Coleman and Voronov, 2003). If managers believe organizational power to be a fixed pie, they are more likely to view the sharing of power as a loss to their own slice of the pie. In fact, even the idea of "power-sharing" seems to imply the need to carve up and distribute some entity of power to others when empowering them. Such a theory can set up a competition for power between supervisors and employees and lead to politicking, power hoarding, and a reliance on compliance strategies of influence which increase the need for continuous scrutiny and control of subordinates.

However, Mary Parker Follett (1924) suggested an alternative view of organizational power as a type of power that can be grown and mutually developed. Follett argued that even though organizations were rife with examples of the use and abuse of "power-over" others (the power of A over B), that it would also be possible and particularly useful to develop the conception of "power-with" others. She envisioned this type of power as jointly developed, coactive and noncoercive (see Follett 1973). Furthermore, Follett suggested that one of the most effective ways to limit the use of coercive power strategies was to develop the idea, the capacity, and the conditions that foster cooperative power.

If managers view power as a resource that can be developed and enhanced in cooperation with employees, they will be more likely to share power and support employee empowerment initiatives. Thus, the belief that organizational power is a fixed-pie entity vs. an expandable resource would be associated with competitive vs. cooperative relations between managers and their employees and lead to an increased withholding of power by individuals in work settings. In other words, viewing organizational power as a fixed-pie entity will lead to an increased sense of competitive interdependence between managers and employees. The considerable body of research on cooperative and competitive interdependence (see Deutsch 1973; Johnson and Johnson 1989, for an overview) has regularly demonstrated their contrasting effects on people's attitudes and behaviors in social relations, including the tendency for competition to foster "attempts to enhance the power differences between oneself and the other" (Deutsch 1973: 30). A variety of other studies have demonstrated the critical role of perceived cooperative interdependence in fostering more constructive power dynamics between employees and managers (Tjosvold 1981, 1985a, 1985b; Tjosvold et al. 1984).

Empirical research on implicit power theories

Over the past decade, the two theories of organizational power have led to a program of empirical research investigating their distinct effects on power-sharing decisions and behaviors in organizations. The first study, conducted in a laboratory, investigated the effects of managers' implicit theories of power in organizations on their willingness to share power with subordinates (Coleman 2004). This study proposed that managers have two different implicit theories of power (IPTs): (1) the belief that organizational power is a scarce resource and as such should be hoarded and accumulated, and (2) the belief that organizational power is an expandable resource and that sharing power with others is not a loss but rather can result in an increased ability to achieve one's goals. The two competing views of power were shown to affect managers' decisions whether to share or withhold resources, as well as the degree to which they reported being willing to involve employees in decisions about work processes. In addition, these two implicit theories were "primed", meaning that one or the other was emphasized and made more salient in the managers' heads through subtle experimental manipulations. As predicted, when cooperative implicit theories were primed (i.e. power is expandable), managers were more likely to share power whereas priming of competitive IPTs (i.e. power is a scarce resource) inhibited sharing of power.

Subsequent research found additional support for the relationship between implicit power theories and power-sharing and extended their effects beyond self-reported decisions to organizational behaviors. In a study conducted in China (Tjosvold et al. 2003), participants portraying managers in an organizational simulation were found to share more power (information and assistance) with subordinates when they were led to believe that their organization had a history of approaching organizational power as an expandable resource than when it was portrayed as traditionally viewing and approaching power as a scarce resource. More recently, two studies found that differences in the accessibility of IPTs (their salience) predicted competitive vs. cooperative orientations between managers and employees and affected managers' willingness to share information, time, and attention (Coleman, under review). These studies showed that operating under the simple assumption that organizational power is a fixed pie can shape how managers interpret their supervisory relationships, influencing their sense of interdependence, responsibility, power dynamics, and ultimately their willingness to make the behavioral changes required of them when instituting programs of employee empowerment. When combined, the findings from these studies are robust and have implications for understanding how different organizational structures and processes can develop and trigger distinct managerial theories of and orientations to power.

The findings from this research not only speak to the potential causal role of implicit power theories in shaping managers' responses to empowerment initiatives, but it emphasizes the critical part that the organizational context plays in triggering and fostering differences in implicit theories. In two of the studies, the different theories (cooperative and competitive) were induced by messages presented in reading passages prior to data collection. This highlights the significant role played by the organizational environment in fostering and triggering these different theories.

Organizational implications

The research on implicit theories of organizational power has several implications for the design of intervention programs for managers and executives. For example, the results indicate that how managers *think* about power may, under certain conditions, significantly affect their behaviors and reactions to power-sharing initiatives. The more competitive managers' conception of power, the less likely they will be to see the sharing of power as a worthwhile opportunity. Therefore, it may be useful for training interventions to be devised that aid in raising the level of awareness of these implicit theories: their sources, their content, and the repercussions of relying on them. Providing managers with an awareness of their own biases and with alternative methods of conceptualizing and approaching power and authority relations could address the limitations that result from relying primarily on more chronic competitive theories.

The results also indicate that the immediate environment can moderate people's use of these theories when interpreting social information by priming and thereby making cooperative or competitive theories more or less accessible to people. It is therefore reasonable to think of organizations as key sources of priming. If competition is consistently emphasized in a system, tasks are structured competitively and outcomes distributed accordingly, "command and control" leadership is modeled from above, and the general climate stresses suspicion and territorialism, then competitive theories will dominate. These primes may come to be institutionalized within a system, automatically triggering the relevant power theories and shaping their chronic content over time. This would imply that interventions directed toward the structure and climate of groups and organizations might also facilitate power-sharing initiatives. For example, structuring cooperative task and reward interdependence among employees, as well as encouraging and training staff in collaborative problem-solving strategies could shift the general work-group or organizational climate toward being less competitive. This, in turn, could influence cognitive processing related to power-sharing. Granted, the amount of variance explained for power-sharing decisions by these implicit theories is modest, but even a small amount of resistance to power-sharing by managers at high levels in an organization over time will have a significant impact on the efficacy of such initiatives. Furthermore, given that the source of these chronic theories is presumed to be primarily from repeated exposure to certain types of social behavior (e.g. competitiveness), altering the prevalence of these behaviors in the organization could, over time, substantially affect the character of the employees' chronic theories about power in that environment.

Conclusion

The realm of social power is vast, and the potential factors that may influence the distribution of power in organizations are innumerable. Yet amidst this complex web of variables, perhaps there are a few core components. This chapter described the important role played by one such factor – implicit power theories – and examined their impact on managerial power-sharing in organizations. Hopefully, such theory and research will lead to more effective power-sharing processes and to their well-documented benefits to organizational life.

References

Appelbaum, S. H., Hebert, D., and Leroux, S. (1999) Empowerment: Power, culture and leadership – A strategy or fad for the millennium? *Journal of Workplace Learning: Employee Counseling Today*, **11** (7), 233–254.

Argyris, C. (1964) *Integrating the individual and the organization*, New York, N.Y.: Wiley.

Argyris, C. and Schon, D. A. (1978) *Organizational learning: A theory of action perspective*, Reading, Mass.: Addison-Wesley.

(1996) *Organizational learning II: Theory, method, and practice*, Reading, Mass.: Addison-Wesley.

Bennis, W. G. and Nanus, G. (1985) *Leaders*, New York, N.Y.: Harper & Row.

Bogner, W. C. (2002) Robert H. Waterman Jr. on being smart and lucky. *The Academy of Management Executive*, **16** (1), 45–50.

Borman, W. C. (1987) Personal constructs, performance schemata, and "folk theories" of subordinate effectiveness: Explorations in an army officer sample. *Organizational Behavior and Human Decision Processes*, **40**, 307–332.

Bradford, D. L. and Cohen, A. R. (1984) *Managing for excellence: The guide for developing high performance organizations*, New York, N.Y.: John Wiley.

Burke, W. W. (1986) Leadership as empowering others. In S. Srivastra, and Associates (Eds.), *Executive power: How executives influence people and organizations* (pp. 51–77), San Francisco, Calif.: Jossey-Bass.

Calder, B. J. (1977) An attribution theory of leadership. In B. M. Staw and G. R. Salancik (Eds.), *New directions in organizational behavior* (pp. 179–204), Chicago, Ill.: St. Clair Press.

Cartwright, D. (1959) *Studies in social power*, Ann Arbor, Mich.: Institute for Social Research.

Chiu, C., Dweck, C. S., Tong, J. Y., and Fu, J. H. (1997) Implicit theories and conceptions of morality. *Journal of Personality and Social Psychology*, **73**, 923–940.

Chiu, C., Hong, Y., and Dweck, C. S. (1997) Lay dispositionism and implicit theories of personality. *Journal of Personality and Social Psychology*, **30**, 19–30.

Coch, L. and French, J. R. P. Jr. (1948) Overcoming resistance to change. *Human Relations*, **1**, 512–532.

Cohen, S. G. and Ledford, G. E. Jr. (1994) The effectiveness of self-managing teams: A quasi-experiment. *Human Relations*, **47**, 13–43.

Coleman, P. T. (2004) Implicit theories of organizational power and priming effects on managerial power sharing decisions: An experimental study. *Journal of Applied Social Psychology*, **34** (2), 297–321.

(Under review) Implicit theories, interdependence, and power sharing: Mindsets as a barrier to empowerment.

Coleman, P. T. and Voronov, M. (2003) Power in groups and organizations. In M. A. West, D. J. Tjosvold, and K. G. Smith (Eds.), *International handbook of organizational teamwork and cooperative working* (pp. 229–254), New York, N.Y.: John Wiley & Sons.

Conger, J. A. and Kanungo, R. N. (1988) The empowerment process: Integrating theory and practice. *Academy of Management Review*, **13**, 471–482.

Dahl, R. P. (1957) The concept of power, *Behavioral Science*, **2**, 201–218.

Dastmalchian, A., Javidan, M., and Alam, K. (2001) Effective leadership and culture in Iran: An empirical study. *Applied Psychology*, **50** (4), 532–558.

Deming, W. E. (1993) *The new economics for industry, government, education*, Cambridge, Mass.: Massachusetts Institute of Technology, Center for Advanced Engineering Study.

Deutsch, M. (1973) *The resolution of conflict: Constructive and destructive processes*, New Haven, Conn.: Yale University Press.

Dweck, C. S. (1996) Implicit theories as organizers of goals and behavior. In P. Gollwitzer and J. A. Bargh (Eds.), *The psychology of action: The relation of cognition and motivation to behavior*, New York, N.Y.: Guilford.

(2006) *Mindset: The new psychology of success*, New York, N.Y.: Random House.

Dweck, C. S., Chiu, C., and Hong, Y. (1995) Implicit theories and their role in judgments and reactions: A world from two perspectives. *Psychological Inquiry*, **6** (4), 267–285.

Dweck, C. S., Hong, Y., and Chiu, C. (1993) Implicit theories: Individual differences in the likelihood and meaning of dispositional inference.

Special issue: On inferring personal dispositions from behavior. *Personality and Social Psychology Bulletin* 19, 644–656.

Dweck, C. S. and Leggett, E. L. (1988) A social-cognitive approach to motivation and personality. *Psychological Review*, 95, 256–273.

Eden, D. and Leviatan, U. (1975) Implicit leadership theories as a determinant of the factor structure underlying supervisory behavior scales. *Journal of Applied Psychology*, 60, 736–741.

Erdley, C. A., Cain, K. M., Loomis, C. C., Dumas-Hines F., and Deweck, C. S. (1997) Relations among children's social goals, implicit personality theories, and responses to social failure. *Developmental Psychology*, 33, 263–272.

Fisher, S. (1989) Stress, control, worry prescriptions and the implications for health at work: A psychological model. In S. L. Sauter, J. J. Hurrell, and C. L. Cooper (Eds.), *Job Control and Worker Health* (pp. 205–236), Chichester: Wiley.

Follet, M. P. (1924) *Creative experience*, New York, N.Y.: Longmans, Green. (1973) Power. In E. M. Fox and L. Urwick (Eds.), *Dynamic administration: The collected papers of Mary Parker Follett* (pp. 66–87), London: Pitman.

French, J. R. P. Jr. and Raven, B. (1959) The bases of social power. In D. Cartwright (Ed.), *Studies in social power* (pp. 150–167), Ann Arbor, Mich.: University of Michigan Press.

Gervey, B. M., Chiu, C., Hong, Y., and Dweck, C. (1999) Differential use of person information in decisions about guilt versus innocence: The role of implicit theories. *Personality and Social Psychology Bulletin*, 25 (1), 17–27.

Glew, D. J., Griffin, R. W., and Van Fleet, D. D. (1995) Participation in organizations: A preview of the issues and proposed framework for future analysis. *Journal of Management*, 21, 395–421.

Harvey, J. B. (1989) Some thoughts about organizational backstabbing. *Academy of Management Executive*, 3, 271–277.

Heider, F. (1958) *The psychology of interpersonal relations*, New York, N.Y.: Wiley.

Henderson, V. and Dweck, C. S. (1990) Motivation and achievement. In S. S. Feldman and G. R. Elliot (Eds.), *At the threshold: The developing adolescent* (pp. 308–329), Cambridge, Mass.: Harvard University Press.

Hollander, E. P. and Offerman, L. R. (1990) Power and leadership in organizations. *American Psychologist*, 45 (2), 179–189.

Home, A. M. (1991) Mobilizing women's strengths for social change: The group connection. *Social Work with Groups*, 14 (3–4), 153–173.

Hong, Y., Chiu, C., Dweck, C., Lin, D. M., and Wan, W. (1999) Implicit theories, attributions, and coping: A meaning system approach. *Journal of Personality and Social Psychology*, 77 (3), 588–599.

Janssen, O., Schoonebeek, G., and van Looy, B. (1997) Cognitions of empowerment: The link between participative management and employees' innovative behavior. *Gedrag en Organisatie*, **10** (4), 175–194.

Jesaitis, P. T. and Day, N. E. (1992) People: Black boxes of many organizational development strategies. *Organizational Development Journal*, **10** (1), 63–71.

Johnson, D. W. and Johnson, R. (1989) *Cooperation and competition: Theory and research*. Edina, Minn.: Interaction Book Company.

Kanter, R. M. (1979) Power failure in management circuits. *Harvard Business Review*, **57**, 65–75.

(1983) *The change masters*, New York, N.Y.: Simon & Schuster.

Kelly, G. A. (1955) *The psychology of personal constructs*, New York, N.Y.: Norton.

Kim, S. (2002) Participative management and job satisfaction: Lessons for management leadership. *Public Administration Review*, **62** (2), 231–241.

Kipnis, D. (1976) *The power-holders*, Chicago, Ill.: University of Chicago Press.

Kirkman, B. L. and Rosen, B. (1999) Beyond self-management: Antecedents and consequences of team empowerment. *Academy of Management Journal*, **42**, 58–74.

Labianca, G., Gray, B., and Brass, D. J. (2000) A grounded model of organizational schema change during empowerment. *Organization Science*, **11** (2), 235–257.

Lasswell, H. D. and Kaplan, A. (1950) *Power and society*, New Haven, Conn.: Yale University Press.

Latham, G. P., Winters, D. C., and Locke, E. A. (1994) Cognitive and motivational effects of participation: A mediator study. *Journal of Organizational Behavior*, **15**, 49–63.

Leana, C. R. (1987) Power relinquishment versus power sharing: Theoretical clarification and empirical comparison of delegation and participation. *Journal of Applied Psychology*, **72** (2), 228–233.

Leana, C. R., Ahlbrandt, R. S., and Murrell, A. J. (1992) The effects of employee involvement programs on unionized workers' attitudes, perceptions, and preferences in decision making. *Academy of Management Journal*, **35**, 861–873.

Leana, C. R., Locke, E. A., Schweiger, D. M., Cotton, J. L., Vollrath, D. A., Lengnick-Hall, M. L., et al. (1990) Fact and fiction in analyzing research on participative decision making: A critique of Cotton, Vollrath, Froggatt, Lengnick- Hall, and Jennings; Rebuttal. *Academy of Management Review*, **15**, 137–153.

Levy, S. R., Plaks, J. E., and Dweck, C. S. (1999) Modes of social thought: Person theories and social understanding. In S. Chaiken and Y. Trope (Eds.), *Dual-process theories in social psychology* (pp. 179–202), New York, N.Y.: Guilford Press.

Levy, S. R., Stroessner, S. J., and Dweck, C. (1998) Stereotype formation and endorsement: The role of implicit theories. *Journal of Personality and Social Psychology*, **74** (6), 1421–1436.

Lewin, K., Lippitt, R, and White, R. K. (1939) Patterns of aggressive behavior in experimentally created social climates. *Journal of Social Psychology*, **10**, 271–301.

Likert, R. (1967) *The human organization: Its management and value*, New York, N.Y.: McGraw-Hill.

Locke, E. A. and Schweiger, D. M. (1979) Participating in decision-making. One more look. In B. M. Staw (Ed.), *Research in organizational behavior I* (pp. 265–339), Greenwich, Conn.: JAI Press.

Lord, R. G., Foti, R. J., and De Vader, C. L. (1984) A test of leadership categorization theory: Internal structure, information processing, and leadership perceptions. *Organizational Behavior and Human Performance*, **34**, 343–378.

McClelland, D. C. (1975) *Power: The inner experience*, New York, N.Y.: Irvington Publishers, Inc.

McGregor, D. (1960) *The human side of enterprise*, New York, N.Y.: McGraw-Hill.

Miles, R. E. (1965) Human relations or human resources? *Harvard Business Review*, July–August, 148–163.

Miller, K. I. and Monge, P. R. (1986) Participation, satisfaction, and productivity: A meta-analytic review. *Academy of Management Review*, **29**, 727–753.

Nacoste, R. W. (1996) How affirmative action can pass constitutional and social psychological muster. *Journal of Social Issues*, **52** (4), 133–144.

Offerman, L. R., Kennedy, J. K. Jr., and Wirtz, P. W. (1994) Implicit leadership theories: Content, structure, and generalizability. *Leadership Quarterly*, **5** (1), 43–58.

O'Toole, J. (1995) *Leading change*, San Francisco, Calif.: Jossey-Bass.

Peccei, R. and Rosenthal, P. (2001) Delivering customer-oriented behavior through empowerment: An empirical test of HRM assumptions. *The Journal of Management Studies*, **38** (6), 831–857.

Peters, T. J. and Austin, N. (1985) *A passion for excellence: The leadership difference*, New York, N.Y.: Random House.

Peters, T. J. and Waterman, R. H. Jr. (1982) *In search of excellence: Lessons from America's best run companies*, New York, N.Y.: Harper & Row.

Pfeffer, J. (1981) Management as symbolic action: The creation and maintenance of organizational paradigms. In L. L. Cummings and B. M. Staw

(Eds.), *Research in Organizational Behavior* (Vol. III, pp. 1–52), Greenwich, Conn.: JAI Press.

Rahim, M. A. (1989) *Managing conflict: An interdisciplinary approach*, New York, N.Y.: Praeger.

Raven, B. H., Schwarzwald J., and Koslowsky M. (1998) Conceptualizing and measuring a power/interaction model of interpersonal influence. *Journal of Applied Social Psychology*, **28**, 307–332.

Rush, M. C., Thomas, J. C., and Lord, R. G. (1977) Implicit leadership theory: A potential threat to the validity of leader behavior questionnaires. *Organizational Behavior and Human Performance*, **20**, 93–110.

Salancik, G. R. and Pfeffer, J. (1977) Who gets power – and how they hold on to it: A strategic contingency model of power. *Organizational Dynamics*, **5**, 3–21.

Schleicher, D. J. and Day, D. V. (1998) A cognitive evaluation of frame-of-reference rater training: Content and process issues. *Organizational Behavior and Human Decision Processes*, **73** (1), 76–101.

Spector, P. E. (1986) Perceived control by employees: A meta-analysis of studies concerning autonomy and participation at work. *Human Relations*, **39** (11), 1005–1016.

Spreitzer, G. M. and Mishra, A. K. (2002) To stay or to go: Voluntary survivor turnover following an organizational downsizing. *Journal of Organizational Behavior*, **23** (6), 707–729.

Sternberg, R. J. (1985) Implicit theories of intelligence, creativity, and wisdom. *Journal of Personality and Social Psychology*, **49**, 607–627.

Stewart, G. L. and Barrick, M. R. (2000) Work team structure and performance: Assessing the mediating role of intrateam process and the moderating role of task type. *Academy of Management Journal*, **43**, 135–148.

Stewart, G. L. and Manz, C. C. (1997) Understanding and overcoming supervisor resistance during the transition to employee empowerment. In W. A. Pasmore and R. W. Woodman (Eds.), *Research in organizational change and development, an annual series featuring advances in theory, methodology, and research* (Vol. X, pp. 169–196), New York, N.Y.: JAI Press.

Tjosvold, D. (1981) Unequal power relationships within a cooperative or competitive context. *Journal of Applied Social Psychology*, **11**, 137–150.

(1985a) The effects of attribution and social context on superiors' influence and interaction with low performing subordinates. *Personnel Psychology*, **38**, 361–376.

(1985b) Power and social context in superior–subordinate interaction. *Organizational Behavior and Human Decision Processes*, **35**, 281–293.

(1987) Participation: A close look at its dynamics. *Journal of Management*, 13, 739–750.

Tjosvold, D., Coleman, P. T., and Sun, H. (2003) Effects of organizational values on leaders' use of information power to affect performance in China. *Group Dynamics: Theory, Research and Practice*, 7, 152–167.

Tjosvold, D., Johnson, D. W., and Johnson, R. T. (1984) Influence strategy, perspective-taking, and relationships between high and low power individuals in cooperative and competitive contexts. *Journal of Psychology*, 116, 187–202.

Vroom, V. H. and Jago, A. G. (2007) The role of the situation in leadership. *American Psychologist*, 62 (1), 17–24.

(1988) *The new leadership: Managing participation in organizations*, Englewood Cliffs, N. J.: Prentice-Hall.

Walls, P. L. (1990) *Human research strategies for organizations in transition*, New York, N.Y.: Plenum Press.

Weber, M. (1947) *The theory of social and economic organization*, New York, N.Y.: Oxford University Press.

Weiss, W. H. (2002) Building and managing teams. *SuperVision*, 63 (11), 19–21.

Yukl, G. A. (1994) *Leadership in organizations*, 3rd edn, Englewood Cliffs, N. J.: Prentice Hall.

PART III

Exchange dynamics and outcomes

9 | Power and social exchange

LINDA D. MOLM

The concept of power has been central to social exchange theory since its early development. Peter Blau (1964) included "power" in the title of his classic theory of exchange; Richard Emerson's (1972a, 1972b) exchange formulation was built upon his earlier analysis of power-dependence relations; and theories and research on power have dominated the contemporary development of the sociological exchange tradition for the past thirty years (see Molm 2000 for a review).

Although social exchange theories are typically formulated at an abstract level designed to apply to different settings and different levels of analysis, several features make them particularly well suited for application to organizations. The participants in social exchange, called *actors*, can be either individual persons or collective actors such as teams or organizations, and either specific entities or interchangeable occupants of structural positions (e.g., the CEO of a firm). Actors are connected to one another in dyadic relations, and those relations are typically embedded in larger exchange networks of variable size and complexity, making social exchange theories appropriate for analysis of both intra- and inter-organizational power relations. Finally, the very concept of exchange is central to most organizational analyses.

Social exchange theory is most appropriately viewed as a framework or theoretical orientation that includes numerous specific theories. All social exchange theories share certain concepts and assumptions, but they also differ in various respects. The theories that I will draw on most extensively in this chapter are power-dependence theory as originally developed by Richard Emerson and Karen Cook, and my own work extending the theory to different bases of power and different forms of exchange. Most of the research discussed in this chapter has been conducted in laboratory experiments, the dominant method used by exchange researchers.

In the following sections I describe the exchange conceptualization of power and then turn to three topics that have been the subject of long-term theoretical research programs: the effects of network structures on power, differences between reward and coercive bases of power, and how power relations are affected by different forms of exchange. I conclude with a discussion of future directions and challenges.

Power and dependence: the exchange conceptualization of power

Social exchange occurs within structures of mutual dependence, in which actors are dependent on each other for valued outcomes. These outcomes include not only the tangible goods and services of economic exchange but also socially valued outcomes such as status or support. Exchange theories assume that actors are motivated to obtain more of the outcomes that they value and others control, that actors provide each other with these valued benefits through exchange, and that exchanges between the same actors are recurring over time, rather than "one-shot" transactions (Molm 2000).

The structural condition that provides the basis for social exchange – the mutual dependence of actors – also provides the basis for power. Thus, relations of dependence bring people together (to the extent that people are mutually dependent, they are more likely to form relations and to continue in them), but they also create inequalities in power that produce inequalities in exchange (unequal dependencies give less dependent actors an advantage in the relation).

The smallest unit of analysis is the *exchange relation* between two actors, consisting of their repeated interactions over some period of time. In an exchange relation between actors A and B, A's *power* over B derives from, and is equal to, B's *dependence* on A (Emerson 1972b). The more dependent B is on A for rewards, the higher the potential cost that A can impose on B by not providing those rewards. Dependence is primarily a function of two variables: resource value and exchange alternatives. B's dependence on A increases with the *value* of the benefits that A can provide for B and decreases with B's access to *alternative* sources of those benefits. The same is true for A; thus, A and B's *mutual* dependence provides the structural basis for their power *over each other*.

Power in the A–B relation can vary on two dimensions: *balance*, or the relative power of A and B over one another, and *cohesion*, or the absolute power of A and B over each other (Emerson 1972b). If two actors are equally dependent on each other, power in the relation is balanced. But if

B is more dependent on A, power is imbalanced and A has a *power advantage* in the relation equal to the degree of imbalance. The greater the mutual or average dependence of the two actors on each other – independent of their power imbalance – the greater their cohesion.

According to this formulation, *power* is a structural potential that derives from the relations of dependence among actors; as such, it is a property of a relation, not an actor. *Power use* is the behavioral exercise of this structural potential, typically measured by the resulting inequality of exchange. Over time, the structure of power produces predictable effects on the frequency and distribution of exchange: Initiations of exchange increase with an actor's dependence; the frequency of exchange in a relation increases with cohesion; and in imbalanced relations, the ratio of exchange changes in favor of the more powerful, less dependent actor.

Emerson (1972b) proposed that imbalanced relations are unstable and lead to "power-balancing" processes, which are strategies to change the structure of imbalanced relations in favor of the disadvantaged actor. Two such power-balancing mechanisms are coalition formation by the disadvantaged actors, which is a means of reducing a powerful actor's alternatives (labor unions are an example), and network extension, which is a means of increasing the alternatives of less powerful actors (for example, through "networking").

Network structures and power

While Emerson's exchange formulation proposed that power and dependence vary as a function of both resource value and actors' alternatives, the contemporary development of the field has focused primarily on the latter – actors' alternatives – and their effects on the opportunity structures that drive the use of power. Actors' access to alternative sources of valued outcomes (e.g., alternative suppliers, business partners, or advisers) depends on their structural position in larger *exchange networks*.

Exchange networks are sets of *connected* exchange relations among actors, in which the frequency or value of exchange in one relation (e.g., A–B) affects the frequency or value of exchange in another (e.g., B–C) (Emerson 1972b). When exchange in one relation *increases* exchange in another relation, the connection between the two relations is *positive*; for example, A may give information to B that makes B's subsequent exchange with C possible. When exchange in one relation *decreases* exchange in another, the connection is *negative*; for example, manufacturer A's exchange with supplier B makes A's exchange with another supplier of the same parts less likely.

Negatively connected networks have received the most attention from researchers because they provide actors with alternative sources of a desired resource (e.g., alternative suppliers of parts for a manufacturer), and variations in actors' alternatives affect power. Actors who have more alternatives, better (more valuable) alternatives, and/or more available alternatives than other actors are less dependent on those others and have more power in the network. The structure of negatively connected networks – their size and shape – determines actors' access to alternative partners and thus determines the structure of power and the inequality that emerges from exchanges between actors in the network.

Network structure not only determines the distribution of power among actors in the network, it drives the *use* of power. A key tenet of the social exchange perspective, originally proposed by Emerson (1972b), is that the use of power is *structurally induced*, without any necessary intent to use power or even awareness of power. An actor who possesses a structural power advantage will, over time, obtain more rewards at lower cost – even if the actor is unaware of his advantage (e.g., unaware that the partner lacks good alternatives), unaware of the effects on the partner (e.g., unaware of the partner's costs), and is simply acting on the opportunities available for exchange with alternative partners. The mechanism that drives this process is the structure of the negatively connected network, which provides power-advantaged actors with access to more or better alternatives than other actors in the network. When advantaged actors pursue exchange with alternative partners, they necessarily impose costs on other (more dependent) partners with whom they do not exchange – that is, they "use power" over them. In the process, they drive up the cost of obtaining the rewards they control, while lowering their own costs of obtaining the partners' rewards. The inequality that results is produced by structural differences in dependence, not by the motives or intentions of exchange actors.

Actors can also use power strategically, by selectively giving and withholding rewards, contingent on the partner's prior behavior. Such strategic power use *is* intentional. Both Lawler (1992) and (Molm 1997) have made strategic power use part of a tripartite conception of power that includes structural power (based on the structure of dependence), power strategies, and power outcomes (Emerson's "power use," defined by an unequal distribution of exchange benefits). Most contemporary theories of exchange and power, however, continue Emerson's emphasis on the structure of exchange, while making minimal assumptions about actors' motives or intent.

Research on power in exchange networks

Programmatic research on exchange relations and networks did not begin until the late 1970s; during the 1980s and 1990s several distinct programs of research on power and exchange emerged. Some of these programs were based on the power-dependence tradition, while others tested new theories – especially new algorithms for measuring power in exchange networks – that developed as competitors to power-dependence theory.

Cook, Emerson and their students conducted the first critical tests of Emerson's power-dependence theory in a laboratory setting which was specifically designed for the study of power in negatively connected networks (Cook and Emerson 1978). In contrast to the reciprocal exchanges envisioned by the classical theorists, subjects in Cook and Emerson's setting negotiated the terms of exchange, through offers and counteroffers, to reach binding agreements. Results of this work confirmed the major predictions of power-dependence theory, showing that networks that create imbalances in structural dependence produce unequal distributions of benefit, in favor of the less dependent actor, while those in which power and dependence is balanced produce equal distributions of benefit. As Emerson proposed, these effects occur even in the absence of actors' knowledge of their relative power positions. When actors are informed of emerging inequalities, normative concerns about the fairness of exchange can inhibit power use. Behavioral commitments between exchange partners, which impede the exploration of alternatives that drives power use, have a similar effect. Later studies showed that disadvantaged actors can improve their bargaining position by forming coalitions, which reduce power imbalance and lead to more equal exchanges (Cook and Gillmore 1984). A pivotal 1983 study (Cook et al. 1983) linked exchange-theory and power-dependence concepts with social network research and provided the impetus for the development of new theories offering network-level predictions of the distribution of power.

These theories, which included network exchange theory (Markovsky et al. 1988), expected value theory (Friedkin 1992), and game theoretic approaches (Bienenstock and Bonacich 1993), introduced a period of sustained theory competition that led to increased precision and accuracy of predictions of power in a wide range of network structures. All of this research was conducted in laboratory settings modeled after the Cook and Emerson setting, and most of it concentrated on a specific problem: predicting how actors divide profits in negatively connected networks of direct exchange when transactions are negotiated and agreements are binding.

I turn now to a consideration of how power and power use are affected when two of these conditions are altered: Power is coercive rather than reward-based, and exchanges are not negotiated.

Bases of power: reward and punishment

The classical exchange theorists explicitly excluded punishment and coercion from their theories, believing that social exchange must be restricted to voluntary, mutually rewarding interactions (Blau 1964; Homans 1961). Following their lead, most contemporary researchers have studied exchange relations in which power is derived from actors' dependence on each other for rewards. When compared with more traditional conceptions of power as coercive, this view of power is quite benign. It is also unnecessarily restrictive; the parallels between rewards and punishments should make it possible to analyze both bases of power from an exchange perspective. Mutual reward exchanges and coercive exchanges are alike in the sense that in both, actors give rewards to another in exchange for something they value: In mutual reward exchanges, each actor gives rewards in exchange for reciprocal rewards; in coercive exchanges, one actor gives rewards in exchange for the other's removal of punishment or threat of harm. Similarly, both reward power and punishment or coercive power are derived from others' dependence on an actor, either for obtaining rewards or avoiding punishment, and they provide actors with parallel ways of affecting other actors' outcomes – by giving and withholding rewards, or by giving and withholding punishments.

This logic provided the foundation for a decade-long program of research that sought to bring coercive power within the scope of social exchange theory, specifically power-dependence theory (Molm

1997). Its focus was exchange relations of some endurance that are imbedded in larger networks, formed and maintained without explicit bargaining or negotiation, by actors who control both rewarding and punishing outcomes for one another.

The original question that this program addressed was whether structures of power that are comparable in all respects *except* the base of power have similar effects on exchange. To answer this question, objectively equivalent structures of reward power and coercive power were created in the laboratory by varying actors' control over gains and losses of a single outcome, money. Results showed that equivalent power advantages on the two bases of power have vastly different effects on their use (Molm 1997). The structure of reward power dominates interaction, with actors rarely using a coercive power advantage. Further studies revealed that different causal mechanisms link structural power and power use for the two bases of power. Unlike reward power, the use of coercive power is not structurally induced by power advantage; that is, the power to punish does not lead automatically to its use. Coercion is a purposive power strategy in which actors knowingly and contingently impose cost on another to compel them to provide rewards. But in relations in which actors have the power to both reward and punish each other, the use of coercion is risky. Being disadvantaged on reward power provides the strongest incentive to use coercion, but it also increases the costs that a partner can impose in retaliation. Justice norms reinforce these effects; that is, actors perceive a partner's coercive tactics as unjust, and as their sense of injustice increases, so does their resistance to coercion. These reactions are strongest when advantaged actors, who expect rewards rather than punishments from their partners, are targets of coercion. Consequently, loss-averse actors typically forgo the use of coercion and its potential gains to avoid loss, and without use, coercive power becomes ineffective.

At the same time, however, experimental results show that coercive power, *when used contingently and consistently,* can be a highly effective means of obtaining greater benefits from an exchange partner, even when that partner is advantaged on reward power (Molm 1997). Thus, in their *effects* on exchange, coercive power and reward power follow the same principles.

This research program demonstrated that it is possible to incorporate punishment and coercion in social exchange theory, and to use the central concepts of the theory – the dependencies of actors on one another, and the potential costs and benefits they can provide for each other – to analyze the use and effects of coercive power. But it also revealed fundamental differences between the two forms of power and showed that coercive power, when embedded in relations in which actors are dependent on one another not only for avoiding punishment but for obtaining valued benefits, is a much weaker force than is usually assumed.

Forms of exchange

Following Cook and Emerson's lead, the vast majority of research on power in exchange networks has concentrated on a specific form of exchange in which actors negotiate the terms of strictly binding agreements. Similarly, most of the newer theories of power developed by exchange theorists have assumed negotiated exchanges. This contemporary shift to the study of negotiated exchange marks a departure from the classical theories of Blau (1964) and Homans (1961). These theorists were concerned, instead, with reciprocal exchanges, in which individuals offer help or advice to one another without negotiation of terms and without knowledge of whether or when the other will reciprocate. Both negotiated and reciprocal forms of exchange are common in natural settings, particularly organizational settings. But they differ on key dimensions that affect both the mechanisms of power use and the relation of structural power to other important outcomes of exchange relationships (Molm 2003).

In *negotiated* exchange, actors engage in a joint-decision process, such as explicit bargaining, in which they reach an agreement, typically binding, about the terms of exchange. Both sides of the exchange are agreed upon at the same time – the flow of benefits is always *bilateral* – and the benefits for both partners comprise a discrete transaction. Most economic exchanges other than fixed-price trades fit in this category, as do some social exchanges.

In *reciprocal* exchange, actors individually initiate exchanges by performing a beneficial act for another (e.g., doing a favor or giving advice) without negotiation and without knowing whether, when, or to what extent the other will reciprocate. In contrast to negotiated exchanges, benefits can flow unilaterally: Actors can initiate exchanges that are not reciprocated, and they can receive benefits without giving anything in return. Exchange relations that develop under these conditions take the form of a series of sequentially contingent individual acts, with the equality or inequality of exchange emerging over time.

While negotiated exchanges are typically associated with business settings and reciprocal exchanges with more informal interactions among friends and family members, both are common in organizations. Since Granovetter's (1985) classic article, research has increasingly documented the extent to which even economic actions are embedded in social relationships. As Uzzi's research (1996) on the garment and banking industries and Larson's study (1992) of alliances between entrepreneurial firms and their partnered organizations illustrate, socially embedded relationships include numerous transactions in which actors unilaterally provide benefits to one another, without discussing the terms or timing of reciprocity, and without binding agreements or other mechanisms to guarantee reciprocity. While organizational studies tend to emphasize the more personal nature of embedded relationships and reciprocal exchange (i.e. the length of the relationship, the recurring nature of contact, and the exchange of social as well as economic resources), experimental research by exchange theorists shows that the *form* of exchange, per se, has pronounced effects on exchange even in relationships that are identical in other respects. These effects include differences in the use of power and in other exchange outcomes – the development of trust, commitment, and affective bonds – that are affected by power.

The use of power

First, the form of exchange affects the mechanisms of power use in negatively connected networks (Molm et al. 1999). In negotiated exchanges, powerful actors impose cost on some partners when they make agreements with other, alternative partners, thus *excluding* some partners from valuable transactions. Exclusion leads those partners to increase their offers in subsequent negotiations and consequently increases the inequality of any agreements made. Power use in reciprocal exchange is also produced by a form of exclusion, the *withholding of rewards* from one partner while pursuing exchange with another. But withholding rewards benefits powerful actors not by driving up partners' offers but by lowering actors' costs. Actors who can maintain one partner's exchange with only intermittent reciprocity have more opportunity to pursue other exchange relations. Powerful actors benefit from both their lower reciprocity and their consequent greater opportunity to pursue other exchanges. These different mechanisms have implications for how some structural dimensions of networks, particularly the availability of alternatives, affect the use of power (see Molm et al. 1999; Molm 2003).

Second, the differences between negotiated and reciprocal exchange affect the uncertainty and risk that actors face. Both the process of bargaining and assurance structures such as contractually binding agreements, warranties, and the like are designed to reduce uncertainty and risk of loss in negotiated exchange. Consequently, the primary risk in negotiated exchange is the *risk of exclusion* – of failing to make an agreement with a desired partner. In reciprocal exchanges, where actors individually give benefits to another without knowing whether or when the other will reciprocate, the primary risk is the *risk of nonreciprocation* – of giving benefit without receiving benefit in return. Efforts by loss-averse actors to reduce these two forms of risk should have *opposite* effects on power use. In negotiated exchange, disadvantaged actors can reduce the probability of exclusion by increasing the amount offered, which *increases* power use by increasing the inequality of the negotiated agreement and increasing the powerful actor's benefits. In reciprocal exchange, disadvantaged actors can reduce the occurrence of nonreciprocity by decreasing unilateral giving – that is, by limiting how often or how much they give to a partner without reciprocation, a response that *decreases* power use by decreasing the inequality in the rate of exchange and decreasing the powerful actor's benefits.

These differences in risk and risk-reduction strategies between the two forms of exchange imply that power use should be lower in reciprocal than in negotiated exchange. Experiments support this logic: Power use is lower for reciprocal exchange under virtually all structures of imbalanced power, and the relation between structural power imbalance and power use is weaker (Molm et al. 1999; Molm et al. 2001).

Trust, commitment, and affective bonds

The most striking effects of the form of exchange are not on power use, however, but on the integrative bonds of trust, commitment, and affective regard that develop from repeated exchanges with the same partners. Reciprocal exchanges generate higher levels of trust, more positive evaluations of the partner, stronger perceptions of fairness, and stronger feelings of commitment and relational solidarity than negotiated exchanges that are structurally equivalent, even after controlling for any differences in the frequency and inequality of exchange (Molm et al. 2000, 2003; Molm et al. 2006, 2007a). These differences are produced by three causal mechanisms that link the form of exchange to integrative bonds: the greater risk of nonreciprocation in reciprocal exchange, which provides the necessary condition for actors to demonstrate their trustworthiness to one another (Kollock 1994; Molm et al. 2000); the expressive value conveyed by acts of voluntary reciprocity, which communicate regard for the partner and the relationship (Molm et al. 2007b; Offer 1997); and the greater salience of conflict and competition in negotiated exchange, which increases actors' sensitivity to injustice and their tendency to perceive the partner in a negative light (Molm et al. 2006).

All of these effects are stronger in relations of unequal power. Unequal power makes reciprocal exchange riskier (particularly for disadvantaged actors), heightens the salience of conflict in negotiated exchange, and increases the expressive value of the partner's reciprocity in reciprocal exchange. When actors are equal in power, these effects are muted. Consequently, differences between reciprocal and negotiated exchange in feelings of trust, commitment, regard, and solidarity are greater in relations of unequal power than in equal power relations (Molm et al. 2007a). Experimental results show that introducing risk in negotiated exchanges, by making agreements nonbinding, is most likely to increase trust when power relations between actors are highly unequal, for example, in relationships between management and labor. By building trust and affective bonds in unequal power relations, some of the more harmful effects of power use also may be avoided.

Future directions and challenges

The exchange approach to power has considerable potential for understanding power relations in organizations. Both fields are developing in ways that promise greater complementarity in the future, particularly by recognizing that most transactions are not "one-shot" affairs but are instead embedded in relationships that involve multiple forms of exchange (reciprocal as well as negotiated) and multiple spheres of exchange (social as well as economic). These relationships are situated in networks that often create differences in power between actors, both within organizations and across organizations. Furthermore, the actors involved in these relationships include both individuals within organizations and organizations engaged in exchanges with other organizations, as corporate actors.

Exchange theory's applicability to both individual and corporate actors, embedded in networks of varying size and shape, makes the framework especially useful for the study of complex organizations. Power-dependence theory, in particular, has often been applied to the analysis of organizational exchange and interorganizational relations (Cook 1977; Cook and Emerson 1984), and principles of the theory underlie the resource dependence perspective in organizational studies (e.g., Pfeffer and Salancik 1978). Organizational theorists typically go beyond the structural sources of power emphasized by exchange theorists, however, to consider various strategies that organizations use to change and adapt to their environments. Many of these strategies (such as joint ventures, specialization, consolidation, and vertical integration) can be analyzed in terms of Emerson's balancing operations.

In addition to theoretical understanding, the exchange perspective also offers implications for practice. Exchange theory's analysis of power-dependence relations suggests strategies for increasing power – through network extension (increasing one's alternatives) or coalition building (decreasing an exchange partner's alternatives) – and emphasizes the importance of recognizing the role that structure plays in determining power outcomes, particularly the structure of reward power. Coercive power can be an effective adjunct to reward power (especially for those disadvantaged on reward power), but its use must be immediate, contingent, and consistent. Evidence that negotiation and other risk-reduction strategies (such as the use of binding contracts) can have negative consequences for relationships should be of particular importance to managers or those seeking to build long-term relations with associates. Reducing risk may safeguard against loss, but at the cost of building trust and affective regard. Embedding negotiated exchange within a relationship that includes reciprocal exchange is likely to produce stronger, more resilient trust and to ease the tensions inherent in relations of unequal power.

Let me briefly address two issues that might be regarded as potential obstacles to further progress in developing the exchange tradition in ways that are fruitful for organizational analysis. One is the key theoretical role of resource value in exchange theory. While contemporary theories of exchange have focused primarily on structural determinants of power, the *value* of the resources exchanged also affects power (Molm et al. 2001). Experimental research either manipulates or controls value by using money – a resource of quantifiable value at a ratio level of measurement – as the exchange benefit. Because money is a general medium of exchange in society, it is reasonable to assume that subjects (especially those recruited on the basis of their desire to earn money) will value and seek to acquire more of it, at least within the range of potential earnings offered in most experiments. But in natural settings, researchers are confronted with multiple resources of varying metrics and actors who differentially value those resources. Measuring value is thus a challenge for researchers who wish to study exchange processes in organizational settings. Emerson's (1987) last published paper emphasized the importance of developing a theory of value in exchange, and recent developments such as Hechter's (1992) call for the endogenous use of values in behavioral explanations and Thye's (2000) status value theory of power in exchange relations signal new developments in the sociological analysis of values in social exchange.

A second obstacle is the relatively narrow scope conditions of many contemporary theories of power in exchange networks. For most organizational scholars, greater breadth and less precision would be more useful. The emphasis on increasing the precision of predictions (and hence on restricting scope) has been important for competitive tests of theories that may not differ in their ordinal predictions (e.g., both may predict higher power use in network A than in network B), but do differ in their predictions of exactly how much benefit actors will obtain from their agreements. The trade-off has been a focus on a relatively narrow set of problems. We know a great deal about power use in negotiated exchanges in negatively connected networks but far less about other topics. Extending the range and scope of exchange theories is particularly important for applications of the theories outside the laboratory. This chapter has discussed some recent efforts at extension, by expanding the bases of power and forms of exchange studied, but others should be explored. I will mention just a few of these here.

First, theories of power in positively connected networks are still in their infancy, with only a few theoretical or empirical studies to date (e.g., Yamagishi et al. 1988). These networks, in which actors exchange information, opinions, and so forth that flow *across* relations and build cooperation and solidarity, play an important role in many organizations and deserve far more systematic analysis and study than they have received from exchange theorists to date. We know that network centrality yields power in positively connected networks, because central actors can serve as "brokers" in cooperative relations, and that the principle of local scarcity of valued resources is involved in this process. But much remains to be learned.

Second, exchange theorists should give more consideration to the *dynamics* of exchange, such as changes in network structures and the evolution of exchange forms. With few exceptions, the large body of research on power in exchange networks has concentrated on the effects of static structures on behavior. But networks are rarely static; they expand and contract, network connections change, and the value of resources attached to different positions varies. Similarly, exchange relations in natural settings often involve histories of both negotiated and reciprocal exchange, occurring either sequentially or concurrently. Studying the effects of such histories would be particularly relevant to organizational studies of embedded relationships, which often undergo change as the relationship develops (e.g., what begins as a contractual relationship may evolve into one that includes elements of reciprocal exchange).

Third, the roles that perception, meaning, and emotions play in power relations have been relatively neglected by contemporary exchange theorists. Recently, however, exchange theorists have been introducing more consideration of cognition and emotion – especially the latter – into analyses of exchange process (see Lawler 2001, and Lawler's chapter in this volume). For some theorists, emotions such as affective attachments are studied primarily as outcomes of exchange relations (e.g., Molm et al. 2007a); for others, affect and emotion play causal roles in determining exchange behaviors (Lawler 2001). Cognitions also play a potentially important role in another understudied aspect of exchange: the role of risk and risk aversion as determinants of exchange. In organizational settings, risk and uncertainty are inevitable features of exchange, and understanding actors' perceptions of risk is important.

Developments along these lines would increase the relevance of exchange theory for the analysis of power and interdependence in organizations. They would also serve the social exchange tradition well, by recapturing some of the breath and richness of the classic exchange formulations but with the added sophistication and rigor that contemporary scholars have brought to the field.

References

Bienenstock, E. J. and Bonacich, P. (1993) Game theory models for social exchange networks: Experimental results. *Sociological Perspectives*, 36, 117–136.

Blau, P. M. (1964) *Exchange and power in social life*, New York, N.Y.: Wiley.

Cook, K. S. (1977) Exchange and power in networks of interorganizational relations. *Sociological Quarterly*, 18, 62–82.

Cook, K. S. and Emerson, R. M. (1978) Power, equity and commitment in exchange networks. *American Sociological Review*, 43, 721–739.

(1984) Exchange networks and the analysis of complex organizations. *Research in the Sociology of Organizations*, 3, 1–30.

Cook, K. S., Emerson, R. M., Gillmore, M. R., and Tamagishi, T. (1983) The distribution of power in exchange networks: Theory and experimental results. *American Journal of Sociology*, 89, 275–305).

Cook, K. S. and Gillmore, M. R. (1984) Power, dependence, and coalitions. In E. J. Lawler (Ed.), *Advances in group processes* (Vol. I, pp. 27–48), Greenwich, Conn.: JAI Press.

Emerson, R. M. (1972a) Exchange theory, part I: A psychological basis for social exchange. In J. Berger, M. Zelditch Jr., and B. Anderson (Eds.), *Sociological theories in progress* (Vol. II, pp. 38–57), Boston, Mass.: Houghton-Mifflin.

(1972b) Exchange theory, part II: Exchange relations and networks. In J. Berger, M. Zelditch Jr., and B. Anderson (Eds.), *Sociological theories in progress* (Vol. II, pp. 58–87), Boston, Mass.: Houghton-Mifflin.

(1987) Toward a theory of value in social exchange. In K. S. Cook (Ed.), *Social exchange theory* (pp. 11–58), Newbury Park, Calif.: Sage.

Friedkin, N. E. (1992) An expected value model of social power: Predictions for selected exchange networks. *Social Networks*, 14, 213–229.

Granovetter, M. (1985) Economic action and social structure: The problem of embeddedness. *American Journal of Sociology*, 91, 481–510.

Hechter, M. (1992) Should values be written out of the social scientist's lexicon? *Sociological Theory*, 10, 214–230.

Homans, G. C. (1961) *Social behavior: Its elementary forms*, New York, N. Y.: Harcourt Brace & World.

Kollock, P. (1994) The emergence of exchange structures: An experimental study of uncertainty, commitment, and trust. *American Journal of Sociology*, 100, 313–345.

Larson, A. (1992) Network dyads in entrepreneurial settings: A study of the governance of exchange relationships. *Administrative Science Quarterly*, 37, 76–104.

Lawler, E. J. (1992) Power processes in bargaining. *Sociological Quarterly*, 33, 17–34.

(2001) An affect theory of social exchange. *American Journal of Sociology*, 107, 321–352.

Markovsky, B., Willer, D., and Patton, T. (1988) Power relations in exchange networks. *American Sociological Review*, 53, 220–236.

Molm, L. D. (1997) *Coercive power in social exchange*, Cambridge: Cambridge University Press.

` (2000) Theories of social exchange and exchange networks. In G. Ritzer and B. Smart (Eds.), *The Handbook of Social Theory* (pp. 260–272), New York, N.Y.: Sage Press.

(2003) Theoretical comparisons of forms of exchange. *Sociological Theory*, 21, 1–17.

Molm, L. D., Collett, J. L., and Schaefer, D. R. (2006) Conflict and fairness in social exchange. *Social Forces*, 84, 2325–2346.

(2007a) Building solidarity through generalized exchange: A theory of reciprocity. *American Journal of Sociology*, 113, 205–242.

Molm, L. D., Peterson, G., and Takahashi, N. (1999) Power use in negotiated and reciprocal exchange. *American Sociological Review*, 64, 876–890.

(2001) The value of exchange. *Social Forces*, 80, 159–185.

Molm, L. D., Schaefer, D. R., and Collett, J. L. (2007b) The value of reciprocity. *Social Psychology Quarterly*, 70, 199–217.

Molm, L. D., Takahashi, N., and Peterson, G. (2000) Risk and trust in social exchange: An experimental test of a classical proposition. *American Journal of Sociology*, 105, 1396–1427.

(2003) In the eye of the beholder: Procedural justice in social exchange. *American Sociological Review*, 68, 128–152.

Offer, A. (1997) Between the gift and the market: The economy of regard. *Economic History Review*, 3, 450–476.

Pfeffer, J. and Salanack, G. R. (1978) *The external control of organizations: A resource dependence perspective*, New York, N.Y.: Harper & Row.

Thye, S. R. (2000) A status value theory of power in exchange relations. *American Sociological Review*, 65, 407–432.

Uzzi, B. (1996) The sources and consequences of embeddedness for the economic performance of organizations: The network effect. *American Sociological Review*, 61, 674–698.

Yamagishi, T., Gillmore, M. R., and Cook, K. S. (1988) Network connections and the distribution of power in exchange networks. *American Journal of Sociology*, 93, 833–851.

10 | *The power process and emotion*

EDWARD J. LAWLER AND CHAD A. PROELL

Introduction

Power is a crucial phenomenon in organizations, both pervasive and somewhat elusive. The study of power in organizations has a long tradition (Crozier 1964), yet the literature on power is fragmented and has been a central focus only intermittently over time. Fundamental assumptions about the role of power vary widely. On the one hand, power can be construed broadly as a negative and divisive force in relations, groups, and organizations. It enables those having power to exert influence over or command the compliance of others through coercion, force, and threats. This is the punitive, manipulative face of power (Deutsch and Krauss 1962; Lawler et al. 1988; Tedeschi et al. 1973). On the other hand, power can be construed as a positive, integrative force enabling those with power to provide rewards, inducements, and reinforcements to others (Bacharach and Lawler 1980; Boulding 1989). It gives those with power the opportunity to promote cooperation and collaboration. The negative view of power emphasizes the harm it can do and the resistance it can generate, whereas the positive view of power emphasizes the role of power in mobilizing concerted action toward collective goals. Implicitly, negative and positive *emotions* (e.g., pleasure, enthusiasm, pride or anger, fear, sadness) are likely to be associated, respectively, with the negative and positive faces of power. This chapter proposes a power-process model for examining the relationship between power and emotion.

Recent work on power and emotion can be found within three disparate lines of theory and research:

1. social-exchange theory in sociology (Lawler and Thye 1999);
2. "approach inhibition" theory in psychology (Keltner et al. 2003);
3. research on negotiations from organizational behavior (Carnevale and Isen 1986).

169

Unfortunately, these literatures have existed largely in isolation. This chapter draws ideas from each and fleshes out the role emotions play in power relations. We provide exemplars of research falling within these research traditions but, due to space limitations, we do not undertake a comprehensive review. Our purposes are primarily conceptual. This chapter presents a power-process model designed to integrate elements from different approaches to power. In the context of this power-process model, we highlight some of the conclusions about power and emotion that can be drawn from work on power dependence structures, the approach/ inhibition effects of power, and the role of emotions, felt or expressed, in negotiation settings. We propose that the power-process model can not only integrate ideas from widely disparate literatures but also reveal gaps and suggest problems and issues for future study.

The first step, however, is to define emotion. A review of the psychological and sociological literatures reveals an almost endless array of variation in how emotion, affect, feelings, moods, and sentiments are used (Lawler 2007). We adopt a commonly used definition of emotions as transitory positive or negative evaluative states with physiological, neurological, and cognitive components (Izard 1991; Kemper 1978). Emotions are a nonconscious response to external stimuli whereas feeling emotions involves at least a minimal awareness of the bodies' response to the stimuli (Damasio et al. 2000). We use the terms "emotions" and "feelings" interchangeably and focus on generalized emotions or feelings that people develop in interaction or exchange with others. Such emotions involve feeling good, feeling pleasure, or feeling happy, rather than more specific emotions directed at self or other such as pride or gratitude (Lawler 2001; Weiner 1985). Affect is generally construed as a broader term than emotion (see Brief and Weiss 2002). It subsumes the generalized feelings of concern described here, as well as more enduring emotional states such as moods (which are diffuse feelings without targets) and sentiments (which target self, other, or groups) (Lawler 2007). Unless otherwise noted, we limit the scope of our analysis to short-term emotional states while recognizing that in dealing with recurrent interactions or exchanges, the distinction between transitory and enduring affective states tends to blur.

A power process model

Most definitions of power focus on *social* power. What makes power social is that it is a property of a relationship between two or more

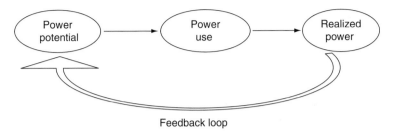

Figure 10.1 Power process model.

individuals, i.e. to have power is to have power over someone else (Brass and Burkhardt 1993; Emerson 1962; French and Raven 1959; Ng 1980). Most concepts of power also include one or more of the following: (1) a capability or potential; (2) behaviors using that capability; (3) the impact of using the capability (actual or realized power and influence). The first typically involves a structure (e.g., network or hierarchy) within which a position provides an actor resources that are of value to one or more others (Cook and Emerson 1978; Emerson 1972). The second typically involves tactics or strategies designed to shape or change the behavior of another (Bacharach and Lawler 1981; Molm 1990). The third involves successful or unsuccessful influence over that other. Lawler (1992) incorporated all three of these facets or dimensions into a "power process model" which informs this paper. This model is diagrammed in Figure 10.1.

In the power-process model, each facet should be thought of as one "moment" of an integrated process. An actor faces a "problem" that involves influencing another; the actor has a resource (capability) that the other values, a range of behavioral options (tactics) for using this resource, and an outcome or result that is desired (Lawler 1992). Power capabilities underlie power use, and power use is the basis for actual power. One advantage of this model is that it makes fewer a-priori assumptions than most power frameworks, especially those that conflate power and its effects (see Dahl 1957). Rather than presuming that a capability is used, this model implies that there may be conditions under which having a capability is sufficient to influence another in the absence of power use. Whether or not it is used becomes a theoretical and empirical question. Rather than assuming that power produces results that favor the more powerful, the model implies that this depends on how the power is used (i.e. the tactics chosen) and the amount and type of resistance generated by lower power actors. For example, low-power actors may have more influence than their power position would suggest because they are highly motivated to devise effective tactics (Bacharach and Lawler 1980), or because they more carefully process and weigh information on the high-power person (Fiske 1993). Thus, by making sharp distinctions between these complementary facets of power, the power-process model poses questions that many other frameworks on power define away.

An implication is that in almost any social relationship, individuals are likely to have some capacity to affect each other, a variety of options for using that capability, and an uncertain probability of success (Lawler 1992: 20). Emotions can enter the power process at all three points. If A has a power capability, it may arouse a fear of negative sanctions or the hope of positive reward; if A uses his or her power, the tactics chosen could affect the emotions felt by the other and perhaps those of the actor using the tactic; and if a successful result is generated, the emotions felt by self and other may depend on the degree that they each receive benefits from A's successful influence. The three moments of the power process and prospective emotional effects can be tied in part to underlying dependencies and interdependencies (Bacharach and Lawler 1980; Emerson 1972; Thibaut and Kelley 1959). These can be fruitfully analyzed from power-dependence theory (Bacharach and Lawler 1981; Emerson 1962, 1972).

Power as dependence

Power-dependence theory, developed originally by Emerson (1962, 1972), is based on a very simple idea: *The power of A is based on the dependence of B on A for valued outcomes, and vice versa.* The degree of A's power over B depends on how much B values what A provides and the degree that B does not have alternative persons or relations from which to acquire these valued outcomes. The relational nature of power dependence emphasizes the point that power relations are two-way, involving mutual dependencies or interdependencies (see also Thibaut and Kelley 1959), and should be analyzed in these terms.

Importantly, Emerson's (1972) framework implies a non-zero-sum conception of power in which each actor's power in a relation can grow or decline; thus an increase in one actor's power does not by definition reduce the other's power. Bacharach and Lawler (1981) developed the non-zero-sum implications of Emerson's (1972) framework by distinguishing the relative power (dependence) of actors from the total power (dependence) in the relationship. Relative power refers to the degree of difference between A's dependence on B and B's dependence on A, whereas total power refers to the sum of each actor's dependence on the other (see also Molm 1987). Total power or dependence in a relation can vary because each actor's alternatives may contract or expand, and the value of the outcomes at stake also may grow or decline over time. Bacharach and Lawler (1981) use the distinction between relative and total power to develop the positive face of power. If actors have equal power and they build greater total power into their relationship, they have more to gain from repeated exchange or collaboration. They can accomplish joint goals together more effectively, more quickly, and with fewer costs. If actors have unequal power but increase the total power or dependence in their relationship, a similar result is likely to occur because there are stronger incentives for collaboration (Piskorski and Tiziana 2006).

A non-zero-sum approach to power has implications for the emotions felt by actors in exchange. All things being equal, one would expect equal power dependence to generate more positive feelings about exchange with another than unequal power. Higher total power in the relation should also produce more positive emotions than lower total power. The rationale for the former is that equal power conditions avoid the issues of justice and legitimacy that tend to occur under unequal power conditions. The rationale for the latter is that the interaction or exchange generates greater joint gain. Overall, it is reasonable to hypothesize that equal power and high total power will enhance the total amount of positive affect in a relationship. Theory and research on relational cohesion suggests how this might occur.

Relational cohesion

Lawler and colleagues (Lawler and Yoon 1993, 1996) developed a theory of relational cohesion that incorporates both zero-sum and non-zero-sum components of power dependence and shows how each of these affect the emotions generated from social exchange. Specifically, they proposed that equal and high total power would generate more frequent exchange, and frequent or repeated exchanges would be a basis for enduring exchange relations because of emotions generated by successful exchanges. This is theorized to occur because coming to an agreement is an accomplishment that makes the actors feel good. These positive emotions, when felt or experienced repeatedly, generate perceptions of a unifying, cohesive relation which the actors are then motivated to maintain net of the effects of the exchange outcomes themselves (see Lawler and Yoon 1993, 1996). The result is commitment behavior directed at the social unit in question (the relation). A series of studies by Lawler and colleagues supports the predictions of relational cohesion theory (e.g., Lawler et al. 2000; Lawler and Yoon 1993, 1996, 1998). In sum, both equal and higher total power produce more positive emotions than unequal and lower total power, and these promote stronger relationships.

It is important to point out, however, that repeated exchanges (frequency) generate positive feelings and more cohesion/commitment even under most unequal power conditions (Lawler and Yoon 1998). As long as exchange generates positive emotions to some degree, repeated exchanges build relations even under unequal power (see Thye et al. 2007). The only exception to this pattern has been when one actor has extremely low power; here exchanges do not generate positive emotions or feelings (see Lawler and Yoon 1998). In terms of the power-process model, this research shows how and when power potential promotes mutually felt positive emotions by repeatedly producing exchange outcomes. These emotional reactions shape whether actors attempt to maintain the relation over time.

There also is research in the exchange tradition suggesting that under unequal power, the results of the power process have different emotional effects on the low- and high-power actors (Lawler and Yoon 1993; Molm 1997). With this in mind, Lovaglia and colleagues (Lovaglia 1994, 1995a, 1995b; Lovaglia and Houser 1996; Willer et al. 1997) investigated the hypothesis that the exercise or demonstration of power should lead to enhanced status for the higher-power actor (Emerson 1962; Lovaglia 1994). The results indicated, however, that the relationship between power and status is complicated by the emotional responses of the low-power actor to the exercise of power by the high-power actor. Specifically, if low-power actors reacted with negative emotions to the exercise of power (defined as garnering higher individual profits), this actually decreased the high-power actor's status and influence (Lovaglia and Houser 1996; Willer et al. 1997). Thus, while Lawler and colleagues' work indicates that exchanges made under unequal power conditions can generate positive emotions separate from the outcome and help to build collaborative relations, the work by Lovaglia and colleagues suggests that negative emotions from the results of exchange may obstruct this process. In terms of the power-process model, the important point is that realized power is connected to the generation of emotions, and these emotions produce feedback effects from the outcome to the future capability.

Use of power

The network-oriented power-dependence approach of Emerson (1972) tends to downplay the tactics of using power. Emerson assumes that if actors have power, they will use power, thereby conflating the first two moments of our power-process model (see Figure 10.1). Extant research explicitly on power and emotion has also downplayed tactics (see Lawler and Yoon 1993, 1996, 1998); an exception is the work by Molm (1991, 1997) who has explicitly compared coercive and reward tactics by high- and low-power actors in a network. She found that coercive tactics evoke negative emotional reactions while reward tactics evoke positive emotions and, importantly, that the negative emotional responses to coercive tactics was stronger than the positive emotional responses to reward tactics. Moreover, she found that those in disadvantaged positions were more likely to use coercive tactics against the higher power actor than vice versa, and that those in a power-advantaged position reacted more negatively to such coercion than those in a power-disadvantaged position (Molm 1997).

Proell (2007) recently used the power-process model to explore an alternative approach to power and status from that of Lovaglia et al. (Lovaglia 1994, 1995a; Lovaglia and Houser 1996; Willer et al. 1997). Drawing upon the French and Raven (1959), Kipnis (Kipnis and Schmidt 1988; Kipnis et al. 1980) and Yukl (Yukl and Falbe 1990; Yukl and Tracey 1992) tradition of influence tactics, as well as Lawler's (1992) broad classification of tactics as positive (signaling cooperative motives) and negative (signaling competition), Proell found that the emotion generated from the exercise of power depended on the type of tactic used. Positive tactics, such as ingratiation, elicited more positive emotions, whereas negative tactics, such as coalitions, elicited more negative emotions. Moreover, reaction to the tactics depended upon the status of the person using the tactic. Coalition tactics by high-status persons evoked more negative reactions from low-status targets than did coalition tactics of low status directed at high-status targets. Thus, it appears that both structurally determined power (Molm 1991) and the status of the actor using the tactic moderate emotional reactions to tactic use.

In terms of the power-process model, both the work of Molm and Proell indicate that emotions are linked to the tactics chosen. This work also indicates why it is important to avoid the conflation of power potential and power use. Emotional reactions to tactics are partially contingent upon the circumstances surrounding the tactic use, including the power potential of the actor engaging in the tactic. Moreover, this research, combined with the findings of Lovaglia and colleagues (1996) and Lawler and colleagues (1993, 1996, 1998), underscores the importance of the positive face of power. Negative tactics generate negative emotions which potentially undermine the stability of an exchange relationship, whereas positive tactics generate positive emotions which should reinforce an exchange relationship. Put differently, feedback loops involving positive emotions from tactics to power potential should strengthen an actor's future power potential, whereas negative feedback loops involving negative emotions should decrease that power potential and ultimately challenge the stability of an exchange relationship.

One salient limitation of work in the exchange tradition is that little attention has been given to the spread of emotions across individuals, i.e. emotional contagion. Emotional contagion is the transfer of emotions from individual to individual (Schoenewolf 1990). A good deal of work demonstrates that the emotions of actors in a relationship tend to converge over time (Bartel and Saavedra 2000; Totterdell 2000; Totterdell et al. 1998). In fact, not only do emotions converge with repeated interaction, but Anderson et al. (2003) show that it is the low-power actor whose emotion converges toward the high-power actor. The implications for repeated exchange are potentially quite large. High-power actors who are happy with their resource gains may actually promote more happy feelings among low-power actors than their outcomes would indicate because their emotions are converging toward those of the high-power actors. This might serve to strengthen the stability or cohesion of unequal power relationships in the workplace. Conversely, an unhappy high-power actor, regardless of the source of unhappiness, may undermine the cohesion of an unequal exchange relationship and even set off conflict spirals similar to those studied by O'Connor and Arnold (2001). Future work should address more systematically the contagion effects that can occur when people interact and exchange to achieve collective goals.

Experiencing power: approach/avoidance processes

Recent work in psychology has used approach/avoidance theory to examine how the experience of power affects the propensity toward initiating action to deal with a problem or issue. In terms of the power-process model, such power-to-action effects capture a process underlying the potential-to-use link. Approach/inhibition work seeks to understand when action is actually undertaken to use power. The approach/inhibition theory of power is inspired in part by the work of Kipnis (1976) in that it is concerned with how the possession of power affects the behavior of the power-holder (see Keltner et al. 2003 for a review).

Put simply, the theory argues that the environment of high-power actors consists of more rewards, opportunities, and freedom. Because high-power agents are enmeshed in a reward-rich environment, with substantial opportunities for and freedom of action, approach-related tendencies are automatically and subconsciously activated (see Keltner et al. 2003 for a review). These approach tendencies are in turn associated with automatic cognition, attention to rewards, and a propensity toward action. Conversely, the environment of low-power actors consists of less freedom, fewer opportunities, and more threat which automatically and subconsciously trigger inhibition-related tendencies. These inhibition tendencies, in turn, are associated with systematic cognition, attention to threats, and a propensity away from action. Important for our purposes, approach tendencies are also associated with positive emotion (Davidson 1992; Higgins 1997) whereas inhibition tendencies are associated with negative emotion (Carver and White 1994). Thus, elevated power leads to the experience and expression of positive emotions, and decreased power leads to the experience and expression of negative emotions.

This work predicts overall that individuals with high-power potential will be more likely to use their power than low-power individuals. Similarly, affect/emotion enters the power process at the power-potential stage of the power-process model. Those high in power potential are also high in positive affect and they express those emotions more freely than those low in potential power. Galinsky et al. (2003) found support for the predicted power-to-action effects – namely that individuals primed with high power and given more potential power in terms of their ability to allocate resources were more likely than those who lacked power to take action to solve a problem. However, this work did not specifically address the emotions involved. Work by Anderson and Berdahl (2002), however, found that individuals assigned to a high-power position on a committee determining resource allocations, experienced approach tendencies and positive emotions while individuals assigned to a low-power committee position experienced inhibition tendencies and negative emotion. Similarly, Berdahl and Martorana (2006) found that high-power actors did experience and *express* more positive emotions and less anger than did low-power actors in a controversial group conversation. Thus, research suggests that the mere experience of high and low power potential has relevant implications for both the power-potential-to-power-use connection as well as the power-potential-to-emotion connection. While there is growing support for the predictions of the approach/inhibition theory of power in general (e.g., Galinsky et al. 2003), the investigation of the power-to-emotion predictions have only recently begun.

Viewing work on approach/inhibition theory from the power-process model, one limitation is that although this research does focus on when power potential may lead to power use, it does not predict which tactics will be chosen when power is used. For example, because high-power actors are also in a more positive affective state, is it the case that they are more likely to engage in positive tactics than low-power actors in a relationship? Conversely, because low-power actors are in a negative affective state, are they prone to select negative or punishing strategies? This is suggested by Molm's (1997) work. Whereas one advantage of this literature over the exchange tradition is that it specifically theorizes and empirically examines the power-potential-to-power-use connection, exchange theory does a better of job of connecting power use to results and results to emotions. These two theoretical approaches are complementary, and emotional processes may be a point of integration. For example, the results or outcomes of exchange may generate approach or inhibition tendencies, as well as the possession or experience of power potential.

Another limitation of the approach/avoidance approach to power is its strong focus on unequal power relationships. The experience of power is based on having more power than someone else. This emphasis on unequal power ignores the non-zero-sum implications of power-dependence theory. Because the total power in a relationship may vary, individuals may experience equal power relationships, yet the individual actors may still be prone to feeling high or low power. A potentially important question is whether this type of relationship translates into the approach/inhibition emotion tendencies described by Keltner et al. (2003). In other words, are the effects of relative and total power consistent with each other? Under higher total power, will both actors have approach tendencies, whereas under lower total power will they both have inhibition tendencies? Questions such as these would move forward research on the experience of power and emotion but could also tie this research more closely to the exchange tradition and potentially create other opportunities for cross-fertilization.

Emotions as a basis for power

Recently, a small body of negotiation research has examined emotions as tactics. The orienting idea is that emotions or emotional expressions can be used strategically or tactically to produce desired outcomes (Frank 1988), thus resulting in increased or decreased power. Applying our power-process model, the focus here is on the use-to-realized-power link. This research tends to involve one-shot negotiations and emphasize realized power, that is, resources produced as a result of negotiation. Thus, the evidence on increasing or decreasing power is indirect, since the emotion-to-power-potential effects presume that realized power in a single negotiation carries over to subsequent negotiations or exchanges. Assuming that an increase in realized power does carry meaning for subsequent exchanges, there are two relevant issues addressed by this literature: (a) value-creation as a result of experiencing emotions and (b) value-claiming as a result of emotional displays. Each is briefly discussed below.

With regard to value creation, a seminal study by Carnevale and Isen (1986) found that negotiators primed with positive affect, via the reading of humorous cartoons, communicated more openly, assessed the other's priorities more accurately, and created more value (i.e. had more integrative agreements) than negotiators not primed with positive affect. These results have been replicated (Baron 1990; Forgas 1998; Kramer et al. 1993) and extended to show that negative affect correspondingly reduces joint outcomes (Allred et al. 1997). This work was extended further in an important way by Anderson and Thompson (2004), who showed that, in unequal power relations, it is the high-power negotiator's positive emotion that leads to a better integrative outcome, not the emotions of the low-power negotiator. Overall, interpreting integrative outcomes as realized *total* power, the experience of positive and negative affect appears to play a central and important role in how much total power a relationship develops, but this is due primarily to the emotion or affect of the high-power negotiator.

Turning to the claiming of value in negotiations, research consistently finds that the display of negative emotion in the form of anger results in the successful claiming of more resources. For example, Van Kleef et al. (2004) found that in computer-mediated negotiations, information about a counterpart's angry emotional state led negotiators to make fewer demands of and more concessions to their counterpart than when information about a counterpart's positive emotions were made available. Importantly however, Sinaceur and Tiedens (2006) show that this effect is moderated by the power positions of the negotiators. Low-power negotiators concede more to an angry counterpart but there are no significant effects for anger display on high power counterparts (Van Kleef et al. 2006). Thus, because high-power negotiators can gain more power and low-power negotiators can lose power via displays of anger, as a strategic tool, anger most likely serves to further exacerbate power inequalities rather than balance power relationships. In sum, the evidence from the negotiations literature suggests that negative emotions (in particular anger) are often effective tactics for generating realized power, whereas positive emotions are effective tactics for creating joint value. These broad implications are generally consistent with social-exchange research on power and emotion in the relational cohesion tradition (e.g., Lawler and Yoon 1993, 1996).

Conclusions

Understanding the relationships of power and emotion is in its infancy, despite significant growth of attention in the fields of sociology, psychology, and organizational behavior. To date, emotion has served primarily as an explanatory mechanism for other processes, such as the emergence of commitment in social exchange (e.g., Lawler and Yoon 1996) or as an ancillary consequence or byproduct of power relations (e.g., Keltner et al. 2003). Using our power-process model as a framework, it is clear that many questions remain unanswered and there are gaps to be filled, theoretically and empirically. It is also clear how disparate work on specific links of the power process model can fit together and be interrelated. There are good reasons for having distinct theories and research on particular parts of the model (e.g., power to action, tactics to power, outcomes to power potential), but it is also important to have a broader framework for integrating distinct lines of work. Future research should theorize more systematically the inter-relationships of these component parts of the power-process model. The distinct moments of our power-process model suggest a wide range of issues and questions to be dealt with in future work. We hope this paper will help to encourage more sustained and systematic attention to the multitude of ways that power and emotion are intertwined.

References

Allred, K. G., Mallozzi, J. S., Matsui, F., and Raia, C. P. (1997) The influence of anger and compassion on negotiation performance. *Organizational Behavior and Human Decision Processes*, 70 (3), 175–187.

Anderson, C. and Berdahl, J. L. (2002)The experience of power: Examining the effects of power on approach and inhibition tendencies. *Journal of Personality and Social Psychology*, 83 (6), 1362–1377.

Anderson, C., Keltner, D., and John, O. P. (2003) Emotional convergence between people over time. *Journal of Personality and Social Psychology*, 84 (5), 1054–1068.

Anderson, C. and Thompson, L. L. (2004) Affect from the top down: How powerful individuals' positive affect shapes negotiations. *Organizational Behavior and Human Decision Processes*, 95 (2), 125–139.

Bacharach, S. B. and Lawler, E. J. (1980) *Power and politics in organizations*, San Francisco, Calif.: Jossey-Bass.

(1981) *Bargaining, power, tactics, and outcomes*, 1st edn, San Francisco, Calif.: Jossey-Bass.

Baron, R. A. (1990) Environmentally induced positive affect: Its impact on self-efficacy, task-performance, negotiation, and conflict. *Journal of Applied Social Psychology*, 20 (5), 368–384.

Barsade, S. G. (2002) The ripple effect: Emotional contagion and its influence on group behavior. *Administrative Science Quarterly*, 47 (4), 644–675.

Bartel, C. A. and Saavedra, R. (2000) The collective construction of work group moods. *Administrative Science Quarterly*, 45 (2) 197–231.

Berdahl, J. L. and Martorana, P. (2006) Effects of power on emotion and expression during a controversial group discussion. *European Journal of Social Psychology*, **36** (4), 497–509.

Boulding, K. E. (1989) *Three faces of power*, Newbury Park, Calif.: Sage Publications.

Brass, D. J. and Burkhardt, M. E. (1993) Potential power and power use: An investigation of structure and behavior. *Academy of Management Journal*, **36** (3), 441–470.

Brief, A. P. and Weiss, H. M. (2002) Organizational behavior: Affect in the workplace. *Annual Review of Psychology*, **53**, 279–307.

Carnevale, P. J. D. and Isen, A. M. (1986) The influence of positive affect and visual access on the discovery of integrative solutions in bilateral negotiation. *Organizational Behavior and Human Decision Processes*, **37** (1), 1–13.

Carver, C. S. and White, T. L. (1994) Behavioral-inhibition, behavioral activation, and affective responses to impending reward and punishment – the bis bas scales. *Journal of Personality and Social Psychology*, **67** (2), 319–333.

Collins, C. (2004) *Interaction ritual chains*, Princeton, N. J.: Princeton University Press.

Cook, K. S. and Emerson, R. M. (1978) Power, equity and commitment in exchange networks. *American Sociological Review*, **5**, 721–739.

Crozier, M. (1964) *The beuracratic phenomenon*, Chicago, Ill.: University of Chicago Press.

Dahl, R. A. (1957) The concept of power. *Behavioral Science*, **2** (3), 201–215.

Damasio, A. R., Grabowski, T. J., Bechara, A., Damasio, H., Ponto, L. L. B., Parvizi, J., et al. (2000) Subcortical and cortical brain activity during the feeling of self-generated emotions. *Nature Neuroscience*, **3** (10), 1049–1056.

Davidson, R. J. (1992) Emotion and affective style: Hemispheric substrates. *Psychological Science*, **3** (1), 39–43.

Deutsch, M. and Krauss, R. M. (1962) Studies of interpersonal bargaining. *Journal of Conflict Resolution*, **6**, 52–76.

Emerson, R. M. (1962) Power-dependence relations. *American Sociological Review*, **27** (1), 31–41.

(1972) Exchange theory, part II: Exchange relations, exchange networks, and groups as exchange systems. In J. Berger, M. Zelditch, and B. Anderson (Eds.), *Sociological theories in progress* (Vol. II, pp. 58–87), Boston, Mass.: Houghton Mifflin.

Fiske, S. T. (1993) Controlling other people: The impact of power on stereotyping. *American Psychologist*, **48** (6), 621–628.

Forgas, J. P. (1998) On feeling good and getting your way: Mood effects on negotiator cognition and bargaining strategies. *Journal of Personality and Social Psychology*, **74** (3), 565–577.

Frank, R. H. (1988) *Passions within reason: The strategic role of emotions*, New York, N.Y.: Norton.

French, J. R. P. Jr. and Raven, B. (1959) The bases of social power. In D. Cartwright (Ed.), *Studies of social power* (pp. 150–167), Ann Arbor, Mich.: Institute for Social Research.

Galinsky, A. D., Gruenfeld, D. H., and Magee, J. C. (2003) From power to action. *Journal of Personality and Social Psychology*, **85** (3), 453–466.

Higgins, E. T. (1997) Beyond pleasure and pain. *American Psychologist*, **52** (12), 1280–1300.

Isen, A. M., Daubman, K. A., and Nowicki, G. P. (1987) Positive affect facilitates creative problem solving. *Journal of Personality and Social Psychology*, **52** (6), 1122–1131.

Isen, A. M., Rosenzweig, A. S., and Young, M. J. (1991) The influence of positive affect on clinical problem-solving. *Medical Decision Making*, **11** (3), 221–227.

Izard, C. E. (1991) *The psychology of emotion*, New York, N.Y.: Plenum Press.

Keltner, D., Gruenfeld, D. H., and Anderson, C. (2003) Power, approach, and inhibition. *Psychological Review*, **110** (2), 265–284.

Kemper, T. D. (1978) *A social interactional theory of emotions*, New York, N.Y.: Wiley.

Kipnis, D. (1976) *The power-holders*, Chicago, Ill.: University of Chicago Press.

Kipnis, D. and Schmidt, S. M. (1988) Upward-influence styles: Relationship with performance evaluations, salary, and stress. *Administrative Science Quarterly*, **33** (4), 528–542.

Kipnis, D., Schmidt, S. M., and Wilkinson, I. (1980) Intraorganizational influence tactics: Explorations in getting ones way. *Journal of Applied Psychology*, **65** (4), 440–452.

Kramer, R. M., Newton, E., and Pommerenke, P. L. (1993) Self-enhancement biases and negotiator judgment: Effects of self-esteem and mood. *Organizational Behavior and Human Decision Processes*, **56** (1), 110–133.

Lawler, E. J. (1992) Power processes in bargaining. *Sociological Quarterly*, **33** (1), 17–34.

(2001) An affect theory of social exchange. *American Journal of Sociology*, **107** (2), 321–352.

(2007) Affect and group attachments: The role of shared responsibility. In C. Anderson, M. Neale, and E. Mannix (Eds.), *Research on managing groups and teams, Vol. IX: Affect and Groups* (pp. 185–216), Amsterdam: Elsevier.

Lawler, E. J., Ford, R. S., and Blegen, M. A. (1988) Coercive capability in conflict: A test of bilateral deterrence versus conflict spiral theory. *Social Psychology Quarterly*, **51** (2), 93–107.

Lawler, E. J. and Thye, S. R. (1999) Bringing emotions into social exchange theory. *Annual Review of Sociology*, **25**, 217–244.

Lawler, E. J., Thye, S. R., and Yoon, J. (2000) Emotion and group cohesion in productive exchange. *American Journal of Sociology*, **106** (3), 616–657.

Lawler, E. J. and Yoon, J. (1993) Power and the emergence of commitment behavior in negotiated exchange. *American Sociological Review*, **58** (4), 465–481.

(1996) Commitment in exchange relations: Test of a theory of relational cohesion. *American Sociological Review*, **61** (1), 89–108.

(1998) Network structure and emotion in exchange relations. *American Sociological Review*, **63** (6), 871–894.

Lovaglia, M. J. (1994) Relating power to status. In E. J. Lawler and B. Markovsky (Eds.), *Advances in group processes* (Vol. XI, pp. 87–111), Greenwich, Conn.: JAI Press.

(1995a) Power and status: Exchange, attribution, and expectation states. *Small Group Research*, **26** (3), 400–426.

(1995b) Status, emotion, and structural power. In J. Szmatka, J. Skvoretz, and J. Berger (Eds.), *Status, network and structure* (pp. 159–178), Stanford, Calif.: Stanford University Press.

Lovaglia, M. J. and Houser, J. A. (1996) Emotional reactions and status in groups. *American Sociological Review*, **61** (5), 867–883.

Molm, L. D. (1987) Extending power dependence theory: Power processes and negative outcomes. In E. J. Lawler and B. Markovsky (Eds.), *Advances in group processes* (Vol. IV, pp. 178–198), Greenwich, Conn: JAI Press.

(1990) Structure, action, and outcomes: The dynamics of power in social exchange. *American Sociological Review*, **55** (3), 427–447.

(1991) Affect and social exchange: Satisfaction in power-dependence relations. *American Sociological Review*, **56** (4), 475–493.

(1997) *Coercive power in social exchange*, Cambridge and New York, N. Y.: Cambridge University Press.

Ng, S. H. (1980) *The social psychology of power*, San Diego, Calif.: Academic Press.

O'Connor, K. M. and Arnold, J. A. (2001) Distributive spirals: Negotiation impasses and the moderating role of disputant self-efficacy. *Organizational Behavior and Human Decision Processes*, **84** (1), 148–176.

Piskorski, M. J. and Tiziana, C. (2006) When more power makes actors worse off: Turning a profit in the american economy. *Social Forces*, **85** (2), 1011–1036.

Proell, C. A. (2007) Movin' on up: A theoretical model of power change. Unpublished manuscript.

Schoenewolf, G. (1990) Emotional contagion: Behavioral induction in individuals and groups. *Modern psycho-analysis*, 15, 49–61.

Sinaceur, M. and Tiedens, L.Z. (2006) Get mad and get more than even: When and why anger expression is effective in negotiations. *Journal of Experimental Social Psychology*, 42 (3), 314–322.

Tedeschi, J.T., Schlenker, B.R., and Bonoma, T.V. (1973) *Conflict, power, and games: The experimental study of interpersonal relations*, Chicago, Ill.: Aldine.

Thibaut, J.W. and Kelley, H.H. (1959) *The social psychology of groups*, New York, N.Y.: Wiley.

Thye, S.R., Lawler, E.J., and Yoon, J. (2007) Social exchange and the maintenance of order in status stratified systems. Unpublished manuscript.

Tiedens, L.Z. (2001) Anger and advancement versus sadness and subjugation: The effect of negative emotion expressions on social status conferral. *Journal of Personality and Social Psychology*, 80 (1), 86–94.

Totterdell, P. (2000) Catching moods and hitting runs: Mood linkage and subjective performance in professional sport teams. *Journal of Applied Psychology*, 85 (6), 848–859.

Totterdell, P., Kellett, S., Teuchmann, K., and Briner, R.B. (1998) Evidence of mood linkage in work groups. *Journal of Personality and Social Psychology*, 74 (6), 1504–1515.

Van Kleef, G.A., De Dreu, C.K.W., and Manstead, A.S.R. (2004) The interpersonal effects of anger and happiness in negotiations. *Journal of Personality and Social Psychology*, 86 (1), 57–76.

Van Kleef, G.A., De Dreu, C.K.W., Pietroni, D., and Manstead, A.S.R. (2006) Power and emotion in negotiation: Power moderates the interpersonal effects of anger and happiness on concession making. *European Journal of Social Psychology*, 36 (4), 557–581.

Weiner, B. (1985) An attributional theory of achievement-motivation and emotion. *Psychological Review*, 92 (4), 548–573.

Willer, D. (2003) Power-at-a-distance. *Social Forces*, 81 (4), 1295–1334.

Willer, D., Lovaglia, M.J., and Markovsky, B. (1997) Power and influence: A theoretical bridge. *Social Forces*, 76 (2), 571–603.

Yukl, G. and Falbe, C.M. (1990) Influence tactics and objectives in upward, downward, and lateral influence attempts. *Journal of Applied Psychology*, 75 (2), 132–140.

Yukl, G. and Tracey, J.B. (1992) Consequences of influence tactics used with subordinates, peers, and the boss. *Journal of Applied Psychology*, 77 (4), 525–535.

11 | Gender inequalities in power in organizations

ALICE H. EAGLY AND AGNETA FISCHER

Even in postindustrial societies, a considerable male–female power gap has remained in most organizations. Men are more likely to be the bosses and women the secretaries, clerks, and assistants. Although some women are present in lower- and middle-management positions in most organizations, they are considerably less well represented as top executives. One can quibble about types of power and say that women, even when in subordinate roles, have power that they exert informally as the secretary sometimes influences her boss and controls others' access to him. However, the secretary's decision-making power is paltry in comparison to that of her boss. It is this typical gender imbalance in organizational power that we examine in this chapter, with a focus on its causes and possibilities for amelioration.

Our claims about men's greater power are easily validated by statistics on managerial roles, which we present for our own countries, the USA. and the Netherlands, to illustrate common situations in Western industrialized nations. In the United States, 42 percent of "legislators, senior officials, and managers" are women, compared with 26 percent in the Netherlands (United Nations Development Program, 2006, Table 25). Within the context of industrialized nations, this representation of women is relatively high in the USA and low in the Netherlands. The comparable statistics for other nations are, for example, 36 percent in Canada, 35 percent in Germany, 33 percent in the United Kingdom, 31 percent in Sweden, and 29 percent in Norway.

A casual consumer of such statistics might think that the USA is close to attaining gender equality in organizational power. But this is not the case. American women occupy managerial positions that have less power and authority, on the average, than those occupied by men, even when their job titles are comparable (Lyness and Thompson 1997; Smith 2002). Illustrating this power imbalance is the statistic that women are 16 percent of corporate executives in the Fortune 500, the 500 US corporations with the largest revenues (Catalyst 2006b).

Among these executives, women are 11 percent of the line officers, who have direct responsibility for profits and losses, and 21 percent of the staff officers, who provide support to the line operation. On the boards of directors that oversee the policies and activities of corporations, the representation of women is 15 percent (Catalyst 2006a).

The Netherlands has an even smaller representation of women in top corporate positions: The percentage of women in the highest decision-making bodies of the fifty largest publicly quoted companies is 7 percent. In contrast, averaged across all European nations, women are 11 percent of these executive groups (European Commission 2006).

In both the USA and the Netherlands, women have more access to power outside of large corporations and especially in the nonprofit sector. In fact, women constitute 24 percent of chief executives in the USA when all organizations are considered (US Bureau of Labor Statistics, 2006). Beyond the business sector, women are 63 percent of educational administrators, 53 percent of the chief executives of foundations and charitable giving programs, and 27 percent of the top federal civil service (Eagly and Carli 2007). In the Netherlands, women are 20 percent of the directors of primary schools, 32 percent of the members of boards of directors of welfare and education organizations, 25 percent of the top management of the largest volunteer organizations, and 12 percent of the top federal civil service (Portegijs et al. 2006). Women's organizational power thus depends on the sector of society but, especially in the Netherlands, it is generally less than men's power.

The mission of this chapter is to evaluate the possible causes of women's lesser access to organizational power, a social pattern that has proven to be very persistent in industrialized countries, despite the positive value placed on equal opportunity for women. We examine whether women's human capital investments, employment discrimination against women, and organizational impediments continue to limit women's ability to ascend organizational hierarchies. Finally, we consider organizational innovations that can foster women's access to power in organizations.

Human capital investments of women and men

An explanation for the gender gap in organizational power drawn from neoclassical economics is that women's human capital investments in

education, training, and work experience are lower than men's, producing generally less successful careers. However, with respect to education, this argument no longer has much force. In the USA and most
European nations, women attain university degrees at higher rates than
men. For every 100 men in post-secondary education, there are 139
women in the USA and 108 in the Netherlands (United Nations
Development Programme 2006).

   In discussions of the effects of human capital on careers, more attention
has focused on women's responsibility for domestic work, which may limit
their employment. It is certainly true that women spend less time than men
in paid employment and more time caring for their homes and children
(Bianchi et al. 2006; Portegijs et al. 2006). In industrialized countries, the
number of children that women have is inversely related to their hours of
paid labor (e.g., Angrist and Evans 1998). Yet, the USA and the
Netherlands differ in the amount of paid work undertaken by women.
The female labor-force participation rate expressed as a percentage of the
male rate is 81 percent in the USA and 76 percent in the Netherlands
(United Nations Development Programme 2006). More striking are these
nations' differences in hours of paid employment: Part-time employees
constitute 8 percent of men and 19 percent of women in the USA and
15 percent of men and 60 percent of women in the Netherlands
(Organisation for Economic Co-operation and Development [OECD]
2005). For employees, the average hours per week of paid work are
forty-two for women and forty-nine for men in the United States but
twenty-three for women and thirty-eight for men in the Netherlands
(Boelens and van Iren 1999). Because hours worked and work experience
foster career success (see meta-analysis by Ng et al. 2005), the larger male–
female differences in employment hours in the Netherlands than the USA
illuminate the larger Dutch gender gap in organizational power.

   These differing employment patterns reflect national differences in
social policies. In the USA, policies strongly reward employment (e.g.,
earned income tax credit), and there is little financial support for caring
activities. In the Netherlands, governmental mandates include a
sixteen-week paid maternity leave, normal benefits and hourly wages
for part-time work, and a statutory right to part-time work (Visser et al.
2004). In the USA, there are no such protections, and part-time work is
deskilled compared with full-time work (Hirsch 2005).

   The Dutch model of supportive work–family policies perpetuates
traditional maternalism, with the majority of married women employed

part-time with correspondingly more limited career success than married men (Orloff 2006; Prowse 2005). In contrast, the American model of incentives for employment, relatively unattractive part-time employment options, and lack of social provision for caretaking (e.g., short, often unpaid maternal leaves) fosters women's full-time employment. Women's labor force participation in turn encourages more egalitarian households in which men contribute more childcare and housework (Hook 2006). Consistent with the greater labor-force participation of American than Dutch women, time-diary studies estimate that the minutes per day that Dutch men devote to household work is 116 (1995 estimate) or 117 (2000 estimate), compared with 149 (1998 estimate) or 129 (2003 estimate) for American men (Hook 2006). Also, the US feminist movement has promoted equal employment opportunity, and the nation has implemented a myriad of legal and regulatory decisions that help insure women equal workplace rights (Orloff 2006). Nonetheless, the consistency and amount of paid labor have remained less for American women than men.

A division of labor that cedes more responsibility to men as family providers fosters labor markets that are segregated by sex, with poorer pay and opportunities in female-dominated jobs (England 2005). In fact, more than half of all workers in the USA and the Netherlands would have to switch jobs to produce an equal distribution of men and women in all jobs (Tomaskovic-Devey et al. 2006; Portegijs et al. 2006). However, consistent with the prevalence of part-time paid labor for women in many European nations, occupational sex segregation is generally more extreme in Europe than in the USA (Bridges, 2003).

A different, more subtle argument about human capital is that women are not motivated to seek positions that confer power because they believe that the demands of such positions are incompatible with their family responsibilities. Employed mothers and wives may be content with *mommy track* positions and avoid *fast track* positions. However, on balance, empirical evidence has not supported this claim (Smith 2002). There are two research methods that have tested this self-selection hypothesis: Examination of (a) whether employed women's family responsibilities affect their actual access to authority and (b) what level of aspiration employed women versus men profess in surveys. Studies using the first method test whether employed women differ in organizational power, depending on the amount of their family responsibilities. Specifically, if employed women self-select because of family responsibilities, they should be less well represented in positions of authority if they are married, have children in the home, and have inegalitarian household arrangements in which the husband does little domestic work. Most tests of these predictions have not yielded supportive findings (Smith 2002). For example, a large cross-national study of the USA, Canada, the United Kingdom, Australia, Sweden, Norway, and Japan did not confirm this self-selection hypothesis, except to some degree in Canada (Wright et al. 1995). Other studies have asked employees about their aspirations to reach top positions. For example, a US survey of Fortune 1,000 executives within two or three reporting levels of the CEO found that the men and women reported equal aspiration to reach the CEO job and no effect of the presence of children on the aspirations of women or men (Catalyst 2004). Also, in nationally representative US survey data, although women assigned less importance to promotion than men, this difference disappeared when controlled for location in the opportunity structures of organizations and for past promotions (Cassirer and Reskin 2000). More women than men held jobs that lacked promotion opportunities in the form of, for example, job ladders and regular promotion procedures.

In the Netherlands, the evidence is more mixed. A large study of managers in five Dutch organizations showed that at higher managerial levels the proportion of women with children was considerably lower than the proportion of men with children, and this female–male difference decreased at middle management levels (Fischer et al. 2000). Yet, the same study showed that men and women did not differ in their self-reported career ambition in service organizations, and women reported even greater ambition than men in commercial and industrial organizations. Moreover, men and women did not differ in the reasons they reported for declining a job at a higher career level (e.g., family responsibilities, stress).

In short, the most basic reason for men's greater organizational power implicates their greater responsibility as family providers and women's as homemakers. The effects of this division of labor include women's lesser job experience and consistency of employment, and these work patterns account for a portion of the gender gap in organizational power. Yet, employed women receive substantially smaller gains in authority than employed men for similar human capital investments (see Smith 2002), despite the fact that they generally report equal ambition once job characteristics are controlled. Such findings raise questions about discrimination also limiting women's rise in organizational hierarchies.

Discrimination that limits women's organizational power

To test for discrimination, studies have determined whether employees' sex still predicts wages or promotions even after the effects of work patterns and other human-capital variables are controlled (see Blau and Kahn 2006; Maume 2004). The gender gap that remains after instituting such controls provides an estimate of sex discrimination. These methods almost always have suggested that women have a discriminatory wage and promotion disadvantage compared with men (see Eagly and Carli 2007).

In a different test of discrimination, some researchers have devised experiments in which participants evaluate individual male or female managers or job candidates whose characteristics are held constant except for their sex. Some of these experiments have presented application materials such as résumés to research participants, with either a male name or a female name attached to the materials. In a meta-analysis of forty-nine such experiments, Davison and Burke (2000) found that men were preferred over equivalent women for masculine jobs such as auto salesperson and sales manager for heavy industry (mean $d = 0.34$), and women over men for feminine jobs such as secretary and home economics teacher (mean $d = -0.26$). For gender-integrated jobs such as psychologist and motel desk clerk, men were also preferred over women, although to a somewhat lesser extent than for masculine jobs (mean $d = 0.24$; Davison 2005, personal communication). Men thus had an advantage over equivalent women except in settings traditionally associated with women.

The more positive evaluations that women receive for female-dominated jobs do not confer organizational power on them because, even in female-dominated fields, men are more likely than women to ascend to positions of authority. The quicker promotions of men than women in female-dominated fields such as social work and nursing has been dubbed the *glass escalator* (Williams 1995). Regardless of whether the context is male-dominated or female-dominated, men gain greater organizational power than women (see Yoder 2002).

In short, research provides persuasive evidence that discrimination is one factor accounting for women's lesser power in organizations. Even with equivalent qualifications, women are less likely to be hired, except for traditionally feminine jobs, and they are less likely to be promoted in organizational hierarchies. Yet, to understand how discrimination comes about, we need to take a closer look at organizational processes.

Organizational processes

Although it may seem to many that organizations provide equal advancement opportunities for women and men, their social structure and culture often pose more challenges to women than men. Organizations' structures are inherent in their formal roles, rules, and procedures, and their cultures reside in their tacit rules and norms of conduct. Men's predominance in higher positions promotes structures and cultures that foster men's greater organizational power.

Generally, two dimensions of organizational cultures have been distinguished: task-orientation (or rational goal cultures), which is associated with masculinity in most cultures, and people orientation (or human-relations cultures), which is associated with femininity (e.g., Fischer and Vianen 2004). Masculine, task-oriented cultures emphasize competition, rationality, efficiency, control, hierarchy, an individual view of success, and priority of career advancement over family concerns. The masculine character of many organizations' cultures makes it difficult for women to advance. We review some of the most important of these impediments (see also Eagly and Carli 2007; Fischer and Vianen 2004).

Demands for long hours and relocation

One common feature of masculine organizational culture is a demand for managers' continuous availability. In general, managerial, professional, and technical workers have longer than average work weeks (Jacobs and Gerson 2004). Very long hours can serve as an important qualification for rising to higher positions, especially if organizations focus on inputs rather than the productivity or quality of employees' work. Working nights and weekends can demonstrate commitment to the organization, even when such efforts are not really necessary (Brett and Stroh 2003; Rapoport et al. 2002). In addition to long hours, managers may encounter demands to relocate when higher positions become available in other locations.

Because long hours reduce the number of highly paid workers that organizations must employ, this pattern can be attractive especially during periods of downsizing. However, requiring more work from fewer employees often creates stress (Armstrong-Stassen 2005) and can reduce organizational performance (McElroy et al. 2001). Moreover, long hours can reflect managers' lack of planning and discipline concerning what work really needs to be done and how to organize to accomplish these tasks efficiently.

Demands for relocations and long hours are obviously problematic for employees with substantial family responsibilities. Women especially experience stresses because they are less likely than men to be able to shift domestic responsibilities to a spouse (Davidson and Fielden 1999). In anticipation of such stresses, women in high-status careers tend to forgo or delay childbearing (e.g., Hewlett 2002), and some quit their jobs when they have a child. For example, one US study found that 37 percent of women with very strong educational credentials voluntarily dropped out of employment at some point, compared with 24 percent of similarly qualified men (Hewlett and Luce 2005). Among women with one or more children, this percentage rose to 43 percent. The main reason that these women relinquished employment was for "family time," but for men it was to change careers. In the Netherlands, 11 percent of women who have their first child stop working and 49 percent reduce their hours of paid work. In contrast, men remain working for as many hours as they did before their first child was born (Portegijs et al. 2006).

Implicit masculine values

Masculine values may be revealed at a more implicit level, for example, in the language that is used or the leisure-time activities that are organized. Consistent with men's emphasis on decisive action, masculine organizational culture often features sports and military terminology. Successful activity is termed a *slam-dunk* or *home run* or *batting one thousand*, and good behavior involves *being a team player*. Militaristic language is prominent as well, as in *uphill battle, sneak attack, getting flack*, and *killing the competition*. Expressions common in Dutch management include *conquering the market, striking your enemy a heavy blow*, and prohibitions against *two captains on one ship*.

Masculine values may also be communicated in the recreational activities pursued by workplace colleagues. For example, in the USA,

Wal-Mart middle managers' meetings included visits to strip clubs and Hooters restaurants. An executive retreat was combined with a quail-hunting expedition at Sam Walton's ranch in Texas. To further emphasize the message about masculine culture, one manager received feedback that she would not advance any further at Wal-Mart because she didn't hunt or fish (Featherstone 2004).

In the Netherlands, organizations' formal policies generally emphasize diversity and equal opportunity, even while their informal cultures encourage traditional attitudes about men and women. For instance, norms often foreclose advancement for those who work fewer than thirty-eight hours a week or reject the opportunity to work abroad. The women employed in those firms are reluctant to complain because company policies explicitly support equal opportunity and the male managers believe that gender does not affect opportunities. This system implies that it is merely women's individual life choices that prevent them from moving up the career ladder.

Women are generally less enthusiastic about masculine organizational culture than men are (Van Vianen and Fischer 2002). Yet, the fact that there are women in top positions shows that women are capable of conforming, for example, by prioritizing their careers over their family responsibility, behaving assertively, and learning the terminology of sports and military conquest. In fact, women in top positions have generally acquired masculine attributes and styles of leadership and communication, suggesting that accommodation is the main way for women to advance in masculine organizations (Van Vianen and Fischer 2002). However, this approach can make women feel that they are not authentically expressing their own identities and preferences (Eagly 2005). Alternatively, some women invent nuanced ways of advancing while working to transform masculine cultures so that they become more inclusive (see Meyerson 2001).

Importance of building social capital

Ample empirical evidence has shown that managers' social capital, especially relationships with people in other organizations, fosters their advancement (e.g., Seibert et al. 2001). Such relationships can yield valuable information, access to help and resources, and career sponsorship. It is therefore notable that women generally have less social capital than men (see review by Timberlake 2005).

Women's deficit in social capital exists even though they acknowledge the importance of networking (e.g., Manuel et al. 1999) and on average have better relational skills than men, as shown, for example, on tests of emotional intelligence (e.g., Brackett et al. 2006; Van Rooy et al. 2005). Women's relational skills are often directed to work that has little bearing on advancement (Fletcher 1999). For example, as managers, women are more likely than men to focus on the development and mentoring of followers and attending to their individual needs (Eagly et al. 2003). Fast-track employees instead generally become associated with high-visibility tasks and not with the less visible relational tasks that are nonetheless crucial for the successful completion of organizational projects. Moreover, many of the relational tasks that women undertake are devalued as easy, such as coordination and planning tasks and the collection of information (De Pater et al. 2007). Ironically, by providing the social glue that helps organizations to function smoothly, women may fail to gain important leadership roles.

Women's deficits in social capital follow in part from the fact that much of the networking that builds social capital increases the long work hours that present obstacles to women (and men) with significant family responsibilities. Social capital can flow, for example, from after-dinner drinks with colleagues or weekend golf outings with potential clients and customers. Even during ordinary work hours, informal networking can be difficult for women who are a small minority, with influential networks composed almost entirely of men. In these contexts, women usually have less legitimacy and influence and therefore benefit less than men from participation.

In organizations that are less segregated by gender, women do not necessarily have fewer networking relationships than men. However, women often network with other women and men with other men. All-women networks are nonoptimal for women's advancement because networks populated by men are generally more powerful. Yet, women do experience gains from relationships with other women, especially in terms of social support, role modeling, and information about overcoming discrimination (see Forret and Dougherty 2004; Timberlake 2005).

One of the benefits of social capital is that it facilitates opportunities to gain appropriately demanding assignments, known as *developmental job experiences*. Becoming recognized for solving problems acknowledged as challenging speeds advancement to upper-level management, but social capital is a prerequisite for winning the chance to take on such projects (e.g., McCauley et al. 1994). Given their generally lesser social capital, it is not surprising that women often lack such opportunities (e.g., De Pater and Van Vianen 2006; Lyness and Thompson 2000).

Women's difficulties in obtaining developmental job experiences are compounded by their occupancy of managerial roles that serve staff functions, such as human resources and public relations, rather than line functions, which are more critical to the success of organizations. Given stereotypical norms about which sex is optimal for various types of management, men are more often channeled into line management, with its better opportunities to ascend into senior leadership.

Despite women's difficulties in obtaining demanding assignments, other evidence shows that some women are placed, more often than comparable men, in highly risky positions, a phenomenon labeled the *glass cliff* (Ryan and Haslam 2007). When companies are facing financial downturns and declining performance, executives have a fairly high risk of failure. Companies may be more willing to have female executives take these risks, and women may be more willing to accept such positions, given their lesser prospects for obtaining more desirable positions. Both this glass cliff as well as fewer developmental job experiences deny women access to the "good" assignments that maximize opportunities for showing oneself as a high-potential manager.

Possibilities for reform

There are many innovations that can allow women to achieve greater access to power in organizations. We consider three of the most important reforms: (1) family-friendly work arrangements, (2) more inclusive organizational cultures, and (3) unbiased selection and promotion.

Family-friendly personnel practices

Proposals include upgrading the wages and responsibility of part-time positions and allowing flexible hours in full-time positions. Giving employees with significant parental responsibility extra time to build their credentials for promotion can also be helpful. Other options practiced by some organizations include job sharing, telecommuting, and dependent-childcare options, sometimes including employee-sponsored on-site childcare. A study of large US firms thus showed that such family-friendly human-resource practices increased the number of women in senior management five years later (Dreher 2003). Another worthy proposal is to allow "on-ramps" that provide mothers with opportunities to return to responsible positions after a period out of the workforce (Hewlett and Luce 2005).

Despite the advantages of family-friendly options, these innovations have mixed impact on women's careers if only women take advantage of them. As we showed earlier in this chapter, women's lesser amount and consistency of employment contribute to their lesser career advancement. Therefore, options such as long parental leaves and reduced hours slow the careers of those who take these benefits. In addition, having many more women than men take such benefits can harm the careers of women in general because of the expectation that they will exercise such options. Reluctance thus grows to give women access to more essential managerial roles (Gupta et al. 2006; Mandel and Semyonov 2005).

More inclusive organizational cultures

Organizational cultures could become less masculine through targeted changes. Most important would be the moderation of hours on-the-job for managerial and professional employees. If executives emphasized efficiency and judicious assignments of tasks, new norms could support work hours that hew more closely to a forty-hour week for full-time employees. Also, informal events that often serve as venues for wheeling and dealing could be made family- and women-friendly. For example, Sunday-evening basketball or drinks after work could be discouraged in favor of Sunday-afternoon picnics and visits to amusement parks and cultural institutions. Norms could also support men's as well as women's occasional absences for family responsibilities (e.g., conferences with children's teachers). With progressive leadership, these and other reforms are fully within the reach of contemporary organizations.

Unbiased performance evaluations and recruitment

To lessen the discrimination that can reduce women's career advancement, the evaluation of candidates for promotion should be based on explicit, valid performance evaluations that limit the influence of decision-makers' conscious and unconscious biases. In addition, recruitment from outside and inside of organizations should involve open processes such as publicity or advertising rather than reliance on informal social networks. Such personnel practices increase women's access to management (Gelfand et al. 2005).

Without objective evaluations and open recruiting, various biases likely contaminate personnel decisions, including the tendency of employees to prefer to associate with others who are similar to themselves. People in authority positions tend to favor individuals who are similar to themselves on characteristics such as gender, race, and religion (e.g., Elliott and Smith 2004). Therefore, smaller proportions of women in higher positions lead to smaller numbers of women subsequently hired to fill such positions. These processes, labeled *homosocial reproduction*, perpetuate traditional elites at the tops of organizations (Kanter 1977).

When clear standards are not applied to all candidates, people making hiring or promotion decisions may rely on stereotypes or their personal preferences. These problems are exacerbated by the tendency for people who hold power to stereotype those who are subject to their power, perhaps because their feeling of entitlement fosters inappropriate confidence in simple beliefs about others (Goodwin and Fiske 2001; Keltner et al. 2003). Therefore, monitoring and oversight of personnel decisions are generally necessary to insure fairness. Structures that assign responsibility for opening up positions to all groups (e.g., affirmative-action plans and diversity committees) have proven to be effective in increasing the number of women in management (Kalev et al. 2006).

Procedures that foster equal access to hiring and promotion often exist at lower managerial levels, where objective qualifications such as educational credentials and experience are important. At executive levels, it is far more difficult to design procedures that insure equal access because selection and promotion are based more on observations of visible performances than on easily quantifiable credentials. For example, executives' qualifications are often established in their presentations to boards and committees and the impressions they make on others in negotiations and informal networking (Ishida et al. 2002).

Conclusion

The lesser organizational power of women than men is a persisting pattern in all industrialized countries. We have documented this situation in two nations and revealed its roots in the contemporary division of labor that still cedes more domestic responsibility to women and provider responsibility to men. This semi-traditional division of labor in which both men and women are usually employed, but women with shorter work hours and lesser continuity, disadvantages women for organizational advancement. Also restricting women's rise in many organizations are sex discrimination, unwelcoming masculine organizational culture, and lack of access to powerful male-dominated networks.

We have described some progressive policies that can allow organizations to change from within, but these reforms are likely to have minor impact compared with change in the family division of labor toward equal sharing of providing and domestic work. US data show shifts in this direction as men have gradually devoted more time to housework and childrearing (Bianchi et al. 2006) and, correspondingly, women have gained workplace authority (Eagly and Carli 2007). Despite these shifts, equal sharing of organizational power between men and women remains a somewhat distant goal as does equality in the domestic division of labor.

References

Angrist, J. and Evans, W. N. (1998) Children and their parents' labor supply: Evidence from exogenous variation in family size. *American Economic Review*, 88, 450–477.

Armstrong-Stassen, M. (2005) Coping with downsizing: A comparison of executive-level and middle managers. *International Journal of Stress Management*, 12, 117–141.

Bianchi, S. M., Robinson, J. P., and Milkie, M. A. (2006) *Changing rhythms of American family life*, New York, N.Y.: Russell Sage.

Blau, F. D. and Kahn, L. M. (2006) The gender pay gap: Going, going … but not gone. In F. D. Blau, M. C. Brinton, and D. B. Grusky (Eds.), *The declining significance of gender?* (pp. 37–66), New York, N.Y.: Russell Sage Foundation.

Boelens, L. R. and van Iren, A. M. (1999) *Werk en leven (Work and life)*, The Hague: Elsevier (Ministry of Work and Social Issues).

Brackett, M. A., Rivers, S. E., Shiffman, S., Lerner, N., and Salovey, P. (2006) Relating emotional abilities to social functioning: A comparison of self-report and performance measures of emotional intelligence. *Journal of Personality and Social Psychology*, 91, 780–795.

Brett, J. M. and Stroh, L. K. (2003) Working 61 hours a week: Why do managers do it? *Journal of Applied Psychology*, **81**, 67–78.

Bridges, W. P. (2003) Rethinking gender segregation and gender inequality: Measures and meanings. *Demography*, **40**, 543–568.

Cassirer, N. and Reskin, B. (2000) High hopes: Organizational positions, employment experiences, and women's and men's promotion aspirations. *Work and Occupations*, **27**, 438–463.

Catalyst (2004) *Women and men in US corporate leadership: Same workplace, different realities?* Retrieved March 12, 2007, from www.catalyst. org/files/full/Women%20and%20Men%20in%20US%20Corporate% 20Leadership%20Same%20Workplace,%20Different%20Realities. pdf.

—— (2006a) *2005 Catalyst census of women board directors of the Fortune 500*. Retrieved May 23, 2006, from www.catalyst.org/files/full/2005% 20WBD.pdf.

—— (2006b) *2005 Catalyst census of women corporate officers and top earners of the Fortune 500*. Retrieved September 2, 2006, from www.catalystwomen.org/files/full/2005%20COTE.pdf

Davidson, M. J. and Fielden, S. (1999) Stress and the working women. In G. N. Powell (Ed.), *Handbook of gender and work* (pp. 413–428), Thousand Oaks, Calif.: Sage.

Davison, H. K. and Burke, M. J. (2000) Sex discrimination in simulated employment contexts: A meta-analytic investigation. *Journal of Vocational Behavior*, **56**, 225–248.

Dreher, G. F. (2003) Breaking the glass ceiling: The effects of sex ratios and work-life programs on female leadership at the top. *Human Relations*, **56**, 541–562.

De Pater, I. E. and Van Vianen, A. E. M. (2006) *Gender differences in job challenge: A matter of task preferences or task allocation?* Paper presented at the annual meeting of the Society for Industrial and Organizational Psychology, New York.

De Pater, I. E., Van Vianen, A. E. M., and Fischer (2007) Gender differences in challenging experiences: The role of task choice. Manuscript submitted for publication.

Eagly, A. H. (2005) Achieving relational authenticity in leadership: Does gender matter? *Leadership Quarterly*, **16**, 459–474.

Eagly, A. H. and Carli, L. L. (2007) *Through the labyrinth: The truth about how women become leaders*, Boston, Mass.: Harvard Business School Press.

Eagly, A. H., Johannesen-Schmidt, M. C., and Van Engen, M. L. (2003) Transformational, transactional, and laissez-faire leadership styles: A meta-analysis comparing women and men. *Psychological Bulletin*, **129**, 569–591.

Elliott, J. R. and Smith, R. A. (2004) Race, gender, and workplace power. *American Sociological Review*, **69**, 365–386.

England, P. (2005) Gender inequality in labor markets: The role of motherhood and segregation. *Social Politics*, **12**, 264–288.

European Commission (2006) *Decision-making in the top 50 publicly quoted companies*. Retrieved March 11, 2007, from http://europa. eu.int/comm/employment_social/women_men_stats/out/measures_out438_en.htm

Featherstone, L. (2004) *Selling women short: The landmark battle for workers' rights at Wal-Mart*, New York, N.Y.: Basic Books.

Fischer, A. H. and Van Vianen, E. A. M. (2004) Corporate masculinity. In P. Essed, D. T. Goldberg, and A. L. Kobayashi (Eds.), *A companion to gender studies* (pp. 342–354), Oxford: Blackwell.

Fischer, A. H., Rodriguez Mosquera, P. M., and Rojahn, K. (2000) *Masculiniteit met een feminien gezicht (Masculinity with a female face)*, The Hague: Elsevier (Ministry of Work and Social Issues).

Fletcher, J. K. (1999) *Disappearing acts: Gender, power, and relational practice at work*, Cambridge, Mass.: MIT Press.

Forret, M. L. and Dougherty, T. W. (2004) Networking behaviors and career outcomes: Differences for men and women? *Journal of Organizational Behavior*, **25**, 419–437.

Gelfand, M. J., Raver, J. L., Nishii, L. H., and Schneider, B. (2005) Discrimination in organizations: An organizational level systems perspective. In R. L. Dipboye and A. Colella (Eds.), *Discrimination at work: The psychological and organizational bases* (pp. 89–116), Mahwah, N. J.: Erlbaum.

Goodwin, S. A. and Fiske, S. T. (2001) Power and gender: The double-edged sword of ambivalence. In R. K. Unger (Ed.), *Handbook of the psychology of women and gender* (pp. 358–366), Hoboken, N. J.: Wiley.

Gupta, D., Oaxaca, N., and Smith, N. (2006) Swimming upstream, floating downstream: Comparing women's relative wage progress in the United States and Denmark. *Industrial and Labor Relations Review*, **59**, 243–266.

Hewlett, S. A. (2002) *Creating a life: Professional women and the quest for children*, New York, N.Y.: Talk Miramax Books.

Hewlett, S. A. and Luce, C. B. (2005) Off-ramps and on-ramps: Keeping talented women on the road to success. *Harvard Business Review*, **38** (3), 43–46, 48, 50–54.

Hirsch, B. T. (2005) Why do part-time workers earn less? The role of worker and job skills. *Industrial and Labor Relations Review*, **58**, 525–551.

Hook, J. L. (2006) Care in context: Men's unpaid work in 20 countries 1965–2003. *American Sociological Review*, **71**, 639–660.

Ishida, H., Su, K-H., and Spilerman, S. (2002) Models of career advancement in organizations. *European Sociological Review*, **18**, 179–198.

Jacobs, J. A. and Gerson, K. (2004) *The time divide: Work, family, and gender inequality*, Cambridge, Mass.: Harvard University Press.

Kalev, A., Dobbin, F., and Kelly, E. (2006) Best practices or best guesses? Assessing the efficacy of corporate affirmative action and diversity polities. *American Sociological Review* 71: 589–617.

Kanter, R. M. (1977) *Men and women of the corporation*, New York, N.Y.: Basic Books.

Keltner, D., Gruenfeld, D. H., and Anderson, C. (2003) Power, approach, and inhibition. *Psychological Review*, **110**, 265–284.

Lyness, K. S. and Thompson, D. E. (1997) Above the glass ceiling? A comparison of matched samples of female and male executives. *Journal of Applied Psychology*, **82**, 359–375.

(2000) Climbing the corporate ladder: Do female and male executives follow the same route? *Journal of Applied Psychology*, **85**, 86–101.

Mandel, H. and Semyonov, M. (2005) Family policies, wage structures, and gender gaps: Sources of earnings inequality in 20 countries. *American Sociological Review*, **70**, 949–967.

Manuel, T., Shefte, S., and Swiss, D. J. (1999) *Suiting themselves: Women's leadership styles in today's workplace*, Cambridge, Mass.: Radcliffe Public Policy Institute and the Boston Club.

Maume, D. J. Jr. (2004) Is the glass ceiling a unique form of inequality? Evidence from a random-effects model of managerial attainment. *Work and Occupations*, **31**, 250–274.

McCauley, C. D., Ruderman, M. N., Ohlott, P. J., and Morrow, J. E. (1994) Assessing the developmental components of managerial jobs. *Journal of Applied Psychology*, **79**, 544–560.

McElroy, J. C., Morrow, P. C., and Rude, S. N. (2001) Turnover and organizational performance: A comparative analysis of the effects of voluntary, involuntary, and reduction-in-force turnover. *Journal of Applied Psychology*, **86**, 1294–1299.

Meyerson, D. E. (2001) *Tempered radicals: How people use difference to inspire change at work*, Boston, Mass.: Harvard Business School Press.

Ng, T. W. H., Eby, L. T., Sorensen, K. L., and Feldman, D. C. (2005) Predictors of objective and subjective career success: A meta-analysis. *Personnel Psychology*, **58**, 367–408.

Organisation for Economic Co-operation and Development (2005) *OECD Employment Outlook 2005 (Statistical Annex)* Paris: OECD Publishing. Retrieved February 20, 2007, from www.oecd.org/dataoecd/36/30/35024561.pdf.

Orloff, A. S. (2006) From maternalism to "employment for all": State policies to promote women's employment across the affluent democracies. In J. D. Levy (Ed.), *The state after statism: New state activities in the age of liberalization* (pp. 230–268), Cambridge, Mass.: Harvard University Press.

Portegijs, W., Hermans, B., and Lalta, V. (2006) *Emancipatiemonitor 2006*, The Hague: Sociaal Cultureel Plan Bureau.

Prowse, V. (2005) *How damaging is part-time employment to a woman's occupational prospects?* (IZA Discussion Paper No. 1648), Bonn: Institute for the Study of Labor.

Rapoport, R., Bailyn, L., Fletcher, J. K., and Pruitt, B. H. (2002) *Beyond work-family balance: Advancing gender equity and workplace performance*, San Francisco, Calif.: Jossey-Bass.

Ryan, M. K. and Haslam, S. A. (2007) The glass cliff: Exploring the dynamics surrounding the appointment of women to precarious leadership positions. *Academy of Management Review*, **32**, 549–572.

Seibert, S. E., Kraimer, M. L., and Liden, R. C. (2001) A social capital theory of career success. *Academy of Management Journal*, **44**, 219–237.

Smith, R. A. (2002) Race, gender, and authority in the workplace: Theory and research. *Annual Review of Sociology*, **28**, 509–542.

Timberlake, S. (2005) Social capital and gender in the workplace. *Journal of Management Development*, **24**, 34–44.

Tomaskovic-Devey, D., Zimmer, C., Stainback, K., Robinson, C., Taylor, T., and McTague, T. (2006) Documenting desegregation: Segregation in American workplaces by race, ethnicity, and sex 1966–2003. *American Sociological Review*, **71**, 565–588.

United Nations Development Programme (2006) *Human development report 2006*, New York, N.Y.: Oxford University Press. Retrieved December 15, 2006, from http://hdr.undp.org/reports/global/2005/pdf/ HDR05_HDI.pdf.

US Bureau of Labor Statistics (2006) *Women in the labor force: A databook.* Report 996. Retrieved December 13, 2006, from www.bls.gov/cps/ wlf-databook2006.htm.

Van Rooy, D. L., Alsonso, A., and Viswesvaran, C. (2005) Group differences in emotional intelligence scores: Theoretical and practical implications. *Personality and Individual Differences*, **38**, 689–700.

Van Vianen, A. E. M. and Fischer, A. H. (2002) Illuminating the glass ceiling: The role of organizational culture preferences. *Journal of Occupational and Organizational Psychology*, **75**, 315–337.

Visser, J., Wolthagen, T., Beltzer, R., and Koot-van der Putte, E. (2004) The Netherlands: From atypicality to typicality. In S. Sciarra, P. Davies, and M. Freedland (Eds.), *Employment policy and the regulation of part-time work in the European Union: A comparative analysis* (pp. 190–223), New York, N.Y.: Cambridge University Press.

Williams, C. L. (1995) *Still a man's world: Men who do women's work*, Berkeley, Calif.: University of California Press.

Wright, E. O., Baxter, J., and Birkelund, G. E. (1995) The gender gap in workplace authority: A cross-national study. *American Sociological Review*, 60, 407–435.

Yoder, J. D. (2002) 2001 Division 35 presidential address: Context matters: Understanding tokenism processes and their impact on women's work. *Psychology of Women Quarterly*, 26, 1–8.

PART IV

Power to influence

12 | *Power and the interpersonal influence of leaders*

GARY YUKL

To be effective, a leader must influence people to carry out requests, support proposals, and implement decisions. In large organizations, the effectiveness of most managers depends on influence over superiors and peers as well as influence over subordinates (Kotter 1985). Two types of constructs that have dominated theory and research on interpersonal influence in organizations are power and influence tactics. This chapter will explain how leaders use influence tactics to accomplish their job responsibilities and how their personal and position power can enhance their effectiveness.

Power and influence outcomes

Power has been defined in many different ways, and there is disagreement about the best way to define and measure it. In this chapter, interpersonal power means the potential influence of one person (the "agent") over the attitudes and behavior of one or more other people (the "targets"). This definition emphasizes potential influence rather than influence behavior or outcomes and specified targets rather than general influence in the organization. It is difficult to describe the power of an agent without specifying the target person(s), the influence objectives, and the time period (Yukl 2006). An agent will have more power over some people than over others and more influence for some types of issues than for others. Furthermore, an agent's power may change over time as conditions change or the effects of an agent's decisions become evident (Hollander 1980; Pfeffer 1981).

Outcomes of influence attempts

Power provides potential influence, but overt attempts to exert power do not necessarily result in the agent's intended outcome. To assess the effects of an influence attempt, it is useful to differentiate among three distinct outcomes (Yukl 2006). Commitment occurs when the target person internally agrees with a decision or request from the agent and makes a concerted effort to carry out the request or implement the decision effectively. Compliance occurs when the target is willing to do what the agent asks but is apathetic about it and will make only a minimal effort. Resistance occurs when the target person is opposed to the agent's proposal or request and tries to avoid carrying it out (e.g., by refusing, by making excuses, delaying action, or seeking to have the request changed). Target commitment is usually considered to be the most favorable outcome, but sometimes compliance is all that is needed to accomplish the agent's objectives.

Power and influence outcomes

Most studies on the implications of power for leadership effectiveness find that leader expert and referent power are positively correlated with subordinate satisfaction and performance (Yukl 2006). The results for legitimate, reward, and coercive power are inconsistent, and many of the correlations with criteria of leadership effectiveness are negative or non-significant rather than positive. Overall, the results suggest that effective leaders rely more on expert and referent power to influence subordinates. However, the field survey research probably underestimates the utility of position power, especially when compliance is an acceptable outcome.

Only a few studies have related power to commitment, compliance, and resistance outcomes. Warren (1968) found that expert, referent, and legitimate power were correlated positively with attitudinal commitment by subordinates, whereas reward and coercive power were correlated with behavioral compliance. In a study by Thambain and Gemmill (1974), the primary reason given for compliance was the leader's legitimate power, and reward power was also an important reason for compliance, even though neither type of power was associated with commitment. Yukl and Falbe (1991) found that legitimate power was the most common reason given for compliance with requests from a boss, even though it was not correlated with task commitment.

The consequences of having power depend greatly on how it is used. Effective leaders are likely to use both personal and position power in a subtle, careful fashion that minimizes status differentials and avoids threats to the target person's self esteem. In contrast, leaders who exercise power in an arrogant, manipulative, domineering manner are likely to engender resentment and resistance (Yukl 2006).

Optimal amount of power

It is obvious that leaders need some power to be effective, but the amount of overall power that is necessary for effective leadership and the mix of different types of power are questions that research has only begun to answer. Clearly the optimal amount of power will depend on what needs to be accomplished and on the leader's skill in using what power is available. Less power is needed by someone who has the skills to use power effectively and who recognizes the importance of concentrating on essential objectives. More influence is necessary when major changes are needed, but there is likely to be strong initial opposition to them. In this situation, an agent needs sufficient power to persuade people that change is necessary and desirable, or to actually implement changes to demonstrate they are effective.

In general, a moderate amount of position power seems optimal for most situations (Yukl 2006). Some coercive power is necessary to buttress legitimate and expert power when a manager needs to influence compliance with rules and procedures that are unpopular but necessary to do the work and avoid serious accidents. Likewise, coercive power is needed to restrain or banish rebels and criminals who would otherwise disrupt operations, steal resources, or harm other members. However, too much position power may be as detrimental as too little. A manager with extensive position power may be tempted to rely on it instead of developing personal power and using influence tactics that are likely to elicit target commitment. The idea that power corrupts is especially relevant for position power, but it also applies to personal power. A person with extensive expert and referent power (e.g., charismatic leader) may be tempted to act in ways that will eventually lead to failure (Zaleznik 1970).

Types of proactive influence tactics

Power provides potential influence, but some researchers have been more interested in studying the specific types of behavior used to exercise influence. The type of behavior used in an effort to influence the attitudes and behavior of another person is called an influence tactic.

When a request is clearly legitimate, relevant for the work, and something the target person knows how to do, then it is often possible to gain target compliance by using a simple, polite request. However, when target resistance is more likely, then the agent may need to use proactive influence tactics.

Proactive influence tactics have an immediate task objective, such as getting the target person to carry out a new task, change work procedures, provide assistance on a project, or support a proposed change. Proactive tactics can be differentiated from impression management tactics, which are used to influence how targets view the agent (e.g., friendly, talented, reliable, powerful). However, an agent's choice of proactive tactics can subsequently affect the agent–target relationship and the agent's power.

Proactive influence tactics can be studied with several research methods, including coding of qualitative descriptions of influence behavior (e.g., from critical incidents or diaries), manipulation of influence tactics in laboratory experiments (e.g., with actors, role-play exercises, or scenarios), and manipulation of influence behavior in field experiments (e.g., with feedback and training). The method used most often to study proactive influence tactics is a behavior-description questionnaire. Since 1980, two different questionnaires were developed for survey research on proactive influence tactics.

Profiles of organizational influence strategies

Kipnis, Schmidt, and Wilkinson (1980) collected descriptions of successful and unsuccessful influence attempts, and the researchers analyzed these critical incidents to identify specific types of influence tactics. Based on their findings, the researchers developed a self-report agent questionnaire called the Profiles of Organizational Influence Strategies (POIS) to measure eight influence tactics. Schriesheim and Hinkin (1990) later conducted a factor analysis of the POIS using data from samples of agents who indicated how often they used each type of tactic in upward influence attempts with their boss. The factor analysis provided support for six of the proposed tactics (i.e. rationality, exchange, ingratiation, assertiveness, coalition, and upward appeal), but not for the other two tactics (blocking and sanctions). The revised agent POIS with six tactic scales was tested in a later study which also involved upward influence (Hochwarter et al. 2000). The results provided only limited support for the tactic scales. The scale reliabilities were low for some samples, and some of the fit statistics for the confirmatory factor analysis were outside the acceptable range.

Both the original and revised versions of the agent POIS have been used in many studies on the determinants and consequences of proactive tactics (e.g., Deluga 1988; Schmidt and Kipnis 1984; Thacker and Wayne 1995; Vecchio and Sussmann 1991; Wayne et al. 1997). However, only a few studies (e.g., Erez et al. 1986; Kipnis et al. 1980) used the POIS to measure how the tactics are used by a leader to influence subordinates or peers. As yet there is little evidence that the scales can accurately measure influence behavior with subordinates or peers. One obvious limitation of the POIS is reliance on agent self-reports of influence behavior. Self-reports of behavior are seldom as accurate as ratings of a person's behavior by other people. Another limitation is the failure to include scales for some proactive tactics that the literature on leadership and power suggests are likely to be important for managers and professionals (e.g., consultation, inspirational appeals, legitimating).

Influence behavior questionnaire

Unlike the POIS, the Influence Behavior Questionnaire (IBQ) was developed as a target questionnaire. The early version of the IBQ included scales for six tactics which are similar to ones in the POIS (rational persuasion, exchange, ingratiation, pressure, coalition, and upward appeals), but new items were developed for these scales rather than merely revising agent items from the POIS. The IBQ also included scales to measure four additional tactics (consultation, inspirational appeals, personal appeals, and legitimating). Early validation research provided support for nine of the ten tactics (Yukl and Tracey 1992). The factor analysis for data from target subordinates and peers indicated that upward appeals were viewed as just another form of coalition tactic, so these two scales were combined. The nine-tactic version of the target IBQ was used in several studies on antecedents and consequences of proactive tactics (e.g., Barbuto and Scholl 1999; Gravenhorst and Boonstra 1998; Douglas and Gardner 2004; Yukl and Tracey 1992). The IBQ was later revised and extended to include two additional tactics. Research with surveys, incidents, and lab experiments verified that the eleven tactics are distinct and meaningful for managers and

Table 12.1 Definition of the eleven proactive influence tactics.

Rational persuasion: using logical arguments and factual evidence to show a proposal or request is feasible and relevant for attaining important task objectives.

Apprising: explaining how carrying out a request or supporting a proposal will benefit the target personally or help advance the target's career.

Inspirational appeals: appealing to values and ideals, or seeking to arouse the target's emotions, to gain commitment for a request or proposal.

Consultation: encouraging the target to suggest improvements in a proposal or to help plan an activity or change that requires the target person's support and assistance.

Collaboration: offering to provide relevant resources and assistance if the target will carry out a request or approve a proposed change.

Ingratiation: using praise and flattery before or during an influence attempt, or expressing confidence in the target's ability to carry out a difficult request.

Personal appeals: asking the target to carry out a request or support a proposal out of friendship, or asking for a personal favor before saying what it is.

Exchange: offering an incentive, suggesting an exchange of favors, or indicating the willingness to reciprocate at a later time if the target will do what the agent requests.

Coalition tactics: enlisting the aid of others to persuade the target to do something, or citing the support of others as a reason for the target to agree.

Legitimating tactics: establishing the legitimacy of a request by referring to rules, policies, contracts, prior agreements, or precedent.

Pressure: making demands or threats, using persistent reminders, or checking frequently on compliance in order to influence the target to carry out a request.

professionals (Yukl et al. 2005; Yukl et al. 2008). The eleven proactive tactics are listed and defined in Table 12.1.

Effectiveness of proactive tactics

Yukl and Tracey (1992) proposed a model to predict the outcomes of using different influence tactics. A tactic is more likely to be successful if the target perceives it to be a socially acceptable form of influence behavior, if the agent has sufficient position and personal power to use the tactic, if the tactic has the capability to affect target attitudes about the desirability of the request, if it is used in a skillful way, and if it is used for a request that is legitimate and consistent with target values and needs. The effectiveness of a tactic also depends on the influence objective and the other tactics used in an influence attempt.

Individual tactics

The relative effectiveness of different proactive influence tactics has been examined in several studies (e.g., Yukl et al. 1996; Yukl et al. 2008; Yukl and Tracey 1992; Yukl et al. 2005). The number of studies on outcomes of using the tactics is small, but similar results were found for different research methods. The results suggest that the most effective tactics (called "core tactics") for influencing target commitment are rational persuasion, consultation, collaboration, and inspirational appeals (Yukl 2006).

Exchange and apprising are moderately effective for influencing subordinates and peers, but these tactics are difficult to use for proactive influence attempts with bosses. Both tactics require resources or information that a boss is more likely to possess than a subordinate. Ingratiation is sometimes useful in an influence attempt with a subordinate or peer, but it is likely to appear manipulative when used with a boss. Ingratiation is usually more effective as part of a long-term strategy for building cooperative relations than to gain compliance with an immediate request.

Personal appeals can be useful for influencing a target person with whom the agent has a friendly relationship. However, this tactic is only relevant for certain types of requests (e.g., to get assistance, to get a personal favor, to change a scheduled meeting), and it is more likely to result in target compliance than in commitment. Pressure and legitimating tactics are not likely to result in target commitment, but these tactics are sometimes useful for eliciting compliance, which may be an acceptable outcome for the influence attempt. Coalition tactics are seldom used to influence subordinates, but sometimes they can be effective for influencing a peer or boss to support a change or innovation, especially if the coalition partners use the core tactics.

Overall, the findings in the research are consistent with the proposition that each tactic can be useful in an appropriate situation. Some tactics tend to be more effective than others, but the best tactics do not always result in task commitment and the worst tactics do not always result in resistance. The outcome of any particular influence attempt is affected strongly by other factors in addition to the type of influence tactics used by the agent (e.g., agent power, the influence objective, the perceived importance of the request, the agent–target relationship, cultural values and beliefs about the proper use of the tactics). How a tactic is actually used is another determinant of its effectiveness. For example, a strong form of rational persuasion (e.g., a detailed proposal, elaborate documentation) is more effective than a weak form of rational persuasion (e.g., a brief explanation, an assertion without supporting evidence). Any tactic can result in resistance if it is not used in a skillful manner, or if it is used for a request that is improper or unethical (Yukl 2006).

Tactic combinations

Influence attempts often involve more than one type of proactive influence tactic. To investigate this question requires a method such as critical incidents or experiments, and only a few studies have examined tactic combinations (e.g., Barry and Shapiro 1992; Case et al. 1988; Falbe and Yukl 1992). Nevertheless, some tentative conclusions can be drawn from the available research. The effectiveness of a combination seems to depend in part on the potency of the individual tactics and how compatible they are with each other. Compatible tactics are easy to use together, and they are likely to improve the influence outcome. For example, rational persuasion is a very flexible tactic that is usually compatible with any of the other tactics. Pressure tactics are likely to be incompatible with personal appeals or ingratiation. When multiple tactics are used in the same influence attempt, the effectiveness also depends on how they are sequenced (see Yukl 2006). Knowing how to successfully combine different influence tactics appears to require considerable insight and skill.

Tactic meta-categories

Some researchers have attempted to group the specific tactics into broadly defined meta-categories. One example is the dichotomy between "hard" versus "soft" tactics (e.g., Van Knippenberg and Steensma 2003). Another example is a taxonomy that adds a third meta-category called "rational tactics" (e.g., Deluga 1992; Falbe and

Yukl 1992; Farmer et al. 1997). Sometimes the classification of specific tactics into meta-categories is based entirely on the judgment of the researchers, and they do not always agree as to whether a specific tactic is hard, soft, or rational. Farmer et al. (1997) used confirmatory factor analysis to test competing models for tactic meta-categories, but the results were weak and inconclusive. The researchers only included the six tactics in the revised agent POIS, and the data only involved upward influence. In research with the IBQ that included a wider variety of specific tactics and target ratings by subordinates and peers as well as bosses, a two- or three-factor model did not get much support (Yukl et al. 2005).

Most researchers who use the hard versus soft meta-categories do not provide a clear rationale for them. Each meta-category should be firmly grounded in a theoretical framework involving different influence processes or mediated effects. Studies on the effects of soft versus hard tactics usually find that only the soft tactics are related to favorable outcomes such as target commitment or satisfaction with the agent. One possible explanation for this finding is that soft tactics involve intrinsic motivation and hard tactics involve extrinsic motivation. Another possible explanation is that soft tactics increase target empowerment and hard tactics reduce it. The two explanations are not mutually exclusive, and to date there has been only a limited effort to verify them.

Meta-categories have several limitations (Yukl and Chavez 2002). When the component tactics in a meta-category are not all related to outcomes (or antecedents) in the same way, and analyses are conducted only for the meta-categories, then these differences will be obscured. The researchers who have used meta-categories seldom report the results for the specific tactics or check to determine if results are consistent for tactics in the same meta-category. For example, exchange and pressure are both regarded as hard tactics by some researchers, but they have somewhat different consequences. Another limitation is that several of the proactive tactics have both harder and softer forms, and this diversity within the tactics is ignored when the tactics are classified simply as either hard or soft. For example, rational persuasion can be done in a very assertive way (e.g., challenging the target's information or reasons for resisting), or in a softer way (e.g., presenting information about different options and letting the target draw the logical conclusion about which is the best one).

Influencer types

Some researchers have advocated that the profile of scores for different tactics can be used to classify people into different influencer types. Kipnis and Schmidt (1988) conducted a cluster analysis of their data and found four influencer types that they labeled shotgun, bystander, tactician, and ingratiator. Farmer and Maslyn (1999) later conducted a partial replication of the study that included some measures of agent attributes that may help to explain the profiles.

The idea that there are different influencer types is worth exploring, but these two studies both have serious limitations (Yukl and Chavez 2002). The researchers failed to rule out the possibility that the profiles indicated by the cluster analysis merely reflect different response biases. The "shotgun" managers had high scores on all tactics, whereas the "bystander" managers had low scores on all tactics. The shotgun profile may be an artifact of a respondent bias to use high scores in ratings on questionnaires involving power and influence, whereas the bystander profile may reflect a bias to use low scores. The credibility of this alternate interpretation is supported by a consistent pattern of scores for these two influencer types on some other self-report measures used by Farmer and Maslyn (1999), such as the perceived power of the boss and the perceived level of organizational politics.

The executives classified as tacticians by Kipnis and Schmidt (1988) used rational tactics more than the other tactics, and they were more successful than executives with other tactic profiles (as indicated by performance ratings and salary levels). However, it is not clear what the tactician profile really means. Tacticians were the only people who reported that they used rational persuasion more than any of the other tactics, but an alternative interpretation of this finding is that they have more self-awareness about their influence behavior. Rational persuasion is easier to use than the other tactics for influencing bosses, especially when there is a good relationship (tacticians reported the highest LMX scores). Since other tactics that can be effective for upward influence attempts were not included in the two studies, the tactician profile may tell us less about influence behavior than about the agent's interpersonal skills. Finally, with regard to the ingratiator profile, Farmer and Maslyn (1999) found it was not stable and was the most difficult one to interpret.

The two studies on types of influencers did not adequately evaluate the construct validity and incremental utility for each tactic profile that was identified. To explore the meaning of the profiles would require research with a broader range of tactics, more accurate measures of influence behavior (e.g., use target ratings in addition to self-ratings), and influence attempts with subordinates and peers as well as bosses. The research should include relevant measures of agent traits, values, and skills that can explain the reason for different tactic profiles. It is essential to verify that the typology can accurately classify most agents, and the researchers should demonstrate that the typology accounts for unique variance in outcomes beyond what could be explained by using individual tactics as predictors.

Power and influence behavior

Research suggests that power and influence behavior are distinct constructs (Hinkin and Schriesheim 1990; Littlepage et al. 1993; Yukl et al. 1996). However, the relationship between specific forms of power, specific influence behaviors, and influence outcomes is not very well understood. Yukl (2006) proposed that power can have different types of effects, and they are not mutually exclusive.

Power can influence the choice of tactics

Some tactics require a particular type of power to be effective, and a leader who has this type of power is more likely to use these tactics. For example, exchange tactics require reward power, which provides an agent with something of value to exchange with the target person. Rational persuasion is more likely to be used when the agent has the knowledge necessary to explain why a request is important and feasible (Yukl and Tracey 1992). The choice of tactics also depends on the relative power of the agent and target. Hard forms of pressure are less likely to be used with a target person who has more position power than the agent (Somech and Drach-Zahvy 2002).

Power can enhance the effectiveness of tactics

Power can be a moderator variable if it enhances or diminishes the effectiveness of proactive influence tactics. This moderator effect is most likely to occur for a type of power directly relevant to the tactics used in an influence attempt. For example, expert power and information power probably moderate the effect of rational persuasion. Reward power probably moderates the effect of exchange tactics. It is also possible for agent power to enhance the success of an influence tactic for which the power is not directly relevant. For example, an agent with strong referent power may be more successful when using rational persuasion or consultation to gain support for a proposal.

Effects of power when there is no overt influence attempt

It is also likely that agent power can influence the target person's attitudes and behavior even when the agent does not make any overt influence attempt. For example, people are likely to act more deferentially and cooperatively toward someone who has high position power, because they realize the person can affect their career and they do not want to risk the person's displeasure. In another example, people are more likely to imitate the behavior of someone with high referent power (e.g., celebrity entertainer, religious leader), even if the agent did not intend nor desire this outcome.

Influence behavior can affect perceived power

An agent's choice of proactive influence tactics can affect target perception of agent power. For example, an agent's use of rational persuasion in support of a proposed change may result in the target person having a stronger appreciation of the agent's expertise if events verify that the agent's claims and predictions were accurate. Research shows that the proactive tactics can affect the quality of the agent–target relationship (and referent power). For example, tactics such as ingratiation, consultation, and collaboration are likely to improve the relationship, whereas frequent use of pressure and legitimating tactics are likely to undermine it (Yukl and Michel 2006). Target perception of agent power can be affected also by the agent's use of impression management tactics (Ammeter et al. 2002).

Summary and research suggestions

Power is the capacity to influence the attitudes and behavior of other people in the desired direction. Research on the use of different forms of power suggests that effective leaders rely more on personal power than on position power. The amount of position power necessary for leader effectiveness depends on the nature of the organization, task, and subordinates. A moderate amount of power may be optimal for most situations.

Influence attempts usually involve proactive influence tactics. The four core tactics (rational persuasion, consultation, collaboration, and inspirational appeals) are the ones most likely to result in target commitment. The other seven tactics are more likely to elicit compliance than commitment, but they are often useful for supplementing the core tactics. Any tactic can elicit resistance if it is inappropriate for the influence objective and situation or it is not used in a skillful, ethical way.

Power and influence behavior can be regarded as separate constructs, but they are interrelated in complex ways. Both constructs are necessary to understand interpersonal influence in organizations. Power can affect an agent's choice of proactive tactics, enhance the effects of tactics used by an agent, or influence the target person even when the agent does not make an overt influence attempt. Over time an agent's influence behavior can subsequently affect target perception of the agent's power.

Social scientists have made good progress in learning about power and influence tactics, but more research is needed on the likely interactions among different forms of power, on the effects of combining different influence tactics, on the joint effects of power and influence tactics, and on the conditions that facilitate the effective use of influence tactics. Future research should also include more effort to understand the underlying psychological processes that can explain the effects of power and influence (e.g., Elangovan and Xie 1999; Farmer and Aguinis 2005). Cross-cultural differences in values relevant to power and influence are another promising area of research (e.g., Kennedy et al. 2003). More research is needed on the way people use influence tactics to resist unwanted influence attempts (e.g., Tepper et al. 1998; Yukl et al. 2003). Finally, there is a need for more theory and research to bridge the gaps between the power/ influence literature and other subjects that involve influence processes, such as leadership, motivation, job satisfaction and stress, negotiations, conflict resolution, group decisions, organizational change, and organizational governance.

References

Ammeter, A. P., Douglas, C., Gardner, W. L., Hochwarter, W. A., and Ferris, G. R. (2002) Toward a political theory of leadership. *Leadership Quarterly*, **13**, 751–796.

Barbuto, J. E. Jr. and Scholl, R. W. (1999) Leaders' motivation and perception of followers' motivation as predictors of influence tactics used. *Psychological Reports*, **84**, 1087–1098.

Barry, B. and Shapiro, D. L. (1992) Influence tactics in combination: The interactive effects of soft versus hard tactics and rational exchange. *Journal of Applied Social Psychology*, **22**, 1429–1441.

Case, T., Dosier, L., Murkinson, G., and Keys, B. (1988) How managers influence superiors: A study of upward influence tactics. *Leadership and Organizational Development Journal*, **9** (4), 25–31.

Deluga, R. J. (1988) Relationship of transformational and transactional leadership with employee influencing strategies. *Group and Organization Studies*, **13** (4), 456–467.

(1992) The relationship of subordinate upward influencing behavior with impression management characteristics. *Journal of Applied Social Psychology*, **21**, 1145–1160.

Douglas, C. and Gardner, W. L. (2004) Transition to self-directed work teams: Implications of transition time and self-monitoring for managers' use of influence tactics. *Journal of Organizational Behavior*, **25**, 47–65.

Elangovan, A. R. and Xie, J. L (1999) Effects of perceived power of supervisor on subordinate stress and motivation: The moderating role of subordinate characteristics. *Journal of Organizational Behavior*, **20**, 359–373.

Erez, M., Rim, Y., and Keider, I. (1986) The two sides of the tactics of influence: Agent vs. target. *Journal of Occupational Psychology*, **59**, 25–39.

Falbe, C. M. and Yukl, G. (1992) Consequences to managers of using single influence tactics and combinations of tactics. *Academy of Management Journal*, **354**, 638–653.

Farmer, S. M. and Aguinis, H. (2005) Accounting for subordinate perceptions of supervisory power: An identity-dependence model. *Journal of Applied Psychology*, **90** (6), 1069–1083.

Farmer, S. M. and Maslyn, J. M. (1999) Why are styles of upward influence neglected? *Journal of Management*, **25**, 653–682.

Farmer, S. M., Maslyn, J. M., Fedor, D. B., and Goodman, J. S. (1997) Putting upward influence strategies in context. *Journal of Organizational Behavior*, **18**, 12–42.

French, J. and Raven, B. H. (1959) The bases of social power. In D. Cartwright (Ed.), *Studies of social power* (pp. 150–167), Ann Arbor, Mich.: Institute for Social Research.

Gravenhorst, K. M. and Boonstra, J. J. (1998) The use of influence tactics in constructive change processes. *European Journal of Work and Organizational Psychology*, 7, 179–197.

Hinkin, T. R. and Schriesheim, C. A. (1989) Development and application of new scales to measure the French and Raven bases of social power. *Journal of Applied Psychology*, 74, 561–567.

 (1990) Relationships between subordinate perceptions of supervisor influence tactics and attributed bases of supervisory power. *Human Relations*, 43, 221–237.

Hochwarter, W. A., Harrison, A. W., Ferris, G. R., Perrewe, P. L., and Ralston, D. A. (2000) A re-examination of Schriesheim and Hinkin's (1990) measure of upward influence. *Educational and Psychological Measurement*, 60 (5), 751–771.

Hollander, E. P. (1980) Leadership and social exchange processes. In K. Gergen, M. S. Greenberg, and R. H. Willis (Eds.), *Social exchange: Advances in theory and research* (pp. 343–354), New York, N.Y.: Plenum Press.

Kennedy, J., Fu, P. P., and Yukl, G. (2003) Influence tactics across twelve cultures. In W. Mobley and P. Dorfman (Eds.), *Advances in global leadership* (Vol. III, pp. 127–148), JAI Press.

Kipnis, D. and Schmidt, S. M. (1988) Upward influence styles: Relationship with performance evaluations, salary, and stress. *Administrative Science Quarterly*, 33, 528–542.

Kipnis, D. Schmidt, S. M., and Wilkinson, I. (1980) Intra-organizational influence tactics: Explorations in getting one's way. *Journal of Applied Psychology*, 65, 440–452.

Kotter, J. P. (1985) *Power and influence: Beyond formal authority*, New York, N.Y.: Free Press.

Kuhn, A. (1963) *The study of society: A unified approach*, Homewood, Ill.: Irwin.

Littlepage, G. E., Van Hein, K. M., and Janiec, L. L. (1993) Evaluation and comparison of three instruments designed to measure organizational power and influence tactics. *Journal of Applied Social Psychology*, 23 (2), 107–125.

Pfeffer, J. (1981) *Power in organizations*, Marshfield, Mass.: Pittman.

Schmidt, S. M. and Kipnis, D. (1984) Manager's pursuit of individual and organizational goals. *Human Relations*, 37, 781–794.

Schriesheim, C. A. and Hinkin, T. R. (1990) Influence tactics used by subordinates: A theoretical and empirical analysis and refinement of the

Kipnis, Schmidt, and Wilkinson subscales. *Journal of Applied Psychology*, 75, 246–257.

Schriesheim, C. A., Hinkin, T. R., and Podsakoff, P. M. (1991) Can ipsative and single-item measures produce erroneous results in field studies of French and Raven's five bases of power? An empirical examination. *Journal of Applied Psychology*, 76, 106–114.

Somech, A. and Drach-Zahavy, A. (2002) Relative power and influence strategy: The effects of agent/target organizational power on superiors' choice of influence strategies. *Journal of Organizational Behavior*, 23 (2), 167–179.

Tepper, B. J., Eisenbach, R. J., Kirby, S. L., and Potter, P. W. (1998) Test of a justice-based model of subordinates' resistance to downward influence attempts. *Group and Organization Management*, 23, 144–160.

Thacker, R. A. and Wayne, S. J. (1995) An examination of the relationship between upward influence tactics and assessments of promotability. *Journal of Management*, 21, 739–756.

Thambain, H. J. and Gemmill, G. R. (1974) Influence styles of project managers: Some project performance correlates. *Academy of Management Journal*, 17, 216–224.

Van Knippenberg, B. and Steensma. H. (2003) Future interaction expectation and the use of soft and hard influence tactics. *Applied Psychology: An International Review*, 52 (1), 55–67.

Vecchio, R. P. and Sussmann, M. (1991) Choice of influence tactics: Individual and organizational determinants. *Journal of Organizational Behavior*, 12, 73–80.

Warren, D. L. (1968) Power, visibility, and conformity in formal organizations. *American Sociological Review*, 6, 951–970.

Wayne, S. J., Liden, R., Graef, I., and Ferris, G. (1997) The role of upward influence tactics in human resource decisions. *Personnel Psychology*, 50, 979–1006.

Yukl, G. (2006) *Leadership in organizations*, 6th edn, Upper Saddle River, N. J.: Prentice Hall.

Yukl, G. and Chavez, C. (2002) Influence tactics and leader effectiveness. In L. Neider and C. Schriesheim (Eds.), *Leadership: Research in Management* (Vol. II, pp. 139–165), Greenwich, Conn.: Information Age Publishing.

Yukl, G., Chavez, C., and Seifert, C. F. (2005) Assessing the construct validity and utility of two new influence tactics. *Journal of Organizational Behavior*, 26 (6), 705–725.

Yukl, G. and Falbe, C. M. (1991) The importance of different power sources in downward and lateral relations. *Journal of Applied Psychology*, 76, 416–423.

Yukl, G., Fu, P. P., and McDonald, R. (2003) Cross-cultural differences in perceived effectiveness of influence tactics for initiating or resisting change. *Applied Psychology: An International Review*, 52, 68–82.

Yukl, G., Kim, H., and Falbe, C. M. (1996) Antecedents of influence outcomes. *Journal of Applied Psychology*, 81, 309–317.

Yukl, G. and Michel, J. (2006) Proactive influence tactics and leader-member exchange. In C. A. Schriesheim and L. Neider (Eds.), *Power and influence in organizations: Research in Management* (pp. 87–103), Greenwich, Conn.: Information Age Publishing.

Yukl, G., Seifert, C., and Chavez, C. (2008) Validation of the extended influence behavior questionnaire. *Leadership Quarterly*, 19 (5), 609–621.

Yukl, G. and Tracey B (1992) Consequences of influence tactics used with subordinates, peers, and the boss. *Journal of Applied Psychology*, 77, 525–535.

Zaleznik, A. (1970) Power and politics in organizational life. *Harvard Business Review*, May–June, 47–60.

13 | Bases of leader power and effectiveness

M. AFZALUR RAHIM

Power is certainly one of the major areas of scientific investigation in organizational behavior and organization theory. The phenomena of social power are pervasive in all groups, organizations, and societies. In an organizational setting, the process of exercising power serves as one of the key characteristics which define the relationship between a supervisor and a subordinate (Pfeffer 1992; Yukl 2006; see also Raven et al. 1998). Acquisition, maintenance, and use of the right types of power are essential for effective leadership.

Power can be defined as the ability of one party to change or control the behavior, attitudes, opinions, objectives, needs, and values of another party (Rahim 1989). Raven et al. (1998: 307) provided a complimentary definition of social power as the "resources one person has available so that he or she can influence another to do what that person would not have done otherwise." These definitions imply that the theory of power for this chapter is limited to interpersonal influence, i.e. the influence of one individual (leader) over another individual (follower). That is, it deals with the interpersonal and not the structural and situational sources of power. The reason behind this restriction is that it is not easily possible to investigate both sources in one chapter. It should be noted that power possessed by a supervisor is important to influence not only subordinates, but also colleagues, supervisors, and people outside the organization.

Power bases differ from *influence attempts* as the former is associated with the capacity to use power and the latter with the actual use of power. Compliance with the wishes of a supervisor is a function of the power possessed as well as power used by a supervisor.

Several classifications of leader or supervisory power have been set forth, but the bases of power taxonomy suggested by French and Raven (1959), coercive, reward, legitimate, expert, and referent, still appears to be fairly representative and popular in application. This five-category power nomenclature has dominated the conceptualization of interpersonal sources of power for nearly five decades. There were attempts to expand this set to include "information" and other power bases, but Gaski (1986: 62) has argued that, "these alleged power sources appear to be already captured by the French and Raven framework." Aguinis et al. (1996), Hinkin and Schriesheim (1989), Pearce and Robinson (1987), Rahim (1988), and Stahelski, Frost, and Patchen (1989) provided empirical evidence of this framework.

The objective of this chapter is to review the diverse literature in order to develop guidelines for enabling leaders to acquire, maintain, and use power bases to effectively influence not only subordinates, but also colleagues, supervisors, and people outside the organization. This was done by reviewing the nature of these power bases, their measures, and how they influence each other and criterion variables, such as compliance with supervisor's wishes, commitment, styles of handling conflict with supervisor, and job performance in the American and cross-cultural contexts.

French and Raven power bases

As discussed by French and Raven (1959), the five types of social power are as follows:

1. Coercive power.
2. Reward power.
3. Legitimate power.
4. Expert power.
5. Referent power.

Coercive power

Coercive power is based on a subordinate's perception that their supervisor has the ability to punish them if they fail to conform to the influence attempt. Firing, suspending, ridiculing, demoting, or reprimanding a subordinate are common ways of using coercive power by a supervisor. In other words, coercive power is a function of the perception of subordinates of the extent to which their supervisors can inflict punishment for undesired behavior.

Reward power

Reward power is based on the perception of subordinates that their supervisor can reward them for desired behavior. Supervisors often use pay raises, promotions, bonuses, or recognition to exert reward power over their subordinates. To be effective, subordinates must value the incentives provided and that the supervisors are able to provide these incentives.

Whereas coercive power is associated with the capacity to inflict punishment for undesirable behavior, reward power is associated with the ability to provide positive inducements for desirable behavior. In other words, reward power can be considered as the flip side of coercive power. Although these are considered two different power bases, one may consider them as two opposite ends of a continuum.

Legitimate power

This power is possibly the most complex of those presented here. It is based on the internalized values of subordinates which dictate that the supervisor has the right to prescribe and control their behavior and they have the obligation to accept the influence. The power is vested in the rights, duties, and responsibilities of the position, not the person who holds position.

Expert power

Expert power is based on the subordinates' belief that their supervisor has adequate professional experience, training, special expertise, and access to knowledge. Accountants, marketing researchers, IT specialists, and engineers may exert significant influence on their subordinates because of their specialized skills.

Referent power

Referent power is based on the desire of subordinates to identify and associate with their supervisor. Identification is the feeling of oneness of a subordinate with their supervisor. Here the control is dependent upon the supervisor's charisma or personal magnetism to attract subordinates to them so that they follow their leadership.

Information power

Raven (1965) expanded the original five-category French and Raven taxonomy by adding another power base: *informational power*. This is associated with one's access to information which is not public knowledge, but which is needed by employees to perform their job adequately. For example, a secretary to a senior executive may have this power. He or she may have access to the information and ability to control the flow of information to and from the senior executive.

Position and personal power bases

Coercive, reward, legitimate, and information power bases are associated with the position that a supervisor holds in an organization. These power bases together constitute the position power of an organization member. The remaining two power bases are associated with a person not a position incumbent. Individuals acquire these power bases through their own effort and together they are called personal power. Rahim (1988) and Yukl and Falbe (1991) provided evidence of factorial independence of the position and personal power bases.

Extension of French and Raven power bases

Raven (1992, 1993) revised and expanded the original taxonomy of power bases and created a power–interaction model of interpersonal influence. This model includes two forms of each of the five original power bases and an informational power base. Raven et al. (1998) designed a forty-four-item instrument (Interpersonal Power Inventory) to measure these eleven power bases. A factor analysis of the mean scores of the eleven power bases resulted in two factors: "harsh" or "strong" bases (personal coercive, impersonal reward, legitimate reciprocity, personal reward, impersonal coercive, legitimate equity) and "soft" or "weak" bases (expert, referent, informational, legitimate dependence, legitimate position).

Further descriptions of these power bases are provided by Raven (1993) and Raven and his colleagues (Erchul et al. 2004; Erchul et al. 2001). Although studies generally conclude that a soft power base is more effective in inducing compliance among subordinates than a harsh power base, a study by Schwarzwald et al. (2001) with police officers who worked with transformational captains reported greater willingness to comply with both harsh and soft power bases than their colleagues who worked with low transformational captains.

Other power bases

Other power bases have been suggested by scholars from time to time, but these conceptualizations did not gain prominence in theory and research. These are as follows:

1. **Affiliation or connection power.** Leaders acquire this power from their association with influential individuals inside or outside the organization. In other words, it is associated with the attributes of the individuals with whom the leader is connected and is probably a source of referent power (Bielous 1995; Benfari et al. 1986).
2. **Credibility power.** This source of power is associated with one's integrity, character, and truthfulness. Employees are more likely to be persuaded by a supervisor with high credibility than a supervisor with little or no credibility. Nesler et al. (1993) suggested and provided evidence for considering credibility as an additional source of power.
3. **Ecological power.** Yukl (2006) suggests another source of power which is associated with control over work design, technology, and physical work environment. This provides an ability to exert indirect influence on employees.
4. **Persuasiveness power.** This is another variation of referent power and is associated with persuasion skills or one's ability to reason effectively (i.e. rational problem solving skills) with others (Yukl and Van Fleet 1992).
5. **Prestige power.** Probably this is another variation of referent power and is associated with the status, esteem, or personal reputation of leaders in organizations (Finkelstein 1992).

Measurement

The development and refinement of the theory of supervisory power has been plagued by measurement and analytic shortcomings. A number of early studies used single-item measures to rank the importance of French–Raven power bases as reasons for compliance with supervisor's wishes (Bachman et al. 1966; Student 1968). These measures had inadequate psychometric properties and, as a result, findings from these studies are questionable (Podsakoff and Schriesheim 1985).

Raven et al. (1998) designed a forty-four-item instrument to measure their expanded eleven-category power bases. After dropping one item from each power category as "some of the items did not hang together" the authors factor-analyzed the means of the eleven indexes of power bases which resulted in two factors: hard and soft power bases. It is not clear why the authors did not use standard practice for instrument development which would involve factor analysis of the forty-four items.

Several measures of power bases are now available with reported psychometric properties and may be used in future studies (Frost and Stahelski 1988; Hinkin and Schriesheim 1989; Pearce and Robinson 1987; Rahim 1988; Yukl and Falbe 1991). Rahim and Magner's study (1996) with three US ($n = 1,474$) and two Bangladesh and South Korean ($n = 978$) samples provided support for the convergent and discriminant validities for the Rahim Leader Power Inventory (Rahim 1988) and the invariance of factor pattern and factor loadings across four organizational levels. This and other studies (Hess and Wagner 1999; Lam 1997) support the construct validity of the instrument. Further studies are needed to gain better understanding of the psychometric properties of the remaining instruments. Data from cross-cultural studies will be of great value.

Yukl (2006: 160) suggests that the findings from the power studies "may be biased due to attributions, social desirability, and stereotypes." However, these problems are not unique to the studies on power as any survey instrument will have some of these shortcomings. In any field study on power, attempts should be made to control these biases. Three instruments designed by Hinkin and Schriesheim, Rahim, and Yukl and Falbe discussed in the preceding paragraph have strong psychometric properties and can be used in future studies.

Interdependence among power bases

The bases of leader power are interdependent and are often used in combination. For example, giving a reward by a supervisor may be attributed to his or her referent power. Raven (1992; see also Yukl 2006) rightly suggested the need for studying how certain power bases influence the existence and use of the remaining power bases. Greene and Podsakoff's field experiment (1981) indicates that a change in the perception of reward power base may affect the perception of coercive, legitimate, and referent power bases but not expert power base. These interrelationships should be explained so that practitioners can acquire and use appropriate power bases to improve their subordinates' job performance and satisfaction. Knowing how power bases influence each other is important as each power base may influence outcomes, not only directly but also through the mediation of its effects on other sources of power (Gaski 1986: 63). It is possible that the position power base influences criterion variables through the mediation of the personal power base. Stated in another way, the position power base influences the personal power base, which, in turn, influences criterion variables. Support for this relationship can be found from Gaski's study of channels of distribution (1986) which reported positive relationships of reward to expert and referent power bases. Similar relationships were reported by Carson et al. (1993), Rahim and Psenicka (1996), and Munduate and Dorado (1998). The studies by Carson et al. and Rahim and Psenicka found positive relationships of legitimate power base to expert and referent power bases. This makes sense, as supervisors who use their legitimate power base may be perceived by their subordinates as competent as well as friendly, considerate, and fair.

Previous studies found that the expert and referent power bases were significantly correlated. Carson et al.'s meta-analysis of the power bases and outcomes (1993), Munduate and Dorado's study with seventy-eight Spanish subjects (1998), and Rahim and Psenicka's study (1996) with 578 employees found positive relationship of expert to referent power base. One possible explanation of this is that subordinates like to identify and associate with a supervisor who possesses expert power. Furthermore, these studies reported that the reverse influence (i.e. referent power influencing expert power) is unlikely to happen. This is very similar to the influence of expert power on the interpersonal attraction of subordinates (Aguinis et al. 1996). In other words, the perception of expert power positively influences the perception of referent power.

Mediating effects of power bases

Several studies indicate that coercive power is generally ineffective in influencing individual outcomes (Podsakoff et al. 1982; Rahim 1989). Studies by Munduate and Dorado (1998) and Rahim and Psenicka (1996), which used structural equations models, indicate that coercive power negatively influences individual outcomes, such as workgroup commitment through the mediation of the expert and referent power bases.

Mossholder et al. (1998) conducted a field study that investigated the mediating effects of procedural justice on the relationships of power bases to job satisfaction and organizational commitment. The study reported consistent mediation effects of justice on the relationships of the coercive, expert, and referent power bases to satisfaction and commitment. Putting it in another way, coercive, expert, and referent power bases influence procedural justice, which in turn, influences the criterion variables. The mediating effects of justice associated with reward and legitimate power bases were not significant.

Correlates of power bases

Oyster (1992) conducted an interesting study on women executives' perception of the power bases used by "best" and "worst" bosses. Results show that male bosses were more likely than female bosses to be identified as the worst bosses, but females and males were equally likely to be identified as the best bosses. The best bosses used more reward, informational, expert, and referent and less coercive and legitimate power bases than the worst bosses. The following review shows that reward, expert, and referent power bases which are used more by the best bosses than worst bosses are better predictors of criterion variables.

Compliance

Ideally, a criterion variable for a study on power would be one that most directly linked to the outcome of power use. The most appropriate criterion measure to use, then, would be some measure of followers' compliance with leaders' influence attempts. Early studies on French and Raven's power typology frequently touched upon subordinates' compliance with supervisors' wishes and effectiveness in relation to the supervisors' particular power bases (Bachman 1968; Bachman et al. 1968; Bachman et al. 1966; Ivancevich 1970; Student 1968). The consensus among these studies was that subordinates perceive a coercive power base as a weak reason for compliance with supervisors' wishes. Reward and legitimate power bases were considered important by the subordinates but they showed no clear relationship with compliance. Expert power base and, in most cases, referent power base consistently correlated with compliance. This lack of consistent relationships between power bases and compliance may be partly attributed to the measurement and sampling deficiencies discussed before.

Studies by Dunne et al. (1978) and Thamhain and Gemmill (1974) indicated that expertise, professional challenge, and formal authority were important reasons for compliance with the requests of project managers. These studies strongly suggested that legitimate power was effective in inducing compliance. In a major study, Warren (1968) found that the use of five types of power by principals was positively associated with total conformity (behavioral and attitudinal) of teachers. The rank-order correlation between referent power and conformity was the highest. Rahim and Afza's study (1993) with 308 US accountants showed that the expert and referent power bases were positively associated with attitudinal compliance, but legitimate and referent power bases were positively associated with behavioral compliance. This study also shows that the expert and referent power bases were negatively associated with propensity to leave a job.

A study by Rahim et al. (1994) with 459 managers in the US and 625 managers in South Korea found that the legitimate, expert, and referent power bases were positively associated with compliance in the US In South Korea, legitimate, referent, and reward power bases were associated with compliance. It is not clear why expert power base was not associated with compliance. One can speculate why reward power is associated with compliance in South Korea and not the US In a collectivistic culture like South Korea, the reward allocation rule is more likely to follow the equality norm rather than the equity norm (Kim et al. 1990). Since rewards are allocated to group members more or less equally under the equality norm, a supervisor's reward power base in a dyadic relation may be seen as a potential source of an incremental influence for gaining compliance and satisfaction with supervision. However, this is speculative and can only be validated by further comparative research on the power bases.

Satisfaction with work and supervision

Satisfaction with work and supervision are important criterion variables for the study of power. This is because one of the principal reasons for the possession and/or use of power is to keep the subordinates satisfied.

A study by Busch (1980) indicated that expert and referent power bases were positively related to satisfaction with supervision of employees. Coercive power base was negatively but not consistently related to their satisfaction with supervision. Reward and legitimate power bases were not consistently related to satisfaction with supervision. This study used a modified version of the single-item instrument designed by Student (1968). Earlier studies on the power bases and satisfaction with work found similar relationships (Bachman 1968; Bachman et al. 1966; Bachman et al. 1968; Burke and Wilcox 1971). Low reliabilities of the power instruments used in the above studies may have attenuated relationships between the power bases and satisfaction with work and supervision.

Studies on leadership by Sims and Szilagyi (1975), Keller and Szilagyi (1976), and Podsakoff et al. (1982) found that performance-contingent reward behavior of the leader was positively correlated with satisfaction with supervision. But the performance-contingent punishment behavior of the leader had no effects on the satisfaction with supervision. Rahim and Afza's (1993) study showed that referent power base was positively associated with satisfaction with supervision among accountants. Another study with 476 managers in the US shows that legitimate power was negatively and expert and referent power bases were positively associated with satisfaction with supervision (Rahim 1989).

A study by Rahim et al. (1994) reported that legitimate power was negatively associated with satisfaction with supervision in the USA and South Korea. Referent power base in the USA and reward, expert, and referent power bases in South Korea were positively associated with satisfaction with supervision.

Organizational commitment

There is great interest among scholars to investigate employee commitment because it is generally viewed as a positive factor for both individuals and organizations. Rahim and Afza's study (1993) showed that referent and expert power bases were positively associated with organizational commitment.

A field study in Bangladesh shows that legitimate and expert power bases were positively associated with organizational commitment (Rahim et al. 1994). A study by Rahim and Psenicka (1996) reported that overall position power base (coercive, reward, and legitimate) influences personal power base (expert and referent); expert power, in turn, positively influences referent power; referent power, in turn, positively influences workgroup commitment. Finally, commitment negatively influences workgroup conflict.

Another study showed that conflict management strategies mediated the relationship between power bases and organizational commitment in the US and Greece (Rahim et al. 2003). The study showed that referent power is more effective than other power bases in influencing criterion variable. Without the qualities associated with referent power, other power bases may not be very effective in changing the behavior of subordinates.

Styles of handling conflict

After reviewing numerous studies, Raven and Kruglanski (1970) concluded that the analysis of power provided a fruitful basis for understanding interpersonal conflict. There is need for investigating how managers' power bases affect their subordinates' conflict management so that supervisors can change or maintain their power bases to achieve optimum results.

A field study with a collegiate sample of 301 management students shows that reward power base was positively associated with integrating (collaborating) and negatively associated with avoiding styles of handling conflict with supervisor (Rahim and Buntzman 1989). Legitimate power was positively associated with dominating (competing) style; expert power was positively associated with integrating and dominating styles, but negatively associated with avoiding style; and referent power was positively associated with integrating, obliging, and compromising styles and negatively associated with dominating style. Another study in the USA, Greece, South Korea, and Bangladesh, which used structural equations models, shows the following:

1. Coercive power was negatively associated with expert power in the US
2. Reward power was positively associated with expert power in all the four countries and it was positively associated with referent power in Greece and Bangladesh.
3. Legitimate power was positively associated with expert power in all the four countries, but it was positively associated with referent power in the USA

4. In all the four countries, expert power was positively associated with referent power, referent power was positively associated with problem-solving approach to conflict management and negatively associated with bargaining approach to conflict management.
5. In the US and Greece, problem-solving strategy was positively and bargaining strategy was negatively associated with propensity to leave a job.

(Rahim and Psenicka 2004)

The lack of relationships between conflict-management strategies and propensity to leave a job in the two collectivistic countries (South Korea and Bangladesh) probably indicates that employees in these countries do not have adequate opportunities to move from one job to another. Results other than these did not differ systematically that could be attributed to the individualism–collectivism dimension of the national culture.

Job performance

A field study in Bangladesh reported that coercive power was negatively associated with the effectiveness (performance, conformance, dependability, and personal adjustment) of employees and expert power was positively associated with the same criterion variable (Rahim et al. 1994). Another study in Bulgaria shows that referent power base was positively associated with effectiveness (Rahim et al. 2000).

A recent study that performed data analysis with LISREL in 398 groups simultaneously examined the relationships of subordinates' perception of the bases of supervisory power to each other and to their own conflict management styles with supervisors, which, in turn, influenced supervisory rating of job performance (Rahim et al. 2001). Employees ($N = 1,116$) completed questionnaires on power and conflict styles, and their job performance was evaluated by their respective supervisors ($N = 398$). Overall, the model suggests that coercive power negatively influenced and reward and legitimate powers positively influenced expert power base, but only legitimate power positively influenced referent power base. Expert power positively influenced referent power which, in turn, positively influenced problem-solving style and negatively influenced bargaining style. The problem-solving style positively influenced job performance, but the bargaining style did not have significant influence on performance.

Discussion

In sum, the literature review suggests that personal power base (expert and referent powers) is associated with effective leadership. Also, effective leaders use performance-contingent reward power to increase job satisfaction and performance of subordinates. They use somewhat legitimate and performance-contingent coercive power bases depending on situations.

As discussed in the interdependence among power bases section, an alternative explanation of the weak relationship between position power and criterion variables is that position power base may influence criterion variables through the mediation of personal power base. Consistent with this review, a model of power bases and subordinates' performance and satisfaction (presented in Figure 13.1) is suggested which can be tested in future studies.

Figure 13.1 shows that coercive, reward, and legitimate power bases influence expert and referent power bases; expert power base influences referent power base, which in turn, influences outcomes. In future studies, other power bases reviewed in this chapter (personal power: affiliation, credibility, persuasiveness, prestige; position power: informational, ecological) may be included in this model. Also other criterion variables, such as motivation, creative behavior, and organizational citizenship behavior may be included in this model.

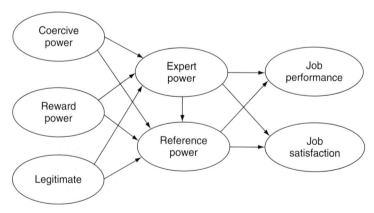

Figure 13.1 A model of bases of leader power and employee performance and satisfaction.

How to acquire, maintain, and use power bases effectively

The studies reviewed in this chapter show that power is very important for leadership effectiveness. Therefore, it is appropriate to discuss what leaders can do to acquire and maintain the right types of power bases and learn how to use them to attain goals. Leaders will become more effective in enhancing positive outcomes and reducing dysfunctional outcomes of subordinates by enhancing their own personal (expert and referent power bases) and position power bases (legitimate and performance-contingent reward power bases). Subordinates' perception of their supervisors' use of these four power bases may have compound positive impact on the subordinates' job performance, satisfaction, and other outcomes.

Personal power base
The challenge of the contemporary organizations is to enhance managers' personal power base. In order to obtain desired results, there should be changes at the individual and organizational levels.

Expert power
Improving managers' expert power would involve basic education and specific job-related training. Education and training should include, among others, familiarity with the organization's culture and on-the-job training to build on this power base. Managers should also be encouraged to enhance their skills through continuous self-learning. They will also need appropriate job experience to build on this power base.

Referent power
Studies reviewed in this chapter show that referent power base is more effective than other power bases in influencing criterion variables. Although this power base has the most potential, it is probably used the least (Benfari et al. 1986). Supervisors who are deficient on this power base may be provided human-relations training so that they learn to be empathetic to the subordinates' needs and feelings, treat them with dignity and ethically, and present their interests to higher-level managers when there is a need to do so. This should enhance a supervisor's base of referent power.

Intervention at organizational level

Organizations should provide appropriate reinforcements for learning and improving their referent and expert power bases. Education and training may be of limited value when it comes to improving referent power base. Organizations may have to adapt the policy of recruiting managers with vision and charisma who are likely to bring an adequate referent power base.

Position power

Training should help managers learn how to use position power base to deal with certain social situations.

Coercive power

Managers may be provided human-relations training so that they use only performance-contingent coercive power to deal with appropriate situations. Whereas in an individualistic culture coercive power base does not have any impact on subordinate outcomes, in a collectivistic culture the acquisition of coercive power can have a negative impact on outcomes.

Reward power

Supervisors may be encouraged to provide various kinds of performance-contingent rewards by granting them the power they need to reward subordinates for their contributions to the organization. Subordinates are more likely to follow a leader's instructions if he or she provides rewards to subordinates contingent upon performance and does not punish them for nonperformance. Although this recommendation is useful for the managers in the individualistic cultures, this is particularly appropriate for the collectivistic cultures.

Legitimate power

Subordinates are more likely to follow a leader's instructions if he or she provides instructions unambiguously, makes sure that instructions are reasonable and appropriate, explains reasons for the instructions, and follows channel of command. Training can help supervisors to follow policies and procedures consistently and to provide instructions, guidance, and advice clearly. There is a "zone of indifference" within which the subordinates will accept directives (Zelditch and Walker 1984). This power is ineffective outside this zone. In other words, subordinates may not carry out directives adequately if they believe the directives are unreasonable or unjustified.

Directions for future research

The model suggested in this chapter may be tested to enhance our understanding of the effectiveness of power bases. An important area of future research concerns carefully designing and evaluating the effects of intervention on supervisory power bases in enhancing subordinates' job performance and satisfaction. Field experiments are particularly useful in evaluating the effects of enhancing the personal power base of supervisors on individual and organizational outcomes. There is also need for scenario-based and laboratory studies that control some of the extraneous variables to better understand the effects of leader power reported in the present study.

References

Aguinis, H., Nestler, M. S., Quigley, B. M., Lee, S. J., and Tedeschi, J. T. (1996) Power bases of faculty supervisors and educational outcomes for graduate studies. *Journal of Higher Education*, **67**, 267–297.

Bachman, J. G. (1968) Faculty satisfaction and the dean's influence: An organizational study of twelve liberal arts colleges. *Journal of Applied Psychology*, **52**, 55–61.

Bachman, J. G., Bowers, D. G., and Marcus, P. M. (1968) Bases of supervisory power: A comparative study in five organizational settings. In A. S. Tannenbaum (Ed.), *Control in organizations* (pp. 229–238), New York, N.Y.: McGraw-Hill.

Bachman, J. G., Smith, C. G., and Slesinger, J. A. (1966) Control, performance, and job satisfaction: An analysis of structural and individual effects. *Journal of Personality and Social Psychology*, **52**, 55–61.

Benfari, R. C., Wilkinson, H. E., and Orth, C. D. (1986) The effective use of power. *Business Horizon*, May–June, 12–16.

Bielous, G. (1995) Seven social power bases and how to effectively use them. *Supervision*, **66** (10), 14–16.

Burke, R. J. and Wilcox, D. S. (1971) Bases of supervisory power and subordinate job satisfaction. *Canadian Journal of Behavioral Science*, **3**, 183–193.

Busch, P. (1980) The sales manager's bases of social power and influence upon the sales force. *Journal of Marketing*, **44** (4), 91–101.

Dunne, E. J. Jr., Stahl, M. J., and Melhart, L. J. Jr. (1978) Influence sources of project and functional managers in matrix organizations. *Academy of Management Journal*, **21**, 135–40.

Carson, P. P., Carson, K. D., and Roe, W. (1993) Social power bases: A meta-analytic examination of interrelationships and outcomes. *Journal of Applied Social Psychology*, **23**, 1150–1169.

Erchul, W. P., Raven, B. H., and Ray, A. G. (2001) School psychologists' perceptions of social power bases in teacher consultation. *Journal of Educational and Psychological Consultation*, **12**, 1–23.

Erchul, W. P., Raven, B. H., and Wilson, K. E. (2004) The relationship between gender of consultant and social power perceptions within school consultation. *School Psychology Review*, **33**, 582–590.

Finkelstein, S. (1992) Power in top management teams: Dimensions, measurement, and validation. *Academy of Management Journal*, **35**, 505–538.

French, J. R. P. Jr. and Raven, B. (1959) The bases of social power. In D. Cartwright (Ed.), *Studies in social power* (pp. 150–167), Ann Arbor, Mich.: Institute for Social Research.

Frost, D. E. and Stahelski, A. J. (1988) The systematic measurement of French and Raven's bases of social power in workgroups. *Journal of Applied Social Psychology*, **18**, 375–389.

Gaski, J. F. (1986) Interrelations among a channel entity's power sources: Impact of the exercise of reward and coercion on expert, referent, and legitimate power sources. *Journal of Marketing Research*, **18**, 62–77.

Greene, C. N. and Podsakoff, P. M. (1981) Effects of withdrawal of a performance-contingent reward on supervisory influence and power. *Academy of Management Journal*, **24**, 527–542.

Hess, C. W. and Wagner, B. T. (1999) Factor structure of the Rahim Leader Power Inventory (RLPI) with clinical female student supervisee. *Educational and Psychological Measurement*, **59**, 1004–1016.

Hinkin, T. R. and Schriesheim, C. A. (1989) Development and application of new scales to measure the French and Raven 1959 bases of social power. *Journal of Applied Psychology*, **74**, 561–567.

Ivancevich, J. M. (1970) An analysis of control, bases of control, and satisfaction in an organizational setting. *Academy of Management Journal*, **13**, 427–436.

Keller, R. T. and Szilagyi, A. D. (1976) Employee reactions to leader reward behavior. *Academy of Management Journal*, **19**, 619–627.

Kim, K. I., Park, H. J., and Suzuki, N. (1990) Reward allocations in the United States, Japan, and Korea: A comparison of individualistic and collectivistic cultures. *Academy of Management Journal*, **23**, 188–198.

Lam, S. S. K. (1997) Validity and reliability of the Rahim Leader Power Inventory: An investigation in Hong Kong. *International Journal of Management*, **14**, 643–645.

Mossholder, K. W., Kemery, E. R., and Wesolowski, M. A. (1998) Relationships between bases of power and workplace reactions: The mediational role of procedural justice. *Journal of Management*, **24**, 533–552.

Munduate, L. and Dorado, M. A. (1998) Supervisor power bases, co-operative behaviour, and organizational commitment. *European Journal of Work and Organizational Psychology*, 7, 163–177.

Nesler, M. S., Aguinis, H., Quigley, B. M., and Tedeschi, J. T. (1993) The effect of credibility on perceived power. *Journal of Applied Social Psychology*, **23**, 1407–1425.

Oyster, C. K. (1992) Perceptions of power: Female executives' descriptions of power usage by "best" and "worst" bosses. *Psychology of Women Quarterly*, **16**, 527–533.

Pearce, J. A. III and Robinson, R. B. Jr. (1987) A measure of CEO social power in strategic decision-making. *Strategic Management Journal*, **8**, 297–304.

Pfeffer, J. (1992) *Managing with power: Politics and influence in organizations*, Boston, Mass.: Harvard Business School Press.

Podsakoff, P. M. and Schriesheim, C. A. (1985) Field studies of French and Raven's bases of power: Critique, reanalysis, and suggestions for future research. *Psychological Bulletin*, **97**, 387–411.

Podsakoff, P. M., Todor, W. D., and Skov, R. (1982) Effects of leader contingent and noncontingent reward and punishment behaviors on subordinate performance and satisfaction. *Academy of Management Journal*, **25**, 810–821.

Rahim, M. A. (1988) The development of a leader power inventory. *Multivariate Behavioral Research*, **23**, 491–502.

(1989) Relationships of leader power to compliance and satisfaction with supervision, Evidence from a national sample of managers. *Journal of Management*, **15**, 545–557.

Rahim, M. A. and Afza, M. (1993) Leader power, commitment, satisfaction, compliance, and propensity to leave a job among American accountants. *Journal of Social Psychology*, **133**, 611–625.

Rahim, M. A., Antonioni, D., Krumov, K., and Ilieva, S. (2000) Power, conflict, and effectiveness: A cross-cultural study in the United States and Bulgaria. *European Psychologist*, **5**, 28–33.

Rahim, M. A., Antonioni, D., and Psenicka, C. (2001) A structural equations model of leader power, subordinates' styles of handling conflict and job performance. *International Journal of Conflict Management*, **12**, 191–211.

Rahim, M. A. and Buntzman, G. F. (1989) Supervisory power bases, styles of handling conflict with subordinates, and subordinate performance and satisfaction. *Journal of Psychology*, **123**, 195–210.

Rahim, M. A., Khan, A. A., and Uddin, S. J. (1994) Leader power and subordinates' organizational commitment and effectiveness: Test of a theory in a developing country. *International Executive*, **36**, 327–341.

Rahim, M. A., Kim, N. H., and Kim, J. S. (1994) Bases of leader power, subordinate compliance, and satisfaction with supervision: A cross-cultural study of managers in the US and S. Korea. *International Journal of Organizational Analysis*, **2**, 136–154.

Rahim, M. A. and Magner, M. R. (1996) Confirmatory factor analysis of the bases of leader power: First-order factor model and its invariance across groups. *Multivariate Behavioral Research*, **31**, 495–516.

Rahim, M. A. and Psenicka, C. (1996) Bases of leader power, workgroup commitment, and conflict: A structural equations model. In M. A. Rahim, R. T. Golembiewski, and C. C. Lundberg (Eds.), *Current topics in management* (Vol. I, pp. 31–47), Greenwich, Conn.: JAI Press.

(2004) A cross-cultural model of power bases, conflict management strategies, and propensity to leave a job. In M. A. Rahim, R. T. Golembiewski, and K. D. MacKenzie (Eds.), *Current topics in Management* (Vol. IX, pp. 185–205), New Brunswick, N. J.: Transaction.

Rahim, M. A., Psenicka, C., Nicolopoulos, A., and Antonioni, D. (2003) *Relationships of leader power to subordinates' styles of handling conflict and organizational commitment: A comparison between the US and Greece.* In M. A. Rahim, R. T. Golembiewski, and K. D. Kackenzie (Eds.), *Current topics in management* (Vol. VIII, pp. 187–204), Piscataway, N. J.: Transaction.

Raven, B. H. (1965) Social influence and power. In I. D. Steiner and M. Fishbein (Eds.), *Current studies in social psychology* (pp. 371–381), New York, N.Y.: Holt, Rinehart & Winston.

(1992) A power/interaction model of interpersonal influence: French and Raven thirty years later. *Journal of Social Behavior and Personality*, **7**, 217–244.

(1993) The bases of power: Origins and recent developments. *Journal of Social Issues*, **49**, 227–251.

Raven, B. H. and Kruglanski, A. W. (1970) Conflict and power. In P. Swingle (Ed.), *The structure of conflict* (pp. 69–109), New York, N.Y.: Academic Press.

Raven, B. H., Schwarzwald, J., and Koslowsky, M. (1998) Conceptualizing and measuring a power/interaction model of interpersonal influence. *Journal of Applied Social Psychology*, **28**, 307–332.

Schwarzwald, J., Koslowsky, M., and Agassi, V. (2001) Captain's leadership type and police officers' compliance to power bases. *European Journal of Work and Organizational Psychology*, **10**, 273–290.

Sims, H. P. Jr. and Szilagyi, A. D. (1975) Leader reward behavior and subordinate satisfaction and performance. *Organizational Behavior and Human Performance*, 14, 426–438.

Stahelski, A. J., Frost, D. E., and Patchen, M. E. (1989) Use of socially dependent bases of power: French and Raven's theory applied to workgroup leadership. *Journal of Applied Social Psychology*, 19, 283–297.

Student, K. R. (1968) Supervisory influence and work-group performance. *Journal of Applied Psychology*, 52, 188–194.

Thamhain, H. J. and Gemmill, G. R. (1974) Influence styles of project respondents: Some project performance correlates. *Academy of Management Journal*, 17, 216–224.

Warren, D. I. (1968) Power, visibility, and conformity in formal organizations. *American Sociological Review*, 33, 951–970.

Yukl. G. (2006) *Leadership in organizations*, 6th edn, Upper Saddle River, N. J.: Pearson Education.

Yukl, G. and Falbe, C. M. (1991) Importance of different power sources in downward and lateral relations. *Journal of Applied Psychology*, 76, 416–423.

Yukl, G. and Van Fleet, D. D. (1992) Theory and research on leadership in organizations. In M. D. Dunnette and Hough, L. M. (Eds.), *Handbook of industrial and organizational psychology* (Vol. III, pp. 147–197), Palo Alto, Calif.: Consulting Psychologists Press.

Zelditch, M. and Walker, H. A. (1984) Legitimacy and the stability of authority. In S. B. Bacharach and E. J. Lawler (Eds.), *Advances in group processes* (Vol. I, pp. 1–25), Greenwich, Conn.: JAI Press.

14 Power tactics preference in organizations
Individual and situational factors

MENI KOSLOWSKY AND
JOSEPH SCHWARZWALD

Introduction

The concepts of power and influence have been of interest to social thinkers even before psychologists began to study the phenomena (Bruins 1999; Carson et al. 1993; Ng 1980). Dahl (1957: 201) believes that from the days of Plato to the more modern thinkers such as Weber, the concept of power has been "as ubiquitous as any that social science can boast." Russell (1938) sees the centrality of power in social sciences as parallel to the concept of energy in the physical sciences. Similar to energy which can manifest itself in different forms, power may be observed in the military, civilian, and judicial domains. Lewin (1951) in his field theory established the foundation for the psychological formulation of social power and influence. He defined the relationship between an influencing agent and a target person acting in a field where opposing forces are said to exist. Lewin's approach had a major impact on French and Raven's taxonomy of social-power tactics (1959) and even more so on Raven's Interpersonal Power Interaction Model (IPIM) (1992).

The chapter integrates previous findings using the IPIM and presents an overall perspective for explaining social-power choice in conflict situations. In terms of our presentation, compliance can be said to occur when the influencing agent's power exceeds the target's resistance. The IPIM's applicability for organizational settings is delineated here by identifying individual and situational factors involved in choosing power tactics to gain compliance. By including relevant moderators and mediators, the presentation allows for expanding the model's theoretical basis, as well as its practical implications. In addition, limitations, conceptual and methodological, are raised, and future directions for ameliorating these deficiencies are suggested.

In their original work in the field, French and Raven (1959) identified five distinct power tactics to which Raven (1965) added, at a later time, information, as a sixth tactic that an influencing agent can exercise for changing attitudes and/or behaviors of a target person:

1. Coercive power: threat of punishment;
2. Reward power: promise of monetary or non-monetary compensation or both;
3. Legitimate power: drawing on one's right to influence;
4. Expert power: relying on one's superior knowledge;
5. Referent power: based on target's identification with influencing agent;
6. Informational power: providing relevant facts and logical justification.

This taxonomy was considered the most popular and sophisticated formulation in the field (Mintzberg 1983; Podsakoff and Schriesheim 1985). It generated research on influence processes in organizations, families, schools, health and medicine, marketing and consumer psychology (Koslowsky and Schwarzwald 2001). This taxonomy continues to serve as a basis for investigations of influence as of this writing (Keshet et al. 2006; Rahim et al. 2001; Teven and Herring 2005).

Based on research findings and as a response to criticism concerning the original formulation (e.g., Kipnis and Schmidt 1985; Podsakoff and Shriesheim 1985), Raven (1992, 1993, 2001) reconceptualized the original taxonomy and proffered a model of eleven tactics. Coercion and reward were separated into personal and impersonal perspectives, and legitimate power was differentiated into four tactics, all of which reflected various social norms. The definitions for expertise, reference, and informational tactics remained true to the original formulation.

1. Impersonal coercion: threat of tangible punishment;
2. Personal coercion: threat of intangible punishment such as disregard or contempt;
3. Impersonal reward: promise of tangible compensation;
4. Personal reward: promise of intangible remuneration such as esteem or approval;
5. Legitimacy of reciprocity: Compliance is insisted as a return for something positive done for the target;

6. Legitimacy of equity: Compliance is demanded as a compensation for either harm or suffering inflicted by the target;
7. Legitimacy of dependence: Compliance is requested in order to provide assistance to the agent who is in need;
8. Legitimacy of position: Compliance is anchored on the principle of authority that comes with one's status or position.

The Interpersonal Power Inventory (IPI)

The new taxonomy called for constructing a scale that would meet both conceptual and psychometric requirements. For this purpose, Raven et al. (1998) devised the Interpersonal Power Inventory (IPI) consisting of thirty-three behavioral items, three from each of the eleven power tactics described in the model (see Table 14.1).

The scale uses an approach similar to a critical incident by asking respondents how reasonable, likely, or often it is for a target person to comply with each behavior. After a short introduction describing a conflict situation, respondents are presented with the items. Typically, they are required to indicate how reasonable it is for a specific item to lead to compliance on the part of a target or how reasonable it is for a specific item to be used by an influencing agent for gaining compliance. The introduction can be rephrased to meet specific goals of a study allowing a researcher to examine responses to different situations. Below is an example of a questionnaire tapping the subordinate's perspective of compliance to a supervisor's request:

Often supervisors ask subordinates to do their job somewhat differently. Sometimes subordinates resist doing so or do not follow the supervisor's directions exactly. At other times, they will do exactly as their supervisor requests. We are interested in those situations that lead subordinates to follow the requests of their supervisor.

Think about a time when you were being supervised in doing some task. Suppose your supervisor asked you to do your job somewhat differently and, though you were initially reluctant, you did exactly as you were told. Please indicate how reasonable (1 "definitely not a reason" to 7 "definitely a reason") it is that you would have complied to the supervisor's request if he/she had used this item.

In Table 14.1, the items are presented from the subordinate's perspective.

Table 14.1 IPI items classified by power strategy and power tactic (subordinate perspective).

Power strategy	Power tactic	Behavioral item
Harsh	Personal reward	I liked my supervisor and his/her approval was important to me.
		My supervisor made me feel more valued when I did as requested.
		It made me feel personally accepted when I did as my supervisor asked.
	Impersonal reward	A good evaluation from my supervisor could lead to an increase in pay.
		My supervisor could help me receive special benefits.
		My supervisor's actions could help me get a promotion.
	Personal coercion	It would have been disturbing to know that my supervisor disapproved of me.
		My supervisor may have been cold and distant if I did not do as requested.
		Just knowing that I was on the bad side of my supervisor would have upset me.
	Impersonal coercion	My supervisor could make things unpleasant for me.
		My supervisor could make it more difficult for me to get a promotion.
		My supervisor could make it more difficult for me to get a pay increase.
	Legitimacy-position	After all, he/she was my supervisor.
		My supervisor had the right to request that I did my work in a particular way.
		As a subordinate, I had an obligation to do as my supervisor said.
	Legitimacy-reciprocity	For past considerations I had received, I felt obliged to comply.
		My supervisor had previously done some good things that I had requested.
		My supervisor had let me have my way earlier so I felt obliged to comply now.
	Legitimacy-equity	By doing so, I could make up for some problems I may have caused in the past.
		Complying helped make up for things I had not done so well previously.
		I had made some mistakes and therefore felt that I owed this to him/her.

Table 14.1 (*cont.*)

Power strategy	Power tactic	Behavioral item
Soft	Expertise	My supervisor probably knew the best way to do the job.
		My supervisor probably knew more about the job than I did.
		My supervisor probably had more technical knowledge about this than I did.
	Referent power	I respected my supervisor and thought highly of him/her and did not wish to disagree.
		I saw my supervisor as someone I could identify with.
		I looked up to my supervisor and generally modeled my work accordingly.
	Information	Once it was pointed out, I could see why the change was necessary.
		My supervisor gave me good reasons for changing how I did the job.
		I could then understand why the recommended change was for the better.
	Legitimacy-dependence	Unless I did so, his/her job would be more difficult.
		I understood that my supervisor really needed my help on this.
		I realized that a supervisor needs assistance and cooperation from those working with him/her.

Psychometric characteristics

Reliability

Internal consistency measures of the individual tactics were quite satisfactory, with a median value of .81. These reliability values are especially notable given the fact that each tactic contained only three items. By incorporating several items for each tactic and illustrating adequate reliability, the scale answered one of the main criticisms concerning the questionable usage of single item formats in power research (Podsakoff and Schriesheim 1985).

Criterion validity

Studies have shown the IPI correlates with attitudinal measures such as job satisfaction and organizational commitment (Koslowsky et al.

2001; Raven et al. 1998). Also, Koslowsky et al. (2001) reported convergent and discriminant validity of five tactics (reward, coercion, referent, expertise, and legitimacy of position) from the IPI that correspond to the tactics included in the Schriesheim et al. (1991) scale. Overall findings provided support for convergent validity and indicated higher discriminant values for the IPI tactics.

Structure
Exploratory/confirmatory factor analysis and smallest space analysis indicated that the eleven tactics are not independent but rather represent two general strategies: harsh/hard versus soft (see Table 14.1 for the tactics subsumed under each strategy). These findings were replicated several times (e.g., Erchul et al. 2001; Schwarzwald et al. 2004; Schwarzwald et al. 2006).

This dichotomy reflects a conceptual distinction with harsh tactics relying on social or organizational resources and soft tactics on personal ones. Harsh tactics stress the influencing agent's advantage over the target because of the ability to reward, punish, or demand compliance by virtue of authority. Moreover, this strategy leaves little leeway for the target's discretion. In contrast, soft tactics provide information or highlight the commonality between the parties involved and by considering targets as more or less equal permits them the freedom to decide (Bruins 1999).

Methodological advantages also accrue to applying the harsh/soft taxonomy rather than relying on individual tactics (Schwarzwald and Koslowsky 2006). First, the reliabilities for the two strategies yield higher reliabilities than individual tactics. Second, as the availability of individual power tactics is context-related and a specific tactic may not be appropriate in all situations, a global measure allows for comparisons across settings. Finally, our studies have indicated that harsh strategies are more informative. When comparing various sub-groups, including gender, conflict content, or leadership style, significant differences were obtained for harsh strategies but not for soft. We attributed the lack of soft strategy differences among sub-groups to the fact that these strategies are more socially acceptable and more frequently used, making it difficult to determine whether the behavior is truthful or simply reflects impression management. In contrast, harsh strategies, which are considered less desirable, and carry a social price of potentially hampering the relationship, reflect a more truthful and revealing response.

Although harsh tactics are indeed less socially desirable, their judicial usage in certain cases may be beneficial without necessarily causing negative repercussions in the relationship. This was illustrated in a study of police officers who reported greater compliance with harsh tactics when used by high transformational captains compared to their high transactional counterparts (Schwarzwald et al. 2001). We inferred from these findings that what matters is the subordinates' interpretation of the leader's behavior. Transactional leaders who exhibit interest in task completion rather than in satisfying subordinates' needs resort frequently to harsh tactics; thus, this behavior is perceived as a personal variable rather than a situational one. Transformational leaders who do display a concern for subordinate needs use harsh tactics infrequently; here, harsh tactics are perceived as situational rather than personal. In practical terms, when a situation requires immediate action and soft tactics are less efficient, compliance can be expected even when the power bases are considered atypical.

The Interpersonal Power Interaction Model (IPIM)

Raven's (1992, 1993, 2001) IPIM includes a set of factors which are involved in the influencing agent's choice of power tactics for gaining compliance in conflict situations.[1] As a consequence of our work with the IPIM and that of several others who have conducted investigations in the area, we have formulated a testable model that specifies antecedents, moderators, and mediators for explaining the choice process. The process is illustrated in Figure 14.1.

Antecedents and moderators

The IPIM delineates the factors that affect the influencing agent's tactic preference for gaining compliance. From our perspective, any of the antecedents can be viewed as a moderator in relationship to any of the other antecedents. As seen in Figure 14.1, the antecedents in the model are defined as general factors that need to be translated into specific variables that would fit the contextual settings under investigation. For

---

[1] The model also explains compliance from the target's perspective. This issue is not within the scope of this chapter.

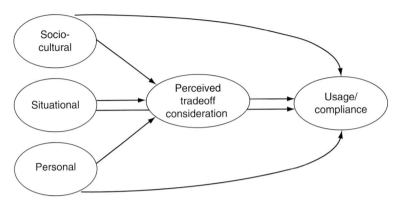

Figure 14.1 The choice of power tactics in the IPIM.

example, the social-cultural factor can be operationalized in different ways such as gender and how it relates to power-tactic preference (Keshet et al. 2006) or religiosity and its impact on power usage in religious versus secular schools (Schwarzwald et al. 2006).

Situational factors can be tested by examining power preferences for different organizational features including setting and status (Koslowsky and Schwarzwald 1993), work type (routine vs. complex; Schwarzwald et al. 2004), inter-group relations (Schwarzwald et al. 2005), and conflict content (Schwarzwald et al. 2006).

The model assumes that power usage can serve as a means for satisfying personal needs. This may be illustrated when an influencing agent prefers harsh tactics, even when soft ones are as effective, so as to elevate the self. In one study, low self-esteem individuals were found to resort more to harsh tactics (Schwarzwald and Koslowsky 1999). In a second one, where professional distance (e.g., similarity in education, experience) between supervisors and subordinates was investigated, findings indicated that subordinates similar to their supervisors were more reluctant to comply (Koslowsky et al. 2001). This reluctance was attributed to the fact that subordinates with similar profiles to their supervisors feel that their opinion is just as legitimate. Alternatively, supervisors with similar qualifications arouse feelings of inequity among subordinates and their refusal to comply serves as a means for restoring equity (Schwarzwald and Goldenberg 1979).

Mediators in the model

Raven suggested that the choice process is influenced by the perceived availability, acceptability, costs, and benefits associated with the various power tactics. For example, coercion while hastening compliance may impede the relationship with the target; legitimacy of dependence reflects possible weakness in the influencing agent's reliance on the target; and reference which endears the target to the influencing agent may be perceived as inappropriate in correctional facilities.

In the present conceptualization, cost–benefit considerations are postulated as mediators that link antecedents with power tactics preference (see Figure 14.1). In one of our studies (elaborated on below), it was found that participants were willing to use harsh tactics to a greater extent when the target was an out-group member as compared with an in-group member. Here, the choice of power tactics reflects differential risk evaluations where individuals are more willing to risk impermanent affiliation with out-group members.

Variable selection in testing the IPIM process

The simultaneous examination of the social-cultural, situational and personal factors allows for investigating whether an additive or interactive process explains greater variance of power-tactic preference. Clearly, the procedure of translating factors delineated in the model into testable variables should be anchored in theory or previous findings. Below are two examples illustrating this procedure.

Example 1

Schwarzwald et al. (2005) investigated group membership (in-group/out-group), influencing agent's status (low, same, high) and gender as antecedents for predicting power tactic preference. Gender represented the social-cultural, group membership, the situational, and status, the personal factor.

Although gender often represents a personal-type factor, its categorization here stems from the universal socialization experiences of men and women. Cross-cultural research shows that the core personality elements of gender stereotypes overlap, to a great extent, across cultures. For example, men are often seen as adventurous, independent, dominant, and strong whereas women as sentimental, submissive, and superstitious (Williams and Best 1982). This gender distinction is labeled by Eagly and Steffen (1984) as "communal" (altruistic and caring for others) when describing the female stereotype and "agentic" (imposing themselves and controlling their environment) for the male stereotype. Thus, men could be expected to use harsh tactics more frequently and soft ones less frequently than women, an expectation that has been confirmed in several studies (Bui et al. 1994; Gruber and White 1986; DuBrin 1991; Eagly and Johnson 1990; Falbo and Peplau 1980; Offerman and Kearney 1988).

Group membership allowed us to inquire whether power-tactic preference, which has been shown to serve as a means for satisfying the personal self also applies to the "social self". Social-identity theory maintains that enhancement of the social self can be achieved by affiliating with in-group members who are perceived as positively distinct from those in the out-group (Tajfel 1982; Tajfel and Turner 1986). As empirical research has shown individuals to discriminate against the out-group so as to create an in-group advantage (Brewer and Kramer 1985; Mullen et al. 1992), we examined whether power tactics preference is also used for this purpose.

As regards status, the IPIM suggests that it affects power preference. Low-status individuals are likely to have less control over valued resources and outcomes and be more dependent on others making them less prone to harsh or authoritarian-type tactics. Consistent with this notion, managers have been shown to apply power tactics differentially toward subordinates and peers with high-status individuals employing more frequently harsh strategies whereas low-status ones employ soft strategies (Fung 1991; Yukl and Falbe 1991).

Our study raised two questions concerning the interplay among the factors:

1. Are the IPIM assumptions applicable for inter-group relations so that power preferences within an organization become a channel for gaining in-group over out-group advantage?
2. Do status and gender moderate power preference in interpersonal and inter-group relations?

These questions were tested on two samples, college students and service workers in various organizations. Participants read scenarios describing a conflict situation between a team leader (influencing agent) whose status is higher, the same or lower than a target person. Group membership was defined by the target's organizational affiliation: either as a permanent, tenured employee (in-group) or as a temporary employee, recruited from a manpower agency (out-group). After reading the scenario, participants completed the IPI which assessed how reasonable it is that the team leader would resort to each of the thirty-three behaviors appearing in the scale, and their responses were categorized into harsh and soft strategies.

Students attributed greater harsh tactics' usage toward out-group than in-group members and more frequent usage of harsh tactics to high-status influencing agents. Workers also attributed greater harsh tactics usage toward the out-group. Yet, the status effect was moderated by participant's gender such that men replicated the pattern found among students while for women, no significant trend was noted. In both samples, soft tactics were not found to be related to the study antecedents.

Our data showed that power tactics are used for creating in-group advantage and concurs with findings indicating a differential treatment favoring the in-group. Implications for power-tactic preference in heterogeneous organizations are clear: Individuals, when deciding on a specific power strategy, perform unique cost–benefit calculations taking into account group affiliation. By resorting to harsh tactics with out-group members, the influencing agent is de-emphasizing potential costs such as harming the relationship. Thus, with temporary workers where the interaction is transitory the costs associated with the application of more expedient tactics are disregarded. In contrast, with in-group workers, where a more permanent affiliation is expected, the risk of harming the relationship becomes more crucial in the choice process. Such differential treatment may also hinder an organization from achieving its organizational goals, as ideas generated by out-group members, even when potentially beneficial, will be ignored.

Example 2

Here, we present a recently completed study demonstrating a mediating process in the IPIM. Managerial style (interpersonal or task orientation) was hypothesized as mediating between social (power) distance and power strategy choice (soft, harsh) (Koslowsky et al. 2007).

Social distance refers to hierarchical conceptualization of human relationships (Hofstede 1991, 2001). It reflects the manner in which less powerful individuals in society or organizations expect and accept unequal distribution of power. In high social-distance cultures, obedience to authority (parent, boss, officials) is the norm, direct supervision is expected, and subordinates feel uncomfortable in freely approaching their boss. In low social-distance cultures, greater equality is emphasized such that subordinates feel at ease challenging senior-management decisions and expect greater job autonomy. As harsh strategies are more authoritative and typify the top-down style of management, we expected these tactics to be more frequently observed in high, rather than low, social-distance environments. It would also follow from social-distance theory that harsh tactics in a high social-distance environment would arouse less resistance and its use be more acceptable to low-status workers.

Managerial style was hypothesized to act as a mediator in the study. The concept was defined as the need perceived by the supervisor in a specific situation to exercise either an employee-centered or a task-centered focus. Similar to the distinctions that have been made previously by several researchers (e.g., Bass and Avolio 1994; Eagly and Karau 1991), and more recently by Anderson et al. (2006), leaders are categorized into two broad categories:

1. employee-oriented leaders who convey warmth and consult with their subordinates or listen carefully to their complaints;
2. task leaders who place the task and its successful completion as the paramount activity in the workplace.

As a mediator, managerial style is expected to explain the relationship between social distance (antecedent) and power strategy (outcome). Accordingly, managerial style should vary as a function of social distance and predict power strategy. Research has already shown that even in hierarchical environments, such as those commonly found in a police force, leadership style varies (Schwarzwald et al. 2001). The assumption here is that social distance influences the way disagreement is perceived. As such, we tested whether in high-social-distance environments a subordinate's disagreement will increase the likelihood of a task-style managerial orientation, which, in turn, increases the likelihood of applying harsh strategies. In contrast, in a low-social-distance environment, the task-oriented leadership style is likely to be deemphasized and the captain will more likely exercise soft tactics.

The investigation, conducted in the Israeli police department, included forty captains and 191 policemen. Participants answered questionnaires assessing social distance, captain's managerial style, and power tactics preference during conflicts between captains and policemen.

First, a principal component analysis yielded a two-factor solution supporting the aforementioned managerial style orientations. Second, findings revealed three patterns:

1. Overall, soft tactics were reported to be used more frequently than harsh ones, a tendency which has been found in nearly all our work.
2. Captains reported greater usage for soft tactics and lesser usage of harsh tactics as compared with their policemen's responses. This was attributed to the supervisor's tendency to describe themselves in a positive light matching their perception of modern managerial style.
3. The overall model was only confirmed for harsh tactics. These three patterns have been described in previous studies as well (e.g., Schwarzwald et al. 2006).

The analysis of the mediation process supports the IPIM assumption that power choice is rational in that the influencing agent's awareness of the present social distance affects managerial style. While the total effect of social distance on harsh tactics usage was found to be .46, the inclusion of managerial style as a mediator significantly reduced the direct effect of social distance on harsh tactics to .18 (see Figure 14.2). Yet, these findings reflect only a partial mediation. Managerial style does not appear to fully explain the social distance-harsh tactics relationship and other variables should be explored (Baron and Kenney 1986; Evans 1997).

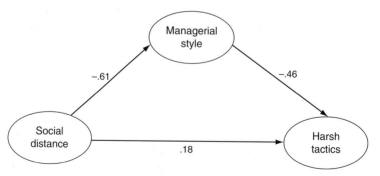

Figure 14.2 The mediational process with harsh tactics as outcome variable.

Future directions

Our studies have shown that the IPIM has promoted the understanding of social-power choice. Nonetheless, several conceptual and methodological issues still need to be investigated. For example, studies including mediators are scarce, and identifying other potential mediators awaits further exploration.

Another research focus that may provide further empirical validity for the power model is to analyze its applicability in diverse organizational settings. As conflicts are inevitable and explaining the dynamics involved would be beneficial, it behooves us to find commonalities and uniqueness across different types of organizations. Etzioni's taxonomy system (1964, 1971), which differentiates between coercive, calculative, and normative systems, is a possible scheme for achieving some of these goals.

Another area that has not been adequately explored is whether supervisors, in trying to gain compliance, relate similarly to all subordinates within a system. In analyzing social-power relationships with the IPIM, the implicit assumption has been that leaders within an organizational unit behave uniformly with all subordinates. However, research findings show that leaders do indeed distinguish between certain types of employees (e.g., preferred or competent subordinates) and others (Dansereau et al. 1975; Graen and Cashman 1975). Future investigations should test whether this variability in behavior is also pertinent to power-tactic choice.

Finally, as most power investigations have employed self-report measures, common method variance, a potential biasing factor, may have produced inflated correlations (Crampton and Wagner 1994). Other designs such as controlled experiments, observation, and quasi-experimental ones in the field would enhance the empirical validity of the IPIM.

References

Anderson, N., Lievens, F., Dam, K. V, and Born, M. (2006) Construct-driven investigation of gender differences in a leadership-role assessment center. *Journal of Applied Psychology*, **91**, 55–566.

Baron, R. M. and Kenny, D. A. (1986) The moderator-mediator variable distinction in social psychological research: Conceptual, strategic, and statistical considerations. *Journal of Personality and Social Psychology*, **51**, 1173–1182.

Bass, B. M. and Avolio, B. J. (1994) *Improving organizational effectiveness through transformational leadership*, Thousand Oaks, Calif.: Sage Publications.

Brewer, M. B. and Kramer, R. (1985) The psychology of intergroup attitudes and behavior. *Annual Review of Psychology*, **36**, 219–243.

Bruins, J. (1999) Social power and influence tactics: A theoretical interdiction. *Journal of Social Issues*, **55**, 81–89.

Bui, K. T., Raven, B. H., and Schwarzwald, J. (1994) Influence strategies in dating relationships: The effects of relationship satisfaction, gender, and perspective. *Journal of Social Behavior and Personality*, **9**, 429–442.

Carson, P. P., Carson, C. K., and Roe, C. W. (1993) Social power bases: A meta-analytic examination of interrelationships and outcomes. *Journal of Applied Social Psychology*, **23**, 1150–1169.

Crampton, S. M. and Wagner, J. A., III. (1994) Percept-percept inflation in microorganizational research: An investigation of prevalence and effect. *Journal of Applied Psychology*, **79**, 67–76.

Dahl, R. A. (1957) The concept of power. *Behavioral Science*, **2**, 201–218.

Dansereau, F. Jr., Graen, G., and Haga, W. J. (1975) A vertical dyad linkage approach to leadership within formal organizations: A longitudinal investigation of the role making process. *Organizational Behavior and Human Performance*, **13**, 46–78.

DuBrin, A. J. (1991) Sex and gender differences in tactics of influence. *Psychological Reports*, **68**, 635–646.

Eagly, A. H. and Johnson, B. T. (1990) Gender and leadership style: A meta-analysis. *Psychological Bulletin*, **108**, 233–256.

Eagly, A. and Karau, S. J. (1991) Gender and the emergence of leaders: A meta-analysis. *Journal of Personality and Social Psychology*, **60**, 685–710.

Eagly, A. H. and Steffen, V. J. (1984) Gender stereotypes stem from the distribution of women and men into social roles. *Journal of Personality and Social Psychology*, **46**, 735–754.

Erchul, W. P., Raven, B. H., and Ray, A. G. (2001) School psychologists' perceptions of social power bases in teacher consultation. *Journal of Educational and Psychological Consultation*, **12**, 1–23.

Etzioni, A. (1964) *Modern organizations*, Englewood Cliffs, N. J.: Prentice-Hall.

(1971) *Comparative analysis of complex organizations*, New York, N.Y.: Free Press.

Evans, G. W. (1997) Moderating and mediating processes in environment-behavior research. In G. T. Moore and R. Marans (Eds.),

Advances in environment, behavior, and design: Towards the integration of theory, methods, research, and utilization (Vol. IV, pp. 255–285), New York, N.Y.: Plenum.

Falbo, T. and Peplau, L. A. (1980) Power strategies in intimate relationships. *Journal of Personality and Social Psychology*, **38**, 618–628.

French, J. R. P. Jr. and Raven, B. H. (1959) The bases of social power. In D. Cartwright (Ed.), *Studies in social power* (pp. 150–167), Ann Arbor, Mich.: Institute for Social Research.

Fung, S. (1991) The effects of power, relationship, and purpose in gaining compliance. *Contemporary Social Psychology*, **15**, 44–57.

Graen, G. and Cashman, J. F. (1975) A role making model of leadership in formal organizations: A developmental approach. In J. G. Hunt and L. L. Larson (Eds.), *Leadership frontiers*, Kent, Ohio: Kent State University Press.

Gruber, K. J. and White, J. W. (1986) Gender differences in the perceptions of self's and other's use of power strategies. *Sex Roles*, **15**, 109–118.

Hofstede, G. H. (1991) *Cultures and organizations: Software of the mind*, London: McGraw-Hill.

(2001) *Culture's consequences: Comparing values, behaviors, institutions, and organizations across nations*, Thousand Oaks, Calif: Sage.

Keshet, S., Kark, R., Pomerantz-Zorin, L., Koslowsky, M., and Schwarzwald, J. (2006) Gender, status, and the use of power strategies. *European Journal of Social Psychology*, **36**, 105–117.

Kipnis, D. and Schmidt, S. M. (1985) The language of persuasion. *Psychology Today*, **19**, 40–46.

Koslowsky, M., Aminov, H., and Schwarzwald, J. (2007) Social distance and managerial style: Predictors of influence tactics usage. Presented at the Conference of the Society of Industrial and Organizational Psychology, New York.

Koslowsky, M. and Schwarzwald, J. (1993) The use of power tactics to gain compliance: Testing aspects of Raven's (1988) theory in conflictual situations. *Social Behavior and Personality*, **21**, 135–144.

(2001) Power interaction model: Theory, methodology, and practice. In A. Lee-Chai and J. Bargh (Eds.), *Use and abuse of power* (pp. 195–214), Philadelphia, Pa.: Psychology Press.

Koslowsky, M., Schwarzwald, J., and Ashuri, S. (2001) On the relationship between subordinates' compliance to power sources and organizational attitudes. *Applied Psychology: An International Review*, **50**, 436–454.

Lewin, K. (1951) *Field theory in social science*, New York, N.Y.: Harper.

Mintzberg, H. (1983) *Power in and around organizations*, Englewood Cliffs, N. J.: Prentice-Hall.

Mullen, B., Brown, R., and Smith, C. (1992) Intergroup bias as a function of salience, relevance, and status: An integration. *European Journal of Social Psychology*, 22, 103–122.

Ng, S. H. (1980) *The social psychology of power*, New York, N.Y.: Academic Press.

Offerman, L. R. and Kearney, C. T. (1988) Supervisor sex and subordinate influence strategies. *Personality and Social Psychology Bulletin*, 11, 286–300.

Podsakoff, P. M. and Schriesheim, C. A. (1985) Field studies of French and Raven's bases of power: Critique, reanalysis, and suggestions for future research. *Psychological Bulletin*, 97, 387–411.

Rahim, M. A., Antonioni, D., and Psenicka, C. (2001) A structural equations model of leader power, subordinates' styles of handling conflict, and job performance. *International Journal of Conflict Management*, 12, 191–211.

Raven, B. H. (1965) Social influence and power. In D. Steiner and M. Fishbein (Eds.), *Current studies in social psychology* (pp. 371–382), New York, N.Y.: Holt, Rinehart, & Winston.

  (1992) A power/interaction model of interpersonal influence: French and Raven thirty years later. *Journal of Social Behavior and Personality*, 7, 217–244.

  (1993) The bases of power: Origins and recent developments. *Journal of Social Issues*, 49, 227–251.

  (2001) Power/interaction and interpersonal influence: Experimental investigations and case studies. In A. Lee-Chai and J. Bargh (Eds.), *Use and abuse of power* (pp. 217–240), Philadelphia, Pa.: Psychology Press.

Raven, B. H., Schwarzwald, J., and Koslowsky, M. (1998) Conceptualizing and measuring a power/interaction model of interpersonal influence. *Journal of Applied Social Psychology*, 28, 307–322.

Russell, B. (1938) *Power: A new social analysis*, London: Allen & Unwin.

Schriesheim, C. A., Hinkin, T. R., and Podsakoff, P. M. (1991) Can ipsative and single-item measures produce erroneous results in field studies of French and Raven's (1959) five bases of power? An empirical investigation. *Journal of Applied Psychology*, 76, 106–114.

Schwarzwald, J. and Goldenberg, J. (1979) Compliance and assistance to an authority figure in perceived equitable or nonequitable situations. *Human Relations*, 32, 877–888.

Schwarzwald, J. and Koslowsky, M. (1999) Gender, self-esteem, and focus of interest in the use of power strategies by adolescents in conflict situations. *Journal of Social Issues*, 55, 15–32.

  (2006) The Interpersonal Power Interaction Model: Theoretical, empirical, and methodological reflections. In D. Chadee and J. Young (Eds.),

Current themes in social psychology, St. Augustine, Trinidad: SOCS, The University of the West Indies.

Schwarzwald, J., Koslowsky, M., and Allouf, M. (2005) Group membership, status, and social power preference. *Journal of Applied Social Psychology*, 35, 644–665.

Schwarzwald, J., Koslowsky, M., and Ochana-Levin, T. (2004) Usage of and compliance with power tactics in routine versus nonroutine work settings. *Journal of Business and Psychology*, 18, 385–402.

Schwarzwald, J., Koslowsky, M., and Agassi, V. (2001) Captain's leadership type and police officers' compliance to power bases. *European Journal of Work and Organizational Psychology*, 10, 273–290.

Schwarzwald, J., Koslowsky, M., and Brody-Shamir, S. (2006) Factors related to perceived power usage in schools. *British Journal of Educational Psychology*, 76, 445–462.

Tajfel, H. (1982) Social psychology of intergroup relations. *Annual Review of Psychology*, 33, 1–39.

Tajfel, H. and Turner, J.C. (1986) The social identity theory of intergroup behavior. In S. Worchell and W.C. Austin (Eds.), *Psychology of intergroup relations*, 2nd edn, Chicago, Ill.: Nelson-Hall.

Teven, J.J. and Herring, J.E. (2005) Teacher influence in the classroom: A preliminary investigation of perceived instructor power, credibility, and student satisfaction. *Communication Research Reports*, 22, 235–246.

Williams, J.E. and Best, D.L. (1982) *Measuring sex stereotypes: A thirty-nation study*, Beverly Hills, Calif.: Sage.

Yukl, G. and Falbe, C.M. (1991) Importance of different power sources in downward and lateral relations. *Journal of Applied Psychology*, 76, 416–423.

15 | Influence triggers and compliance
A discussion of the effects of power, motivation, resistance, and antecedents

JOHN E. BARBUTO, JR. AND
GREGORY T. GIFFORD

This chapter describes a framework for understanding target compliance. The framework draws from the leadership, influence, and motivation literatures to identify target-based influence triggers and the moderating variables that lead to target compliance. The chapter discusses the proposed relationships and provides directions for future research.

Introduction

The role of power and influence on individual behavior is a necessary consideration in the organizational behavior and organizational theory literatures (Barbuto 2000b; Pfeffer 1981). Looking only at an agent's behaviors in trying to enact behavioral change in targets is, in many ways, like looking only at the behaviors of a truck driver who encounters a deer in the road and has to decide how to avoid an accident. The driver may consider several options to prevent a collision: flash the high-beam headlights, sound the horn, apply the brakes, or turn out of the path of the deer. Each choice is derived entirely from the truck driver's perspective, and none of them usually work to prevent an accident. The optimum solution to avoiding an accident, however, lies in understanding the behaviors of the deer, which will freeze when bright lights shine in its eyes. When the headlights are turned off, the deer will unfreeze and react to the vibrations of the road and the sight and sound of the oncoming truck, thus fleeing from the truck and avoiding the accident. Because many agents take the same approach as the truck driver (i.e. thinking only about what they would do and not considering what the deer might do), they may never understand their targets well enough to choose the best courses of action.

This example is not intended to imply that targets are merely deer on the highway, as this would be far too simplistic. However, most behavioral scientists would agree that agents capable of understanding the target's perspective will have a greater chance of enacting desired changes than agents who lack this capacity. The role that power plays in its kinetic and active form becomes central in understanding the influence process. Over the past fifty years, examination of the agent-target phenomenon almost exclusively from the agent's perspective has left a void in power and influence research that can be diminished only with greater attention to theory and research developed from the target's vantage point.

This work describes a framework that clarifies the connection between agents' power bases and influence and identifies the contributing factors in the influence process, from the targets' perspective, to help explain why targets comply with implied and explicit directives. More specifically, this work examines the characteristics of the target, agent, and situation that result in a target's compliance or noncompliance with a target's influence attempts.

Influence triggers are the input variables for the proposed framework (Figure 15.1). A trigger is defined from the target's standpoint as the instantaneous reaction to an influence attempt and describes the essence

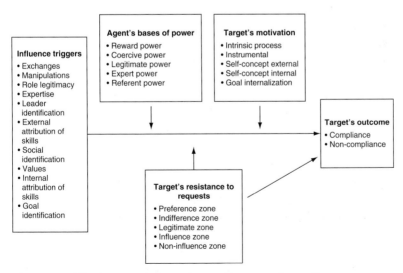

Figure 15.1 The framework for understanding targets' compliance.

or reason for compliance. Triggers result from an agent's intentional or unintentional inducements (House et al. 1996). Although leadership and influence behaviors describe the types of interventions made by agents, triggers, on the other hand, explain the types of reactions that targets experience upon an agent's intervention. Several moderating variables affect the relationship between influence triggers and target compliance. These variables include the target's resistance to the agent's directives, the target's sources of motivation, and the agent's bases of social power.

We begin with a general overview of the framework (Figure 15.1) and identify specific influence triggers from the literature on motivation, leadership, influence, and power. Next, we describe the moderating variables, beginning with the target's resistance, followed by the target's motivation and the agent's bases of social power. Third, we explore an integration of the influence triggers with the moderating variables explaining their relationships and combined effects on target compliance. Finally, we summarize the model, discuss future research opportunities, and explore practical implications for the framework.

The framework

An agent's implicit or explicit messages and behaviors may tap a target's influence triggers. In this sense, an agent does not use influence triggers to affect a target's behavior, but instead uses behaviors that are interpreted by the target and lead to influence triggers. These triggers will then, depending on the target's general resistance to the intervention, the target's sources of motivation, and the agent's bases of social power, lead to target compliance (or noncompliance). In this framework, the influence triggers act as input variables for targets' compliance, while three moderating variables – the target's resistance level, the target's sources of motivation, and the target's perception of the agent's power – act in conjunction with the influence triggers to determine the target's compliance or noncompliance.

For each influence trigger, the likelihood of that trigger leading to the target's compliance will depend on the compatibility of the influence trigger with the target's sources of motivation and the agent's power bases, in addition to the degree of the target's resistance. Influence triggers compatible with the target's motivation favor conditions for compliance. Influence triggers compatible with the agent's bases of power favor conditions for compliance. If the target's resistance level to the tasks or goals is low, this also favors conditions for compliance.

Triggers identified from the influence and leadership literature will be described in more detail in the upcoming sections. The target's resistance levels will be explained using Barbuto's (2000a) concentric zones of resistance and will be described with connections to influence triggers. The target's sources of motivation, as described by Leonard et al. (1999) and operationalized by Barbuto and Scholl (1998, 1999) will be described with links to influence triggers. The agent's bases of social power as described by French and Raven (1959) and operationalized by Hinkin and Schriesheim (1989) will be described in more detail with connections to influence triggers.

Influence triggers

Unlike leadership styles or influence tactics in which interventions are most typically examined from the agent's behaviors, an influence trigger is understood as a target's reaction to an influence attempt. Each time an agent attempts to influence a target, some type of trigger will occur for the target. These triggers may or may not reflect the agent's intent.

Ten influence triggers are identified from recurring themes in the literature (Barbuto 2000b). These triggers can be categorized into three types: power-derived, relations-derived, and values-derived. Power-derived triggers include exchanges, manipulations, role legitimacy, expertise, and leader identification. Relations-derived triggers include external attribution of target skills and social identification. Values-derived triggers include value approach, internal attribution of target skills, leader identification, and goal identification.

Power-derived triggers

Several triggers are derived from perceptions surrounding agents' uses of social power. In these instances, targets' attributions or perceptions of the agent's behaviors precede the manifestation of each of these influence triggers.

Exchange triggers
Exchange triggers occur when a target is inclined to comply with an agent's directives because the agent has attached contingent rewards to

goal or task completion. Targets believe there is an instrumental tie to goal accomplishment and are motivated to achieve organizational goals or perform requested tasks in anticipation of desired rewards, only if they believe the agent can administer such rewards (Hinkin and Schriesheim 1989). Examples of exchange triggers are especially common in commission-based industries. For example, car salespersons are inclined to pursue sales because tangible rewards are attached to each car they sell.

If targets comply with requests because of feelings of obligation or indebtedness (e.g., if they are reminded of past favors, then reciprocal exchange triggers may be present) (Barbuto 2000b). Here, the targets comply with the agent's directives because they feel indebted toward the agent, because of the agent's past favors or considerations.

Manipulative triggers

Manipulative triggers occur when targets are inclined to comply with an agent's requests because they believe noncompliance will result in negative consequences. Targets believe if they do not pursue specified goals or tasks, they will be demoted, reprimanded, publicly defamed, fired, transferred, or receive some other undesirable punishment and only if they believe the agent can/will administer such punishments. An example of this influence trigger can be found in organizations where an agent may casually mention that the organization needs to become "leaner" and remind workers that all options will need to be explored. A target may interpret this as an ultimatum, and a manipulative trigger is tapped within the target. Targets are influenced by threats of punishment because they believe the agent can and will invoke negative consequences – regardless of whether the agent had intended to send such a message.

Role legitimacy triggers

Role legitimacy triggers occur when targets are inclined to comply with an agent's requests based on role expectations, awareness of cultural values, and acceptance of social structure. Targets comply with behavioral directives of agents because they believe job requirements, position power, organizational culture, and normative roles in the organization are consistent with the requests the agent has made. An example of role-legitimating triggers can be found quite readily in most families. Children often will obey their parents, not because they agree with the parents' decisions or fear any retribution, but simply because "they are the parents."

Expertise triggers

Expertise triggers occur when targets are inclined to comply with an agent's directives because they believe the agent has information, knowledge, or unique expertise in the necessary area. Targets comply with directives because they respect the unique knowledge and experience of the agent and trust the agent to act in the collective interests. An example of expertise triggers may be in research and development where scientists have free rein to pursue new product breakthroughs. Trust is needed for expertise triggers to take effect because without it, targets will question the agent's motives and limit compliance.

Leader identification triggers

Leader identification triggers occur when targets are inclined to comply with an agent's directives because the agent has developed widespread appeal and targets feel great loyalty toward the agent. Targets comply because they identify with and seek approval from the agent and believe that compliance will gain this approval. Martin Luther King, Jr. was able to effect incredible change and stir great emotional commitment from his targets because of the symbolic and charismatic effects he had developed.

Relations-derived triggers

Some influence triggers rely on the target's relationship with peers. These relations-derived triggers include external attribution and social identification influence triggers. In these cases, the social pressures of peer groups instigate the manifestations of these influence triggers.

External attribution triggers

External attribution triggers occur when targets are inclined to comply with an agent's directives because they believe doing so will cause others to recognize their talents and abilities. Public awareness and recognition of their contributions to the success of the organization will motivate targets to comply. Examples of external attribution triggers can be found frequently in organizational settings where some workers prefer to work on highly visible projects because they see opportunities to enhance their reputation among peers and superiors.

Social identification triggers

Social identification triggers occur when targets are inclined to comply with the agent to derive social benefits or social rewards. Targets are motivated to pursue the organization's goals for socially desirable outcomes, such as acceptance or admiration among peers and increased social influence. If targets place a high value on being part of a group and have a natural desire for acceptance, social identification triggers will lead to compliance.

Values-derived triggers

Some influence triggers rely on personal values, standards, and shared ideals; these include values-based, internal attribution, and goal identification triggers. These values-derived triggers are sourced within the individual.

Values-based triggers

Values-based triggers occur when targets are inclined to comply with the agent's directives because they see links between goal attainment or task performance and their personal values. Targets believe the organization's goals are congruent with their value system and receive the message "the goals of this organization are congruent with my values; therefore, pursuing these goals will support my values." An example of a values-based trigger can be readily found when nurses find themselves working with undesirable bosses or in difficult working conditions, but are still influenced to perform the tasks assigned because of a deep-rooted value for caring for and nurturing others.

Internal attribution triggers

Internal attribution triggers occur when targets are inclined to comply with an agent's directives because they link task performance or goal attainment to their personal standards of traits and skills. Targets comply because they believe their skills are necessary to perform the tasks and achieve the organization's goals. An example of an internal attribution trigger may be commonly found among new product engineers in the automobile industry, who are continually challenged to design new products and improve existing ones.

Goal identification triggers

Goal identification triggers occur when targets comply with an agent's directives because they share an organization's vision and are convinced compliance will help the organization reach its goals. Targets comply with an agent's requests because they identify with organizational goals and believe the behaviors requested by the agent would help the organization reach its goals. An example of the goal identification influence trigger may be found in charitable organizations with humanitarian missions.

Moderating variables

Each influence trigger may be evident and may lead to compliance in different settings. The likelihood of compliance when targets experience influence triggers depends upon the interaction of these triggers with moderating variables (target's resistance to the agent's requests, target's source of motivation, and agent's bases of power; see Figure 15.1). Targets asked to perform tasks or pursue goals to which they have little resistance will more likely comply than if resistance is moderate or high. Similarly, influence triggers that tap into targets' sources of motivation are more likely to lead to compliance than triggers that do not tap into targets' motivation. Also, if influence triggers complement the agent's bases of social power, there will be a greater likelihood targets will comply with directives than if these triggers are not consistent with the agent's bases of social power. Each of the moderating variables is discussed in this section, leading to propositions that reflect their expected interactions with influence triggers that favor compliance.

Target's resistance to agent's directives

A target's resistance can be understood as the target's degree of willingness to perform specific task directives or pursue communicated directions of agents (Figure 15.2). The more inclined targets are to accept a given request, the less resistance will affect compliance. The greater the target's resistance, the greater the required influence from agents to successfully gain compliance in an influence attempt.

Understanding the target's resistance requires an assessment of how willing the target is to perform the specific behaviors or pursue the specific goals requested. A series of concentric circles or zones,

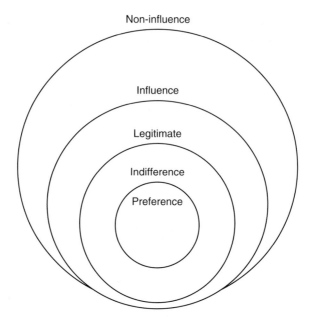

Note: Resistance increases as behaviors or goals fall farther from the center (preference zone).

Figure 15.2 Targets' resistance to behavioral directives.

extending Barnard's (1938) zones of indifference, can further illustrate this willingness to comply with directives (see Figure 15.2). Barnard (1938) originally articulated resistance levels to behavioral directives in two general zones: those to which targets would be indifferent and those to which targets would not be indifferent but, in fact, resistant. In this sense, this construct is similar to the attitudinal measure of latitude of acceptance (Sherif 1964). Managers can easily induce targets to perform tasks to which targets merely feel indifferent; however, tasks to which targets feel not indifferent, but resistant, require much greater inducements. These two general zones of indifference articulated by Barnard (1938) are further separated into five levels, or zones, of resistance in recent work (Barbuto 1997, 2000a).

   If all behaviors are plotted in a multilayered circle, the farther from the center a behavior lies, the greater the target's resistance (see Figure 15.2). Each circle represents a concentric zone or level of target resistance. These zones (moving from the center outward) are termed preference zone, indifference zone, legitimate zone, influence zone, and non-influence zone. Each zone constitutes different levels of target resistance to behavioral directives. These zones explain why some individuals require greater inducements to perform specific tasks than do others. Resistance increases as behaviors fall farther from the center of the concentric zones. When agents ask targets to perform specific tasks, the concentric zone into which the requested behavior falls will affect the likelihood of gaining compliance.

In instances where the agent's requests fall into the target's inner three zones, preference, indifference, and legitimate, far less inducement is necessary than when the agent's requests fall into the target's outer two zones, influence and non-influence (Figure 15.2).

Behaviors that fall into the preference zone are those a person intends to do anyway, prior to any influence or agent inducement. If the desired behavior falls within a target's preference zone, agent inducements are unnecessary (Barbuto 2000a). For example, asking workers to perform their favorite tasks will almost always lead to compliance. In many cases, targets would perform these tasks without agents even mentioning them.

Behaviors that fall into the indifference zone are those a person is willing to do prior to any exertion of influence but does not intend to do. In the absence of any influence attempt, a person will not engage in behaviors in this zone. If the desired behavior falls within a person's indifference zone, however, influence may be easily exerted through mere suggestion from the agent. There are many tasks targets are not averse to performing and do not require great inducements from agents to gain compliance.

Behaviors that fall into the legitimate zone are those that an individual is likely to consider reasonable. With inducements, agents can influence the target's behaviors in this zone. In the absence of an influence attempt, the target will not exhibit behaviors in this zone because they must be consistent with the individual's role definition or adequate role behavior. An example of legitimate zone behaviors will vary from job to job. For an office secretary, certain tasks such as filing, letter writing, scheduling appointments, and other administrative tasks would likely fall in the legitimate zone.

Behaviors that fall into the influence zone are those that an individual is likely to consider unreasonable. Targets will require substantive inducements to perform such behaviors. Even in the presence of an influence attempt, behaviors in this zone may still not occur. Behavior in this zone could be compared to performance beyond expectations or extra role behavior.

Behaviors that fall in the non-influence zone are those that an individual is likely to consider off-limits. The target will not be willing to perform these behaviors, even with strong inducements, and will not compromise or perform behaviors in the non-influence zone. Agents will be unsuccessful in attempting to induce workers to perform such behaviors. In instances where requests fall in a target's non-influence zone, no inducements will generate compliance.

Zones of resistance and the influence process

Several scholars have examined the types of tasks performed by workers, in terms of resistance levels and expectation levels. Of the ten influence triggers described in the previous section, value-based, expertise, external-attribution, internal-attribution, leader-identification, and goal-identification triggers each can be classified as interpersonal or value driven. These types of triggers would be most effective when the target's resistance falls in the influence zone, suggesting that exchange and manipulative triggers would be least likely to lead to compliance with behaviors or goals that fall into a target's influence zone.

Target's sources of motivation

The target's sources of motivation constitute another set of moderating variables in this framework. Beyond the target's resistance, the relative success of an influence trigger depends, in part, on the target's sources of motivation. Sources of motivation in this framework explain how certain influence triggers are successful if they tap into a target's salient motives.

Five sources of motivation

The five sources of motivation applied in this model were originally proposed by Leonard et al. (1999) and were further developed and used to predict agents' behaviors (Barbuto and Scholl 1998, 1999). The five sources of motivation are intrinsic process, instrumental, self-concept external, self-concept internal, and goal internalization.

Intrinsic process motivation occurs when a target is motivated to perform certain kinds of work or to engage in certain types of behavior for the sheer fun of it. The work itself, not the task outcome, provides the incentive because targets genuinely enjoy what they are doing. Instrumental rewards motivate targets when they believe their behaviors will lead to certain tangible, extrinsic outcomes, such as pay or promotions. Self-concept external motivation tends to be externally based; targets attempt to meet the expectations of others by behaving in ways that elicit social feedback consistent with their self-concept. Targets behave in ways that satisfy reference group members, first to gain acceptance, then status. Self-concept internal motivation occurs when a target sets internal standards of traits, competencies, and values that become the basis for the ideal self. Targets are motivated to engage in behaviors that reinforce these internal standards and later achieve higher competency. Goal internalization motivation induces targets to adopt attitudes and behaviors based entirely on their personal value systems. Goal internalization is different from the previous four sources of motivation because it involves the absence of self-interest. Motivation occurs because targets believe in the cause. With goal internalization, however, targets do not require any strong inducements beyond a belief that the goals of the organization can be attained with their assistance. If targets believe in the articulated goals, they will be motivated to perform whatever tasks are necessary to achieve these goals.

Sources of motivation and the influence process

The effect of motivation on the influence process will depend on whether the influence trigger has tapped into the target's source(s) of motivation. In instances where an influence trigger taps into targets' motives, the likelihood of compliance will increase. Conversely, if influence triggers fail to tap into the target's source(s) of motivation, the likelihood of compliance will decrease. More than one source of motivation may be driving behavior at a given time. Agents who are able to tap into multiple sources of motivation when articulating goals and necessary tasks to be performed will increase the likelihood of gaining a target's compliance.

Agent's bases of social power

A third moderating variable for understanding the influence process is the agent's base of social power. Over the years, a number of power typologies have been proposed, the most influential perhaps being that of French and Raven (1959), who distinguished among reward, coercive, legitimate, referent, and expert power. Their typology is the framework most frequently used in power research. A major criticism of the French and Raven (1959) typology is that the power bases described lack conceptual consistency regarding the source or origin of influence, making it difficult to operationalize the construct and sample the domains of interest (Hinkin and Schriesheim 1989; Yukl 2005). Hinkin and Schriesheim (1989) reconceptualized French and Raven's (1959) taxonomy to improve the theoretical definitions and make them practical for research efforts.

Five bases of power

For this framework, the five bases of power operationalized by Hinkin and Schriesheim (1989) serve as moderating variables to explain the relationship between influence triggers and the target's compliance. These bases of power, developed by French and Raven (1959) include reward, coercive, legitimate, referent, and expert power.

Reward power is the ability to administer things desired or to remove undesirable things. Agents have gained reward power once targets believe agents can control rewards. Coercive power is the ability to administer punishments, which may take the form of demotion, termination, transfer, and emotional or physical hostility. Legitimate power is the ability to elicit feelings of obligation from others. If targets believe their job responsibilities, rank, and position are consistent with the agent's requests, the agent has legitimate power over the targets. This base of power has also been described as position power and structural power. Referent power is the ability to elicit feelings of personal acceptance or approval in others. If targets emulate their agents, feel admiration toward them, or harbor a strong desire for acceptance from them, then agents have gained referent power. When this base of power is operationalized as identification with and emulation of the agent, it tends to resemble charismatic influences (Conger and Kanungo 1987). Similarly, when this base of power is operationalized and evident in a target as identification with a social group or a desire to belong, it tends to resemble social identity theory (Ashforth and Mael 1989). Expert power is the ability to administer to others information, knowledge, or expertise. If targets believe that agents have expertise or unique qualifications for asserting claims or making requests, then agents have expert power. There are two key aspects of expert power: Targets must have mutual goals, and targets must trust agents to act in the best interest of the collective. If either of these two rungs is missing, then expert power will not be given.

Bases of social power and the influence process

Hinkin and Schriesheim's (1989) application of French and Raven's (1959) power bases is conceptualized from the target's perspective, with the implication that power exists only as it is perceived by the target. This assumption is not challenged in this model, and it is applied in the conceptual framework. The bases of power described previously affect both the likelihood that influence triggers will lead to the target's compliance and the relative success or failure of an influence attempt. If an agent's base(s) of power are aligned with influence triggers experienced by targets, the likelihood of compliance will increase. In instances that influence triggers are not grounded in the agent's power bases, targets will question the instrumentality of inducements and will be less likely to comply with requests.

Moderating variables

The typologies of influence triggers have been derived from the motivation, power, leadership, and influence literatures. The likely outcome for each influence trigger depends on the target's resistance to an agent's directive, the target's source of motivation, and the agent's bases of power. The moderating variables will interact with the influence triggers and serve to lessen or heighten the likelihood of compliance. Combinations of moderating variables will produce the most favorable conditions for compliance (Figure 15.1). When some moderating variables are compatible but others are not (e.g., the exchange trigger is in effect, the target has high instrumental motivation, but the agent lacks reward power), the likelihood of compliance is lessened. When none of the moderating variables are compatible with the influence trigger experienced by the target (e.g., an exchange trigger is in effect, but the target has low instrumental motivation, the agent lacks reward power, and the target's resistance is in the influence or non-influence zones), then the likelihood of compliance is lowest.

Antecedents of influence triggers

Leadership scholars have recently explored the antecedents of leadership (see Avolio 1994; Barbuto et al. 2005; Grams and Rogers 1989). Antecedents offer insight into previously established schemata by which individuals base actions and reactions. Exploring the antecedents of

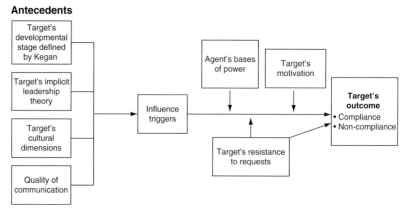

Figure 15.3 Framework for understanding the effect of antecedents on influence triggers and target compliance.

influence triggers would be useful in anticipating how targets manifest intent. It may also inform agents to optimally initiate appropriate influence triggers. The antecedent component has been included in an expanded framework (see Figure 15.3).

Antecedents of influence triggers

Stages of development
Kegan (1982) proposed stages of ego construction that described ways of meaning making in a six-stage model. These stages included

1. incorporative (the beginning stages of development involving reflexes, motions and senses);
2. impulsive (one's impulses drive one's actions);
3. imperial (individuals are aware of their own and others needs but have no sense of being responsible for those needs);
4. interpersonal (individuals operate on a set of values, ideals and beliefs and are able to understand another's point of view even if it conflicts with one's own view);
5. institutional (individuals defined who they are and have developed internal rules and regulations for actions);
6. interindividual (individuals realize that deeper meanings exist than the categorical systems that have been developed to describe the world, thus individuals view the world in shades of gray).

Targets at lower stages of development interpret meaning of influence triggers with a lower order than targets operating at higher levels. Kegan's (1982) work purported a constellation of internal cognitions that interact in such a way that individuals form mental organizations through which triggers manifest. The interpretations of influence triggers are dependent upon targets' level of constructive development.

Cultural differences

In the expanded framework, individuals process influence triggers through a number of filters one of which is societal culture. Hofstede (1980) argued that individuals filter behaviors relying on characteristics of their culture, which include: power distance (the degree that individuals accept power differences); individuality (the degree that individuals act in their self-interest); masculinity (the degree that competitiveness and assertiveness are paramount); uncertainty avoidance (the degree that individuals need low risk) and long-term orientation (the degree that individuals focus on long-term impacts versus short-term goals).

Hofstede's work discussed the importance of cultural differences in most leadership processes. As workplaces diversify, the cultural filter that plays in the influence process will be increasingly salient (Hooijberg and DiTomaso 1996).

Implicit theories

An individual's interpretation of events, actions, and behaviors utilizes pre-existing mental structures and schemata to interpret and classify behaviors (Lord and Maher 1991). Targets use implicit theories of leadership behavior to classify agents' actions (Eden and Levitan 1975). Based upon pre-existing mental schemata, targets may interpret influence triggers differently than the agent intended it to be. Individuals develop prototypes of leaders and interpret leader behaviors based on those prototypes (Hogg and Abrams 1988).

Quality of communication

Adler and Elmhorst (2002) presented a model of communication in which communication between employees is affected by context, the encoding and decoding of the sender and the receiver and three different types of interfering noise – physical background noise, physiological noise, and psychological noise. The model suggested that messages are filtered by context and noise resulting in the quality of communication impacting interpretations of influence intentions.

The quality of the communication between agents and targets filters the influence triggers being experienced by the target in this expanded framework.

Summary

This framework is derived from the target's perspective, focusing on the reactions of targets to influence attempts rather than the actual behaviors or interventions of agents. Influence triggers represent a reaction or internal mechanism that responds to implied or explicit messages from agents. This framework explains how influence triggers will be moderated by several factors. These moderating variables include the target's resistance to the requested behaviors or goals (Barbuto 2000b), the target's sources of motivation (Barbuto and Scholl 1998), and the target's perception of the agent's bases of social power (French and Raven 1959; Hinkin and Schriesheim 1989). The research from which this framework was derived has focused on agents' behaviors but needs to be studied within a target context. The proposed relationships between influence triggers, combined with the moderating variables, and target outcomes were explored and explicit propositions can be developed to guide future research efforts.

The most significant contribution of this chapter is the description and application of influence triggers. Influence triggers offer an alternative explanation of the power and influence process, focusing on the target's perspective and the target's reactions to an agent's influence interventions. A second substantive contribution of this work is the conceptualization and extension of Barnard's (1938) zones of indifference in the development of concentric zones of behaviors to explain a target's resistance to directives. The concentric zones of behavior more usefully articulate a target's resistance to influence attempts and provide researchers with a salient target-based variable for understanding the inducement process. A third contribution of this chapter is the conceptualization of both the target's motivation and the agent's bases of power as moderating variables for understanding target compliance. Use of this framework may shed some light on the roles of power, motivation, concentric zones of resistance, the influence process, and inducements in understanding influence triggers and compliance.

References

Adler, R. B. and Elmhorst, J. M. (2002) *Communicating at work: Principles and practices for business and the professions*, 7th edn, New York, N.Y.: McGraw-Hill.

Ashforth, B. and Mael, F. (1989) Social identity theory and the organization. *Academy of Management Review*, **14**, 20–39.

Avolio, B. J. (1994) The "natural": Some antecedents to transformational leadership. *International Journal of Public Adminstration*, **17** (9), 1559–1581.

Barbuto, J. E. (2000a) Comparing leaders' ratings to targets' self-reported resistance to task directives: An extension of Chester Barnard's zones of indifference. *Psychological Reports*, **86** (2), 611–621.

(2000b) Influence triggers: A framework for understanding follower compliance. *Leadership Quarterly*, **11** (3), 365–387.

(1997) *Motivation and leadership: Towards a predictive model of leader influence behavior*, Ann Arbor, Mich.: University of Michigan Press.

Barbuto, J. E., Cundall, S., and Fritz, S. M. (2005) Motivation and transactional, charismatic, and transformational leadership: A test of antecedents. *Journal of Leadership and Organizational Studies*, **11** (4), 26–40.

Barbuto, J. E. and Scholl, R. W. (1999) Leader's motivation and perception of follower's motivation as predictors of leader's influence tactics used. *Psychological Reports*, **84**, 1087–1098.

(1998) Motivation sources inventory: Development and validation of new scales to measure an integrative taxonomy of motivation. *Psychological Reports*, **82**, 1011–1022.

Barnard, C. (1938) *The functions of the executive*, Cambridge, Mass.: Harvard Press.

Conger, J. A. and Kanungo, R. N. (1987) Toward a behavioral theory of charismatic leadership in organizational settings. *Academy of Management Review*, **12**, 637–674.

Eden, D. and Levitan, U. (1975) Implicit leadership theory as a determinant of the factor structure underlying supervisory behavior scales. *Journal of Applied Psychology*, **80** (6), 736–741.

French, J. P. R. and Raven, B. (1959) Social bases of power. In D. Cartwright (Ed.), *Studies in social power*, Ann Arbor, Mich.: University of Michigan Press.

Grams, W. C. and Rogers, R. W. (1989) Power and personality: Effects of Machiavellianism, need for approval and motivation on use of influence tactics. *The Journal of General Psychology*, **117** (1), 71–82.

Hinkin, T. R. and Schriesheim, C. A. (1989) Development and application of new scales to measure the French and Raven (1959) bases of social power. *Journal of Applied Psychology*, **74**, 561–567.

Hofstede, G. (1980) *Culture's consequences: International differences in work-related values*. Newbury Park, Calif.: Sage.

Hogg, M. A. and Abrams, D. (1988) *Social identifications: A social psychology of intergroup relations and processes*, London: Routledge.

Hooijberg, R. and DiTomaso, N. (1996) Leadership in and of demographically diverse organizations. *Leadership Quarterly*, 7 (1), 1–19.

House, R. J., Shane, S. A., and Herold, D. M. (1996) Rumors of the death of dispositional research are vastly exaggerated. *Academy of Management Review*, 21, 203–224.

Kegan, R. (1982) *The evolving self*, Cambridge, Mass.: Harvard University Press.

Leonard, N., Beauvais, L., and Scholl, R. (1999) Work motivation: The incorporation of self-concept-based processes. *Human Relations*, 52, 969–998.

Lord, R. G. and Maher, K. J. (1991) *Leadership and information processing: Linking perceptions and performance*, Boston, Mass.: Routledge.

Pfeffer, J. (1981) *Power in organizations*, Boston, Mass.: Pitman.

Sherif, C. W. (1964) Social categorization as a function of latitude of acceptance and series range. *Journal of Abnormal and Social Psychology*, 67, 148–156.

Yukl, G. A. (2005) *Leadership in organizations*, 6th edn, Englewood Cliffs, N. J.: Prentice Hall.

16 Leadership and conflict

Using power to manage conflict in groups for better rather than worse

RANDALL S. PETERSON AND SARAH HARVEY

Introduction

One of the greatest challenges for leaders is to use their power in ways that effectively manage conflict. Conflict pervades the life of all groups. Sometimes, conflict benefits the group and its members by providing new information and helping members to see new ways of thinking about their work. However, conflict also typically feels uncomfortable and may be interpreted as a personal attack or a personality clash, even when it benefits the quality of a group's decision-making. The challenge for team leaders is, therefore, to exercise power in a way that promotes the potential information-processing benefits of conflict while minimizing the relationship risks associated with expressions of power to resolve conflict. To achieve this, we argue that leaders are more likely to lead their groups to better performance with indirect expressions of power such as managing group process rather than outcomes, because indirect expressions of power are both less likely to elicit reactance on the part of the team members and more likely to create a sense of psychological safety between leaders and followers.

Anyone who has worked in a team – from an amateur sports team to a community task force to a professional consulting team – will have experienced some amount of conflict. Conflict is inevitable in group life because people have different backgrounds, experiences, values, personalities and ideas that cannot help but influence the way that members interact with each other. One of the key challenges facing team leaders is, therefore, how to deal with and resolve conflict in a way that benefits rather than harms the interests of the group and its members. The way that a leader exercises power to meet this challenge influences the nature of conflict in the group.

Early research and theory on conflict in groups viewed it as an exclusively harmful process for groups (see De Dreu and Weingart 2003; cf. Brown 1983; Gladstein 1984; Hackman and Morris 1975).

This literature suggests that intragroup conflict leads to hurt feelings for those directly involved, creates tension for others in the group, and distracts everyone from the work at hand (De Dreu and Weingart 2003; Jehn 1995). Given the variety of negative outcomes suggested, it is not surprising that the instinct of some managers may be to either ignore conflict or to try to actively smother it. We will argue, however, that these strategies are ultimately damaging for a team. In smothering or ignoring conflict, managers ignore a key resource available to the team for making good decisions – the ideas, information, and judgments of its members, each of whom has a different contribution to make to group decisions.

Research now suggests, for example, that conflict can actually be helpful for groups under certain conditions, making group members more creative (e.g. Nemeth 1986), more committed to group decisions and therefore more satisfied (e.g. Amason 1996; Peterson 1999; Thibaut and Walker 1975), more knowledgeable about one another and their interests (see Ronson and Peterson 2007 for a review) and, overall, can achieve higher levels of performance, particularly in complex decision-making tasks (Jehn 1995).

Realizing these outcomes, however, requires that the conflict be carefully managed. The benefits of conflict to group decisions can be swamped by the problems it creates when it leads to interpersonal conflict that disrupts cohesion and trust amongst team members. Moreover, the power that a leader has over the group, and the way in which this power is exercised, influences the effectiveness of group conflict. This creates a dilemma for managers. As managers become increasingly powerful, they are more likely to take active steps to address a conflict (Galinsky et al. 2003; Kipnis 1976). However, when leaders are heavy-handed in exercising their power over the group, this can lead group members to react with increased conflict with the leader, and it can create a lack of psychological safety that more broadly disrupts group outcomes. Similarly, if leaders try to improve group decisions by stepping in and forcing a particular outcome rather than dealing with the conflict, the decision and the group process will be worse (Peterson 1997).

In this chapter, we first introduce some of the key sources of conflict in groups and the role that leaders play in effectively managing those conflicts. We suggest that conflict arises from differences in values, interests, and information, and that these are associated with three types of conflict: task conflict, relationship conflict, and process conflict. We then identify the ways in which the exercise of power may exacerbate conflict in groups. Finally, we propose three strategies that leaders can use in exercising power in indirect ways to encourage the group to deal with conflict productively and to ensure that their group benefits from task-related conflict without letting that conflict devolve into harmful relationship problems for the group.

Matching sources and types of conflict in groups

Sources and types of conflict

Conflict in groups comes in many forms. Group members disagree with fellow team members for different reasons and in different ways. We argue here that there are at least three distinct sources of conflict in most teams: information, goals, and values. The first source of conflict is differences in information between group members, based on their experiences, backgrounds, and skills. The second is differences in interests that require team members to compete for the same scarce resources. The third is the result of underlying differences in values. When people differ in their basic or backstop values, they find if difficult to compromise on these values (e.g., Rokeach 1979; Tetlock 1986).

Differences between group members based on these three sources of conflict in groups results in three types of conflict. Research has long recognized the existence of task and relationship conflict as two distinct types of conflict (e.g., Guetzkow and Gyr 1954). For example, by asking members of management and production teams to describe the types of conflict that occur in their unit, and observing these teams, Jehn (1997) found two distinct types of conflict.

1. Task-based conflict is disagreement over ideas or opinions that are related directly to the content of the task or decision at hand (Jehn 1995; Simons and Peterson 2000; Guetzkow and Gyr 1954).
2. Relationship conflict is a reflection of interpersonal differences or incompatibility, and results in negative affect in the group – anger, frustration, or annoyance directed at another individual in the group (Jehn 1995; Simons and Peterson 2000; Guetzkow and Gyr 1954).

Jehn's (1997) data further revealed another distinct type of conflict that occurs when groups disagree over how the task should be accomplished, or the processes surrounding how the group should work together to accomplish the task goal (i.e. process conflict) (Jehn 1997; Jackson et al. 2002).

The consensus in the literature over the past ten years has been to view relationship conflict as harmful to groups but task conflict as often harmful yet potentially beneficial if managed appropriately (De Dreu and Weingart 2003). Task conflict can improve the decision-making ability and creativity of group members under the right conditions (e.g., cooperative decision-making à la Johnson and Johnson 1997; Tjosvold 1991). When disagreement exists over the content of the task, individual group members – including the leader – become exposed to new ways of thinking and new perspectives from which to view decisions. For example, when individuals are exposed to a minority of people who disagree, they tend to think more divergently and see a wider variety of possible alternatives (Nemeth 1986). In samples of self-managing teams and cross-functional teams, De Dreu and West (2001) found that exposure to minority dissent lead to higher levels of innovation, in teams where members had high levels of participation in decision-making. In addition, conflict can stimulate the uncovering and discussion of information (Stasser and Titus 1987), so that the group has all of the necessary facts at its disposal and can make a more informed decision. Task conflict also provides all group members with an opportunity to have an input into group decisions, which makes individual members more committed to the group's decision (Coch and French 1948; Vroom and Jago 1988) and therefore more likely to work hard to achieve group goals. This can also improve the effectiveness of decision implementation by the group (Peterson 1997; Peterson et al. 2007); in a sample of seventy-eight top management teams working in the hospitality industry, Peterson et al. (2007) found that intense discussion of ideas promoted by the use of a consensus-decision rule improved the implementation success of key strategic decisions.

Conflict can also, of course, result in negative consequences for groups. Relationship conflict in particular produces tension and frustration that interfere with group processes, which disrupts interpersonal relationships between group members and diverts attention away from the task (Jehn 1995; De Dreu and Weingart 2003; Simons and Peterson 2000). The result is lower satisfaction for individual group members and generally lower productivity (Jehn 1995; Saveedra et al. 1993;

Gladstein 1984). Jehn (1995) found that for groups performing routine tasks in a sample from the transportation industry, for example, high levels of interpersonal conflict were associated with decreased satisfaction and lower levels of liking of other members of the group. Groups in which members differ significantly from one another in terms of underlying values, assumptions, and backgrounds tend to have more conflict and less cohesion and satisfaction (Williams and O'Reilly 1998; Mohammed and Ringseis 2001). For example, groups that differ in terms of members' values have been found to have lower satisfaction, less commitment to the group, and lower intent to remain in the group, because the differences in member values lead to interpersonal conflict (Jehn et al. 1999).

Matching sources and types of conflict

We argue that different sources of conflict are likely to result in different types of conflict and thus need to be managed by leaders in different ways. We suggest that differences in information are most likely to result in task conflict that can be resolved by sharing information with one another with minimal amounts of emotional involvement, while differences in interests and values are likely to be more difficult to resolve because of an increased likelihood of emotion and relationship conflict. For differences in interests to be resolved, at least one person must compromise on his or her goals and subordinate his or her goals to the interests of others, which may provoke process conflict, where allocation of resources can be agreed amicably only if members first agree on a fair process (i.e. see procedural justice work of people like Tom Tyler and Allan Lind, e.g. Lind and Tyler 2003).

Differences in *values* are most likely to directly provoke *relationship conflict* because their resolution requires major change or compromise on the part of one or all people involved in the conflict. People both resist making choices between important values and find it difficult when forced into a situation where choices need to be made (e.g., Tetlock 1986). Such differences in values are likely to be high in emotion, fraught with potential to become personalized, and potentially toxic for groups to handle.

These different types of conflict vary substantially in, (a) how difficult they are to resolve, (b) the potential value they offer to the group for improved decision-making, and (c) the degree of risk that they expose the group to in terms of damage to its current and future functioning. Differences based on information are the easiest to resolve by simply sharing the information; they also offer a benefit to the task as they broaden the information available for the decision, and they are unlikely to produce significant interpersonal issues between group members. Since differences in interests may require compromise, they are likely to be harder to resolve. However, differences of interest are also likely to lead to discussion of deeper, underlying priorities and assumptions than are differences in information and therefore could provide a significant benefit to the task if they can be resolved. The process conflict in resolving them is key, however, to ensuring that it does not result in igniting relationship conflict. Finally, differences in values are the hardest to resolve. Resolving these value differences is likely to pose a serious challenge to group members' relationships, since values are deeply held and personal, so that a disagreement with one's values may feel like a personal problem with a particular individual. However, if differences in values can be resolved, they can provide a rich understanding of the problem (e.g., Tetlock 1986).

While many scholars view task conflict and a moderate and initial amount of process conflict as beneficial, and relationship conflict as harmful, the challenge is that these things are not easy to disentangle in an ongoing and interacting group, and recent work suggests that group members do not always separate their views of different types of conflict so easily (De Dreu and Weingart 2003). When a colleague disagrees vigorously with our opinions, for example, we ask ourselves whether it is from a genuine belief that they are supporting an idea that will benefit the group or whether it might be personal. Heated debates over the task can easily be misinterpreted as interpersonal conflict (Simons and Peterson 2000).

The challenge for leaders, then, is to manage the group to extract the benefits of task-related conflict, while minimizing the problems of interpersonal conflict. In particular, the discussion thus far suggests that leaders should hope to maximize differences in information and encourage information-sharing, manage differences in interests by ensuring fair process, and minimize differences in underlying values where possible. However, we argue that not all efforts toward conflict resolution will be effective. When leaders use direct forms of power to try to manage conflict, it can actually create more conflict and an unsupportive interpersonal environment. Instead, we propose three indirect strategies for leaders to leverage potential benefits and minimize the risks of intragroup conflict.

The exercise of power in conflict

Leaders have a great deal of power that can be leveraged to help groups manage conflict for good rather than ill in their teams. Indeed, one could argue that conflict management is their key responsibility in successfully leading a team. Leaders may be tempted to use their power directly to resolve group conflict, for example by taking over a task, making a decision themselves, or instructing others in the group to take certain actions. People high in power tend to be more action oriented (Galinsky et al. 2003) and to express their views in groups more (Islam and Zyphur 2005). For example, Galinksy et al. (2003) conducted a series of experimental studies and found that people high in power were more likely to perform actions such as acting out against an annoying environmental stimulus. Leaders may, therefore, be more likely to exercise their power decisively when conflict arises.

However, exercising their power to alleviate conflict poses something of a dilemma for leaders, since the use of direct power can also *exacerbate* conflict in the group. Specifically, there are three ways that the direct exercise of power in a conflict situation can enhance future conflict – by creating negative feelings toward the leader, by causing people to temporarily hide their true opinions, and by disrupting group cohesion.

First, direct use of power can lead to negative feelings between the group leader and members of the team. When one person exercises power over another, it tends to amplify the differences between the two and, consequently to lead to negative feelings and the potential for conflict. For example, subordinates' perceptions of the power of their supervisors influence the quality of the subordinate–supervisor relationship, such that when supervisors are perceived to have power that they do not use in service of subordinates, subordinates can become withdrawn (Farmer and Aguinis 2005). In other words, using power to overcome a conflict can shift the conflict to leaders themselves. In addition, teams in which members are low in power can outperform teams in which members are high in power due to a lack of trust that occurs in high power teams (Greer and Caruso 2007). This suggests that highlighting the status hierarchy in the group in this way may create less trust in the group.

The second effect of using power directly is that it may reduce the conflict in the short term but lead to longer-term disagreement and lack of trust. When a leader intervenes to take control of a task or decision, other group members may go along with the leader due to pressure to conform (Janis 1982), and keep their disagreements to themselves. However, differences of opinion may resurface as more harmful inter-personal conflict in the future, when group members feel that their views have not been taken into account. People who are low in power in the organizational hierarchy have also been found to be less likely to be forgiving and to reconcile following a dispute than people high in power (Aquino et al. 2006), suggesting that the additional conflict may be harder to resolve.

The third effect of power on conflict is less direct. People tend to feel a greater affiliation toward others who have a similar level of power as themselves; for example, in an experimental study, Dijke and Poppe (2004) found that subjects indicated that they shared group membership to a greater degree with others who had equal power to themselves than unequal others. Thus, when leaders display their power over the group in a direct way, it enhances the perception of the leader's power over the team and may therefore reduce the overall cohesion of the group.

The most potent weapons for achieving a positive influence over group conflict, therefore, are the ones that leaders most often ignore. That is, team leaders have at their disposal a great deal of indirect power in the form of control over group membership and process, in addition to traditional and more direct forms of power (e.g., issuing of direct orders) (Peterson 2001). In another sense, however, team leaders' power may be limited. In many settings, participating in the team may be only one of many functions that each team member fulfils within the organization. In such instances, team leaders may have little ability to provide tangible rewards to team members or to coerce them by with-holding resources or rewards. Drawing on French and Raven's classifi-cation (1959) of the bases of power, leaders may be limited in their ability to use coercive or reward-based power and therefore must be strategic in drawing on their legitimate authority, referent power, and expert power.

In addition to minimizing the risk of creating additional conflict, the use of indirect forms of power provides two other benefits to leaders. First, when leaders directly influence the group's task and out-come, they fail to resolve the conflict that exists between group mem-bers. When the leader uses indirect forms of power to shape the group's process, the group tends to make better decisions and in general to have a higher quality interaction (Peterson 1997).

Second, direct power displays by leaders also tend to create a negative interpersonal atmosphere in the group. When group leaders issue direct orders, group members may feel uncomfortable expressing their views, because the leader may criticize them or challenge their ideas. This creates a lack of psychological safety in the group. Psychological safety is necessary for group members to engage in activities that are central to good decision-making in groups, such as asking questions, challenging one another, and experimenting (Edmondson 1999). A lack of psycho-logical safety between the leader and group members can be particularly damaging for the group, because the leader will not be exposed to alternative views. The leader then has less information on which to base the decision and is not challenged to think through the decision thoroughly. In other words, direct displays of power can reduce the ability of the group to make good decisions.

We therefore identify here three key indirect forms of expressing power or influence for the purpose of shaping and improving team outcomes: structuring the group, directing group process, and mana-ging the external boundaries of the group.

Three strategies for leaders to leverage potential benefits and minimize the risks of intragroup conflict

Structuring the group

One way that leaders can exert power over a group without being directive is by creating or altering group structure. Even where leaders have relatively restricted authority over group members, they retain the legitimate power to compose the group and group processes as they see fit. Exercising this type of legitimate power can indirectly influence conflict in the group.

Structural solutions for leading groups through conflict deal with ways in which the group can be composed and run in order to minimize the degree of relationship conflict and to maximize the useful aspects of task-related conflict. In particular, structural solutions can be used to align group members' underlying interests and to facilitate agreement over the task. Two aspects of group structure can help to bring group members' interests into alignment with one another. First, the task can be designed to create interdependence between group members, such that when one team member achieves her goals, all team members achieve their goals (Deutsch 1949). This minimizes the opportunity for conflict to arise from differences in underlying interests. Interdependence can be created either by dividing the work in such a way that group members must rely on one another to accomplish the task (Wageman 1995; Wageman and Baker 1997; Johnson and Johnson 1997), or the reward structure may be set up such that the reward that members receive for their part of the task is dependent on the performance of the group as a whole (Wageman 1995; Johnson and Johnson 1989). In either situation, what is good for one member of the group benefits other members of the group, so that conflict over underlying differences is minimized.

Structural solutions can also facilitate potentially beneficial task conflict in groups. In order to have task conflict, group members must first have different resources and information to draw on, and they must then use their unique informational resources to inform the group decision. Groups that are high in informational diversity have been found to have higher levels of performance (Jehn et al. 1999). The first structural solution for leaders in promoting task conflict, then, is to divide the task in such a way as to promote differences in information. However, there must still be sufficient overlap in the knowledge of the group so that group members can understand and use one another's information. Bunderson and Sutcliffe (2002) found that groups in which members are highly specialized in different functional silos tend to exchange less information because members do not believe that others can understand their information and fail to see how their information will be useful to others. In contrast, groups that are high in functional diversity but where group members are generalists with experience across a range of functions share more information and have higher levels of performance.

Once group members have a diverse informational source from which to draw, members must share their uniquely held information and use it to inform group decisions. However, groups are not particularly good at sharing and integrating their information in this way (Stasser and Titus 1985). Again, the structure of the group can facilitate the sharing of information. One structural solution is to make it clear to members of the group how information is held within the group – when group members are familiar with one another (Gruenfeld et al. 1996), or when they are told who holds what expertise in the group (Stewart and Stasser 1995) they tend to be more effective at sharing information with one another. Another structural intervention is to manipulate how group members perceive the task itself – when group members believe that a correct answer to the problem exists, they are more likely to search for that answer and therefore, to share more information (Stasser and Stewart 1992). Also, when group members are told to focus on a different aspect of the task they are more likely to uncover unshared information; for example, Brodbeck (2003) found that when group members with different information were told to focus on documenting information, they were more likely to uncover their uniquely held facts. Thus, by altering the goal of the group, leaders can promote the emergence of relevant information that can lead to task conflict.

Directing an inclusive group process

Sometimes structural solutions will be insufficient to align group member interests – in some situations, there is simply no opportunity for overlap in interests or values; that is, sometimes the interests and values of group members will be incompatible with one another (Cronin and Weingart 2007). However, leaders can also prevent differences in interests and values from deteriorating into destructive relationship conflict by creating an inclusive group process. Although leaders who are overly directive have long been identified as problematic for group processes and the cause of poor group decision-making (e.g., Janis 1982; Lippitt and White 1952), leaders who direct the group *process* rather than dictate the outcome for the group are actually associated with more positive group interactions (Peterson 1997). In using this strategy, leaders are drawing on referent power to persuade the group (French and Raven 1959) rather than appealing directly to their authority. Interpersonal influence can often be an equally or more important form of power than traditional coercive power (see Westphal and Bednar 2006), and referent power has been associated with job effectiveness (Rahim et al. 2000).

In particular, group leaders should encourage members to discuss all possible alternatives, should be good listeners, and should respect the concerns and feelings of group members. Leaders who direct the process of the group in this open-minded manner are likely to facilitate the emergence of task conflict in such a way that the group can integrate differing points of view and share information, and thus benefit from the experience.

High levels of task conflict are typically associated with high levels of relationship conflict, because in the process of engaging in heated debates over the decision at hand, group members may make comments or take actions that can easily be misattributed as a personal attack (Simons and Peterson 2000). This process of misattribution is most likely to happen when team members do not trust one another – when there is no trust between people, any ambiguous statements or actions made by one individual will at least be suspect. When an individual's actions are misinterpreted in this way, he is also more likely to reciprocate with mistrust of the other (Zand 1972). Trust or mistrust in a group thus creates an environment in which each group member's behavior is interpreted (Simons and Peterson 2000). Leaders, then, must foster an environment of trust in the group. When trust between group members is high, teams can benefit from constructive task-related conflict, without this conflict devolving into harmful relationship conflict.

In some situations, however, it may be impossible to remove all differences in interests between group members. Individuals in organizations have a variety of motivations that may transcend their interests as they relate to a particular group. For example, a member of a task force that represents one division of a company may feel a greater commitment to represent his or her division than the task force, and the group leader may have little control over this broader set of motivations. In these situations, other group process solutions can help bridge these gaps. In particular, using a consensus decision rule encourages group members to discuss their opinions, defend their ideas, and voice their concerns, because with a consensus rule, each group member has the opportunity to veto the group decision (Peterson et al. 2007). This sort of open discussion exposes each group member to their differences and enables them to see things from one another's perspective, potentially finding points of shared concern. Consensus rules have consistently been associated with group satisfaction (e.g., Miller 1989; Rawlins 1984), and, more recently, with decision commitment and implementation success (Dooley et al. 2000). When group members must come to consensus, they are more likely to recognize different preferences and the underlying reasons for those preferences, and, in order to make a decision, they resolve or compromise on those differences (Holloman and Hendrick 1972; Mohammed and Ringseis 2001). In this way, consensus decision-making may help to bring group member interests into alignment.

Managing the external boundaries

The broader environment in which a group operates also has a significant impact on the performance of the group (e.g., Ancona 1990). The external environment is both a source of information that can and often should inform group decisions, as well as the setting in which the group's performance will be evaluated. The leader can again play a central role in managing the boundary between the team and its external environment, in order to both draw out task conflict and to minimize relationship conflict.

Peterson and Behfar (2003) demonstrated that conflict is a reaction to, as well as cause of, feedback about group performance. When groups receive initial negative feedback about their performance, their levels of both task and relationship conflict increase (Peterson and Behfar 2003). Negative feedback reduces group efficacy and threatens group cohesion (Staw et al. 1981), and increases interpersonal tension (Peterson and Behfar 2003). One important function for the leader, therefore, is to provide a filtered amount of feedback about group performance – enough to promote some degree of task conflict but not so much as to promote relationship conflict. This requires leaders to draw on some expert power, so that group members see the feedback as credible and don't look for alternative signals of group performance. It also requires the leader to use charisma and persuasion to deliver the message in a way that highlights needs for development while motivating the group to improve its performance.

The external environment can also be an important source of information for the group. In a qualitative study of five teams in the consulting industry, Ancona (1990) found that teams that used information from the environment effectively to inform their decisions and actions and that promoted the accomplishments of their team within the organization, tended to have higher levels of success than teams that ignored their environment or interacted with it in a more passive way. One way to facilitate this kind of external interaction is to compose the group of members from a range of functional specialties, so that they can interact and exchange knowledge with many groups outside of the team itself (Ancona and Caldwell 1992; Cummings 2004). Thus, the leader should think carefully about how to compose the group to enable it to work across organizational boundaries and should encourage this type of external interaction.

Each of these three indirect uses of power effectively promotes more positive group processes and better group outcomes. They either allow leaders to manage things that are outside of the group, such as the external environment, or that occur before group interaction, such as group composition or task structure, or they encourage group members to be involved in the resolution of conflict. These indirect forms of power therefore have two advantages for groups. First, it is unlikely that group members will react negatively to these actions, creating additional conflict between the leader and members of the group. Second, both by resolving the existing conflict and by improving the group process, these indirect effects will create a psychologically safe interpersonal atmosphere that will promote effective decision-making.

Conclusion

Conflict is a fact of life for people working in small groups. It is, therefore, a major challenge for leaders. While conflict can both help and damage a group's members, decisions, and performance, the challenge for leaders is to facilitate beneficial task conflict while minimizing harm to the inter-personal relationships between group members. In this chapter, we argue that the way that leaders use their power to manage this conflict has a serious impact on their success – when leaders use direct displays of power, they may actually increase the amount of conflict in the group and generate an unsupportive group environment. We offer three indirect strategies for how group leaders may manage this task effectively: by developing the right structure, by directing an inclusive group process, and by managing how the group interacts with its external environment.

References

Amason, A. (1996) Distinguishing the effects of functional and dysfunctional conflict on strategic decision making: Resolving a paradox for top management teams. *Academy of Management Journal*, **39**, 123–148.

Ancona, D. G. and Caldwell, D. F. (1992) Bridging the boundary: External activity and performance in organizational teams. *Administrative Science Quarterly*, 37, 634–665.

Ancona, D. G. (1990) Outward bound: Strategies for team survival in an organization. *Academy of Management Journal*, 33, 334–365.

Aquino, K., Tripp, T. M., and Bies R. J. (2006) Getting even or moving on? Power, procedural justice, and types of offense as predictors of revenge, forgiveness, reconciliation, and avoidance in organizations. *Journal of Applied Psychology*, 91, 653–668.

Brodbeck, F. (2003) How to improve group decision making in hidden profile situations. Presentation at Small Groups Meeting, Amsterdam.

Brown, L. D. (1983) *Managing conflict at organizational interfaces*, Reading, Mass.: Addison-Wesley.

Bunderson, J. S. and Sutcliffe, K. M. (2002) Comparing alternative conceptualizations of functional diversity in management teams: Process and performance effects. *Academy of Management Journal*, 45, 875–893.

Coch, L. and French, J. (1948) Overcoming resistance to change. *Human Relations*, 1, 512–532.

Cronin, M. and Weingart, L. (2005) Conflict in diverse teams: The problem of representational gaps and the solution of cognitive and affective integration. Working paper.

(2007) Representational gaps, information processing, and conflict in funtionally diverse teams. *Academy of Management Review*, 32 (3), 761–773.

Cummings, J. (2004) Work groups, structural diversity, and knowledge sharing in a global organization. *Management Science*, 50, 352–364.

De Dreu, K. W. and West, M. A. (2001) Minority dissent and team innovation: The importance of participation in decision making. *Journal of Applied Psychology*, 86, 1191–1201.

De Dreu, K. W. and Weingart, L. R. (2003) Task versus relationship conflict, team performance, and team member satisfaction: A meta-analysis. *Journal of Applied Psychology*, 88, 741–749.

Deutsch, M. (1949) A theory of cooperation and competition. *Human Relations*, 2, 129–152.

Dijke, M. V. and Poppe, M. (2004) Social comparison of power: Interpersonal versus intergroup effects. *Group Dynamics: Theory, Research, and Practice*, 8, 13–26.

Dooley, R. S., Fryxell, G. E., and Judge, W. Q. (2000) Belaboring the not-so-obvious: Consensus, commitment, and strategy implementation speed and success. *Journal of Management*, 26, 1237–1257.

Edmondson, A. (1999) Psychological safety and learning behavior in work teams. *Administrative Science Quarterly*, 44, 350–383.

Farmer S. M. and Aguinis H. (2005) Accounting for subordinate perceptions of supervisor power: An identity-dependence model. *Journal of Applied Psychology*, 90, 1069–1093.

French, J. R. P. and Raven, B. (1959) The bases of social power. In D. Cartwright (Ed.), *Studies in social power* (pp. 150–167), Ann Arbor, Mich.: Institute for Social Research.

Galinsky, A. D., Gruenfeld, D. H., and Magee, J. C. (2003) From power to action. *Journal of Personality and Social Psychology*, 85, 453–466.

Gladstein, D. L. (1984) A model of task group effectiveness. *Administrative Science Quarterly*, 29, 499–517.

Greer, L. L. and Caruso, H. M. (2007) Are high-power teams high performers? Linking team power to trust, interpersonal congruence, and decision-making performance. *Academy of Management Proceedings, 2007*, 1–6.

Gruenfeld, D. H, Mannix, E. A., Williams, K. Y., and Neale, M. A. (1996) Group composition and decision making: How member familiarity and information distribution affect process and performance. *Organizational Behavior and Human Decision Processes*, 67, 1–15.

Guetzkow, H. and Gyr, J. (1954) An analysis of conflict in decision-making groups. *Human Relations*, 7, 367–381.

Hackman, J. R. and Morris, C. G. (1975) Group tasks, group interaction processes, and group performance effectiveness: A review and proposed integration. *Advances in Experimental Social Psychology*, 8, 45–99.

Holloman, C. R. and Hendrick, H. W. (1972) Adequacy of group decision as a function of the decision-making process. *Academy of Management Journal*, 15, 175–184.

Islam, G. and Zyphur, M. J. (2005) Power, voice, and hierarchy: Exploring the antecedents of speaking up in groups. *Group Dynamics: Theory, Research, and Practice*, 9, 93–103.

Jackson, K. M., Mannix, E. A., Peterson, R. S., and Trochim, W. M. K. (2002) A multi-faceted approach to process conflict. JACM 15th Annual Conference.

Janis, I. L. (1982) *Groupthink*, 2nd edn, Boston, Mass.: Houghton Mifflin.

Jehn, K. A. (1997) A qualitative analysis of conflict types and dimensions in organizational groups. *Administrative Science Quarterly*, 42, 530–557.

(1995) A multimethod examination of the benefits and detriments of intragroup conflict. *Administrative Science Quarterly*, 40, 256–282.

Jehn, K. A., Northcraft, G. B., and Neale, M. A. (1999) Why differences make a difference: A field study of diversity, conflict and performance in workgroups. *Administrative Science Quarterly*, 44, 741–764.

Johnson, D. W. and Johnson, F. P. (1997) *Joining together: Group theory and group skills*, Needham Heights, Mass.: Allyn & Bacon.

Johnson, D. W. and Johnson, R. (1989) *Cooperation and competition: Theory and research*, Edina, Minn.: Interaction.

Kipnis, D. (1976) *The powerholders*, Chicago: University of Chicago Press.

Lind, E. A. and Tyler, T. R. (2003) *The social psychology of procedural justice*, New York, N.Y.: Plenum.

Lippitt, R. and White, R. K. (1952) An experimental study of leadership and group life. In G. E. Swanson, T. M. Newcomb, and E. L. Hartley (Eds.), *Readings in social psychology*, New York, N.Y.: Holt, Rinehart & Winston.

Miller, C. E. (1989) The social psychological effects of group decision rules. In P. B. Paulus (Ed.), *Psychology of group influence*, 2nd edn, (pp. 327–355), Hillsdale, N. J.: Lawrence Erlbaum Associates.

Mohammed, S. and Ringseis, E. (2001) Cognitive diversity and consensus in group decision making: The role of inputs, processes, and outcomes. *Organizational Behavior and Human Decision Processes*, 85, 310–335.

Nemeth, C. J. (1986) Differential contributions of majority and minority influence. *Psychological Review*, 93, 23–32.

Peterson, R. S. (1999) Can you have too much of a good thing? The limits of voice in improving satisfaction with leaders. *Personality and Social Psychology Bulletin*, 25, 313–324.

(1997) A directive leadership style in group decision making can be both virtue and vice: Evidence from elite and experimental groups. *Journal of Personality and Social Psychology*, 72, 1107–1121.

(2001) Toward a more deontological approach to the ethical use of social influence. In J. Darley, D. Messick, and T. R. Tyler (Eds.), *Social influences on ethical behavior in organizations* (pp. 21–36), Mahwah, N. J.: Erlbaum.

Peterson, R. S. and Behfar, K. J. (2003) The dynamic relationship between performance feedback, trust, and conflict in groups: A longitudinal study. *Organizational Behavior and Human Decision Processes*, 92, 102–112.

Peterson, R. S., Simons, T. L., Rodgers, M. S., and Harvey, S. (2007) Bridging troubled waters: Consensus decision rules attenuate the negative impact of low trust on decision implementation in top management teams. Working paper.

Rahim, M., Antonioni, D., Krumov, K., and Ilieva, S. (2000) Power, conflict, and effectiveness: A cross-cultural study in the United States and Bulgaria. *European Psychologist*, 5, 28–33.

Rawlins, W. K. (1984) Consensus in decision-making groups. In J. T. Wood (Ed.), *Emergent issues in human decision-making* (pp. 19–39), Carbondale, Ill.: Southern Illinois University Press.

Rokeach, M. (1979) *Understanding human values*, New York, N.Y.: Free Press.

Ronson, S. and Peterson, R. S. (2007) The paradox of conflict in groups: Cooperation as a basis for positive group experience and group performance. In B. A. Sullivan, M. Snyder, and J. L. Sullivan (Eds.), *Cooperation: A powerful force in human relations*, Malden, Mass.: Blackwell.

Saavedra, R., Earley, P. C., and Van Dyne, L. (1993) Complex interdependence in task-performing groups. *Journal of Applied Psychology*, 78, 61–72.

Simons, T. L. and Peterson, R. S. (2000) Task conflict and relationship conflict in top management teams: The pivotal role of intragroup trust. *Journal of Applied Psychology*, 85, 102–111.

Stasser G. and Titus W. (1987) Effects of information load and percentage of shared information on the dissemination of unshared information during group discussion. *Journal of Personality and Social Psychology*, 53, 53–81.

Stasser, G. and Stewart, D. (1992) Discovery of hidden profiles by decision-making groups: Solving a problem versus making a judgment. *Journal of Personality and Social Psychology*, 63, 426–434.

Stasser, G. and Titus, W. (1985) Pooling of unshared information in group decision making: Biased information sampling during discussion. *Journal of Personality and Social Psychology*, 48, 1467–1478.

Staw, B. M., Sandelands, L. E., and Dutton, J. E. (1981) Threat-rigidity effect: A multilevel analysis. *Administrative Science Quarterly*, 26, 501–524.

Stewart, D. D. and Stasser G. (1995) Expert role assignment and information sampling during collective recall and decision-making. *Journal of Personality and Social Psychology*, 69, 619–628.

Tetlock, P. E. (1986) A value pluralism model of ideological reasoning. *Journal of Personality and Social Psychology*, 50, 819–827.

Thibaut, J. and Walker, L. (1975) *Procedural justice: A psychological analysis*. Hillsdale, N. J.: Lawrence Erlbaum Associates.

Tjosvold, D. (1991) *The conflict-positive organization*, Boston, Mass.: Addison-Wesley.

Tusi, A. S. and Barry, B. (1986) Interpersonal affect and rating errors. *Academy of Management Journal*, 29, 586–599.

Vroom, V. H. and Jago, A. G. (1988) *The new leadership: Managing participation in organizations*, Englewood Cliffs, N. J.: Prentice-Hall.

Wageman, R. and Baker, G. (1997) Incentives and cooperation: The joint effects of task and reward interdependence on group performance. *Journal of Organizational Behavior*, 18, 139–158.

Wageman, R. (1995) Interdependence and group effectiveness. *Administrative Science Quarterly*, 40, 145–180.

Westphal, J. D. and Bednar, M. K. (2006) How top managers use interpersonal influence to neutralize the effects of institutional ownership. *Academy of Management Proceedings, 2006*, 1–6.

Williams, K. and O'Reilly, C. (1998) Demography and diversity in organizations: A review of 40 years of research. *Research in Organizational Behaviour*, 20, 77–140.

Zand, D. E. (1972) Trust and managerial problem solving. *Administrative Science Quarterly*, 17, 229–239.

17 | Organizational change

LOURDES MUNDUATE AND
FRANCISCO J. MEDINA

If we review the finance section of any newspaper, we are bound to find news about changing business structures (merging, downsizing, acquisition or expansion), or changes in the way things are done or organizations are managed (implementing new technologies, flattening of hierarchies, standardization of production based on quality criteria, etc.). These past few years have been particularly prolific in terms of business mergers and takeovers. According to market analysts Thomson Financial, the value of business mergers and takeovers in 2006 totaled 3.79 billion dollars, representing an increase of 38 percent compared to 2005. To give some examples, the pharmaceutical multinational Pfizer is to close several research centers and factories around the world, laying off nearly 10,000 workers as a reaction to the increased competition from new pharmaceutical companies offering generic alternatives. As for business takeovers, there are the examples of Google's takeover of YouTube or AT&T's of BellSouth. Everything suggests that 2007 and 2008 will be particularly busy in terms of business mergers and takeovers in key economic sectors, such as electricity in Europe (ENEL and Endesa or Suez-Gaz de France), or the car industry worldwide. In short, changing business patterns in strategic sectors of the economy, caused by pressure on organizations to adapt to changing market demands, has accelerated sharply in recent years as a result of globalization and market competition.

These changes force companies to adjust to the new situations. Organizations will only survive if they have the flexibility to react to the constantly changing demands and if they are adept enough at redirecting, orientating, and exploiting their resources efficiently.

In this chapter, we make a detailed analysis of the effects of organizational change on employees and the positive and negative reactions it produces in them. We look at how the use of power by the agents directly involved in change process may induce a proactive attitude toward change, and, finally, we will look at specific strategies that may facilitate a positive disposition toward change.

The influence of organizational change on employees

Research has demonstrated that employees' positive attitudes toward change are a "necessary initial condition for successful planned change" (Miller et al. 1994: 60). An important factor for determining employees' acceptance of organizational change lies in their perception of whether the change will be beneficial or not to them. Some argue that employees normally react negatively to the adverse consequences of the change rather than to the change itself (Dent and Goldberg 1999). However, employees' attitudes in change situations are normally fairly negative. Even if a change leads to job enrichment or additional rewards, it may put new adaptation demands on employees, creating uncertainty and concern about failure, control, and adjustment. Organizational change produces a great feeling of uncertainty in employees for different reasons:

1. Organizational change may threaten employees' job security. A perceived threat to job security leads to very adverse emotional reactions in employees (Burke and Greenglass 2001).
2. Organizational change may involve a shake-up in the distribution of power within the organization. Changes in tasks and responsibilities normally mean that some gain greater power within the organizational structure to the detriment of others.
3. Organizational change normally involves an increase in occupational demands because the employee has to adapt to a new way of doing things and to a new business culture (Spector 2002).
4. Employees lose psychological control over many aspects of their work. The disorder generated by raising previously settled questions about how to perform one's work jeopardizes reliability, threatens individual sense-making and paves the way for the rupture of employees' psychological contracts (Ledford et al. 1990).
5. In the same way, some employees will feel that the changes have made their jobs less interesting, with less task diversity, or less autonomy. Thus, task distribution produced by changes may threaten the intrinsic motivation of employees (Oreg 2006).
6. Organizational change and restructuring are recognized as being highly stressful for employees (e.g., Rafferty and Griffin 2006).

The consequences are negative reactions closely associated to the change itself, such as cynicism (Wanous et al. 2000) or resistance to change (Kotter and Schlesinger 1979). Organizational cynicism is a complex attitude that includes cognitive, affective, and behavioral aspects that increases beliefs of unfairness and feelings of distrust. Research conducted in the USA revealed that between 45 and 50 percent of the workforce displays cynical behavior (Wanous et al. 2000) and that these employees filed more grievances, had lower job satisfaction, did not believe their supervisor or top management, and were not motivated to create positive change (Reichers et al. 1997).

Resistance to change is a three-dimensional (negative) attitude toward change, which includes affective, behavioral, and cognitive components (Piderit 2000). The affective component concerns how workers feel about the change (angry, anxious); the cognitive component involves what they think about the change (its necessity, pertinence); and the behavioral component involves actions or intended actions in response to the change (complaining about the change, trying to convince others about the negative aspect of change). High resistance to change is linked to less satisfaction, greater intention to leave the organization and less organizational commitment (Oreg 2006).

Although the outlook for organizational change looks somewhat gloomy, the organization can develop strategies to ensure that changes are effective. In the following we will look at the variables that predict a positive attitude in employees, the role played by change agents to attract people to this process and how power can be used by them to succeed in such a task.

A positive picture about organizational change

Some researchers have provided an optimistic and positive view of organizational change, analyzing positive reactions related to change, such as participants' openness to the change (e.g., Wanberg and Banas 2000), readiness for change (Madsen et al. 2005), or commitment (Fedor et al. 2006). These positive reactions are more than a mere favorable disposition to change; they imply a proactive attitude to organizational change, which is crucial if change is to be effective. In the following we shall describe these possible positive reactions to change, to focus subsequently on the way in which the exercise of power may encourage the emergence of these favorable attitudes.

Openness to change involves willingness to support the change and positive feelings about the potential consequences of change (such as feelings that the change will be beneficial in some way) (Wanberg and Banas 2000). Readiness for change is more than just understanding or believing in the change. Individuals are ready for change when they understand, believe and intend to change because of a perceived need (Madsen et al. 2005). Employees' commitment to change is defined as a willingness to exert effort on behalf of the change and its successful implementation. Commitment reflects a proactive intent that is different to an absence of resistance to change. In short, commitment represents a behavioral intention to work toward success of the change, rather than just reflecting a favorable disposition toward it (Fedor et al. 2006).

Power in change processes

Analyses of the role played by power in organizational change are increasing in intensity, scale and impact (Munduate and Bennebroeck-Gravenhorst 2003). One of the aspects that has received much attention is the role played by the change agent. As Weick and Quinn (1999) indicated, change is the result of a set of actions occurring at different levels within the organization; moreover, this is the essence of a continuous, evolving and incremental change process. Within this process, change agents have the potential to forge a transformational dynamic that gradually attracts people to this process of adaptation and permanent adjustment. Therefore, there is an important question regarding how the change agent manages to attract employees and evolve them toward permanent adjustment.

The power of the change agent is not the only source of the different social forces that generate and maintain processes of organizational change, but it is essential for understanding employees' reactions to the change process (Dorriots and Johansson 1999). However, research has underestimated the dynamics of power relations and their effects on organizational change. In an attempt to contribute to filling this void we shall distinguish first between power and influence in the change processes, and, second, we shall look at the different responses that the change agents may elicit in their targets, to concentrate subsequently on those responses that provide a better platform for organizational change.

In trying to understand how change is achieved, social psychologists have used the concepts of social power and influence (Raven 1999).

Social power reflects the repertoire of tools available to a person to influence the environment or the other party, while influence refers to the actual usage of a certain tool in a specific situation. French and Raven (1959) defined influence as a force one person (the leader) exerts on someone else (follower) to induce a change in the latter, including changes in behaviors, attitudes, and values. Social power was subsequently defined as the potential ability of a person to influence someone else. Therefore, to understand the role of the change agent in promoting organizational change, we need to consider first of all the responses elicited in the followers that involve a proactive disposition toward change, and second, the repertoire of tools available to the change agent to influence followers. There is a clear difference between yielding to direct or indirect social pressure from a leader and being genuinely persuaded. For example, the leader's influence may be strong enough to wield control over the followers' behavior, ensuring public agreement, regardless of whether they are privately convinced. On other occasions, the influence process may change followers' private attitude or opinion and make them committed to the leader's request. Therefore, social psychologists proposed different types of influence processes. The most important was Kelman's distinction (1961) between compliance, internalization, and identification. Compliance refers to a surface change in behavior and expressed attitudes, often as a consequence of coercion or the followers' desire to obtain a reward. As compliance does not reflect internal change, it usually only persists while behavior is under surveillance. In contrast to compliance, internalization means subjective acceptance that produces true internal change that persists in the absence of surveillance. The inner norm becomes an internalized standard for behavior. There is genuine support for the leader's proposals because they appear to be intrinsically desirable and are suited to the followers' values and beliefs. Identification is based on the leader's attractiveness to the followers, who imitate his or her behavior and attitudes in order to gain his or her approval. The maintenance of a close relationship with the leader involves the followers' need for acceptance and esteem (Hogg and Vaughan 1995).

To understand the way in which the change agent manages to promote these responses, we look at the potential ability or repertoire of tools available to the leader to influence followers. The potential ability refers to the various bases and sources of power. French and Raven (1959) proposed a well-known taxonomy of power that considered six bases of power: reward, coercion, legitimacy, reference, expertise, and information. A leader possesses some or all of these resources and can use them to change the beliefs, attitudes, or behaviors of followers. Reward and coercive power rely on others believing the leader can provide them with the desired rewards or can punish them, respectively. Using either of these bases will induce only a superficial change in the followers. Only compliance is obtained, the continuation of which depends on successful surveillance of the followers by the leader. A person possesses legitimate power when others believe that he or she has a legitimate right to exert influence over them, and they are obliged to adhere to his or her influence attempts. Referent power refers to followers' identification with the leader. It leads to private acceptance by followers by enabling them to maintain a satisfactory relationship with the leader and to see themselves as similar to the leader in certain important areas. Expert power depends on the followers' perception of expertise or knowledge in a specific domain. If a follower perceives a leader as an expert, this will result in private acceptance on the part of the follower. Finally, informational power leads to internalized and lasting changes in the followers' beliefs, attitudes, or values. Compared to other social-power bases, the changed behavior resulting from information is maintained without continued social dependence on the leader and is instead based on the perceived importance and validity of the information. Only informational power leads to cognitive change in followers, as it immediately becomes independent of the leader (Munduate and Bennebroeck-Gravenhorst 2003).

Another related dimension of power refers to sources of power. When dealing with the bases of power, the focus was the repertoire of tools available to a person to influence the other party or the environment. In terms of sources of power, the focus points toward the way a person comes to control these tools. Two different sources of power have been identified: position and personal power. Position power arises from the formal position held in a group or organization, while personal power arises from personal attributes and the kind of relationship established with the other party. In the former source of power, potential control is derived from legitimate authority, and in the latter it stems from task expertise or the opportunity to access certain information that is important for other members of the group or organization.

These two types of power have different consequences for organizational dynamics. The difference in power between superiors and subordinates has a bearing on the influence processes used in this relation (e.g., Yukl and Falbe 1991; Yukl and Tracey 1992). When position is used to influence subordinates, the perception of social distance between both parties increases, paving the way for submission or open conflict (e.g., Coleman and Voronov 2003). Where there is a great difference in power, the leader becomes perceptually separated from the rest of the group through structural role differentiation grounded in social attraction and attributional processes. The leader is seen as an "other" in relation to the rest of the group. An inevitable consequence of role differentiation is that the leader gradually realizes that he or she is effectively treated by followers as an out-group member. A sense of rejection by the group and distancing and isolation may occur, that allows the leader to gain compliance but not internalization through the exercise of power over others. A consequence of this situation is that high-power managers use more competitive behaviors to influence subordinates than low-power managers (Hogg and Reid 2001; Somech and Drach-Zahavy 2002). Similar results are found in the realm of conflict management. Power differences between superiors and subordinates lead to greater use of threats and punishment (De Dreu et al. 1998). In the same way, managers in high-power conditions devalued the worth of their subordinates (Kipnis 1984). Participants given greater power were significantly more deceitful, often competing after promising to cooperate (Lindskold and Aronoff 1980). In a situation such as this we can only expect a significant deterioration in relations between superiors and subordinates and a reduced likelihood of the latter having favorable attitudes toward change.

The opposite happens when the leader exercises influence over personal power bases. Leaders perceived as having high personal power can still have influence without resorting to the use of hierarchy (Hogg and Reid 2001). Leaders may accumulate idiosyncratic credit with the group by conforming to group norms (Hollander 1985). Thus, a leader's authority stems from influence and the formation of norms within the group. An individual can gain authority through leadership where he or she convinces group members that their opinions are valid or that authority can be conferred by formal agreement, customs, or norms inherent in group identity (Turner 2005). As the power of authority expresses the collective will of the group, even obedience can produce pride and a sense of empowerment when the group's collective identity is salient (Turner 2005). Personal power bases are grounded in trust

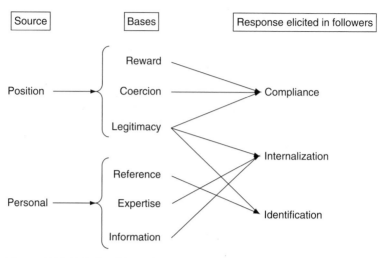

Figure 17.1 Relationships of power sources, bases, and responses elicited in followers.

(Coleman and Voronov 2003). Furthermore, the presence of trust in team members allows increased communication (Carson et al. 1993), improves employees' commitment (Kidd and Smewing 2001), and reduces dysfunctional conflict (Tjosvold 2000).

So far, we have identified two sources of power, six bases of power, and three responses elicited in followers. Figure 17.1 presents the relationships between these aspects of power.

How to facilitate organizational change through the exercise of power

As we have seen in the previous section, findings suggest the importance of cultivating personal power to gain cooperation from others by eliciting internalized responses from followers. In this sense, change agents who use their charisma and experience to influence followers, have special knowledge and experience of the tasks, or manage information appropriately, make team management easier without generating subordinate resistance. In this section we shall describe the set of tools that research has shown to facilitate a positive disposition toward change. These tools come from the use of personal power and include using transformational leadership styles, developing procedural justice,

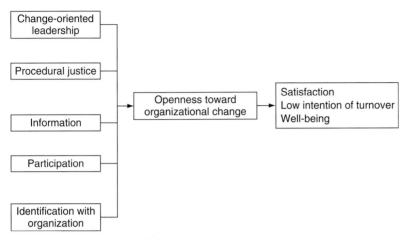

Figure 17.2 Conceptual model of predictors and outcomes of an employee's proactive attitude toward change.

promoting employee participation in change processes, and creating feelings of organizational identification (see Figure 17.2).

Developing a change-oriented leadership

Yukl developed the concept of the change-oriented leader in the three-dimensional leadership model (Yukl 2006; Yukl et al. 2002). Yukl and colleagues add the change dimension to the well-known bi-factorial taxonomy in leadership (task and relationship). The change dimension is compatible with the transformational and charismatic leadership theories (Bass 1985; Conger and Kanungo 1988). The transformational leader uses power to ensure that organizational goals are accomplished. This involves sharing power with subordinates and seeing them as empowered partners (Lowe et al. 1996). According to this model, a change-oriented leader can use the following behaviors: (a) monitoring the environment; (b) encouraging innovative thinking; (c) taking personal risks; and (d) envisioning change.

Leaders have to monitor the environment and identify threats and opportunities for the organization. Information stems from concerns of clients and customers, strategy of competitors, political trends, and economic or technological conditions. A thorough analysis of information is needed to identify problems and opportunities and propose solutions (Yukl et al. 2002). This way, interpreting events and explaining why change is required is a key behavior in most change models (e.g., Kotter 1995, 2002).

Encouraging innovative thinking in employees is like a keystone in the change process (Yukl et al. 2002). It is also a central characteristic of transformational leadership (Lowe et al. 1996) and a necessary condition for the development of innovation in organizations (West et al. 2004). Mumford et al. (2002) identify three leadership characteristics that stimulate team innovation: domain specific expertise, social and problem solving skills, and transformational leadership behaviors. Leader experience contributes to the stimulation of the cognitive resources of the group and its problem-solving capacity (Mumford et al. 2002). Leaders could use their power to protect minority views, to be receptive to followers' information, and to delay their own opinions as long as possible (West et al. 2004). To sum up, to increase innovation, leaders should listen rather than refute, assume responsibility for accurate information, be sensitive to unexpressed feelings, protect minority views, keep the discussion moving, and develop team skills (Maier 1970).

Leaders must also have an inspirational vision of the future. This is a key element of transformational and charismatic leadership. A vision is more effective in influencing followers' commitment to a proposed strategy or change if it is relevant for employees' values, is communicated with enthusiasm and confidence and is perceived as feasible (Tucker and Russell 2004; Yukl et al. 2002).

The exercise of leadership using personal power bases does not just allow the appearance of proactive behaviors toward change but also the reduction of those factors that may hinder it, such as cynicism toward change. An important organizational antecedent of cynicism is the effectiveness of one's own supervisor (Wanous et al. 2000). If supervisors are perceived as being generally ineffective, it is more likely that they will be held responsible for failed change instead of attributing the failure to factors beyond their control. Moreover, leaders may want to actively involve employees in the change process, because participation reduces and prevents cynicism due to the shared responsibility in decision-making. To sum up, some leader behaviors may increase effectiveness in change processes: providing information, listening effectively, being accessible, showing concern for followers and increasing participation in decision-making (Wanous et al. 2000).

Increasing the perception of organizational justice

The way management treats and involves employees during change has received much attention from change researchers and it has been shown to be a powerful determinant of individuals' reactions to major organizational change (Brockner et al. 1994). Organizational justice literature tends to distinguish between distributive justice and procedural justice (Cropanzano and Folger 1991). Distributive justice is based on equity theory (Adams 1965) and is concerned with the fairness of outcomes, whereas procedural justice can be defined as the fairness of procedures enacted by an authority when making allocation decisions (Brotheridge 2003). Research suggests a strong link between power and organizational justice. Subordinates that perceive a low power distance with superiors have strong personal connections and a better understanding of their interests.

Procedural justice is an important tool for the change agent during change processes for two reasons (Tyler and De Cremer 2005). The first is that leaders can gain acceptance for their vision and motivate their followers through leadership using fair procedures. In this sense, when change participants perceive that implementation has been handled fairly, reactions to the change and to the organization are more favorable (Novelli et al. 1995; Wanberg and Banas 2000). The second argument is that when change agents apply fair procedures, they encourage people to identify with organizations, leading to voluntary and willing cooperation (De Cremer and Van Knippenberg 2002).

Tyler and De Cremer (2005) demonstrate that in the process of change, the leader's use of fair procedures will determine whether employees consider the leader to be a legitimate decision-maker and if the leader can be trusted to deal with matters competently. Legitimacy is the employees' assumption that leaders are likely to be right about the matter in hand, that they do their job properly and fairly, and, as a consequence, their decisions ought to be accepted. This perception is important because it leads employees to voluntarily accept the decision and strategies chosen by their leaders (Tyler and Blader 2000, 2003). In this context, employees are more likely to accept changes if they perceive that their leaders are entitled to have their strategic decision accepted. Trust in leader competence reflects the perception that managers understand how to keep the company successful and competitive (Tyler and De Cremer 2005), and that they will propose relevant and useful ideas (Salam 2004).

Summing up, the tools that leaders can use to increase fairness of aspects during a change process include practices such as:

(a) providing advanced notice of changes;
(b) showing respect for the affected individuals;
(c) being open and considerate toward participant concerns;
(d) providing individuals with the opportunity for inputs that can affect ultimate outcomes;
(e) giving group members a voice in the decision-making processes;
(f) being accurate in evaluations leading to a decision;
(g) acting consistently across time and people;
(h) impartiality;
(i) implementing mechanisms to correct inappropriate decisions.

(Leventhal 1980)

These tools are a sign of a low power distance between superiors and subordinates.

Providing sufficient and adequate information

Lewis and Seibold (1998: 96) defined change as a communication problem: "Communication processes are inherently a part of these implementation activities, including announcement of change programs, training of users, and users' interaction and feedback regarding change programs." A successful outcome to the organizational change will depend on whether organizational communication about the change has allowed managers to address employees' concerns and interests. Inefficient handling of information provided to employees leads to rumor and an exaggeration of the negative aspects of change (DiFonzo et al. 1994). In contrast, positive handling of information reduces uncertainty and encourages employee acceptance of change. On this point, research data presented by Schweiger and DeNisi (1991) showed that uncertainty was lower in the group that was exposed to a systematic information process about changes. A timely, accurate and trustworthy communication, provided directly by the supervisor, giving reasons and details about the change process, is crucial for preventing or reducing uncertainty (Bordia et al. 2004a, 2004b).

Promoting employee participation in the change process

Participation refers to giving employees the chance to make inputs in a change process. The change agent needs to attract and gradually involve employees in this process of adaptation and permanent adjustment. The use of personal power develops support and a proactive behavior in subordinates. A higher level of participation increases involvement and the perception that the change would be beneficial (Wanberg and Banas 2000).

Create feelings of identification with the organization

The theory of social identity explains how the individual conception of the self is affected by belonging to certain social groups (e.g., Hogg 2003; Tajfel and Turner 1986). In this sense, identification with the organization reflects the perception of belonging to an organization, where people define themselves in terms of the organization to which they belong (Mael and Ashforth 1992). As identification with the organization leads to activities that are congruent with the identity, high levels of identification are normally associated to a greater probability that these individuals will adhere to organizational norms and values (Van Knippenberg et al. 2006), and a greater interest in organizational change information (Van Knippenberg et al. 2006). Identification is related to employees' attitudes about change, the likelihood of intergroup conflict, and the psychological state of employees after change. As people come to value this conception of the self, they may resist change when they perceive that the change entails an identity transformation (Fiol 2002). For this reason, it is important to ensure a sense of continuity of identity in the change processes (Van Knippenberg et al. 2008). Group identity unifies and empowers people by giving them a common self-interest and the power of collective action, a power to pursue shared goals much greater than the one of any isolated individual (Turner 2005). This power can be used in favor or against change.

Acknowledgments

The authors thank Barbara Van Knippenberg for her helpful contributions to this chapter.

References

Adams, J. S. (1965) Inequity in social exchange. In L. Berkowitz (Ed.), *Advances in experimental social psychology* (Vol. II, pp. 267–299), New York, N.Y.: Academic Press.

Bass, B. (1985) Leadership: Good, better, best. *Organizational Dynamics*, 13, 26–40.

Bordia, P., Hobman, E., Jones, E., Gallois, C., and Callan, V.J. (2004a) Uncertainty during organizational change: Types, consequences and management strategies. *Journal of Business and Psychology*, 18, 507–532.

Bordia, P., Hunt, E., Paulsen, N., Tourish, D., and DiFonzo, N. (2004b) Uncertainty during organizational change: Is it all about control? *European Journal of Work and Organizational Psychology*, 13, 345–365.

Brockner, J., Konovsky, M., Cooper-Schneider, R., Folger, R., Martin, C., and Bies, R.J. (1994) Interactive effects of procedural justice and outcome negativity on victims and survivors of job loss. *Academy of Management Journal*, 37, 397–409.

Brotheridge, C.M. (2003) The role of fairness in mediating the effects of voice and justification on stress and other outcome in climate of organizational change. *International Journal of Stress Management*, 10, 253–268.

Burke, R.J. and Greenglass, E.R. (2001) Hospital restructuring and nursing staff well-being: The role of perceived hospital and union support. *Anxiety, Stress and Coping: An International Journal*, 14, 93–115.

Carson, P.P., Carson, K.D., and Roe, C. (1993) Social power bases: A meta-analytic examination of interrelationships and outcomes. *Journal of Applied Social Psychology*, 23, 1150–1169.

Coleman, P.T. and Voronov, M. (2003) Power in group and organizations. In M. West, D. Tjosvold, and K.G. Smith (Eds.), *International handbook of organizational teamwork and cooperative working* (pp. 229–254), Chichester: John Wiley & Sons.

Conger J. and Kanungo, R.N. (1988) *Charismatic leadership in organizations*, Thousand Oaks, Calif.: Sage.

Cropanzano, R. and Folger, R. (1991) Procedural justice and worker motivation. In R.M. Steers and L.W. Porter (Eds.), *Motivation and work behavior*, 5th edn (pp. 131–143), New York, N.Y.: McGraw-Hill.

De Cremer, D. and Van Knippenberg, D. (2002) How do leaders promote cooperation: The effects of charisma and procedural fairness. *Journal of Applied Psychology*, 87, 858–866.

De Dreu, C.K., Gielbels, E., and Van de Vliert, E. (1998) Social motives and trust in integrative negotiation: The disruptive effects on punitive capability. *Journal of Applied Psychology*, 83, 408–422.

Dent, E.B. and Goldberg, S.G. (1999) Challenging "resistance to change." *Journal of Applied Behavioral Science*, 35, 25–41.

DiFonzo, N., Bordia, P., and Rosnow, R.L. (1994) Reining in rumours. *Organizational Dynamics*, 23, 47–62.

Dorriots, B. and Johansson, I. L. (1999) Communicative power: A linguistic approach to the study of microdynamics of organizations. *Scandinavian Journal of Management*, 15, 193–211.

Fedor, D. B., Caldwell, S., and Herold, D. M. (2006) The effect of organizational changes on employee commitment: A multilevel investigation. *Personnel Psychology*, 59, 1–29.

Fiol, C. M. (2002) Capitalizing on paradox: The role of language in transforming organizational identities. *Organization Science*, 13, 653–666.

French, J. R. P. Jr. and Raven, B. H. (1959) The bases of social power. In D. Cartwright (Ed.), *Studies in social power* (pp. 150–167), Ann Arbor, Mich.: Institute for Social Research.

Hogg, M. A. (2003) Social identity. In M. R. Leary and J. P. Tangney (Eds.), *Handbook of self and identity* (pp. 462–479), New York, N.Y.: The Gilford Press.

Hogg, M. A. and Reid, S. A. (2001) Social identity, leadership and power. In A. Y. Lee-Chai and J. A. Bargh (Eds.), *The Use and Abuse of Power* (pp. 159–180), Ann Arbor, Mich.: Psychology Press.

Hogg, M. A. and Vaughan, G. M. (1995) *Social psychology: An introduction*, London: Prentice-Hall/Harvester Wheatsheaf.

Hollander, E. P. (1985) Conformity, status and idiosyncratic credit. *Psychological Review*, 65, 117–127.

Kelman, H. C. (1961) Processes of opinion change. *Public Opinion Quarterly*, 25, 57–78.

Kidd, J. M. and Smewing, C. (2001) The role of the supervisor in career and organizational commitment. *European Journal of Work and Organizational Psychology*, 10, 25–40.

Kipnis, D. (1984) The use of power in organizations and in interpersonal settings. *Applied Social Psychology Annual*, 5, 179–210.

Kotter, J. P. (1995) Leading change: Why transformation efforts fail. *Harvard Business Review*, 57, 106–114.

(2002) *The heart of change: Real-life stories of how people change their organization*, Cambridge, Mass.: Harvard Business School Press.

Kotter, J. P. and Schlesinger, L. A. (1979) Choosing strategies for change. *Harvard Business Review*, 41, 59–67.

Ledford, G. E. Jr., Mohrman, S. A., Mohrman, A. M., and Lawler, E. E. (1990) The phenomenon of large-scale organizational change. In A. M. Mohrman et al. (Eds.), *Large scale organizational change* (pp. 1–31), San Francisco, Calif.: Jossey-Bass.

Leventhal, G. (1980) What should be done with equity theory? In K. Gergen, M. Greenburg, and R. Wills (Eds.), *Social exchange: Advances in theory and research* (pp. 27–55), New York, N.Y.: Plenum.

Lewis, L. K. and Seibold, D. R. (1998) Reconceptualizing organizational change implementation as a communication problem: A review of literature and research agenda. In M. E. Roloff (Ed.), *Communication yearbook* (Vol. XXI, pp. 93–151), Thousand Oaks, Calif.: Sage.

Lindskold, S. and Aronoff, J. (1980) Conciliatory strategies and relative power. *Journal of Experimental Social Psychology*, **16**, 187–196.

Lowe, K. B., Kroeck, K. G., and Sivasubramanian, N. (1996) Effectiveness correlates of transformational and transactional leadership: A meta-analytic review of the MLQ literature. *Leadership Quarterly*, **7**, 385–425.

Madsen, S. R., Miller, D., and John, C. (2005) Readiness for organizational change: Do organizational commitment and social relationships in the workplace make a difference? *Human Resource Development Quarterly*, **15** (2), 213–233.

Mael, F. A. and Ashforth, B. E. (1992) Alumni and their alma mater: A partial test of the reformulated model of organizational identification. *Journal of Organizational Behavior*, **13**, 103–123.

Maier, N. R. (1970) *Problem solving and creativity: In individuals and groups*, Monterey, Calif.: Brooks Cole.

Miller, V. D., Johnson J. R., and Grau, J. (1994) Antecedents to willingness to participate in a planned organizational change. *Journal of Applied Communication Research*, **22**, 59–80.

Mumford, M. D., Scott, G. M., Gaddis, B., and Strange, J. M. (2002) Leading creative people: Orchestrating expertise and relationships. *Leadership Quarterly*, **13**, 705–750.

Munduate, L. and Bennebroeck-Gravenhorst, K. (2003) Power dynamics and organizational change. *Applied Psychology: An International Review*, **52**, 1–13.

Novelli, L., Kirkman, B. L., and Shapiro, D. L. (1995) Effective implementation of organizational change: An organizational justice perspective. In C. Cooper and D. Rousseau (Eds.), *Trends in organizational behavior* (Vol. II, pp. 15–36), John Wiley and Sons.

Oreg, S. (2006) Personality, context and resistance to organizational change. *European Journal of Work and Organizational Psychology*, **15**, 73–101.

Piderit, S. K. (2000) Rethinking resistance and recognizing ambivalence: A multidimensional view of attitudes toward an organizational change. *Academy of Management Journal*, **25**, 783–794

Rafferty, A. E. and Griffin, M. A. (2006) Perception of organizational change: A stress and coping perspective. *Journal of Applied Psychology*, **91**, 1154–1162.

Raven, B. H. (1999) Reflections on interpersonal influence and social power in experimental social psychology. In A. Rodrigues and R. Levine (Eds.),

Reflections on 100 years of experimental social psychology (pp. 114–134), New York, N.Y.: Basic Books.

Reichers, A. E., Wanous, J. P., and Austin, J. T. (1997) Understanding and managing cynicism about organizational change. *Academy of Management Executive*, 11, 48–59.

Salam, S. C. (2004) Foster trust through competence, honesty, and integrity. In E. A. Locke (Ed.), *Handbook of principles of organizational behaviour* (pp. 274–288), Oxford: Blackwell.

Schweiger, D. M. and DeNisi, A. S. (1991) Communication with employees following a merger: A longitudinal field experiment. *Academy of Management Journal*, 34, 110–135.

Somech, A. and Drach-Zahavy, A. (2002) Relative power and influence strategy: The effects of agent/target organizational power on superior's choices of influence strategies. *Journal of Organizational Behavior*, 23, 167–179.

Spector, P. E. (2002) Employee control and occupational stress. *American Psychological Society*, 11, 153–166.

Tajfel, H. and Turner, J. C. (1986) The social identity theory of inter-group behavior. In S. Worchel and L. W. Austin (Eds.), *Psychology of intergroup relations*, Chicago, Ill.: Nelson-Hall.

Tjosvold, D. (2000) Power in cooperative and competitive organizational contexts. *The Journal of Social Psychology*, 130, 249–258.

Tucker, B. A. and Russell, R. F. (2004) The influence of the transformational leader. *Journal of Leadership and Organizational Studies*, 10, 103–111.

Turner, J. C. (2005) Explaining the nature of power: A three-process theory. *European Journal of Social Psychology*, 35, 1–22.

Tyler, T. R. and Blader, S. L. (2000) *Cooperation in groups*, Philadelphia, Pa.: Psychology Press.

(2003) The group engagement model: Procedural justice, social identity, and cooperative behavior. *Personality and Social Psychology Review*, 7, 349–361.

Tyler, T. R. and De Cremer, D. (2005) Process-based leadership: Fair procedures and reactions to organizational change. *The Leadership Quarterly*, 16, 529–545.

Van Knippenberg, B., Martin, L., and Tyler, T. (2006) Process-orientation versus outcome orientation during organizational change: The role of organizational identification. *Journal of Organizational Behavior*, 27, 685–704.

Van Knippenberg, D., Van Knippenberg, B., and Bobbio, A. (2008) Leaders as agents of continuity: Collective self-consistency and resistance to change. In F. Sani (Ed.), *Self Continuity: Individual and collective perspectives* (pp. 175–187), Mahwah, N. J.: Lawrence Erlbaum Associates.

Wanberg, C. R. and Banas, J. T. (2000) Predictors and outcomes of openness to changes in a reorganizing workplace. *Journal of Applied Social Psychology*, 85, 132–142.

Wanous, J. P., Reichers, A. E., and Austin, J. T. (2000) Cynicism about organizational change: Measurement, antecedents, and correlates. *Group and Organization Management*, 25, 132–153.

Weick, K. E. and Quinn, R. E. (1999) Organizational change and development. *Annual Review of Psychology*, 50, 361–386.

West, M. A., Hirst, G., Richter, A., and Shipton, H. (2004) Twelve steps to heaven: Successfully managing change through developing innovative teams. *European Journal of Work and Organizational Psychology*, 13, 269–299.

Yukl, G. (2006) *Leadership in organizations*. Upper Saddle River, N. J.: Prentice Hall.

Yukl, G. and Falbe, C. M. (1991) The importance of different power sources in downward and lateral relations. *Journal of Applied Psychology*, 76, 416–423.

Yukl, G. and Tracey, J. B. (1992) Consequences of influence tactics used with subordinates, peers, and the boss. *Journal of Applied Psychology*, 77, 525–535.

Yukl, G., Gordon, A., and Taber, T. (2002) A hierarchical taxonomy of leadership behavior: Integrating a half century of behaviour research. *Journal of Leadership and Organizational Studies*, 9, 15–32.

PART V

Leading with values

18 Servant-leadership, key to follower well-being

DIRK VAN DIERENDONCK, INGE NUIJTEN, AND IMKE HEEREN

The true test of a servant leader is this: Do those around the servant-leader become wiser, freer, more autonomous, healthier, and better able themselves to become servants?

Robert K. Greenleaf

For years, the general thinking on leadership was that the real leader was a person who had a vision, was highly practical and had an inspirational presence (Graham 1991). Charismatic leaders, recent examples being Lee Iacocca and Jack Welch, dominated our thinking of the ideal leader. These leaders used their power and influence to motivate people within the organization to turn a vision into reality. In recent years, however, there has been a shift in the managerial ideal type. Incidents such as at Enron have emphasized the importance of ethically responsive leaders for the long-term benefit of companies. *Fortune* magazine's yearly list of "The 100 Best Companies to Work For" emphasizes the importance of employees' needs and values for successful organizational leadership and performance. Moreover, Collins (2001) showed that building great companies for the long run takes a leader who combines strength with humility. Therefore, more than ever before, organizations are seeking to recruit leaders who use their power in a positive way.

Of course, leaders are only leaders if they are followed. Effective and successful leadership depends on a leader's ability to inspire, influence, and mobilize followers toward their and their organization's goals (Yukl 2006). In this respect, more established leadership theories, such as transformational leadership, emphasize the importance of listening to, appreciating, valuing, and empowering people (Bass and Avolio 1994). Therefore, being interested in people and their needs appears to be a prerequisite for good leadership (i.e. making the right decisions, building commitment, and motivating and mobilizing followers) (Ilies et al. 2005). People-centered leadership has gained even

319

more momentum with evidence showing that companies with leaders who empower people, have more satisfied, more committed, better performing employees (Liden et al. 2000).

Apparently people are looking for more ethical conduct and personal consideration in business settings. Servant-leadership might cater to these people's needs. Therefore, servant-leadership is worthwhile exploring as an alternative perspective on using power and influence within organizations. The remainder of this chapter will clarify the concept and show how it leads to a different way of looking at power and interdependence relationships. Building on Greenleaf's quote at the beginning of this chapter, the aim of this chapter is to introduce a model for servant-leadership that links servant-leadership behavior to follower well-being.

What is servant-leadership?

The term "servant-leadership" was coined by Robert Greenleaf (1904–1990) in his seminal work, *The Servant as Leader*. After spending forty years working at AT&T, he retired in 1964 as Director of Management Research. For another twenty-five years, Greenleaf worked as author, teacher, and consultant. The inspiration for the servant-leader came out of reading Herman Hesse's *Journey to the East* (Greenleaf 1977). In this book, the first-person narrator is part of a group of men traveling on a mythical journey. One of the persons in the group is Leo, a servant who takes care of the menial chores, plays music, and sustains the group with his spirit. At a certain moment, Leo disappears, and the group falls into disarray. Years later, the first-person narrator again contacts the Order to which the group belonged. It turns out that Leo is, and was, the titular head of the Order, its spiritual guide and leader. Through this story, Greenleaf realized that it is possible to combine the roles – servant and leader – in one person. Combining these aspects within oneself may even be the mark of a true great leader.

The main thing to understand about servant-leadership in the context of interdependence, is that a servant-leader is *primus inter pares* (i.e. first among equals). Most importantly, being a servant-leader means going beyond one's self-interest; the servant-leader is governed by something more important: serving one's fellow men and women (Luthans and Avolio 2003). This was described by Greenleaf as follows: "The servant-leader is servant first. It begins with the natural feeling that one wants to serve. Then conscious choice brings one to aspire to lead" (Spears 1998: 1). This can be related to McClelland (1975), who, when describing the need for power, already indicated that it can also be used in a beneficial way. More recent work on the helping power motivation explicitly describes people who do have a need for power but want to use it to help people and care for humanity (Frieze and Boneva 2000).

Working from a need to serve doesn't mean that "the inmates are running the prison". On the contrary, a servant-leader has very clear and established ideas about where the journey should be headed. The difference is that a servant-leader doesn't strive for this mission in a charismatic way but builds a learning organization where each person in the group can be valuable in his or her own way. Helping others develop in this way not only benefits the people in question but potentially also everyone around them and, therefore, the organization and society as a whole.

The biggest distinction with other leadership styles is that a servant-leader is genuinely concerned with serving followers (Greenleaf 1977), while other types of leaders have a greater concern for getting followers to engage in and support organizational objectives. Moreover, servant-leaders focus more on the people who are their followers, while other types of leaders focus primarily on organizational goals (Stone et al. 2004). When the main focus of a leader is on the people within the organization, it sets the stage for safe and secure relationships within the organization. Furthermore, servants that are chosen to be leaders are greatly supported by their employees, because they have committed themselves and are trusted (Greenleaf 1998). By providing meaning, paying genuine attention, caring and showing appreciation, servant-leaders empower followers to be the best they can be and run to greater purpose.

Our model is shown in Figure 18.1 and will be explained in the paragraphs below. The different elements in the model are based on a mixture of existing leadership approaches combined with recent insights derived from exploring optimal individual psychological states within organizations (Luthans and Avolio 2003). The model consists of a specific combination of these elements that is unique for servant-leadership. The model is visually depicted as a mandala that one enters through a need to serve. The word "mandala" is of Hindu origin and means "circle". Its symmetrical shape tends to draw the attention

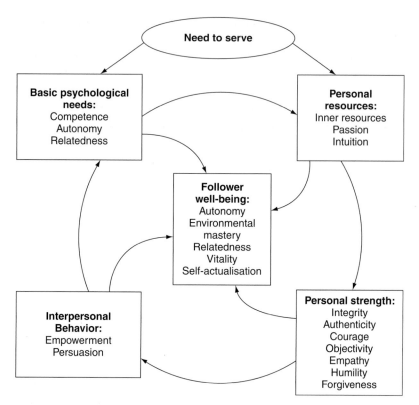

Figure 18.1 Servant-leadership and follower well-being.

toward the centre. Mandalas can be used as objects for meditation to help a person grow toward wholeness. Dovetailing this image, in our model, leadership forms the outward boundary that influences – through a continuing spiral – follower well-being in the centre. It builds on earlier theorizing on servant-leadership (Van Dierendonck and Heeren 2006) and extends it with the follower's perspective. The model focuses on the basic personal qualities of the servant-leader, on the behavior that characterizes the servant-leader, as well as on what servant-leadership means in terms of follower well-being.

Self-determination: basic psychological needs

Although it starts with a need to serve, we propose that in itself that is not enough to be a servant-leader. An important precondition is to be "self-determined". To be "self-determined" means to experience a sense of choice in initiating and regulating one's own actions (Deci and Ryan 2000). After over three decades of research on human motivation, Ryan and Deci (2004) concluded that self-determination follows from fulfilling three basic psychological needs. According to them, the innate psychological needs are: feeling competent, feeling connected to others, and feeling autonomous. When these needs are satisfied, enhanced self-motivation and mental health follow. A self-determined person will be better able to use personal resources, build strong and positive relationships and help others develop their self-determination. Therefore, instead of exerting power by controlling and directing people in an authoritarian way, self-determined leaders are able to work from an integrated perspective where power is not sought for its own sake. Self-determined people feel valuable for being who they are and not for doing particular things. As such, the power that comes with a leadership position is used to provide others with the opportunity to become self-determined as well.

Personal resources

The basic needs are innate psychological nutrients essential for ongoing psychological growth and well-being (Deci and Ryan 2000). As such, needs move a leader to action, whereby our model proposes that for servant-leadership they do so by encouraging the development and use of three specific personal resources. Resources, and personal resources in particular, have been suggested as essential elements for actively creating a world that will provide pleasure and success (Hobfoll 1989). Personal resources can be defined as personal characteristics that are valued by the individual, or that serve as a means for the attainment of personally valued objects, characteristics and conditions. For servant-leadership these personal resources include inner resources, passion, and intuition.

One feature of a servant-leader is the awareness and expression of inner resources as well as the recognition of the inner strength of other people (Van Dierendonck and Heeren 2006). Inner resources reflect the centre of our existence, the core of the self. They function as an inner strength of a person that produces an individualized awareness of one's inner self and a sense of being part of a deeper spiritual dimension (Richardson Gibson and Parker 2003). This gives a feeling of strength when facing the challenges of day-to-day living. Working from inner resources implies being in harmony whereby the inner and the outer self are integrated (Van Dierendonck and Mohan 2006).

The second personal resource is passion. Passion makes a person experience a feeling of new energy while performing a task, which stimulates completing the task at hand. An individual who shows passion in his work can inspire and motivate others. Passionate leaders will touch the heart of others in a positive way by addressing the latter's own motivation. They are a source of inspiration to others, because they have a clear-cut vision. They set a target that goes beyond the everyday tasks and makes the job a challenge and meaningful as well (Goleman et al. 2002).

Intuition is the third personal resource of a servant-leader. There are essentially two different ways in which people make decisions: intuitively and analytically (Hogarth 2001). Trusting one's feelings, intuitive signals, is an important aspect of effective management and leadership. Usually there is a wide gap between the hard facts available and the information someone actually needs. The art of leadership lies partly in the ability to bridge that gap through intuition (Greenleaf 1977; Khatri and Ng 2000). Intuitive processes are the result of learning processes and consist of the mass of facts, patterns, concepts, techniques, abstractions, and anything else that can be traced back to formal knowledge, derived from our thoughts (Khatri and Ng 2000). Intuition is a feeling for patterns, the ability to distil a general pattern from previous experiences that takes place at a subconscious level (Greenleaf 1991). Intuition means being able in a particular situation to use anything you have seen, felt, tasted, and experienced before in similar situations (Khatri and Ng 2000) and then just know what the decision or answer should be.

To conclude, we propose that the basis of servant-leadership lies within a need to serve that can be expressed through satisfying the needs for competence, autonomy, and relatedness within a person. The fulfillment of these needs allows for a different use of the power that comes with the leadership position. It strengthens one's inner resources, builds a passionate attitude toward work, and allows for a greater trust in one's intuition. Together, this heightened sense of self-awareness and strength enables a person to develop as a servant-leader as expressed through one's attitude and behavior.

Servant-leadership behavior

Having discussed what it takes to be(come) a servant-leader, we now turn to describing the behavior which is exemplary of a servant-leader. Moreover, we will elaborate on how we can recognize servant-leadership behavior. Central in trying to understand servant-leadership is the razor's edge that such leaders need to walk on. Power is the ability to influence other people. However, as a servant-leader, the use of power can seem to be counterintuitive by being focused on putting other people first. A true servant-leader needs to give power to followers and enable them to influence their own work to a large extent. Meanwhile, the organizational needs of productivity, survival, and profits need to be met too.

The ten characteristics most commonly associated with servant-leadership are: listening, empathy, healing, awareness, conviction, conceptualization, foresight, stewardship, stimulating personal growth, and building a community (Russell and Stone 2002; Spears 1998). Unfortunately, however, although we intuitively understand these characteristics, these characteristics have never been accurately operationalized, making a valid and reliable study based on these characteristics difficult. Thus, for quantitative research, we decided to come up with a different way to describe servant-leadership behavior.

Various authors have recently introduced variations to the ten characteristics mentioned above. Based on an extensive literature search, Laub (1999) developed six clusters of servant-leadership characteristics. A similar model was developed by Page and Wong (2000). One of the most extensive models is that of Russell and Stone (2002), who distinguished between nine functional characteristics and eleven additional characteristics of servant-leadership. Furthermore, Sendjaya (2003) proposed a model of six clusters. Most recently, Barbuto and Wheeler (2006) suggested to measure servant-leadership using five scales. After studying both the servant-leadership literature and the above-mentioned models, we searched for dimensions or clusters that both reflect the core of servant-leadership and show a certain level of independence. In our model, we distinguish between personal strengths and interpersonal behavior. Personal strengths include those characteristics that build on inner resources, passion, and intuition. These personal strengths capture the essence of a "servant" way of being. It is most notably here, where the servant-leader concept differs most from other leadership theories: Servant-leadership is more a way of life than a strategy (Marinho 2006). It is through these personal strengths that a leader can show servant behavior in the workplace; they inspire, engage, and empower followers.

Personal strengths

The personal-strength level comprises seven dimensions. The first one is integrity. According to Ryan and Deci (2000) fulfillment of the three basic needs will result in a feeling of integrity and well-being. Integrity is defined as the adherence to a generally perceived moral code (Russell and Stone 2002). This morality enhances ethical aspirations of both leader and employee (Sendjaya 2003). Thus, integrity is interrelated with ethical behavior (Russell and Stone 2002). A servant-leader's integrity manifests itself in various aspects: visibility within the organization, honesty (Russell and Stone 2002), and vulnerability (Luthans and Avolio 2003).

The second dimension is authenticity. Authenticity is closely related to expressing the "true self," expressing oneself in ways that are consistent with inner thoughts and feelings (Harter 2002). It focuses on owning one's personal experiences, be they thoughts, emotions, needs, wants, preferences, or beliefs. The usual view of authenticity distinguishes between "outer" behavior and an "inner" realm of intentions, needs, interests, beliefs, and desires which are seen as causing behavior. Authenticity is also a matter of living in such a way that your life has cumulativeness and purpose as a whole (Heidegger 1962). There is a strong sense of accountability to self and others. One takes responsibility for one's life and for the choices made. The importance of authenticity for leadership is best exemplified by Avolio and Gardner's (2005) work on authentic leadership. Within the organizational perspective it can be defined as behaving in such a way that professional roles remain secondary to what the individual is as a person (Halpin and Croft 1966). This implies that the authenticity and integrity of servant-leaders allows them to rely more on referent power instead of on legitimate or coercive power. Moreover, their followers are willing to do what is necessary because they like the leader as a person, not because their leader has authority or is in a specific position.

The third dimension is courage. Greenleaf (1991) argues that servant-leaders distinguish themselves from others through courage.

Courage is pro-active behavior and reveals itself for instance in the form of pioneering. Pioneering implies creating new ways, new approaches to old problems, and relying on strong values and convictions that govern a person's actions (Russell and Stone 2002), rather than waiting for what is to come (Goleman et al. 2002). Moreover, the pioneer is the first to take the risk (Greenleaf 1991). Courage is also found in admitting mistakes (daring to be vulnerable) and allowing extraordinary freedom for followers to exercise their own abilities (Patterson et al. 2003). Since servant-leaders believe in human development, they don't undermine others to feel powerful but, rather, empower them by being courageous and through courageous behavior.

The fourth dimension is objectivity. Objectivity means a servant-leader must be able to be unbiased and maintain an overview. Here, awareness is highly important (Greenleaf 1991).

Awareness gives one the basis for detachment, the ability to stand aside and see oneself in perspective in the context of one's own experience amid the ever present dangers, threats, and alarms. Then one sees one's own peculiar assortment of obligations and responsibilities in a way that permits one to sort out the urgent from the important and perhaps deal with the important. (Greenleaf 1977: 41)

Moreover, servant-leadership implies knowing how to distinguish between matters of greater and matters of lesser importance. Influence, and therefore power, comes from focusing on the greater, more important matters.

The fifth characteristic is humility. Humility is the ability to look at one's own accomplishments and talents in their proper perspective (Patterson 2003). Servant-leaders dare admit they are not omniscient and can learn from others. One of the aspects of humility is serving, the first and foremost priority of a servant-leader. It is not the leader's fate, but a privilege (Russell and Stone 2002). Serving is offering time, energy, care, and compassion to employees (Patterson 2003). A second aspect of humility is modesty. Servant-leaders retreat into the background when a task has been successfully accomplished and give their employees all the credit for it. However, when their performance is less satisfactory, servant-leaders will assume full responsibility and address the matter at hand. This shows that servant-leaders do not give away their power, they just use it in a different way.

The sixth dimension is empathy, recognizing the emotions of others. Empathy is the ability to understand and experience the feelings of others (George 2000). Empathy includes the ability to cognitively adopt the psychological perspective of other people and experience feelings of warmth, compassion, and concern for others. Empathic people have an eye for subtle social signals that indicate what other people need or want, which enables them to recognize the felt, but unspoken, emotions in a person or group (Goleman et al. 2002). Empathy helps leaders to better understand and describe their followers' behavior. By understanding their followers' emotional side, and reacting with compassion and empathic concern, leaders are able to develop high-quality interpersonal relationships.

The seventh and last personal strength is forgiveness. Forgiveness is the ability to forgive things such as offences, differences of opinion, and mistakes. It means letting go of perceived wrongdoings and not carrying a grudge into other situations (McCullough et al. 2000). For servant-leaders it is important to create an atmosphere of trust where people feel accepted, are free to make mistakes and know that they won't be rejected (Ferch 2005). They do not strive for revenge or try to get even. Given the importance of high-quality personal relationships within the workplace, the ability to forgive and be forgiven, can help cleanse situations so that the best in people comes out.

Interpersonal behavior

The behavioral level of servant-leadership has two dimensions: empowerment and persuasion. Empowerment is a motivational concept focused on enabling people (Conger 2000). Empowerment aims at fostering a proactive, self-confident attitude among followers and giving followers a sense of personal power. Furthermore, empowerment means that employees can choose how to achieve goals and are allowed to make mistakes. Empowering leadership behavior encompasses aspects such as delegation of authority and responsibility, encouragement of self-directed decision-making, information-sharing, and coaching for innovative performance (Konczak et al. 2000). At the core stands a servant-leader's belief in the intrinsic value of each individual; it is all about recognition, acknowledgment and the realization of each person's abilities and what the person can still learn (Greenleaf 1998).

The second dimension is persuasion. More than any other influence tactic, servant-leaders rely on persuasion in their discussions with followers (Greenleaf 1998). Position or personal power is seldom used to get people to comply with the leader's position. There is a strong focus on striving toward consensus in teams. Persuasion combines several of the influence tactics described by Yukl (2006): the use of explanations, logical arguments and factual evidence, apprising, inspirational appeals, and consultations. In the end, people follow a servant-leader voluntarily, "because they are persuaded that the leader's path is the right one for them" (Greenleaf 1998: 44). Using persuasion as the most important influence tactic means that coercion and manipulation are not used; one trusts the others' intuitive sense to discover for oneself what the right path to take is.

Follower well-being

With the advent of positive leadership approaches, the realization of the importance of leadership for follower well-being is growing (Ilies et al. 2005). Its importance for organizations is also acknowledged by research showing that enhanced well-being of followers is related to better organizational performance (Fulmer et al. 2003). Given the central role of leaders in the social setting of most organizations, the behavior shown by leaders toward their followers plays an important role in how supportive a work setting is perceived. There is abundant evidence that a controlling, less supportive leadership style where responsibilities are not clarified and feedback is lacking, is related to lower levels of well-being (Cartwright and Cooper 1994; Sosik and Godshalk 2000; Van Dierendonck et al. 2004). On the other hand, a supportive environment provides positive affect, a sense of predictability, and recognition of self-worth (Cohen and Wills 1985). As such, it is likely that servant-leadership behavior characterized by integrity, authenticity, courage, objectivity, empathy, humility, forgiveness, empowerment, and persuasion can enhance the well-being of subordinates. Obviously, this focus on well-being asks for a different way to use power. Well-being cannot be enforced or directly influenced; it can – at most – be facilitated. The focus on well-being implies a shift from creating dependency to encouraging personal freedom.

Our model, and most notably the spiral function suggested by the model, builds on, among others, Frederickson's (1998) broaden-and-build theory that describes how experiencing positive emotions builds physical, intellectual, and social resources. Similarly, Hobfoll's conservation-of-resources theory (1989) suggests a process with so-called gain spirals. According to this theory, people strive to use their positive energy to enhance their resources. Translated to our model, it is suggested that the four basic dimensions of servant-leadership as depicted in the outer ring (i.e. psychological needs, personal resources, personal strengths, and interpersonal behavior) reinforce each other and follower well-being in the centre, in a continuing self-reinforcing upward spiral.

Since followers are people first and employees second, we link follower well-being to theories of general well-being. In defining well-being, two schools can be distinguished, that is hedonic well-being and eudaimonic well-being (Ryan and Deci 2000). The hedonic view, advocated by the Greek philosopher Aristippus (fourth century BC) states that life is about achieving pleasure. Hedonism states that well-being comes from experiencing as much joy as possible and avoiding pain and discomfort (Kahneman et al. 1999). The eudaimonic view, in contrast, encompasses more than happiness in the hedonic sense (Ryff 1989). Aristotle made a clear distinction between positive feelings that come out of activities we do just because they give us pleasure and activities that are an expression of the best within ourselves. Eudaimonic well-being comes from doing things in life that ask us to be the best in life we can be. It means to live in accordance with one's "True Self" (Waterman 1993). Defined this way, well-being refers to optimal psychological functioning.

The starting point of our definition of follower well-being is the seminal work of Ryff (1989). She developed an integrated theoretical framework of eudaimonic well-being on the basis of an extensive literature review. In defining follower well-being we combined this general model with the conceptualizations of self-determination theory (Deci and Ryan 2000), worker well-being by Warr (1994), and worker empowerment by Thomas and Velthouse (1990). Combining these valuable insights, our dimensions of follower well-being include autonomy, environmental mastery, relatedness, vitality, and self-actualization.

Autonomy

Central for autonomous people is a feeling of independence and making one's own decisions. Autonomy refers to being able to choose whether or not to conform to social norms (Ryff 1989). The life of an autonomous individual is rooted in personal norms, needs, and values. It gives a person responsibility to initiate and regulate one's own actions. Perceived choice through autonomy produces greater flexibility, creativity, initiative, and self-regulation (Thomas and Velthouse 1990). Besides, autonomy is a central element of self-determination theory (Deci and Ryan 2000), and, therefore, one of the basic needs to be fulfilled in order to be able to be(come) a servant (leader). As such, by stimulating the autonomy of followers, they, in accordance with the test of servant-leadership, are more likely to become servants themselves.

Environmental mastery

Environmental mastery is suggested by Ryff and Singer (1998) as a secondary dimension of positive psychological health. It implies a sense of mastery, competence, and trust in handling the environment. This dimension evolves over time, when somebody's life becomes more meaningful and a deep connection with others develops (Ryff and Singer 1998). Environmental mastery leads to more self-respect, a sense of competence and personal growth. Self-respect and mastery help establish a meaningful interpretation of life and of high-quality personal relations.

Relatedness

Having and maintaining qualitatively good human relationships is the third key dimension of well-being. Baumeister and Leary (1995), in their review article, give abundant empirical evidence of the need to belong as a fundamental human motive. The lack of human ties is related to the deterioration of one's health, a diminished capacity to adjust and diminished well-being. Jahoda (1958) already described the capacity to love as a key dimension of positive mental health. Finally, Ryan and Deci (2004) also acknowledged the need for relatedness.

Vitality

Recently, several researchers emphasized the importance of studying the sense of energy, engagement and vigor that people experience in a work setting (Schaufeli et al. 2002). Vitality was coined by Ryan and

Frederick (1997) as a specific psychological experience of possessing a subjective feeling of aliveness, enthusiasm, and positive energy. It is an indicator that the activities in life are in concordance with deeply held values and needs. Ryan and Frederick (1997) suggest that experiencing vitality is associated with experiencing life as autonomous and personally expressive. People experience more vitality when they have less inner conflict, feel less controlled by forces outside themselves, and have confidence in their ability to do the things they want to do.

Self-actualization

Self-actualization has a central spot in the thinking of psychologists such as Rogers, Fromm, Maslow, and Allport (Jahoda 1958). According to these authors, striving for self-actualization and personal growth is a central motivator in a person's life. It refers to a feeling of continuous personal development and of realizing one's potential. It is related to having self-respect and self-acceptance, a positive attitude toward oneself, and to accepting one's positive and negative qualities (Ryff 1989). Self-actualization gives life meaning. Meaningfulness through self-actualization includes a sense of wholeness and purpose in life (Ryff and Singer 1998).

Conclusion

Our model proposes that servant-leadership holds key elements that determine follower well-being within organizations. Until now, although research shows that follower well-being is important for organizational performance (Fulmer et al. 2003), this link between leadership and follower well-being has not been widely researched. Similarly, within the power literature, the focus has been mainly on the influence tactics used by leaders. Servant-leadership asks for a different way of thinking. The challenge is no longer how to get followers to do what you want them to do, but leadership becomes the art of encouraging them to bring out the best in themselves. The implicit assumption underlying this thinking is that by bringing out these inherent talents, the organization will profit from it. Servant-leadership is a process where employees follow without being pressured or manipulated. Given the ongoing "war for talent" on the job market (Michaels et al. 2001), one can even speculate that soon servant-leadership will no longer be perceived as a luxury but as a necessity for the long-term survival of organizations.

Servant-leaders differ from other leaders in their use of power in that the starting point of their leadership is their need to serve. This is combined with self-determination: working from a base grounded in fulfilled psychological needs, inner resources, intuition, and passion. Their leadership behavior is reflected in various characteristics at various levels. On the personal-strength level, a servant-leader is characterized by integrity, authenticity, courage, objectivity, empathy, humility, and forgiveness. On the behavioral level, these characteristics include empowerment and persuasion. Both these attitudinal and interpersonal aspects create a safe and nourishing environment that helps people fulfill their need for autonomy, environmental mastery, relatedness, vitality, and self-actualization, that builds on their strengths, and, therefore, that provides personal growth and well-being.

References

Avolio, B. J. and Gardner, W. L. (2005) Authentic leadership development: Getting to the root of positive forms of leadership. *The Leadership Quarterly*, **16**, 315–338.

Barbuto, J. E. Jr. and Wheeler, D. W. (2006) Scale development and construct clarification of servant leadership. *Group and Organization Management*, **31**, 300–326.

Bass, B. M. and Avolio, B. J. (1994) *Improving organizational effectiveness through transformational leadership*, Thousand Oaks, Calif.: Sage.

Baumeister, R. F. and Leary, M. R. (1995) The need to belong: Desire for interpersonal attachments as a fundamental human motivation. *Psychological Bulletin*, **117**, 497–529.

Cartwright, S. and Cooper, C. L. (1994) *No hassle: Taking the stress out of work*, New York, N.Y.: Academic Press.

Cohen, S. and Wills, T. A. (1985) Stress, social support and the buffering hypothesis. *Psychological Bulletin*, **98**, 310–357.

Collins, J. (2001) *Good to Great*, New York, N.Y.: HarperCollins Publishers.

Conger, J. A. (2000) Motivate performance through empowerment. In E. A. Locke (Ed.), *The Blackwell handbook of principles of organizational behavior* (pp. 137–149), Oxford: Blackwell.

Deci, E. L. and Ryan, R. M. (2000) The "what" and "why" of goal pursuits: Human needs and the self-determination of behavior. *Psychological Inquiry*, **11**, 227–268.

Ferch, S. (2005) Servant-leadership, forgiveness, and social justice. *The International Journal of Servant-Leadership*, **1**, 97–113.

Frederickson, B. L. (1998) What good are positive emotions? *Review of General Psychology*, **2**, 300–319.

Frieze, I. H. and Boneva, B. S. (2000) Power motivation and motivation to help others. In A. Y. Lee-Chai and J. A. Bargh (Eds.), *The use and abuse of power* (pp. 75–89), Philadelphia, Pa.: Psychology Press.

Fulmer, I. S., Gerhart, B., and Scott, K. S. (2003) Are the 100 best better? An empirical investigation of the relationship between being a "great place to work" and firm performance. *Personnel Psychology*, **56**, 965–993.

George, J. M. (2000) Emotions and leadership: The role of emotional intelligence. *Human relations*, **53**, 1027–1055.

Goleman, D., Boyatzis, R., and McKee, A. (2002) *Primal Leadership: Realizing the power of emotional intelligence*, Boston, Mass.: Harvard Business School Press.

Graham, J. W. (1991) Servant-leadership in organizations: Inspirational and moral. *The Leadership Quarterly*, **2**, 105–119.

Greenleaf, R. K. (1977) *Servant leadership: A journey into the nature of legitimate power and greatness*, New York, N.Y.: Paulist Press.

(1991) *The servant as leader*. Indianapolis, Ind.: The Greenleaf Center.

(1998) *The power of servant-leadership*, San Francisco, Calif.: Berret-Koehler Publishers.

Halpin, A. and Croft, D. (1966) Organizational climate of schools. In A. Halpin (Ed.), *Theory and research in administration* (pp. 131–249), New York, N.Y.: Prentice Hall.

Harter, S. (2002) Authenticity. In C. R. Snyder and S. J. Lopez (Eds.), *Handbook of positive psychology* (pp. 382–394), New York, N.Y.: Oxford University Press.

Heidegger, M. (1962) *Being and time*, New York, N.Y.: Harper & Row. (Originally published in 1927.)

Hobfoll, S. E. (1989) Conservation of resources: A new attempt at conceptualizing stress. *American Psychologist*, **44**, 513–524.

Hogarth, R. M. (2001) *Educating intuition*, Chicago, Ill.: University of Chicago Press.

Ilies, R., Morgeson, F. P., and Nahrgang, J. D. (2005) Authentic leadership and eudaimonic well-being: Understanding leader-follower outcomes. *The Leadership Quarterly*, **16**, 373–394.

Jahoda, M. (1958) *Current concepts of positive mental health*, New York, N. Y.: Basic Books.

Kahneman, D., Diener, E., and Schwarz. N. (1999) *Well-being: The Foundations of hedonic psychology*, New York, N.Y.: Russell Sage Foundation.

Khatri, N. and Ng, H. A. (2000) The role of intuition in strategic decision making. *Human Relations*, 53, 57–86.

Konczak, L. J., Stelly, D. J., and Trusty, M. L. (2000) Defining and measuring empowering leader behaviors: Development of an upward feedback instrument. *Educational and Psychological Measurement*, 60, 301–313.

Laub, J. A. (1999) *Assessing the servant organization: Development of the organizational leadership assessment (OLA) instrument*, Boca Raton, Fla.: Dissertation.

Liden, R. C., Wayne, S. J., and Sparrowe, R. T. (2000) An examination of the mediating role of psychological empowerment and the relations between the job, interpersonal relationships and work outcomes. *Journal of Applied Psychology*, 85, 407–416.

Luthans, F. and Avolio, B. (2003) Authentic leadership development. In K. S. Cameron and J. E. Dutton (Eds.), *Positive organizational scholarship* (pp. 241–254), San Francisco, Calif.: Berrett-Koehler.

Marinho, R. (2006) The servant-leader and the team: Love without measure! *The International Journal of Servant-Leadership*, 2, 261–285.

McClelland, D. (1975) *Power: The inner experience*, New York, N.Y.: Irvington Publishers.

McCullough, M. E., Hoyt, W. T., and Rachal, K. C. (2000) What we know (and need to know) about assessing forgiveness constructs. In M. E. McCullough, K. I. Pargament, and C. E. Thoresen (Eds.), *Forgiveness: Theory, research, and practice* (pp. 65–88), New York, N.Y.: Guilford Press.

Michaels, E., Handfield-Jones, H., and Axelrod, B. (2001) *The war for talent*, Boston, Mass.: Harvard Business School Press.

Page, D. and Wong, P. T. P. (2000) A conceptual framework for measuring servant leadership. In S. Adjibolosso (Ed.), *The human factor in shaping the course of history and development*, Lanham, Md.: University Press of America.

Patterson, K. (2003) Servant leadership: A theoretical model. *Servant Leadership Roundtable*.

Patterson, K., Redmer, T. A. O., and Stone, G. A. (2003) Transformational leaders to servant leaders versus Level 4 leaders to Level 5 leaders: The move from good to great. Retrieved March 7, 2007, from www.cbfa.org/papers/2003conf/Patterson.pdf.

Richardson Gibson, L. M. and Parker, V. (2003) Inner resources as predictors of psychological well-being in middle-income African American breast cancer survivors. *Cancer Control*, 10, 52–59.

Russell, R. F. and Stone, A. G. (2002) A review of servant leadership attributes: Developing a practical model. *Leadership and Organization Development Journal*, 23, 145–157.

Ryan, R. M. and Deci, E. L. (2000) On happiness and human potentials: A review of research on hedonic and eudaimonic well-being. *Annual Review of Psychology*, 52, 141–166.

(2004) An overview of self-determination theory: An organismic-dialectical perspective. In E. L. Deci and R. M. Ryan (Eds.), *Handbook of self-determination research* (pp. 3–33), Rochester, N.Y.: The University of Rochester Press.

Ryan, R. M. and Frederick, C. (1997) On energy, personality, and health: Subjective vitality as a dynamic reflection of well-being. *Journal of Personality*, 65, 529–565.

Ryff, C. D. (1989) Happiness is everything, or is it? Explorations on the meaning of psychological well-being. *Journal of Personality and Social Psychology*, 57, 1069–1081.

Ryff, C. D. and Singer, B. (1998) The contours of positive human health. *Psychological Inquiry*, 9, 1–25.

Schaufeli, W. B., Salanova, M., Gonzalez, R., and Bakker, A. B. (2002) The measurement of engagement and burnout: A two sample confirmatory factor analytic approach. *Journal of Happiness Studies*, 3, 71–92.

Sendjaya, S. (2003) Development and validation of servant leadership behavioral scale. *Servant Leadership Roundtable*.

Sosik, J. J. and Godshalk, V. M. (2000) Leadership, mentoring functions received, and job-related stress: A conceptual model and preliminary study. *Journal of Organizational Behavior*, 21, 365–390.

Spears, L. (1998) Introduction. In R. K. Greenleaf, *The power of servant leadership* (pp. 1–15), San Francisco, Calif.: Berret-Koehler.

Stone, A. G., Russell, R.F., and Patterson, K. (2004) Transformational versus servant leadership: A difference in leader focus. *Leadership and Organizational Development Journal*, 25, 349–361.

Thomas, K. W. and Velthouse, B. A. (1990) Cognitive elements of empowerment: An "interpretive" model of intrinsic task motivation. *Academy of Management Journal*, 4, 666–681.

Van Dierendonck, D., Haynes, C., Borrill, C., and Stride, C. (2004) Leadership behavior and subordinate well-being. *Journal of Occupational Health Psychology*, 9, 165–175.

Van Dierendonck, D. and Heeren, I. (2006) Toward a research model of servant-leadership. *The International Journal of Servant-Leadership*, 2, 147–164.

Van Dierendonck, D. and Mohan, K. (2006) Some thoughts on spirituality and eudaimonic well-being. *Mental Health, Religion and Culture*, 9, 227–238.

Warr, P. (1994) A conceptual framework for the study of work and mental health. *Work and Stress*, 8, 84–97.

Waterman, A. S. (1993) Two conceptions of happiness: Contrasts of personal expressiveness (eudaimonia) and hedonic enjoyment. *Journal of Personality and Social Psychology*, **64**, 678–691.

Wilson, S. M. (1993) The self-empowerment index: A measure of internally and externally expresses teacher autonomy. *Educational and Psychological Measurement*, **53**, 727–737.

Yukl, G. (2006) *Leadership in organizations*, 6th edn, Englewood Cliffs, N. J.: Prentice Hall.

19 Ethical leadership
The socially responsible use of power

ANNEBEL H. B. DE HOOGH AND
DEANNE N. DEN HARTOG

Powerful leaders can have a substantial impact on the lives of followers and the fate of groups, organizations, and even societies. The potential for beneficial use or misuse of power has led researchers to focus on the ethical aspects of leadership. A recent series of unprecedented media scandals regarding ethical lapses of high-level business managers has placed the ethical aspects of leadership at the forefront of everyone's attention. Despite this growing interest, however, there is very little theoretically driven research that examines which types of leader behavior should be seen as ethical. Moreover, although preliminary research on ethical leadership suggests positive effects of such leadership (e.g., Brown et al. 2005), it does not yet explain when and why ethical leadership has its effects. Finally, why some people in a leadership situation choose to behave in a principled and ethical manner whilst others (at times) do not, is not yet sufficiently clear. Here, we deal with these points from a power and influence perspective.

The use of power and leadership are intertwined concepts, the power to influence others forms a part of most definitions of leadership. Thus, not surprisingly, the power concept contributes to our understanding of ethical leadership in important ways. First, the socially responsible use of power is a key element of ethical leadership, and, in this chapter, we discuss ethical leadership from this perspective. We discuss multiple forms of ethical leader behavior (i.e. integrity and fairness, ethical role clarification, caring behavior, power-sharing, and concern for sustainability) through their link to different connotations of the socially responsible use of power. Second, leader-motive research indicates that power motivation and a personal concern for social responsibility are important antecedents of ethical leadership. We subsequently address these and other possible antecedents of ethical leader behavior in this chapter. Third, looking at the process by which ethical leadership may have its effects, it seems likely that ethical leadership contributes to expert, reward, and referent power of leaders,

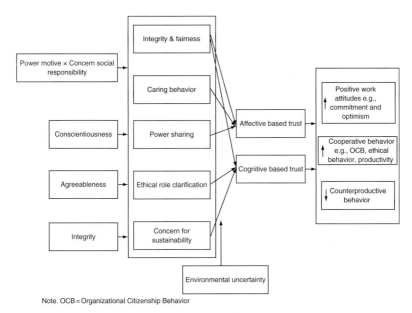

Note. OCB = Organizational Citizenship Behavior

Figure 19.1 A model of antecedents, effects, and processes of ethical leadership.

enhancing subordinates' trust in the leader and, in turn, desirable outcomes. In this chapter, we discuss how and when ethical leadership may have a positive impact on followers, focusing both on the role of power and trust in the leader–follower relationship in bringing these positive effects about. Figure 19.1 depicts a model of the propositions on ethical leadership and its antecedents and consequences presented in this chapter.

As Figure 19.1 shows, we propose several traits and motives as potential antecedents of ethical leader behaviors. Positive relationships between ethical leader behavior and several favorable follower attitudes and behaviors are expected. Affective and cognitive forms of trust in the leader are proposed as mediating mechanisms in the relationship between ethical leader behavior and these outcomes. Finally we discuss uncertainty as a potential contextual moderator.

Defining ethical leadership and power

Ethics and the socially responsible use of power received relatively little attention in leadership research until the morality of exceptional leaders such as charismatic or transformational leaders became an issue (Treviño et al. 2003). Theories of charismatic and transformational leadership overlap considerably in their descriptions of an inspiring, values-based leadership style that includes ethical content (Brown and Treviño 2006a). Thus, some kind of ethical conduct seems part of transformational and charismatic leadership. Bass (1985), however, noted that transformational leaders could use their power toward ethical as well as unethical ends. Accordingly, researchers have differentiated between personalized (unethical) and socialized (ethical) charismatic leadership (House and Howell 1992; see also Howell 1988; Howell and Shamir 2005), and authentic and pseudo-transformational leadership (e.g., Bass and Steidlmeier 1999), taking the social versus self-oriented use of power and the morality of the means and ends of the leaders into account.

Alongside the discussion about the morality of transformational and charismatic leadership, a more general increased attention for the ethical aspects of leadership emerged fuelled by the high-profile cases of management failure and leadership misconduct reported on in the media. Theories about leadership styles such as authentic leadership (e.g., Luthans and Avolio 2003), spiritual leadership (e.g., Fry 2003) and servant leadership (Graham 1991) emerged, all paying attention to the moral aspects of leadership. Moreover, recently researchers have also begun to consider ethical leadership as a set of behaviors or a behavioral style in itself rather than focusing only on ethical aspects of other leadership styles (Brown et al. 2005; De Hoogh and Den Hartog 2008; Kanungo 2001; Kanungo and Mendonca 1996, 2001).

So far, however, there is no clarity about how to define ethical leadership and how to determine which types of leader behaviors should be seen as ethical. Brown et al. (2005) take a social learning approach to ethical leadership and focus on the exemplary behavior of the leader toward followers within the firm. They stress the importance of normative appropriateness of the leader behavior in the eyes of the followers: "those who are perceived to be ethical leaders model conduct that followers consider to be normatively appropriate" (Brown et al. 2005: 120). They define ethical leadership as "the demonstration of normatively appropriate conduct through personal actions and interpersonal relationships, and the promotion of such conduct to followers through two-way communication, reinforcement, and decision-making" (Brown et al. 2005: 120). Thus, ethical leadership is operationalized in terms of behavior intended to benefit employees (cf. Brown et al. 2005). Potential other stakeholders such as customers or society at large are not included.

Other scholars have portrayed ethical leadership more generally by taking into account the purpose of the behavior of the leader and the consequences of this behavior for oneself and others rather than its perceived normative appropriateness (e.g., Turner et al. 2002). For example, Kanungo (2001) states that the leader, in order to be ethical, must engage in virtuous acts or behaviors that benefit others and must refrain from evil acts or behaviors that harm others. Moreover, Kanungo holds that these acts must stem from the leader's altruistic rather than egoistic motives. Such underlying motives may of course be mixed and are not always easy to ascertain. In contrast, Locke argues that ethical egoism or a focus on one's self-interest can in fact produce highly ethical behavior and may at times provide a better guide for ethical conduct than altruism (Avolio and Locke 2005).

Here, we take a social-influence perspective and define ethical leadership as the process of influencing in a socially responsible way the activities of an organized group toward goal achievement. This characterization draws on Stogdill's (1950) general leadership definition and in addition to the three elements that can be discerned in most definitions of leadership – influence, group and goal (Bryman 1992) – it includes an emphasis on leaders' *socially responsible* use of power. Thus, we emphasize the means through which ethical leaders attempt to achieve their own and collective goals and the ways in which they use their power. To us, the essence of ethical leadership is the element of social responsibility of power use.

Ethical leader behaviors

Different leader behaviors have been suggested as part of ethical leadership, including acting fairly and honestly, demonstrating integrity, promoting ethical conduct in others, allowing followers voice and sharing power (Brown et al. 2005; De Hoogh and Den Hartog 2008; Den Hartog and De Hoogh 2008). Here, we will distinguish between such related forms of ethical leader behavior through their link to different connotations of the socially responsible use of power and provide a comprehensive set of dimensions of ethical leader behavior.

One connotation of the term "social responsibility" is responsibility as an obligation or dependability which implies that a person feels an inner obligation to do what is known to be right, "means it," is dependable, and can be "counted upon" (e.g., Blasi 1983; Hoffman 1982; Sartre 1947; see also Winter 1991b). Taken in this way, the socially responsible use of power would suggest that ethical leaders make principled and fair choices, act with integrity, are trustworthy and honest, do not practice favoritism, treat others with respect, and structure work environments justly. We label this part of ethical leadership integrity and fairness.

Most authors see demonstrating fairness and integrity as an integral and core element of ethical leader behavior. For example, Treviño and colleagues found that leader behaviors reflecting fair treatment of employees contributed to perceptions of ethical leadership (Treviño et al. 2003; Treviño et al. 2000). Ethical leadership is also seen to include principled decision-making (Avolio 1999), leaders' personal integrity (Resick et al. 2006), honesty (Brown et al. 2005; Craig and Gustafson 1998), and setting ethical expectations for followers (Treviño et al. 2003). Howell and Avolio (1992) found that honesty differentiated ethical from unethical charismatic leaders.

Next, the socially responsible use of power also has the connotation of awareness of the consequences of one's actions and is used in reference to acknowledging or "owning" one's actions, as in "being responsible" for something or for someone else (e.g., Winter 1991b). Ethical leaders will take responsibility for their own and their followers' actions and will guide employees' behavior by engaging in open communication and clarifying expectations and responsibilities so that employees are clear on what is expected from them. Treviño et al. (2000) found that setting expectations and holding oneself and others accountable was associated with perceptions of ethical leadership. Brown et al. (2005) also hold that ethical leaders are transparent and engage in open communication, promoting and rewarding ethical conduct among followers. This part of ethical leadership can be labeled (ethical) role clarification.

The socially responsible use of power also has the connotation of altruism or pro-social motivation (e.g., Winter 1991b). This pro-social motivation suggests that ethical leaders are concerned about and considerate toward their employees. We label this part of ethical leadership caring behavior (Kalshoven et al. 2008). This operationalization is in line with Treviño et al.'s finding (2003) that a concern for people is particularly important in the attribution of ethical leadership by observers. Brown et al. (2005) also describe ethical leaders as people-focused and caring.

Furthermore, the connotation of the socially responsible use of power as pro-social motivation suggests that ethical leaders allow followers a say in decision-making and listen to their ideas. We label this component power-sharing (De Hoogh and Den Hartog 2008). The importance and effects of power-sharing are also discussed in work on employee empowerment (e.g., Spreitzer 1995). Feldman and Khademian (2003) suggest that inclusive processes such as power-sharing enable employees to make their work more meaningful. In sum, we distinguish integrity and fairness, ethical role clarification, caring behavior and power-sharing as components of ethical leadership at work.

Finally, as ethical leadership is expected to direct organizational members toward goals which are not only beneficial to the organization and its members but also to other stakeholders and even society (see Kanungo 2001), the socially responsible use of power may also be broadened to mean *societally* responsible. In other words, caring about the wider impact of actions on society and the environment is also part of ethical leader behavior (Kalshoven et al. 2008). This component of ethical leadership is labeled "concern for sustainability".

Only a few scales exist which were specifically developed to measure this set of ethical leader behaviors. Brown et al. (2005) combine several ethical leader behaviors (acting fairly and honestly, allowing followers voice, and rewarding ethical conduct) in a ten-item scale. Theoretically, however, these behaviors are rather different and may have different effects. Although their short scale is useful, combining all ethical leader behaviors into a single undifferentiated syndrome may cloud our view on the mechanisms through which ethical leadership may be effective. Recently, we have started developing a new ethical leader behavior questionnaire able to measure an overarching ethical leadership construct as well as to distinguish between different components, including leader integrity and fairness, caring behavior, power-sharing, concern for sustainability, and ethical role clarification (Kalshoven et al. 2008). This more detailed measurement will allow for a more fine-grained analysis of ethical leader behavior and its effects on followers.

Personality, power motivation, and ethical leadership

As stated, to us the essence of ethical leadership is the socially responsible use of power. In personality theory, four dispositions have been described that seem to be of considerable importance to the socially responsible use of power, namely power motivation and a personal concern for social responsibility, conscientiousness, agreeableness, and integrity. These personality traits are depicted as antecedents of ethical leadership behavior in Figure 19.1.

The power motive is defined as the desire to have impact on other people, to affect their behavior and emotions (Winter 1992b). This motive is drawn from Murray's (1938) human motivation taxonomy and is suggested to represent one of the most important dimensions of human motivated behavior (Atkinson 1958). Originally assessed via thematic content analysis of Thematic Apperception Test (TAT) stories, Winter (1991a) recently refined the method, so that any form of imaginative running text or speech can now be used as the basis for power motivation content analyses. Research shows that leaders tend to be high on power motivation (e.g., Greene and Winter 1971). However, high power motivation by itself is expected to lead to destructive, unethical behavior (House and Howell 1992; Winter 1991b; Winter and Barenbaum 1985). In line with this, Winter (1987) content-coded the inaugural addresses of US presidents to assess power motives and found that power motivation was related to leading the country into war. Also, in a sample of historical leaders, O'Connor et al. (1995) found coded power motivation to be positively related to personalized charismatic leadership.

Winter and Barenbaum (1985) developed and validated a measure of personal concern for social responsibility that is expected to moderate the expression of the power motive into either responsible or profligate channels (for an overview of validation studies, see Winter 1991b, 1992a). This measure can be coded in TAT stories or running text and focuses on an inner obligation to do what is right, taking responsibility for oneself and others, being dependable, instilling self-control and having awareness of the consequences of action as represents of the responsibility disposition. Leaders with a high personal concern for social responsibility are believed to use power in an altruistic and collectively oriented manner, behave ethically, and be concerned about the consequences of their own actions on others.

In line with this, research found special relevance of the combination of coded power motivation and a personal concern for social responsibility for charismatic leaders of voluntary organizations (De Hoogh et al. 2005b). Engaging in morally responsible action, emphasizing ideological values, and behaving in ways that reinforce the values inherent in the mission seem especially important for the attribution of charisma to leaders in this ideologically driven context. Moreover, De Hoogh and Den Hartog (2008) examined the relationships of leader's coded personal concern for social responsibility with different aspects of ethical leadership as rated by followers (morality and fairness, role clarification, and power-sharing) as well as with despotic leadership. They found leaders high on a personal concern for social responsibility rated higher on ethical leader behaviors and lower on despotic leadership. Thus, although further research is necessary, research so far implies that a personal concern for the socially responsible use of power is crucial for ethical leadership.

Although the Big Five personality traits have been widely used in research on personality characteristics of effective leaders (e.g., De Hoogh et al. 2005a; Judge and Bono 2000; Judge et al. 2002), so far little research has focused on the Big Five personality traits in relation to ethical leadership. Several Big Five personality dimensions, however, seem important. Conscientiousness, for example, reflects the tendency to be dependable, responsible, dutiful, and thoughtful (McCrae and Costa 1987). Also, individuals high on conscientiousness tend to adhere to standards of conduct and agreed-upon regulations (Costa et al. 1991). Such characteristics play an important role in being socially responsible and are thus likely to be very important for the socially responsible use of power and ethical leadership. High conscientiousness may cause ethical leaders to be fair, dependable, and act with integrity, to clarify expectations and responsibilities for subordinates and to hold themselves and others accountable.

Furthermore, agreeable individuals are altruistic, warm, generous, and trusting (Costa and McCrae 1992; McCrae and Costa 1987). This pro-social aspect of agreeableness may be important for ethical leaders as it induces them to be caring and concerned with others' interests. Also, research has found agreeableness to be positively related to a preference for participative styles of management (Stevens and Ash 2001). To be able to delegate and share sensitive information, one needs to be trusting and straightforward, which both are facets of agreeableness. Thus, agreeableness may also be important for the socially responsible use of power and ethical leadership.

Finally, integrity, a trait that is encompassed by a recently proposed potential sixth dimension of personality, namely honesty-humility (see for example Ashton and Lee 2001, 2005), seems also crucial for ethical leadership. Individuals high on integrity are honest, sincere, fair, adhere to high moral standards, and are devoted to principle (Audi and Murphy 2006). As such, individuals high on integrity are likely to show ethical leader behavior. Future research has, however, yet to provide evidence. Further research on ethical leaders' traits and motivations is necessary to help explain why some leaders show more ethical leadership than others.

Effects and processes of ethical leadership

Ethical leaders are believed to have positive effects on the attitudes and conduct of others in the organization and ultimately even on organizational performance (e.g., Aronson 2001; Brown et al. 2005; Kanungo 2001). Empirically based knowledge about the effects of ethical leadership in organizations is limited though. Research shows positive relationships between ethical leadership and employee attitudes, such as satisfaction and commitment (e.g., Brown et al. 2005; De Hoogh and Den Hartog 2008; Den Hartog and De Hoogh 2008; Khuntia and Suar 2004). Many proposed links with employee behavior, however, remain to be tested. Moreover, extant research has little to say about the process by which the effects of ethical leadership are ultimately realized. Basically, we do not yet know enough about how or why ethical leadership works. Here, we propose a model of how ethical leadership yields its effects (see Figure 19.1).

As stated, we propose a central role for the socially responsible use of power. One major effect of the socially responsible use of power by leaders may be enhancing employees' trust. Thus, we argue that trust likely plays a central role in the positive effects of ethical leaders on their followers. Followers are likely to perceive themselves as being in a high-quality relationship with their ethical leader, whose fair and caring treatment of them would result in strong trust in the leader. Consequently, followers will experience feelings of personal obligation, wish to reciprocate and be inclined to go above and beyond the call of duty (e.g., Brown and Treviño 2006b). Furthermore, due to their perceived trustworthiness, ethical leaders are expected to be seen as a reliable source of both expert and reward power (cf. Yukl and Falbe 1991) and, consequently, are more likely to influence subordinates' pro-social conduct. Also, subordinates are believed to be attracted to and admire trustworthy and upright leaders (Yukl 2006). A leader who is well liked and admired can have considerable influence (or in other words referent power) by setting an example of proper and desirable behavior for subordinates to imitate (Treviño and Brown 2007). In sum, we expect the socially responsible use of power and ethical leader behavior to result in positive work attitudes such as commitment and optimism and cooperative employee behaviors, such as increased citizenship behavior, ethical employee behavior and productivity, and decreased counterproductive behavior. Moreover, we expect trust in the leader to play a central role or, in other words, to act as a mediator in this process.

Two forms of trust seem especially relevant for the influence process involved in ethical leadership, namely cognitive- and affective-based trust (McAllister 1995). Whereas cognitive-based trust is formed on the basis of inferences about the leader's character, affective trust is based on inferences about the relationship with the leader. Cognitive-based trust is important to followers' sense of vulnerability to the leader; the leader has significant influence over work-related issues so followers' inferences about the character of the leader will have consequences for work behavior and attitudes. Affective-based trust is related to desirable outcomes through principles of social exchange; individuals who feel that their leader will demonstrate care and consideration will reciprocate in the form of desired behaviors (cf. Dirks and Ferrin 2002).

Building on this distinction, we propose that ethical leadership may have effects through both forms of trust. First, the socially responsible use of power and ethical leadership may enhance cognitive trust. Based on available knowledge, followers may perceive the leader's character as trustworthy and as mentioned may see their leader as a reliable source of expert and reward power. Second, ethical leaders are likely to generate affective-based trust. Followers may see the relationship with their ethical leader as desirable, such that the parties operate on the basis of trust and they reciprocate the perceived care. Furthermore, ethical leadership may affect outcomes by means of both cognitive- and affective-based trust; inferences about both the leader's character as well as the relationship may result in admiration of a well-liked, trusted leader with strong referent power, and in a desire to please and imitate the leader. Moreover, specific components of ethical leadership may affect particular outcomes through enhancing cognitive- or affective-based trust in the leader, or both (e.g., integrity and fairness through both, caring behavior through affective trust). This model is depicted in Figure 19.1. Although it remains to be tested, this proposed model provides one idea of how ethical leadership yields its strong positive effects.

Ethical leadership and context

The effects of leadership in general are found to be highly dependent on the context. For example, research has shown that charismatic leaders are most effective in less favorable or more challenging situations (e.g., De Hoogh et al. 2004; Den Hartog et al. 2007). When ethical leader behavior will be most (or least) successful in changing employees' behaviors and attitudes, and under which conditions the socially responsible use of power might translate into greater organizational effectiveness has, however, not yet received sufficient attention. We conclude this chapter by offering some first thoughts about when ethical leader behavior will have its strongest impact on others.

An important context element in leadership theory concerns the degree of situational strength as a moderator of leader effects (e.g., Shamir and Howell 1999). Situations characterized by few situational cues, few constraints, and few reinforcers to guide behavior – that is, weak situations – offer more room for leaders to maneuver and affect followers. Moreover, in weak situations, followers are likely to be more open to someone who provides direction (Shamir and Howell 1999). As a result, leaders are likely to be more effective in weak situations than in strong situations. Drawing on situational strength theory, we propose that ethical leadership is likely to be more strongly related to effectiveness and other outcomes under conditions of low situational strength than under conditions of high situational strength.

One example of a situation characterized by low situational strength is environmental uncertainty induced by organizational or technological change (cf. De Hoogh et al. 2004). Uncertain environments provide high latitude of decision discretion and ample opportunities to demonstrate leadership. Moreover, uncertainty is likely to raise a sense of vulnerability for followers. The greater the uncertainty or vulnerability in the context, the more mindful individuals may be of the socially responsible use of power and trust. Followers will have a strong orientation need to reduce their sense of vulnerability (Lind and Van den Bos 2002; Shamir and Howell 1999). Therefore, the greater the uncertainty in the context, the more open individuals may be of ethical leadership and the greater its impact on outcomes. Thus, we expect ethical leadership to have a greater impact on outcomes under conditions of environmental uncertainty (see Figure 19.1). Future research is needed to shed light on these and other potential situational differences in the relationship between ethical leadership, socially responsible power use, and outcomes.

To conclude

Concerns about ethics and the misuse of power have dominated headlines in the media about business and public leaders and have shaken public trust in organizations. Now more than ever knowledge about the responsible use of power and ethical leadership is needed. In this chapter, we examined ethical leadership from a power perspective. We argued that the socially responsible use of power is a key element of ethical leadership. Attempts to describe why and when ethical leadership has its effects on followers led us to examine the role of power and trust in the ethical leadership process and to focus on environmental uncertainty as one potentially important moderator of the relationship between ethical leadership and effectiveness. Moreover, we developed several testable propositions with regard to personality characteristics of ethical leaders to be investigated in future research. Thus, there is much work ahead. With such an important topic as the ethical and socially responsible use of power, it seems imperative that rapid progress is made.

References

Aronson, E. (2001) Integrating leadership styles and ethical perspectives. *Canadian Journal of Administrative Sciences*, 18, 244–256.
Ashton, M. C. and Lee, K. (2001) A theoretical basis for the major dimensions of personality. *European Journal of Personality*, 15, 327–353.

(2005) Honesty-Humility, the Big Five, and the Five-Factor Model. *Journal of Personality*, 73, 1321–1354.

Atkinson, J. W. (Ed.) (1958) *Motives in fantasy, action and society*, Princeton, N. J.: Van Nostrand.

Audi, R. and Murphy, P. E. (2006) The many faces of integrity. *Business Ethics Quarterly*, 16, 3–21.

Avolio, B. J. (1999) *Full leadership development: Building the vital forces in organizations*, Thousand Oaks, Calif.: Sage.

Avolio, B. J. and Locke, E. A. (2005) Should leaders be selfish or altruistic? Letters on leader motivation. In J. B. Ciulla (Ed.), *Ethics: The heart of leadership*, 2nd edn, Westport, Conn.: Praeger.

Bass, B. M. (1985) *Leadership and performance beyond expectations*, New York, N.Y.: Free Press.

Bass, B. M. and Steidlmeier, P. (1999) Ethics, character, and authentic transformational leadership behavior. *The Leadership Quarterly*, 10, 181–217.

Blasi, A. (1983) Moral cognition and moral action: A theoretical perspective. *Developmental Review*, 3, 178–210.

Brown, M. E. and Treviño, L. K. (2006a) Socialized charismatic leadership, values congruence, and deviance in work groups. *Journal of Applied Psychology*, 91, 954–962.

    (2006b) Ethical leadership: A review and future directions. *The Leadership Quarterly*, 17, 595–616.

Brown, M. E., Treviño, L. K., and Harrison, D. A. (2005) Ethical leadership: A social learning perspective for construct development and testing. *Organizational Behavior and Human Decision Processes*, 97, 117–134.

Bryman, A. (1992) *Charisma and leadership in organizations*, London: Sage.

Costa, P. T. Jr. and McCrae, R. R. (1992) *Revised NEO Personality Inventroy (NEO-PI-R) and NEO Five-Factor Inventory (NEO-FFI) professional manual*, Odessa, Fla.: Psychological Assessment Resources.

Costa, P. T. Jr. Mccrae, R. R., and Dye, D. A. (1991) Facet scales for agreeableness and conscientiousness: A revision of the NEO personality inventory. *Personality and Individual Differences*, 12, 887–898.

Craig, S. B. and Gustafson, S. B. (1998) Perceived leader integrity scale: An instrument for assessing employee perceptions of leader integrity. *The Leadership Quarterly*, 9, 127–145.

De Hoogh, A. H. B. and Den Hartog, D. N. (2008) Ethical and despotic leadership, relationships with leader's social responsibility, top management team effectiveness and subordinates' optimism: A multi-method study. *The Leadership Quarterly*, 19, 297–311.

De Hoogh, A. H. B., Den Hartog, D. N., and Koopman, P. L. (2005a) Linking the five factors of personality to charismatic and transactional leadership; Perceived dynamic work environment as a moderator. *Journal of Organizational Behavior*, **26**, 839–865.

De Hoogh, A. H. B., Den Hartog, D. N., Koopman, P. L., Thierry, H., Van den Berg, P. T., Van der Weide, J. G., and Wilderom, C. P. M. (2004) Charismatic leadership, environmental dynamism, and performance. *European Journal of Work and Organizational Psychology*, **13**, 447–471.

(2005b) Leader motives, charismatic leadership and subordinates' work attitude in the profit and voluntary sector. *The Leadership Quarterly*, **16**, 17–38.

Den Hartog, D. N. and De Hoogh, A. H. B. (in press) Empowerment and leader fairness and integrity: Studying ethical leader behavior from a levels-of-analysis perspective. *European Journal of Work and Organizational Psychology*.

Den Hartog, D. N., De Hoogh, A. H. B., and Keegan, A. E. (2007) The interactive effects of belongingness and charisma on helping and compliance. *Journal of Applied Psychology*, **92**, 1131–1139.

Dirks, K. T. and Ferrin, D. L. (2002) Trust in leadership: Meta-analytic findings and implications for research and practice. *Journal of Applied Psychology*, **87**, 611–628.

Feldman, M. S. and Khademian, A. M. (2003) Empowerment and cascading vitality. In K. S. Cameron, J. E. Dutton, and R. E. Quinn (Eds.), *Positive organizational scholarship: Foundations of a new discipline* (pp. 343–358), San Francisco, Calif.: Berret-Koehler.

Fry, L. W. (2003) Toward a theory of spiritual leadership. *The Leadership Quarterly*, **14**, 693–727.

Graham, J. W. (1991) Servant-leadership in organizations: Inspirational and moral. *The Leadership Quarterly*, **2**, 105–119.

Greene, D. L. and Winter, D. G. (1971) Motives, involvements, and leadership among Black college students. *Journal of Personality*, **39**, 319–332.

Hoffman, M. L. (1982) The development of prosocial motivation: Empathy and guilt. In N. Eisenberg (Ed.), *The development of prosocial behavior* (pp. 281–313), New York, N.Y.: Academic Press.

House, R. J. and Howell, J. M. (1992) Personality and charismatic leadership. *The Leadership Quarterly*, **3**, 81–108.

Howell, J. M. (1988) Two faces of charisma: Socialized and personalized leadership in organizations. In J. Conger and R. Kanungo (Eds.), *Charismatic leadership: The illusive factor in organizational effectiveness* (pp. 213–236), San Francisco, Calif.: Jossey-Bass.

Howell, J. M. and Avolio, B. J. (1992) The ethics of charismatic leadership: Submission or liberation? *Academy of Management Executive*, **6**, 43–54.

Howell, J. M. and Shamir, B. (2005) The role of followers in the charismatic leadership process: Relationships and their consequences. *Academy of Management Review*, 30, 96–112.

Judge, T. A. and Bono, J. E. (2000) Five-factor model of personality and transformational leadership. *Journal of Applied Psychology*, 85, 751–765.

Judge, T. A., Bono, J. E., Ilies, R., and Gerhardt, M. W. (2002) Personality and leadership: A qualitative and quantitative review. *Journal of Applied Psychology*, 87, 765–780.

Kalshoven, K., Den Hartog, D. N., and De Hoogh, A. H. B. (2008) *Measuring ethical leadership at work. Presented at the 23rd Annual Meeting of the Society of Industrial and Organizational Psychology*, San Francisco, California.

Kanungo, R. N. (2001) Ethical values of transactional and transformational leaders. *Canadian Journal of Administrative Sciences*, 18, 257–265.

Kanungo, R. N. and Mendoca, M. (1996) *Ethical dimensions of leadership*, Thousand Oaks, Calif.: Sage.

(2001) Ethical leadership and governance in organizations: A preamble. *Canadian Journal of Administrative Sciences*, 18, 241–243.

Khuntia, R. and Suar, D. (2004) A scale to assess ethical leadership of Indian private and public sector managers. *Journal of Business Ethics*, 49, 13–26.

Lind, E. A. and Van den Bos, K. (2002) When fairness works: Toward a general theory of uncertainty management. In B. M. Staw and R. M. Kramer (Eds.), *Research in Organizational Behavior* (Vol. XXIV, pp. 181–223), Greenwich, Conn.: JAI Press.

Luthans, F. and Avolio, B. J. (2003) Authentic leadership: A positive developmental approach. In K. S. Cameron, J. E. Dutton, and R. E. Quinn (Eds.), *Positive organizational scholarship* (pp. 241–261), San Francisco, Calif.: Barrett-Koehler.

McAllister, D. J. (1995) Affect- and cognition-based trust as foundations for interpersonal cooperation in organizations. *Academy of Management Journal*, 38, 24–59.

McCrae, R. R. and Costa, P. T. Jr. (1987) Validation of the five-factor model of personality across instruments and observers. *Journal of Personality and Social Psychology*, 52, 81–90.

Murray, H. A. (Ed.) (1938) *Explorations in personality*, New York, N.Y.: Oxford University Press.

O'Connor, J., Mumford, M. D., Clifton, T. C., Gessner, T. L., and Connelly, M. S. (1995) Charismatic leaders and destructiveness: A historiometric Study. *The Leadership Quarterly*, 6, 529–555.

Resick, C. J., Hanges, P. J., Dickson, M. W., and Mitchelson, J. K. (2006) A cross-cultural examination of the endorsement of ethical leadership. *Journal of Business Ethics*, 63, 345–359.

Sartre, J. P. (1947) *Existentialism*, trans. B. Frechtman, New York, N.Y.: Philosophical Library.

Shamir, B. and Howell, J. M. (1999) Organizational and contextual influences on the emergence and effectiveness of charismatic leadership. *The Leadership Quarterly*, 10, 257–283.

Spreitzer, G. M. (1995) Psychological empowerment in the workplace: Dimensions, measurement, and validation. *Academy of Management Journal*, 38, 1442–1465.

Stevens, C. D. and Ash, R. A. (2001) Selecting employees for fit: Personality and preferred managerial style. *Journal of Managerial Issues*, 4, 500–517.

Stogdill, R. M. (1950) Leadership, membership and organization. *Psychological Bulletin*, 47, 1–14.

Treviño, L. K. and Brown, M. E. (2007) Ethical leadership: A developing construct. In C. L. Cooper and D. Nelson (Eds), *Positive organizational behavior: Accentuating the positive at work* (pp. 101–116), Thousand Oaks, Calif.: Sage.

Treviño, L. K., Brown, M., and Hartman, L. P. (2003) A qualitative investigation of perceived executive ethical leadership: Perceptions from inside and outside the executive suite. *Human Relations*, 56, 5–37.

Treviño, L. K., Hartman, L. P., and Brown, M. (2000) Moral person and moral manager: How executives develop a reputation for ethical leadership. *California Management Review*, 42, 128–142.

Turner, N., Barling, J., Epitropaki, O., Butcher, V., and Milder, C. (2002) Transformational leadership and moral reasoning. *Journal of Applied Psychology*, 87, 304–311.

Winter, D. G. (1987) Leader appeal, leader performance, and the motive profiles of leaders and followers: A study of American presidents and elections. *Journal of Personality and Social Psychology*, 52, 196–202.

(1991a) Manual for scoring motive imagery in running text. *University* of Michigan, Ann Arbor, Mich.

(1991b) A motivational model of leadership: Predicting long-term management success from TAT measures of power motivation and responsibility. *The Leadership Quarterly*, 2, 67–80.

(1992a) Scoring system for responsibility. In C. P. Smith (Ed.), *Motivation and personality: Handbook of thematic content analysis* (pp. 506–511), Cambridge: Cambridge University Press.

(1992b) A revised scoring system for the power motive. In C. P. Smith (Ed.), *Motivation and personality: Handbook of thematic content analysis* (pp. 311–324), Cambridge: Cambridge University Press.

Winter, D. G. and Barenbaum, B. B. (1985) Responsibility and the power motive in women and men. *Journal of Personality*, **53**, 335–355.

Yukl, G. (2006) *Leadership in organizations*, 6th edn, Englewood Cliffs, N. J.: Prentice Hall.

Yukl, G. and Falbe, C. M. (1991) The importance of different power sources in downward and lateral relations. *Journal of Applied Psychology*, **76**, 416–423.

20 | *The* Tao *of value leadership and the power of interdependence*

PING PING FU AND CAROLINE FU

Introduction

The power impulse has two forms: explicit, in leaders; implicit, in their followers. When men willingly follow a leader, they do so with a view to the acquisition of power by the group which he commands, and they feel that his triumphs are theirs.

(Russell 1938: 16)

The above averment by Bertrand Russell, the recipient of the 1950 Nobel Prize for literature, resonates with the Tao of value leadership. In his *Book of Tao (Tao-Te-Ching)*, Lao-Tze says, "when people speak about a good emperor, they would say: 'He has done this and he has done that.' But when they speak of a superior emperor, they would say: 'We have done it all ourselves'" (Siu 1980: 32).[1] By the *Tao* of value leadership, we refer to the ultimate realm as well as the most desirable level leadership can reach: the level when leaders and followers share the same values and become truly interdependent and do their best to achieve their goals. In that process, leadership power, like energy in physics (Russell 1938), acts as a special type of force, not as "abilities" (e.g., Etzioni 1961; Pfeffer 1992) or "potential influence" (e.g., French and Raven 1959), enabling the leader to achieve the highest level.

Leadership power is "a special form of power," which consists of two interrelated essentials "motive and resource" (Burns 1979: 12). "Lacking motive, resource diminishes; lacking resource, motive lies idle; lacking either one, power collapses" (Burns 1979: 12). Like energy in physics

---

[1] Lao-Tze is an ancient Chinese philosopher and one of the major ancient Chinese saints who lived over 2,500 years ago. He authored the *Book of Tao (Tao Te Ching)*, also known as *di wang xue* (a book on the monarch) because it deals with the Tao of the majesty of the country, the highest position of power in today's sense. Through the ages, Taoism, the school that Lao-Tze represents, has played an important role in Chinese people's mental life just as Confucianism has presided over Chinese social life (Peng 2004).

being generated by different types of sources, leadership power, too, is generated by different types of sources. For example, French and Raven (1959) identified five different sources of power, including reward, coercive, legitimate, expert, and referent, reflecting five different types of resources: materials, information, authority, expertise, and characters. The motives for power moderate the effect of the different types of leadership power on followers' attitudes and behaviors (McClelland and Boyatzi 1982).

Leaders' personal values channel the sources of power and drive the motives. Leaders who practice value-based leadership create organizational integrity by emphasizing the acceptable values that reinforce the purposes and promoting those values. When collectively shared, rather than espoused, these values energize people, uplift spirit and create synergy in organizations (Vaill 1998). The synergy of integral values makes leaders and followers become truly interdependent: Trusting and empowering each other result in achieving the organization's highest performance. Leaders who can achieve that synergy are the most effective; therefore, their organizations become more powerful (Vaill 1998). Leadership power is found in the leaders' ability to foster such interdependency, get everyone to collectively embrace the organization's core values, creating a confluence of resources and motives.

However, unlike energy, which works equally effectively regardless of how it is generated, leadership power that comes from different sources produces very different effects on followers because the values channeling the sources of power and driving the motives are different. The five types of power are also grouped into personal power and position power, depending on the origin. The days when leaders could make followers work by exercising position-related power (reward, coercive, and legitimate) are long gone. Since the type of power the leaders hold or the motive they have behind the power affect the type of power source they use, we need to start from the leader's values and motives when examining the effectiveness of leadership power.

This seemingly complicated relationship becomes simple when we follow the *Tao*, the ultimate virtue in the universe. The *Tao*, the complementarity of the yin-yang, demonstrates "striking parallels to modern scientific premises" and leadership theories (Couto and Fu 2004). Using Whitehead's analogy in explaining the logic of interdependence – "King James said, 'No bishops, no king.' ... 'No logic, no science'" (Whitehead 1957: 108) – we follow Whitehead and Russell's logic to explain the Tao of value leadership philosophically: "No followers, no leader", "No congruent individual-organizational values, no interdependence", and "No leader-follower interdependence, no power."

The concept of *Tao*, though ageless, is enigmatic: it has an embedded message inviting us to look for the nonobvious realm of reality. The message repeatedly reminds us that the power of an organization resides in its ability to sustain the complementarity of opposites and turn conflicts into advantageous challenges. The ancient Chinese philosopher Lao-Tze uses the concept of *Tao* to illustrate why shared values result in interdependence between followers and leaders and that interdependence generates leadership power. British Sinologist Joseph Needham says, "A Chinese thought without Taoism is like a tree without roots" (quoted in Peng 2004: 249). Similarly, Tao shows that talking about leadership power without referring to leadership values is like having "a tree without roots."

The ancient wisdom can be integrated with modern leadership theory. In the following sections, we will first briefly review the literature on value leadership and leadership power, and then introduce Lao-Tze and his *Tao Te Ching* (*Book of Tao*). Finally, using the philosophy of *Tao*, we will show how leadership based on respectable values lead to leader–follower interdependence, which in turn generates leadership power to achieve organizational goals. With the help of our ancient sages' wisdom, we discuss the paradoxical relationship between power and values and hope to contribute to the existing leadership literature by eventually going beyond tautological arguments while explaining the dynamics of the leadership power. We also hope the philosophy of *Tao* will help convince our business leaders of what it takes to lead effectively and help make them better leaders.

Value leadership and leadership power

Values are desirable, trans-situational goals that vary in importance as guiding principles in people's lives (Rokeach 1973). Leadership values are the silent power in organizational life (Posner and Schmidt 1992) because they underlie everything leaders say or do, or all the decisions they make. Every enterprise is driven by its leaders' individual and collective values, whether those values are consciously understood or unconsciously influenced, spoken or unspoken, written or unrecorded (Bean 1993). These values function as a cognitive hierarchy (Behr 1998; Ravlin and Meglino 1987) and the hierarchy of values has been used to explain the differences in organizational outcomes (Meglino and Ravlin 1998). Most leadership theories, including charismatic leadership (e.g., House 1977; Conger and Kanungo 1988), transformational leadership (e.g., Avolio et al. 1991; Bass and Avolio 1990), visionary leadership (e.g., Nanus 1992; Westley and Mintzberg 1989), and Leader-Member exchange (LMX) theory (e.g., Graen 1976), take leader values as important sources through which the leader exerts impact on the followers.

Values coming from senior leaders permeate all levels of the organization (e.g., Hambrick and Finkelstein 1987; Schein 1992) and form the shared values that give everyone in the organization "an internal compass that enables them to act independently and interdependently, responsibly and publicly" (Kouzes and Posner 1993: 53). Various researchers argue that certain values are essential to the value systems of good leaders. For example, Snyder et al. (1994) delineated five essential personal values of leadership: service to others, humility, integrity, honesty, and hard work. Schwartz (1994) identified two basic bipolar dimensions: openness to change versus conservation, and self-enhancement versus self-transcendence. The first one emphasizes one's own independent thought and action and favoring change versus submissive self-restriction, preservation of traditional practices, and protection of stability. The second dimension opposes values pursuing one's own success and dominance over others to those pursuing enhancement of others and transcendence of selfish interests and emphasizing the acceptance of others as equals. Empirical research has found self-transcendent values to be directly relevant to transformational leadership (e.g., Agle et al. 1999; Sosik 2005; Jung and Avolio 2000).

When integrated into their personal value systems, these values serve as leaders' blueprints or foundations for making decisions, solving problems, and resolving conflicts (Kouzes and Posner 1993). Therefore, the stronger the leaders' altruistic motive, the more likely they will engage in transformational leadership, a behavior aimed at transforming followers' needs, values, preferences, and aspirations from self-interests to collective interests (e.g., House and Shamir 1993). Value leadership becomes powerful when leaders can effectively instill their values into followers and followers not only accept those values but also internalize them and fully commit themselves to the collective goals. In Burns's (2003: 211) words, "The stronger the value systems, the more strongly leaders can be empowered and the more deeply leaders can empower followers."

We define leadership power as a force derived from shared values that is necessary for leaders to effectively empower followers and mobilize them to work for the shared vision. Unlike the effect of energy in physics, which is independent of any humane factors, leadership power is generated, maintained, and lost in the context of relationships with followers. Leadership power as a force would not exert any influence by itself. Leaders have to exercise or use it in order to achieve the desired effect. Like a captain who has to want to navigate the ship and has to know the destination, a leader also has to have the motive as well as the purpose to exercise power. Power motive is defined as the desire to influence, to have an impact on, or to control another person, group of people, or the world at large (Winter 1973). Power motives are dichotomized into personalized or socialized power. Personalized power motive refers to when expressions of power for the sake of personal aggrandizement become paramount, while socialized power motive refers to "plans, self-doubts, mixed outcomes and concerns for others," which is seen to be a more desirable attribute than personalized power in terms of the organization for power-associated leadership behavior (McClelland 1975; McClelland and Burnham 1995). Self-transcendent values are rooted in the altruistic motive (Kanungo and Mendonca 1996), or in the intent to benefit others, which is consistent with socialized power motive.

Empirical research has shown that leader behaviors have to be consistent with the values they hold in order to be effective. For example, Sosik (2005) found that traditional, collectivistic work, self-transcendent, and self-enhancement values related positively to charismatic leadership, which predicted managerial performance and followers' extra effort and organizational citizenship behavior. Fu and her associates found that the level of middle-manager commitment was the highest when CEO values were self-transcendent and their behaviors were transformational; the commitment level decreased when the CEO had self-enhancing values and exhibited transformational leadership. The results supported the interaction effects between CEO values and their behaviors on middle-manager commitment measured contemporaneously and eighteen months later. These findings suggest that followers interpret both transformational and transactional behaviors positively when the CEO values are self-transcendent but not when the CEO values are self-enhancing (Fu et al. 2006).

Values have "an emotional charge" (Vaill 1989: 54). Executives, recognizing the power of values, can direct a value-laden emotional charge toward achieving an organization's collective goals. Value leadership, although relatively new as a theory, has deep roots in the concept of *Tao*, which concept that has been around for centuries. In the *Book of Tao*, Lao-Tze, the author and a master of leadership paradox, used the concept of balancing values in order to guide value-laden behavior. To really understand the power of value, we feel the urge to borrow the concept of *Tao*, the influence of which, despite the elapse of the 2,500-plus years, still permeates Asia.

As China emerges as a growing economic power, more and more business leaders in and outside China are seeking help from the ancient master because the *Tao*, dealing with the very essential nature of things, aggregates all paradoxical relationships of "Being," including that of leaders and followers across different cultures. Interdependence – harmony between leader and followers, between individual and organization – is the essential nature of the *Tao* of value leadership. According to the *Tao*, leaders have to cultivate their own morals and maintain their integrity. When they do so, they will be more effective instilling their values into their followers. And when followers embrace the values and internalize them, they give their leaders the power to lead effectively toward achieving the organization's goals. The dynamic power of interdependence induces positive psychological and physiological changes that empower people (whether they are leading or following) to "pursue happiness" collectively (Burns 2003: 240) and create a harmonious organizational climate.

Tao, the ancient Eastern philosophical perspective of leadership

Most people think of the symbol of *Tao*, the 5,000-year-old symbol of *Tai ji* (or great supreme) as a symbol of duality in balance (see Figure 20.1). The symbol, in fact, portrays the "primal beginning" (Wilhelm and Baynes 1950: 298), the "Supreme Ultimate" (Capra 1991: 107). *Tao* is the "Chinese hypothesis on transformations in nature resulting from the interactions of the polar contraries," the yin and the yang (Siu 1971: 7). In the symbol, the black stands for the *yin* and the white the *yang*. There is a black dot in the white and vice versa, a white dot in the black that signifies there is *yin* in *yang* and *yang* in *yin*. The *yin* and the *yang* form an inseparable oneness and interdependency. They represent the rotation of Earth's day–night cycle, as day folds into night and night into day.

Figure 20.1 The symbol of *Tao*.

The concept of *Tao* is a difficult idea to express in words as it represents "the unknowable source of all things" or the "way" that brings into being, by various stages, the whole of creation, physical, mental, and spiritual (Billington 1997: 89). "Way" is just a convenient translation of the word *Tao*, which is also translated as rules, method, nature, spirit, truth, pattern, metaphysics, and perspectives (Liu 1990). The fact that one word allows so many interpretations makes the concept of Tao extremely illusive; nevertheless, *Tao Te Ching* still speaks "across the centuries and cultures," and it "continues to speak to us and to challenge us to re-examine our thoughts and ways" (Billington 1997: 89).

To modern philosophers, "the so-called *Tao* has two meanings, namely, Ontology and Cosmology [...] that 'All the things in this world come from Being, and Being comes from Non-being'" (Fu 1953). The universality of *Tao* is described in the following manner:

> There is no base where *Tao* comes from; there is no hole into which *Tao* goes. There is actuality but no place; and there is length but no beginning and end. That from which *Tao* comes is called reality (noumenon).
> That which has actuality but no place and is called Yu (space); and
> That which has been long but has no beginning and end is called Chou (time).
> (Fu 1953; Wu 1995)

Following the *yin-yang* polarity, self-enhancing and self-transcendent bipolar values form an integral oneness. One cannot totally deny self-enhancement, which is associated with self-interest; however, when one focuses on the organization whole rather than the self the organization does well and the self will naturally benefit. Likewise, self-transcendence is also an essential value for all members: only when one can excel in what one does, will one have the ability to help others. When the values of leader and followers are in balance with each other, they create powerful transformative dynamics that naturally align the organization to achieve the highest attainable performance. Thus, value leadership is in accord with nature's order, constantly balancing the bipolar values of self-enhancement and self-transcendence to manifest as one ontological and cosmological being in *Tao*.

Before leaving these philosophical notions, we are compelled to mention Confucianism because of its known influence. Confucianism and Taoism appear to be paradoxical, but they are complementary. Confucianism promotes maintaining social order while Tao practice emphasizes returning to nature's spontaneity (Capra 1991). The former strives to instill social and leadership order – the explicit *yang* – whereas the latter encourages leaders to embrace chaos and change in nature – the implicit *yin*. While Confucianism explicates the *Tao* in the form of social order for people to grasp, Tao concept itself is more implicit while Confucianism more explicit. Thus, Confucianism teaches people how to behave while Tao practice teaches how to think; Confucianism is concrete whereas Tao concept is more abstract. Being closer to the origin of *Tao or* in the *Tao* encourages leaders to contemplate the meaning behind the social order. As a whole, like the *Tao* symbol tells us, *yin* contains *yang* and *yang* embraces *yin*, both concepts are in unison with the *Tao*.

A *Tao* perspective of the power of empowerment

Power has many forms. When appearing in a different form, it "must be regarded as continually passing from any one of its forms into any other" (Russell 1938: 13). Flowing reciprocally between its wielder and receiver, the notion of power itself is very complex as it manifests with various intensities and influences in human interactions and in various organizations. From ancient civilizations to modern societies, power often associates with leadership, "love of power is the cause of the activities that are important in social affairs" (Russell 1938: 12). Russell links love of power to leadership from a non-obvious followership perspective, because it is "disguised, among the more timid, as an impulse of submission to leadership, which increases the scope of the power-impulses of bold men" (Russell 1938: 14). Once leaders are bestowed with power, then morality becomes the topic of concern, as very often they indulge in power and forget those followers who have empowered them in the first place. Maslow, in the *Eupsychian Management*, cautions us to be leery of leaders in love with power: "The person who seeks power for power, is the one who is just exactly likely to be the one who shouldn't have it. Such people are apt to use power very badly; to overcome, over-power, use it for their own selfish gratifications" (Maslow 1998: 152).

It is in the light of *Tao* that we see complementarity of power and empowerment in the leader–follower relationship. The leader, as an individual, empowers values that are deeply engrained in people's belief systems (the universe). Leaders, in order to lead, must also empower themselves with the same values as well as those which the people collectively bestow upon them. Power without empowerment entropies to organizational lethargy and loses its potential to achieve high performance, while chaos and anarchy result when leaders are unable to empower themselves. For these reasons, modern high-performing companies are "values-driven" enterprises (Peters and Waterman 1982). In such enterprises, "leadership is not domination, but the art of persuading people to work toward a common goal" (Goleman 1995: 149). Corporate futures are now depending on talented leaders who can become "virtuoso[s] in interpersonal skills" and have "the ability to get into flow states" (Goleman 1995: 149). Leadership is about fostering a "flow" state in organizations, in which everyone shares vision, value, purpose, and meaning; "when goals are clear, feedback relevant, and challenges and skills are in balance, people's attention becomes ordered and fully invested" (Csikszentmihalyi 1997: 31). Thus, collectively embraced enterprise values drive organizational performance.

The *Tao* of interdependence

Leaders and followers are interdependent. In the new "post-industrial paradigm," Rost (1993: 109) found that when the purposes of "followers and leaders" are mutual, they form one relationship that is leadership. According to Rost, "Metaphorically, their activities are two sides of the same coin, it takes two to tango, the composer and musicians making music, the female and male generating new life, the yin and the yang" (1993: 109); both "flow" and influence one another (1993: 112). When leaders and followers focus on the collective values, power and empowerment become mutual and interdependent. Paradoxically, the interdependence can happen only when followers empower the leader to lead. Lao-Tze states philosophically that the highest attainment of leadership is when a leader can take pride that every member embracing the collective goals is empowered to lead respectively to achieve the mission:

The best rulers are scarcely known by their subjects;
The next best are loved and praised;
The next are feared;
The next despised:
They have no faith in their people,
And their people become unfaithful to them.
When the best rulers achieve their purpose
Their subjects claim the achievement as their own.

(Merel 1995)

Senge (1990: 341) vividly paraphrased the above paradoxical teaching: "The great leader is he who the people say 'We did it ourselves'." Pride and ownership belong to the people. In this instance, the leaders included everyone. The paradox of leadership-followership becomes a natural leading-following oneness: "The Burns Paradox [leadership-followership] ultimately disappears if, instead of identifying individual actors simply as leaders or simply as followers, we see the whole process as a system" in which there is profound interchange between leader and follower as they move in and out of the leadership role (Burns 2003: 185).

Power should be open to all. In a democratic social system, "the posts [that] confer power will be occupied by people who differ from the average in being exceptionally power-loving" (Russell 1938: 14). Acquiring resources to satisfy people's physiological needs may be the starting point in the human "basic need hierarchy," which provides motivation (Maslow 1987: 15). People's basic needs often invoke "unconscious impulses" (Maslow 1987: 12–13) that may become a hidden motive for power. Different motives, triggered by physiological and psychological resource needs, can invoke the love of power either emotionally or intentionally. Love of power, though one of the strongest of human motives, "is very unevenly distributed, and is limited by various other motives, such as love of ease, love of pleasure, and sometimes love of approval" (Maslow 1987: 14). The unevenness of power distribution upsets harmony in business, induces competition, and fosters unintended consequences. Siu, in *The Master Manager*, pointed out about balancing power distribution: "From a practical standpoint, no one can retain power for long without keeping the constituency happy by providing a satisfactory net service of some kind" (Siu 1980: 67). By "net service," Siu meant the amount of benefit actually experienced by the constituency from all that is believed to be available less what is used up in the leader's exercise of power (Siu 1980: 67). The dynamic inter-play between leadership power and followership satisfaction are reciprocally enforcing, to the extent they determine the power of inter-dependence, leadership effectiveness, and business success.

People have vested interests in knowing how their efforts are valued or recognized as contributing to the organization's effectiveness and performance. Vaill (1989: 191) identifies a view of the organization as this "five-dimensional, intertwined stream" or five value ingredients consisting of: "the *economic*, the *technical*, the *communal*, the *adaptive*, and the *transcendent*" (Vaill 1989: 199) in defining an organization's effectiveness: The first four ingredients are more transactional in nature, i.e. though the leadership values may be shared, the binding between leader and followers is an example of "at-the-moment" synergy. However, the fifth ingredient, the "Transcendental," is transforma-tional and therefore has a long-term effect. The organization's uplift spirit lingers in most of the members' intellectual memory years after work events brought them together. Very often, the memory brings intelligence to leaders' emotional moments when dealing with decision-making.

In the *Tao* of value leadership, transactional and transformational leadership form a collective oneness. Transactional leadership "exchanges" or substitutes people's wants for needs while transform-ational leadership has people experience a "metamorphosis" (Burns 2003: 24). For example, all people join companies for a tangible work-compensation exchange. If they experience metamorphous transformation leadership during their employment, they fulfill their initial transactional needs and also obtain satisfaction with their contributions to success. Value leadership enables a company to attain that metamorphous transformation at the same time ful-filling its transactional commitments. Thus, transactional and trans-formational leadership are complementary.

Value leadership, when East meets West

Values that have long been considered spiritual ideals, such as integrity, honesty, and humility, are eternal and universal. These values, demon-strated to have an effect on leadership success (Reave 2005), have stood the test of time and space. In fact, these universal values perpetuate all the widely known writings. The "law of reciprocity," for example, expresses a common human belief and is regarded as the rule of Confucianism (Confucius 1959): "Don't do to others as you don't want them to do to you." The same is true with Christianity's "Golden Rule," the expression of which can be found in an abridged Western Greek translation: "Do unto others as you want them to do unto you." We can take this universality of the law of reciprocity and expand it to apply to value-laden leader–follower relationship. We can interpret the relationship as, "Lead me as you would want to be led."

The evidence of universal consensus is also found in modern research. The Global Leadership and Organizational Behavioral Effectiveness (GLOBE), which was conducted by 170 researchers from sixty-two societies, empirically established the cross-culturally shared conception of leadership, referred to as cultural endorsed implicit theories of leadership (CLT). Basically, the GLOBE findings show that members of cultures share common observations and values concerning what constitute effective and ineffective leadership. Of the six *global* CLT leadership styles, value-based leadership is generally reported to contribute to outstanding leadership, with scores ranging from 4.5 to 6.5 on a 7-point scale among sixty-one GLOBE countries. The findings demonstrate that the attributes of value-based leadership – visionary, inspirational, self-sacrificing, integrity, decisive, and performance-orientation – were universally viewed as facilitating leadership effectiveness (House et al. 2001).

Leadership that respects the values of followers creates empowerment rather than dependency, sustainability rather than short-term success (Reave 2005). In other words, it generates positive power. To develop power, according to *Tao*, leaders must first of all cultivate their own virtues, establish their own value systems, and make sure that these values are inspiring to their followers. Then, leaders need to have the drive to want to exercise that power. They need to not only practice what they preach but also repeatedly to communicate them to their followers, trying to align the values with their own. Moral leaders with self-transcendent values will commit themselves to the development of the followers and demonstrate concerns for them, which, according to the reciprocity law, will naturally result in credibility and win the heart of the followers. When followers feel trusted and trust their leaders, they will feel proud to share the values and will want to internalize these values and work with the leaders to achieve the goals. Leaders who can achieve that are the most powerful.

Conclusion

Leadership power is "moldable" for intellectual enjoyment (Whitehead 1961: 57) and can be leveraged for the benefit of human happiness on earth (Siu 1971: 8). As there are limits to leadership power, understanding the limits and the "purpose of power" can assist leaders to "pursue" their own and others' "general happiness" collectively (Russell 1938: 139). Leaders need to fully recognize the impact of the ultimate purposes, the importance of maintaining a balance between self-transcendent and self-enhancing values, as well as cognition of the interdependence between themselves and their followers. Leaders' strong alignment is defined as a high number of value matches between the personal values of employees and the values of the organization (Reave 2005: 673–674).

The *Tao* of value leadership offers us a way to leverage empowerment-power and leader–follower interdependence, to increase organization effectiveness, and to pursue happiness as a collective goal. As Vaill (1989: 177–178) points out when referring to Taoist management, "it is possible that wu-wei [nonaction] is a more powerful idea about taking action in conditions of permanent white water than anything that we have produced in the West." "Perhaps at some level below conscious thought, Western managers and other action takers might be better at 'going with the flow' and 'moving with the available energy' than we like to think." The power of interdependence is rooted in the congruence of leaders' and followers' personal values and convictions and their willingness to act on those convictions while struggling with high levels of uncertainty. Basically, "no action" when applied to leadership does not mean that leaders do nothing but that they follow the laws of nature when leading, creating a harmonious environment, being empathetic and supportive in cultivating and developing the followers. Organizations are immersed in the society. When leaders succeed in making their followers believe that "they did it themselves," leaders create happiness for their followers, who in turn will perform their best and make the general population happy by making the organization successful. "While leadership is necessary at every stage, beginning with the first spark that awakens people's hopes, its vital role is to create and expand the opportunities that empower people to pursue happiness for themselves" (Burns 2003: 240).

References

Agle, B. R., Mitchell, R. K., and Sonnenfeld, J. A. (1999) Who matters to CEOs? An investigation of stakeholder attributes and salience, corporate performance, and CEO values. *Academy of Management Journal*, **42** (5), 507–525.

Avolio, B. J., Waldman, D. A., and Yammarino, F. J. (1991) Leading in the 1990s: The four I's of transformational leadership. *Journal of European Industrial Training*, **15** (4), 9–16.

Bass, B. M. and Avolio, B. J. (1990) Developing transformational leadership: 1992 and beyond. *Journal of European Industrial Training*, **14**, 21–27.

Bean, W. C. (1993) *Strategic planning that makes things happen: Getting from where you are to where you want to be*, Amherst, Mass.: Human Resource Development Press.

Behr, E. T. (1998) Acting from the center. *Management Review*, **87** (3), 51–55.

Billington, R. (1997) *Understanding Eastern Philosophy*, London and New York, N.Y.: Routledge.

Burns, J. M. (1979) *Leadership*, New York, N.Y.: Harper & Row.

(2003) *Transforming leadership: A new pursuit of happiness*, New York, N.Y.: Grove/Atlantic, Inc.

Capra, F. (1991) *The Tao of physics: An exploration of the parallels between modern physics and eastern mysticism* (3rd edn), Boston, Mass.: Shambhala. (Originally published 1975.)

Confucius (1959) *Four books: The great learning, the doctrine of the mean, Confucian analects, and the works of Mencius*, trans. J. Legge, Taipei: Latitude Longitude Publishing. (Originally written down 500 BCE.)

Conger, J. A., R. Kanungo, et al. (1988) *Charismatic leadership: The elusive factor in organization effectiveness*, San Francisco, Calif.: Jossey-Bass.

Couto, R. A. and Fu, C. (2004) The authentic leadership of sacred texts. Paper presented at the Gallup Leadership Institute Summit, Omaha, Nebraska.

Csikszentmihalyi, M. (1997) *Finding flow in everyday life*, New York, N.Y.: Basic Books.

Etzioni, A. (1961) *A comparative analysis of complex organizations: On power, involvement, and their correlates*, New York, N.Y.: The Free Press.

French, J. R. P. Jr. and Raven, B. H. (1959) The bases of social power. In D. Cartwright (Ed.), *Studies in Social Power* (pp. 150–167), Ann Arbor, Mich.: Institute for Social Research.

Fu, P. Y. (1953) *Philosophy of Chuangtse*. Thesis, National Taiwan University, Taipei.

Fu, P. P., Tsui, A., Liu, J., Hui, C., Song, J.W., Jia, L. D., and Li, L. (2006) CEO personal values and middle manager responses: The mediating role of leadership behavior and organizational culture. Paper presented at the Academy of Management Conference, August, Atlanta.

Goleman, D. (1995) *Emotional intelligence*, New York, N.Y.: Bantam Books.

Graen, G. (1976) Role making processes within complex organizations. In M. D. Dunette (Ed.), *Handbook of Industrial and Organizational Psychology*, Chicago, Ill.: Rand-McNally.

Greer, L.L. and Caruso, H. M. (2007) Are high power teams really high performers? The roles of trust and status congruency in high power team performance. *Academy of Management Proceedings*.

Hambrick, D. C. and Finkelstein, S. (1987) Managerial discretion: A bridge between polar views of organizational outcomes. *Research in Organizational Behavior*, 9, 369–406.

House, R. J. (1977) *Theory of charismatic leadership*. In J. G. Hunt and L. L. Larson (Eds.), *Leadership: The cutting edge* (pp. 189–207), Carbondale, Ill.: Southern Illinois University Press.

House, R. J. and Shamir, B. (1993) Toward the integration of charismatic, visionary and transformational leadership theories. In M. M. Chemers and R. Ayman (Eds.), *Leadership theory and research: Perspectives and directions* (pp. 81–107), San Diego, Calif.: Academic Press.

House, R. J., Hanges, P. J., Javidan, M., Dorfman, P. W., Gupta, V., and Associates, G. (2001) *Cultures, leadership, and organizations: GLOBE, a 62 nation study*, Thousand Oaks, Calif.: Sage.

Jung, D. I. and Avolio, B. J. (2000) Opening the black box: An experimental investigation of the mediating effects of trust and value congruence on transformational and transactional leadership. *Journal of Organizational Behavior*, 21 (8), 949–964.

Kanungo, R. N. and Mendonca, M. (1996) *Ethical dimensions of leadership*, Thousand Oaks, Calif.: Sage Publications, Inc.

Kouzes, J. M. and Posner, B. Z. (1993) Credibility: How leaders gain and lose it, Why People Demand It. San Francisco, Calif.: JosseyBass Publishers.

Liu, B. (1990) Press Freedom: Particles in the Air. In C. C. Lee (Ed.), *Voices of China: The Interplay of Politics and Journalism*, New York, N.Y.: Guilford Press.

Maslow, A. H. (1987) *Motivation and personality*, New York, N.Y.: Harper & Row. (Originally published 1954).

(1998) *Maslow on management*, New York, N.Y.: John Wiley & Sons. (Originally published 1961 as Eupsychian management by Maslow).

McClelland, D. C. (1975) Power motivation and organizational leadership. In D. C. McClelland (Ed.), *Power: The inner experience* (pp. 253–271), New York, N.Y.: Irvington Publishers.

McClelland, D. C. and Burnham, D. H. (1995) Power is the great motivator. *Harvard Business Review*, 73 (1), 126–135.

McClelland, D. C. and Boyatzis, R. E. (1982) Leadership motive pattern and long-term success in management. *Journal of Applied Psychology*, 67 (6), 737–743.

Meglino, B. M. and Ravlin, E. C. (1998) Individual values in organizations: Concepts, controversies, and research. *Journal of Management*, 24 (3), 351–389.

Merel, P. A. (1995) TaoDeChing. Retrieved May, 2007, from www.china-page.com/gnl.html#17.

Nanus, B. (1992) *Visionary leadership: Creating a compelling sense of direction for your organization*, San Francisco, Calif.: Jossey-Bass.

Peng, K. (2004) *New readings in culture psychology*, New York, N.Y.: Wiley.

Peters, T. J. and Waterman, R. H. (1982) In search of excellence: Lessons from America's best-run companies, New York, N.Y.: Harper & Row.

Pfeffer, J. (1992) Understanding power in organizations. *California Management Review*, 34 (2), 29–50.

Posner, B. Z. and Kouzes, J. M. (1993) Psychometric properties of the Leadership Practices Inventory. *Educational and Psychological Measurement*, 53 (1), 191–199.

Posner, B. Z. and Schmidt, W. H. (1992) The values of American managers: An update, *California Management Review, 1992*, 34, 80–94.

Ravlin, E. C. and Meglino, B. M. (1987) Effect of values on perception and decision making: A study of alternative work values measures. *Journal of Applied Psychology*, 72 (4), 666–673.

Reave, L. (2005) Spiritual values and practices related to leadership effectiveness, *Leadership Quarterly*, 16 (5), 655–687.

Rokeach, M. (1973) *The nature of human values and value systems* (pp. 3–25), New York, N.Y.: Free Press.

Rost, J. C. (1993) *Leadership for the twenty-first century*, Westport, Conn.: Praeger.

Russell, B. (1938) *Power: A new social analysis*, New York, N.Y.: Norton.

Schein, E. H. (1992) *Organizational Culture and Leadership*, San Francisco, Calif.: Jossey-Bass Publishers.

Schwartz, S. H. (1994) Are there universals in the content and structure of values? *Journal of Social Issues*, 50 (4), 19–45.

Senge, P. M. (1990) The fifth discipline, the art & practice of the learning organization, New York, N.Y.: Doubleday.

Siu, R. H. G. (1971) The Tao of science: An essay on western knowledge and eastern wisdom (Vol. 1). Cambridge: The Massachusetts Institute of Technology. (Originally published 1957.)

(1980) *The master manager*, Washington, D.C.: John Wiley & Sons.

Snyder, N. H. Jr, Dowd, J. J., and Houghton, D. M. (1994) *Vision, values, and courage: Leadership for quality management*, New York, N.Y.: The Free Press.

Sosik, J. J. (2005) The role of personal values in the charismatic leadership of corporate managers: A model and preliminary field study. *The Leadership Quarterly*, **16**: 221–244.

Vaill, P. B. (1989) *Managing as a performing art: New ideas for a world of chaotic change*, San Francisco, Calif.: Jossey-Bass.

Vaill, P. B. (1998) *Spirited leading and learning: Process wisdom for a new age*, San Francisco, Calif.: Jossey-Bass.

Westley, F. and Mintzberg, H. (1989) Visionary leadership and strategic management. *Strategic Management Journal*, **10**: 17–32.

Whitehead, A. N. (1957) *The aims of education and other essays*, New York: The Free Press, Macmillan. (Originally published 1929).

(1961) *Adventures of ideas*, New York: The Free Press. (Originally published 1933).

Wilhelm, R., and Baynes, C. F. (1950) *The I Ching or book of changes*, Princeton, N. J.: Princeton University Press.

Winter, D. G. (1973) A revised scoring system for the power motive, *The Power Motive* (pp. 249–264), New York: The Free Press.

Wu, K., (1955) *Lao Chuang philosophy*, Taipei: Taiwan Business Affair Publishing.

Index